The Transformation of the Christian Churches in Western Europe 1945-2000

La transformation des églises chrétiennes en Europe occidentale

KADOC Studies on Religion, Culture and Society 6

The Transformation of the Christian Churches in Western Europe

1945|2000

La transformation des églises chrétiennes en Europe occidentale

Leo Kenis, Jaak Billiet & Patrick Pasture, eds

Leuven University Press

Leuven University Press/Presses Universitaires de Louvain/Universitaire Pers Leuven
Minderbroedersstraat 4 bus 5602, B-3000 Leuven (Belgium)

ISBN 978 90 5867 665 8
D/2010/1869/8
NUR: 694

Contents

The Transformation of Christian Churches in Western Europe
An Introduction

Patrick Pasture & Leo Kenis

The Western European religious landscape underwent major changes after World War II. Not the least of these relate to the Christian churches. While admittedly the Christian churches were not as omnipresent as they once had been and their position had been undermined by the development of rationalism and secularism as well as through the great socio-economic transformations of the nineteenth century, by the mid-twentieth century in major parts of the continent they still, or rather once again, occupied a central position in society, though admittedly not everywhere nor among every social group or class: urban centres and middle and working class were usually far less religious than peasants in the countryside, though religious patterns varied widely throughout Europe and the dichotomy between secular industrial areas and pious countryside is far too simplistic.[1] In large parts of Europe, including some major urban and industrial areas such as the Rhineland, Christian churches indeed profoundly influenced the lives of millions, probably more intensively than ever before in history, regulating daily life patterns up to the most intimate. Women especially felt appealed by the churches, though men too were given a role in the ideal religious lives promoted by the Christian churches.[2]

The theory of functional differentiation argues that politics and economy (as well as other spheres) dissociated from religious tutelage, though it actually also means that while politics secularised, religion and economy depo-

1 McLeod, *Secularisation in Western Europe*; Idem, *Religion and the People of Western Europe*.
2 Van Osselaer, *The Pious Sex*; Idem and Buerman, "Feminization Thesis"; Pasture, "Beyond the Feminisation Thesis".

liticised.[3] But modern history does not show such a neat evolution, and in reality churches played a major part in politics again, especially from the late nineteenth century onwards, albeit not as constituent component of state power but via the personal beliefs of rulers, politicians and administrations or via confessional political parties (particularly in Catholic or religiously mixed areas). Claiming to be heirs of the Enlightenment, secularists or anti-clericals, as they were usually called, vehemently opposed Church interference in politics: this opposition generated one of the most salient political cleavages in large parts of (continental) Europe. However, nowhere in Europe state and church were totally separated, though the relations between most secularist regimes such as France after 1905 and countries with state churches could vary tremendously.[4] Moreover in many countries churches, Catholic as well as Protestant, organised social welfare (see Wilhelm Damberg & Patrick Pasture in this book).

While the fate of the Christian churches had fluctuated considerably in the course of the nineteenth and twentieth centuries, as Hugh McLeod reminds in the first chapter of this volume, by the 1960s this dominating position started to fundamentally change, even if Christian Democracy in the post-war years broke through to become the single most important political force in continental Western Europe.[5] While Christian Democracy can be interpreted either as an example of the secularisation of politics - as Christian Democrats operated as politicians in the political sphere, without directly 'representing' a Church - or as an illustration of the impact faith could still have in politics[6], its development in the first place points at another major shift within Christendom, the rise to prominence of the laity, illustrative of major changes not only between the laity and the hierarchy but also within the religious institutions about the relation with God and the world. Paradoxically the salience of the political divisions focused on the role of the churches in politics and society in Europe evaporated after World War II, not the least as the result of

3 For a recent restatement see Ziemann, "The Theory of Functional Differentiation and the History of Modern Society".

4 An overview with regard to contemporary developments in Madeley and Enyedi, eds., *Church and State in Contemporary Europe*. See also Motzkin and Fischer, eds., *Religion and Democracy in Contemporary Europe*.

5 An overview of the most recent general literature in Kaiser, "Review Article: Christian Democracy in Twentieth Century Europe", to be complemented with Kaiser and Wohnout, eds., *Political Catholicism in Europe*, and Gehler and Kaiser, eds., *Christian Democracy in Europe since 1945*.

6 An example of the first interpretation is Kalyvas, *The Rise of Christian Democracy in Europe*, e.g. 261, examples of the latter view include Conway, "Introduction"; Gehler and Kaiser, eds., *Christian Democracy in Europe since 1945*.

an increased pressure towards public organisation of social welfare. In the United States in contrast, Jon Butler recalls, political cleavages and allegiances gradually eclipsed traditional denominational divisions: the realignment of conservatives and liberals started already in the early 1950s but sharpened in the 1960s, culminating in the culture wars of the 1980s and '90s. All churches went through major processes of change in the post-war period, though none as spectacular and mediatised as the Roman Catholic Church, as illustrated by the much publicised Second Vatican Council - whose actual meaning remains subject to discussion, however. The Church of Rome nevertheless fundamentally altered its relation to the secular world as well as its rites and rituals and its presentation to the public.

What in the end stroke most, however, is the decline of participation and integration of ordinary faithful and the exodus of clergy, again mostly and most dramatically affecting the Catholic Church, leading to an acute sense of crisis (see data in Karel Dobbelaere & Jaak Billiet). Several dimensions of this decline can be acknowledged. Church affiliations constitute a clear indication: they dropped everywhere where they were recorded somewhere from the 1950s onwards (the actual chronology varies considerably between the different countries, but the trend is similar). Likewise, participation in Christian rites, in particular church attendance, fell down, even if rites de passage resisted much more to the downward slope - indeed to a certain extent illustrating a continuing need for sacralisation. The mainline churches also witnessed an exodus of clergy, though perhaps none as spectacular as the Roman Catholic Church. At the same time the grip of the churches on the life of the faithful, of youth in particular, weakened. Pop music, partying, and movies, though condemned or at least discouraged, appeared far more attractive than the activities the churches proposed. Traditional gender patterns were abandoned: especially young women saw no future in what traditional society and the churches taught about a life devoted to raising children at home. Modern contraception gave young women means to escape from the enforced life cycle, paid work offered them the means to become more autonomous and to choose for another lifestyle.[7] To be sure not only churches defended this 'traditional' - actually 'modern' - gender pattern, but they did so more radically and grounded their view in theological arguments. This allowed feminists to adopt strong anti-clerical and secularist positions, but also facilitated other movements and ideologies to adapt more smoothly. The issue, as Anne-Marie

7 This argument was most powerfully formulated by Brown, *The Death of Christian Britain*. A recent overview of the literature in Starkey, "Women Religious and Religious Women".

Korte demonstrates, had repercussions in the organisation of the Catholic Church as well, crystallising around the question of ordination and leadership.

The sense of urgency came most to the fore in the sixties, but a discourse on crisis had been subjacent during the whole twentieth century and particularly in the immediate post-war years (see some observations by Étienne Fouilloux).[8] Theologians and philosophers have been looking for different ways to conceive the relations between church and society ever since the Enlightenment raised new challenges to the Christian faith and the way the churches accommodated with the worldly powers. Some dreamed of a new alliance between Church and society, a *Nouvelle chrétienté*, though the term itself already indicates that in this thinking often continuity actually prevails, the reason why others certainly rejected the term or at least avoided using it (see the contributions of Étienne Fouilloux, Gerd-Rainer Horn, and Lodewijk Winkeler). Churches responded to the crisis of the 1940s mainly by missionary initiatives and moral crusades, which incidentally not seldom also aimed at reinforcing the clerical grip on the laity[9], but these missionary initiatives, even the whole concept of mission itself, were increasingly perceived as inefficient and no longer adequate in the 1950s and '60s, among mainline Protestants as well as among Catholics. In a secular environment, Christians should rather act like yeast in the dough, and engage with the world to ameliorate human conditions. Moreover, in an era of decolonisation and emancipation of the Third World the Eurocentric Christian idea of mission as 'saving souls' seemed totally out of tune.[10] (One could observe that in the USA, evangelicals did not give up their missionary ambitions, quite to the contrary, even if they adopted a more inclusive stance as denominational boundaries diluted.)

The Second Vatican Council was seen as an answer to this sense of crisis in the Catholic Church and the perception that she no longer disposed of the right tools and language to address the challenges of the time - hence the need for an 'aggiornamento'. The Council effectively anticipated some major social developments such as consumerism, care for the environment and the need for sustainable development, and raised expectations and true enthusiasm among believers as well as beyond its own constituency. On many subjects a 'Copernican revolution' (Marie-Dominique Chenu) was signalled, perhaps most clearly so in the recognition of the values of pluralism (including democracy and human rights). According to Lodewijk Winkeler, Pope

8 See in particular Fouilloux, *Une Église en quête de liberté*.

9 Pasture, "Modèles internationaux d'action ouvrière catholique".

10 Neckebrouck, *De stomme duivelen*.

John XXIII even adopted 'modernist' ideas. But the latter statement in fact reveals that the Council actually responded less to the current challenges of the times than it focused on some old controversies, and that even these were not all definitively settled. Another matter was that not all of the promises of the Council were effectively put in practice.[11]

Several contributions in this volume examine the question as to what extent the change that the Council seemed to herald was implemented in the actual practice of church life. Such reception of the Council was first of all directed inwardly, into the organisational structure and decision processes of the Catholic Church (Jan Grootaers). One of the major tasks put on the Council's agenda concerned the introduction of collegiality, the participation of local church leaders in the government of the Church. The issue divided the Council fathers in two opposite groups, and after the Council, the division remained present. During the pontificate of John Paul II it became clear that, despite some realisations of collegial decision-making, the former situation was largely consolidated. With regard to the post-conciliar attempt to reform the Roman curia, the Church's central administration, the preservation of the status quo was even more clear (Philippe Chenaux). Impulses to reform this apparatus eventually lead to limited changes. Also at the basis of the Church, the reception of the Council showed an ambivalent character, as could be noticed, e.g., in the evolution of religious orders in the Church (Joachim Schmiedl). In the wake of the Council, many orders and congregations seized the opportunity to renew their life, e.g. by a return to the charisma of their founder. This renewal succeeded fairly well, but it could not prevent a serious crisis in attractiveness and membership. Crisis and renewal went together, and chances to survive were especially presented to those religious institutes that transferred the centre of their recruitment and activities from Europe to other continents. As regards women, the Church neither during nor after the Council gave any indication that women ever could be ordained, but the internal democratisation did open up opportunities for women to take on leadership positions, which they did - what, as Anne-Marie Korte reminds, did not fundamentally change the masculine power structure. In the area of interfaith relations the positive reception of the Second Vatican Council was more real than in other fields of church life. The Council's turn to a more positive attitude towards other churches in fact created complete new relations among Christian churches, particularly with Protestantism (André Birmelé).

11 Among the more critical authors see esp. Pelletier, *La crise catholique*; Greeley, *The Catholic Revolution*.

So in the end the Council certainly did not meet the (divergent) expectations of the faithful. Moreover, the world in the 1960s was changing quickly. A new decolonisation wave gave the last blow to the remaining dominating position of Europe, even if European artists and thinkers still played a major role in the intellectual debate - which had little affinity with the preoccupations of the churches. Intellectuals, Lodewijk Winkeler argues, played a major role in the distribution and spread of new (as well as older) church critical views among the population: what was true for the Netherlands no doubt also applied, perhaps not to the same extent though, to other West European countries as well (see also Wilhelm Damberg & Patrick Pasture). Affluence and increased means of communication - the television that brought American consumer lifestyles into the living rooms of rural Bavaria, Brittany and Flanders - altered the lifestyles of all (Western) Europeans, from the German city dweller to the most remote Sicilian peasant. For the youth, girls and boys alike, it was party time! At least after school was out, as education democratised and nearly everyone learned to read and write - and to decide for oneself about the do's and don'ts: all forms of authority were questioned and in need of legitimacy. For churches that had learned to determine and control the lives of their flock up to the most intimate detail, it was a hard wake up. Notwithstanding its attempt to an 'aggiornamento', the Catholic Church more than many other major churches or denominations refused to surrender to the demands of modern times and set clear moral limits to the will of self-determination as regards sexual behaviour as well as views on priesthood and church life. The Church tried to stick to the old forms in 1968 in both Pope Paul VI's encyclical *Humanae vitae* and his *Credo* of 30 June 1968, in which the pontiff explicitly confirmed the basics of Catholic faith, criticising those who 'humanised' its basic principles up to diluting it. The authoritarian tone even more than the content - arguably few took the effort to actually read any of these church documents - provoked widespread protest and increased the crisis in all respects, particularly among the disillusioned clergy itself. Hence the Church's admonitions mainly provoked anger and protest, and were hardly followed except by the clergy, and more than the occasional few of the latter threw off the cowl. While this obviously captured public imagination and especially *Humanae vitae* possibly enhanced the alienation of many faithful, it did not provoke the crisis in the Catholic Church, as the decline set in considerably earlier, in several countries already before 1960, and similar disaffiliations occurred in other denominations (see also Karel Dobbelaere & Jaak Billiet).

A perhaps somewhat less obvious feature of the disintegration of the mainline churches is the blurring of boundaries, by which their sense of distinctiveness evaporated, most outspokenly in the eyes of ordinary believers.[12] A convergence in outlook between all mainline churches was partly due to the recognition of Protestant theologies for Catholicism and vice versa. The influence of theologians and opinion leaders such as Dietrich Bonhoeffer, Rudolf Bultmann, Johann Baptist Metz, Hans Küng, Jürgen Moltmann, John A.T. Robinson (*Honest to God*, 1963), Edward Schillebeeckx and the so-called Liberation Theology originating in Latin America but with its roots firmly in post-war West European Left Catholicism reached far beyond their denomination.[13] But the 'protestantisation' of Roman Catholicism went much further and came to the fore in the 'Copernican revolution' which in many ways transformed the Church, especially in its most visible features, such as the use of the vernacular instead of Latin, the importance attached to the Word of God, the simplified forms in architecture and liturgy style, the position and dress of the clergy, etc. More fundamental than the changes in outlook - even if they reveal more important underlying transformations - was the reconciliation with the modern world and the recognition of pluralism. Through growing ecumenical contacts, churches acquired a new sensitivity for the reality of religious plurality. In large institutional bodies such as the World Council of Churches, religious plurality became a crucial issue (Hans Ucko). Interchurch dialogue developed in the direction of genuine relationships between churches. From a theological point of view, this interchurch development, in which also the Catholic Church participated, was explicitly valued as a fundamental transformation that reshaped religious identity (Anton Houtepen). Ecumenical openness paved the way for interreligious encounter and led to the fundamental revision of theological views. According to Houtepen, during the second half of the twentieth century, western theology, inspired by enlightened criticism, arrived at a veritable "metamorphosis of the idea of God": God was no longer seen as a power, but rather understood in terms of participation and relatedness.

In the meantime, while theologians and church officials debated the opportunities of ecumenism and possible joint celebrations, the faithful since the 1960s - though in practice rather in the following decades - went much further and gradually decided for themselves that the differences between churches and denominations were man made, not really God's work, and hence no real obstacle existed to more intense crossovers such as mixed

12 Pasture, "Christianity in a De-traditionalising World"; Idem, "Religion in Contemporary Europe"; Idem, "Christendom since the Sixties".

13 On these antecedents see Horn, *Western European Liberation Theology*.

marriages or, in mixed areas, participating in each other services. That indeed happened increasingly, especially in the USA (Jon Butler).

The convergence actually did not stop between religious denominations, but included secular forces as well. As secular objectives took prevalence over religious ones, there was no longer need for the separate organisation of the faithful. This allowed for a recomposition of the socio-political landscape, which, for example, in the Netherlands materialised in the merger of the different Christian parties (1980) and of the Catholic and socialist trade union confederations (1977) after years of intense collaboration. The involvement with the world and the increased claims of solidarity indeed brought Christians on one line with socialists. This had already been the case with the so-called left-Catholics in the immediate after-war (see Gerd-Rainer Horn), but became mainstream in the late 1960s and 1970s, with political theology and liberation theology as its spearhead. It lead to claims of Progressive Fronts and Labour Unity.[14] But notwithstanding the prominence of progressive Christians in the media, conservatives actually associated more effectively in the USA as well as in Europe. Moreover, the lay leaders of confessional socio-political associations, invoking their autonomy in the world, did not always follow the appeals for unity. The Dutch 'de-pillarisation', by which the Catholic 'pillar' disintegrated - as was the case with the socialist, liberal, and albeit to a lesser extent the Protestant pillar -, which was often perceived as the model at the times, in hindsight actually constituted the exception: elsewhere, the confessional and secular subcultures, though profoundly changing, persisted.[15]

In the meantime the world became more plural and fragmented, also, and in particular, in religious perspective.[16] Relatively closed and homogenous socio-religious communities were broken up when people were confronted with many different lifestyles, even if only through television.[17] Moreover people no longer continued to live in their familiar parishes and neighbourhoods but migrated between the countryside and the expanding towns, cities and their expanding suburbs. Life partners in particular were increasingly found outside the familiar locality - though relations more and more lasted less than a lifetime, as 'alternative lifestyles', other than the traditional hetero-

14 Pasture, "Diverging Paths".

15 Hellemans, *Strijd om de moderniteit*; Idem, "Zuilen en verzuiling in Europa"; Pasture, "Christendom since the Sixties". See also ch. 3.

16 Graf and Große Kracht, "Einleitung: Religion und Gesellschaft im Europa des 20. Jahrhunderts", and Knippenberg, "Europäische Religionsgeschichte".

17 Hervieu-Léger, *Religion as a Chain of Memory* (originally: *La religion pour mémoire*).

sexual marriage, gained popularity. In addition, especially when they lived in more urban and industrial environments, people were confronted with migrants from other regions and countries, from within Europe but in the 1950s and '60s increasingly from other continents. These migrants, since the 1960s mostly Moslems, had different customs and beliefs, but apparently in contrast to the USA, these did not spread much beyond the migrant communities themselves. For the migrants, their faith remained a source of certainty and identity in an often hostile or at least not always very welcoming environment: integration was a particularly difficult process that took several generations. In this process, at least the Catholic migrants from Eastern and Mediterranean Europe in the more prosperous north-western regions gradually lost their distinctiveness, something still not (yet) happening with the Moslems who arrived in Europe since the 1960s. In addition to Islam, in the wake of hippie culture Eastern religions such as Hinduism and Buddhism appeared on the European scene in the late 1960s and 1970s. As far as it concerned middle class youth and intellectuals - not 'guest workers' or refugees - these often arguably contributed to a certain "Easternisation" (Colin Campbell) expressed best in New Age.[18] These Eastern religions, in particular Zen Buddhism, did also influence Christian traditions, though the extent and complex ways through which remain understudied (Liliane Voyé offers a first assessment). To a remarkably limited extent also Christian charismatic and healing practices were introduced in Europe, closely associated with American examples and in the 1990s also by African migrants.[19] These charismatics did gradually influence mainstream Christian churches in the 1990s, though also this development largely remains uncharted territory.

The mainstream churches became more plural themselves as a result of different interpretations and increased individualism. Catholic liturgical practices, for example, became quite varied since Vatican II introduced the vernacular and opened the door for cautious renewal. Often this lead to widespread experiment which ended the existing uniformity. This situation provoked a schism between the Church of Rome and some renegades opposing the renewals of Vatican II, grouped around the conservative French bishop Msgr. Marcel Lefebvre, who was excommunicated in 1988.[20] But overall, these distinctions within the changing religious landscape should not obliterate that the impact of the established churches as well as the new religious movements on society decreased, even if the churches did express them-

18 Campbell, *The Easternization of the West*; Graff and Große Kracht, "Einleitung", 29.
19 Jenkins, *God's Continent*, 93-102; Coleman, *The Globalisation of Charismatic Christianity*.
20 Pasture, "Christendom since the Sixties".

selves in politics regularly and loudly. Only by the end of the millennium, it appeared that their voice may have had an impact, paradoxically most so where they were officially curtailed and prevented from a public role.
In Western Europe the decline of traditional institutional religiosity, be it in new forms, did not necessarily lead to a disappearance of religiosity altogether. Instead, as Liliane Voyé describes, syncretist forms of spirituality developed, both outside and inside the Christian traditions, composed of individual ritualistic practices and referring to religious symbols originating in various (often Eastern religious) contexts.[21] According to Staf Hellemans, they expressed a 'longing without belonging'[22], while Anton van Harskamp observes that they did not have much impact on fundamental orientations of life[23], though especially the latter view may mainly express the incapacity of traditional sociology to come to terms with these new forms of believing.[24] Colin Campbell in this respect has argued for a more positive approach that looks for the inner logic and coherence of contemporary spiritualism, of which he emphasises its immanent character as a sign of 'Easternisation'. The latter interpretation may - or not - be a crude overstatement, but at least offers some interesting perspectives for further research, also with regard to liturgical, ritualistic and meditative practices in mainline churches, a hitherto neglected topic.[25]

The transformation of the religious landscape in Europe has been the subject of research and speculation.[26] Until the 1980s the dominating paradigm no doubt was the secularisation thesis, whose origins go back to the great classical social thinkers - from Max Weber and Emile Durkheim over Sigmund Freud and Karl Marx to August Comte and Herbert Spencer - and which got a new boost in the 1960s with authors such as David Martin, Bryan Wilson and Peter Berger. Even in its most sophisticated formulations, distinguishing between different sociological levels[27], it argues that modernisation causes religion to marginalise, being relegated to the private sphere and loosing relevance both for the public and for individual life. Karel Dobbelaere, for example, distin-

21 See also Campbell, *The Easternization of the West*; de Groot, "Three Types of Liquid Religion"; Heelas, Woodhead et al., *The Spiritual Revolution*; Luckmann, *The Invisible Religion*.
22 Hellemans, "From 'Catholicism Against Modernity' to the Problematic 'Modernity of Catholicism'", 124 (the idea of "longing without belonging" was originally formulated by Boym, *The Future of Nostalgia*, 252).
23 Van Harskamp, "Simply astounding. Ongoing secularization in the Netherlands?".
24 Campbell, The Easternization of the West, 69.
25 Ibidem.
26 A discussion on the different theoretical perspectives in Hellemans, "Die Transformation der Religion und der Grosskirchen".
27 Sommerville, "Secular Society Religious Population".

guishes between the social process by which (1) different 'spheres' become autonomous and religion becomes irrelevant in politics, economy, the arts, etc., (2) individuals disaffiliate from churches and (3) religious concepts loose their original meaning.[28] As a meta-narrative explaining long term changes, the gradual 'secularisation' of modernising societies since the seventeenth century - or a 'Golden Age of Faith' situated somewhere since or even in the European Middle Ages - has been fallen in desuetude, notwithstanding the powerful restatements of it by Steve Bruce.[29] Among the alternatives, rational choice ranks high. Largely inspired by the success of Christian denominations in the USA it argues that in a religious 'free market', created by the separation between church and state, religions compete and those that find the best ways to present themselves and fulfil the religious needs of the people - assumed to be constant - would succeed. In that perspective, religious pluralism creates a dynamic context in which religions prosper, as evangelicals in the USA testify.[30] But, as Karel Dobbelaere and Jaak Billiet demonstrate in the present volume, because of the absence of real competition between religions, the theory in its classic formulation does not apply to Europe, and secularisation theory, especially referring to rationality and societalisation, far more explains the decline of religious practices and orthodoxy. Hence the secularisation thesis seems to regain some of its credibility, at least as regards present-day developments in Europe.[31] Connecting long-term, medium-term and short-term factors, Hugh McLeod recently explained the religious crisis of the 1960s as the end of Christendom, arguing in this volume that there are some important features particular to the present crisis since the 1960s.[32] Nevertheless, there exist other meta-narratives for long-term developments

28 Dobbelaere, *Secularization: an Analysis at Three Levels*. A recent reassessment is Dobbelaere, "Assessing Secularization Theory". A more historical assessment in Tschannen, *Les théories de la sécularisation*.

29 Bruce, *God is Dead*, and Idem, *Religion in the Modern World*. Compare Nash, "Reconnecting Religion with Social and Cultural History".

30 The main proponents of the theory are Rodney Stark, Roger Finke and Laurence R. Iannaccone. A summary in Stark and Finke, *Acts of Faith*, and Finke, "The Illusion of Shifting Demand". For a critical assessment, see Young, *Rational Choice Theory and Religion*. A radical sociological critique in Bruce, *Choice and Religion*, and more recently (and less critical), the special issue of *Social Compass*, 15 (2006) 5. Most recent studies of secularisation also contain a critical examination and rebuttal of rational choice theory. See, apart from Bruce's work, Norris and Inglehart, *Sacred and Secular*, 95-103. Especially the association between religious pluralism and religious growth has been subject to sharp criticisms, see Chaves and Gorski, "Religious Pluralism and Religious Participation".

31 For a recent restatement see Ziemann, "The Theory of Functional Differentiation and the History of Modern Society"; Idem, *Sozialgeschichte der Religion*; Pollack, "Religion und Moderne"; Idem, *Säkularisierung - ein moderner Mythos?*

32 McLeod, *The Religious Crisis of the 1960s*; McLeod and Ustorf, eds., *The Decline of Christendom in Western Europe*.

than the secularisation thesis or a rational choice perspective. Building upon the theoretical framework of Franz-Xaver Kaufmann and Karl Gabriel, in his recent work increasingly connecting with axial age theory of Karl Jaspers, Staf Hellemans interprets the transformations of mainline churches as modernisations, arguing that they adapt and participate in the modernisation processes. The period since the 1960s then offers a new phase in that process, during which the churches present themselves as one religious option among others, and act accordingly.[33] Danièle Hervieu-Léger however emphasised the impossibility to maintain a *lignée croyante*, the chain of memory which in her view constitutes the core of religion, in a society that was opened up by affluence and increased communication. These generated a crisis of formal and informal education, leading to a *société amnésique*, where the traditional confessional culture - Catholic in the France that she studies - evaporated.[34] But this situation leaves room for a search for new religious expressions. This points at another important development, the broadening of the perspective away from the churches to include a larger socio-religious landscape, a result of the declined impact of the religious institutions and the importance of other and non-institutional religious expressions, which come to the fore in the syncretism that Liliane Voyé assesses. Patrick Pasture elsewhere connected this idea with Grid-Group Cultural Theory developed initially by Mary Douglass to assess the fluctuating interactions between society and religion which lead to different, often even contradictory religiosities and spiritualities.[35]

This does not, however, imply the disappearance of the mainline churches. To be sure, they attract less and less followers, and their entanglement with other institutions - which also weakened - diminished. In response to the pluralisation of the religious landscape, mainly as a result of migration by Moslems, also in Europe the idea of a more radical separation between church and state found its way into political practices, though still not absolute: state-church relations rather seem to be evolving towards complex relations of various forms of conditional support for certain religious expressions (within one country), with not all faiths treated exactly the same way, - not that of secularist systems, as existed in the former communist East European

33 Hellemans, "How Modern is Religion in Modernity?"; Idem, "From 'Catholicism Against Modernity' to the Problematic 'Modernity of Catholicism'"; Idem, "Die Transformation der Religion und der Grosskirchen"; Idem, *Het tijdperk van de wereldreligies*.

34 Hervieu-Léger speaks of the "ex-culturation of Catholicism": Hervieu-Léger, *Catholicisme, la fin d'un monde*, 96-97, 268, 277, 285-286, 312-313. For a more theoretical approach, see Idem, *Religion as a Chain of Memory*; Davie, *Religion in Modern Europe*.

35 Pasture, "Christianity in a De-traditionalising World"; Idem, "Religion in Contemporary Europe".

countries or France.[36] But churches since the 1960s and especially the 1980s intervened again more directly, albeit more as bearers of moral authority and with regard to social ethics (see Johan Verstraeten), in principle accepting the autonomy and plurality of the political - though especially the Catholic Church's public interventions do not leave much room for manoeuvre and should be quite compelling to the faithful, be it that these no longer consider the Church's directives as such. However, not only in politics the faithful decide for themselves about the do's and don'ts: syncretism and religious bricolage belong to the standard elements of religious practice in every context. Also in the liturgy, especially during rites de passage, ordinary believers, not the clergy become the designers of ceremony, following loosely the Church's prescripts.

The present volume does not address all of the issues and questions mentioned in these introductory pages. Most somehow do appear. The first chapters provide historical and sociological analyses of the transformations of the position of the churches in post-war Europe - and one, by Jon Butler, concerning the United States as counterpoint - from different perspectives. The following chapters focus on some major issues that the churches dealt with: social ethics, the position of women, and ecumenism. Jaak Billiet, Karel Dobbelaere and Bart Cambré adopt an altogether different issue assessing the relationship between church commitment, religious pluralism and tolerance, and the attitude towards migrants in Europe. The last part is entirely dedicated to a major momentum in the history of the Catholic Church, the Second Vatican Council and its impact.

This volume results from a conference held in Leuven in September 2002. We wish to thank KADOC for turning this collection of papers into a nice book, and all the authors for taking in account the suggestions of the editors, as well as for their patience, as finalising this manuscript took far more time as could be expected.

36 The overall convergence includes in particular traditional Protestant, Anglican and Catholic countries. If it includes also Orthodox countries is less clear, though, as Silvio Ferrari observed, it is significant that none of the post-communist countries where Orthodoxy dominates has opted to adopt the Greek state-church system. Ferrari, "State Regulation of Religion in the European Democracies", esp. 107-108. See also Madeley and Enyedi, eds., *Church and State in Contemporary Europe*.

I
Continuities and Discontinuities in Religiousness

The Present Crisis in Historical Context

Hugh McLeod

Historians divide between those who see fundamental changes as products of gradual long-term evolution, and those who focus on short periods of revolutionary upheaval. To the former party belongs Alan Gilbert. In *The Making of Post-Christian Britain* he begins his story in the thirteenth century. Secularisation is almost as slow as the geological processes that built the Himalayas, and just as inexorable. The religious crisis of the 1960s and 1970s was merely the logical conclusion of developments which began in the distant past.[1] Other historians have reached the same conclusions by different routes. For instance, a very similar evolutionary model of progressive religious decline appears to underlie the work of the distinguished Marxist historian, Eric Hobsbawm. This is reflected in the amount of space devoted to religion in successive volumes of his series of histories of the world since 1789 (focusing initially on Europe, but gradually extending more widely). In the volume covering the years 1789-1848 religion gets a chapter. In the volume on 1848-1875 it is reduced to five pages, prefaced by the comment that "Compared to secular ideology religion in our period is of slight interest, and does not deserve extended treatment". By the twentieth century Christianity is reduced to a few scattered pages, though Islam gets slightly more attention. The underlying assumptions are stated in the first of these volumes, namely that religion is "no longer dominant (to use a biological analogy)" but "recessive", and that even in periods when it appeared to be advancing it was really declining.[2]

In recent years the approaches embodied in their different ways by Gilbert and Hobsbawm have come under widespread attack, not only because of a

1 Gilbert, *The Making of Post-Christian Britain*.
2 Hobsbawm, *The Age of Revolution*, 261; Idem, *The Age of Capital*, 271; Idem, *The Age of Extremes*.

priori objections to their determinism, but also on more empirical grounds. One of the main themes of recent research on modern European religion has been to suggest that histories which have subordinated all else to the master theme of secularisation have seriously underestimated the significance of religion, the churches, and indeed the religious generally in the eighteenth and nineteenth centuries and the first half of the twentieth century.[3] The most outspoken of these critics is Callum Brown, according to whom "Gilbert felt empowered by the intellectual bravado of 1970s sociology to vacuum up vast swathes of history in his own contestable generalisations".[4] As against Gilbert's vision of a British Christianity in long slow decline, Brown argued that a hitherto healthy patient had suddenly met with a catastrophic (and quickly fatal) accident in the 1960s. He therefore starkly entitled his book *The Death of Christian Britain*. Brown emphasised the dominant role of Christianity, and especially of Evangelical Protestantism, in nineteenth-century Britain, and its continuing influence up to the 1950s especially in areas of personal morality and views of the self. He argues that the 1960s brought sudden and drastic change, as a result, especially, of women's rejection of older concepts of femininity, and the emergence of a rebellious youth culture. These changes were reflected in a rapid decline in participation in the rites of passage and in the numbers of young people joining the church, as well as in the 'sexual revolution'.

Brown believes the changes in the 1960s to be entirely beneficial. But his chronology is not so different from that of some traditionalist Christian historians. For instance, Cholvy and Hilaire in their classic narrative of religion in modern France refer to the years 1930-1960 as French Catholicism's "Thirty Glorious Years", but they depict the 1960s as a disaster. They blame it mainly on the mistakes made by those clergy who took the ideas of the Second Vatican Council to harmful extremes, who engaged in mistaken pastoral experiments, or who were seduced by the spirit of '68.[5]

But the approach which focuses on sudden and drastic changes also has its problems. In order to highlight the extent of the changes in the 1960s and 1970s Brown tends to overstate the extent of Christian, especially Evangelical, influence in earlier periods. And in order to emphasise the suddenness of

3 For an overview of more recent 'revisionist literature', see McLeod, "New Perspectives on the Religious History". A striking example is Blaschke, "Das 19. Jahrhundert".

4 Brown, *The Death of Christian Britain*, 201.

5 Cholvy and Hilaire, *Histoire religieuse de la France contemporaine 1930-1988*, 282-290, 311-312, 315-324, 328-330.

the changes around 1960s, he gives insufficient attention to the longer-term preconditions for the changes at that time.

My aim in this paper is to put the religious crisis of the 1960s in the context of earlier religious crises, in order to assess which aspects were new, and which were a continuation of long-established trends. As against those like Brown who see the present crisis as uniquely damaging to the Christian churches, I want to stress the seriousness of earlier crises and their traumatic impact upon contemporaries. As against those who stress continuity, I want to say that some aspects of the present crisis really are new, and do thus present the Christian churches with problems they never faced before.

In the first part I will look at some of the major crises faced by West European Christianity during the eighteenth and nineteenth centuries and the first half of the twentieth century, and at how they were experienced by contemporaries. I shall place these in three categories: intellectual and cultural developments; social change; and politics. In the second part I will look at what is new in the present situation.

Crises faced by West European Christianity

In England the abolition of censorship in 1694 precipitated what has been called 'the deist crisis'. Within a short period, a number of books were published which attacked orthodox Christianity from a deist point of view. Similar ideas were already being published in the Dutch Republic. In France, where publication was impossible, they were being circulated through manuscripts. The first half of the eighteenth century saw the development of an educated public opinion suspicious of Christian orthodoxy, whether from a deist, an atheist or (more often, probably) from a 'rational Christian' point of view.[6] All forms of 'enthusiasm' and 'superstition' were under attack, together with such 'gloomy' doctrines as that of Original Sin. *Christianity not Mysterious* was the title of one of the most famous works in this genre, and the overt intention of this literature was not so much directly to attack Christianity, as to jettison all those aspects of traditional doctrine that were deemed incompatible with modern enlightened reason, in order to preserve a kernel of truth. However, it is clear that in private there was a section of the intellectual and social elite which was

6 For a maximalist view of the conflict between Christianity and Enlightenment, see Gay, *The Enlightenment*. More nuanced is Porter and Teich, eds, *The Enlightenment in National Context.*

prepared to go much further in distancing itself from any form of Christianity. In 1736 the philosopher and Anglican bishop, Joseph Butler, claimed that it was "taken for granted by many persons that Christianity is not so much a subject of inquiry, but it is at length discovered to be fictitious".[7]

By the second half of the century there were evident signs of a significant degree of alienation from the Christian churches or from Christianity generally among a section of the intellectual, social and political elite. For the first time in many centuries avowed unbelievers, such as Frederick the Great of Prussia or Pombal in Portugal sat on thrones or acted as chief ministers. The 'Enlightened Absolutism' fashionable among monarchs of that era, while not anti-Christian, aimed to cut back the economic and social role of the church, and was hostile both to many aspects of popular piety, and to such central aspects of Catholic and Orthodox religious life as monasticism. (Admittedly the Protestant churches less often found themselves in conflict with 'enlightened' authority, though 'orthodox' Protestants found themselves in conflict with 'modernising' church leaders, backed by the state or social elites.)[8] Also new was the prominence of unbelievers, sceptics or those who were highly unorthodox in their religious position among the leading writers of the period. While we have little evidence for other countries, it is clear that in German cities the second half of the eighteenth century saw a severe decline in religious practice - quite as sharp in fact as anything that has happened in more recent years. In the extreme case of Hanover the number of communions in the year per 100 Protestants fell from 150 in 1750 to 20 in 1800. In other cities the drop was less spectacular, but still substantial - for instance, from 100 to 45 in Hamburg, and from 150 to 40 in Berlin. The reasons for this severe decline have not yet been investigated in any great detail, but it is clear that falling participation in the church was not only a facet of small intellectual elites, but was spread more widely.[9]

Christianity was back in fashion after 1815. But it was not long before the doubters returned to the attack.[10] The assault had at least three dimensions. First there was the attack on the credibility of the Bible. Second, there were claims that science had completely superseded theology. Third, there was a new religion of art and literature, whose devotees claimed to have discovered truths inac-

7 Butler, *The Analogy of Religion*, Advertisement.

8 A good example is Scotland, where ministers of the established Church played a leading part in the Enlightenment, while facing considerable opposition from the evangelical "Popular Party". See Sher, *Church and University in the Scottish Enlightenment*.

9 Hölscher, "Säkularisierungsprozesse", 244; Idem. "Hannover in the 19th century", 407.

10 Useful overviews include Chadwick, *The Secularization of the European Mind*; Nipperdey, *Deutsche Geschichte*, 403-451; Wilson, *God's Funeral*.

cessible either through science or through more traditional forms of religion. While Nietzsche in 1882 proclaimed the death of God, many of his contemporaries were saying the same thing in less colourful terms. As early as 1844 Marx had stated that in Germany the criticism of religion was complete. "Science has become a religion for us", the Berlin medical scientist, Rudolf Virchow, declared in 1865.[11] Meanwhile for Richard Wagner, traditional religion had become "artificial", but music offered "the essence of religion freed from all dogmatic fictions". Music would give modern civilisation "a soul", "a new religion".[12]

No doubt certain groups - for instance, scientists and musicians - were much more influenced by such claims than the population in general. But again, these ideas spread far beyond small circles of intellectuals. In Germany the adoption of Darwinism by the Social Democratic Party meant that some knowledge both of Darwin and of various anti-religious, but also completely non-Socialist, scientific writers spread to wide sections of the working class. In France Jules Ferry, Minister of Education at the time of the secularisation of the school system in the 1880s, was a disciple of Auguste Comte, and Comte's Positivism was one of the influences on the national school system as it developed at that time.[13] Again, it was probably among the educated middle class in the cities of northern Germany that the impact of these ideas was greatest. Berlin in the 1880s was said to be "the most irreligious city in the world", and levels of church-going in Berlin, Hamburg or Bremen were low not only by the standards of the later nineteenth century, but by those of the later twentieth century.[14]

Two important qualifications need to be made, however, when talking about the religious alienation of the educated middle class in the nineteenth century. First there are major differences between countries, or even between different regions of the same country. For instance, this alienation had gone further in Germany among Protestants and Jews than among Catholics, and further in Germany generally than in Britain. British visitors to Germany and German visitors to Britain in the nineteenth century both commented unfavourably on the religious situation - though for opposite reasons.[15] And Gunilla-Frederike Budde in a study comparing the upbringing of bourgeois children in England and Germany, contrasted the very high levels of church-going recorded in English

11 Nipperdey, *Deutsche Geschichte*, 496.
12 Obelkevich, "The Religion of Music", 562.
13 McLeod, *Secularisation in Western Europe*, 120-121, 154-156.
14 Ribbe, "Zur Entwicklung und Funktion der Pfarrgemeinden", 251; McLeod, *Piety and Poverty*, 10, 83; for comprehensive data on German Protestant religious practice, see Hölscher, ed, *Datenatlas zur religiösen Geographie*.
15 McLeod, "Comparing Secularisations", 185.

autobiographies and diaries with the much lower levels suggested by similar documents from Germany.[16] The second point is that in all countries there were significant gender differences. In 1842 the Bishop of Chartres told the women of his diocese "You are almost, at least in the parts where we live, the Church's only consolation". In fact the proportion of women receiving Easter Communion in his diocese was not remarkably high, but by comparison with the very low proportion of men doing so, it did seem a relatively 'consoling' figure.[17] Wherever in nineteenth-century Europe church congregations were declining, men were leaving at a faster rate than women. And even when women seldom went to church, they often continued to pray, read the Bible or sing hymns at home, to visit shrines, and to pass on their religious beliefs to their children.[18] Indeed, Paul Drews writing of the big cities of Saxony in 1902 went so far as to claim that the population was divided into "two great camps" of pious women and religiously indifferent men. Granting an element of exaggeration here, it would still be valid to suggest, as Charles Booth did, writing in the same year about working-class districts of London, that religion had a bigger place in the home than in the workplace.[19] This needs to be borne in mind in any assessment of the extent of secularisation in this period.

In northern Germany, the decline in religious practice preceded industrialisation and rapid urbanisation. There were many parts of Europe, however, where social and economic change in the nineteenth century undermined long established traditions of piety. Most obviously the growth of cities presented the churches with big logistical problems, as they struggled to build churches and schools and to provide sufficient clergy and other church workers for the new centres of population.[20] The relentless growth in parish size during the nineteenth century and the deterioration in ratios of clergy to people are both well known. Equally the giant cities of the nineteenth century provided space for subcultures of many diverse kinds, baffling all efforts by the church or authorities of any other kind to impose common moral standards. Thieves and prostitutes had always been familiar parts of the urban scene. Exiles, immigrants and communities of foreign merchants and artisans also had a long-standing presence in many cities. By the eighteenth century there is evidence of homosexual subcultures in London and Paris.[21] In the nineteenth century any large city was likely to

16 Budde, *Auf dem Weg ins Bürgerleben*, 386.

17 Gadbois, "'Vous êtes presque la seule consolation de l'Église'", 321; Gibson, *A Social History of French Catholicism*, 174.

18 McLeod, *Secularisation in Western Europe*, 124-136.

19 Drews, *Das kirchliche Leben*, 365; Booth, ed, *Life and Labour of the People in London*, I, 27-28.

20 See McLeod, ed, *European Religion in the Age of Great Cities*.

21 Sibalis, "Paris", 13; Trumbach, "London", 89-102.

include not only a bohemian element, but also a wide variety of exotic political and religious groups. So shocked or excited were observers by the image of the 'godless' city, that they were inclined to overlook the fact that the cities were also major centres for more conventional religious activities.[22] Inevitably, however, the proportion of the population engaged was not so great as in smaller towns and rural areas where the established church faced less competition. It should also be noted that in some countries the relative weakness of established religion in the major cities was compensated for by the strength of Dissenting or immigrant churches. In England, for instance, the Anglican church was stronger in the countryside than the city, but the Catholic church was mainly urban, and Baptists, Congregationalists, Methodists and other Dissenters also flourished in the cities: competition between them left a legacy of over-provision of religious buildings which is still visible in English cities today.[23] In Scotland in 1851 average levels of church-going were actually higher in urban than in rural areas.[24]

But the most important aspect of social change in the nineteenth century was the intensification of class conflict - and this affected many agricultural or industrial villages as much as the cities. Proletarianisation, arising from mechanisation and the increasing size of units of production, affected agriculture as well as industry. Indeed some of the starkest social contrasts in Europe were found in the regions of large estates in southern Spain, Portugal and Italy.[25] Laissez-faire economics and harsher treatment of the poor, embodied in such measures as England's New Poor Law of 1834, also had a general impact. On the other hand, it was in urban and industrial areas that working-class consciousness and organisation developed fastest. Strikes and lockouts were often the occasions on which the working class sense of their own 'otherness' crystallised. These struggles left a lasting sense of bitterness, which could find expression in resentment against the church and clergy, if the latter were perceived as being too close to 'the bosses'.[26] Thus in the 1905 Ruhr miners' strike, where the Protestant churches mainly tried to adopt a mediating role, they were criticised for being insufficiently supportive of the strikers, and it was subsequently claimed that the strike marked a turning point in relations between the church and the miners.[27] It may well be

22 For the range of religious options in nineteenth century French cities, see Kselman, "The Varieties of Religious Experience in Urban France".

23 See Gill, *The Myth of the Empty Church*.

24 Brown, *Religion and Society in Scotland*, 60.

25 For the religious alienation of many of the rural poor in southern Spain, see Lannon, *Privilege, Persecution and Prophecy*.

26 For an overview, see McLeod, *Piety and Poverty*, 103-147.

27 Brakelmann, "Evangelische Pfarrer", 314. See also Davies, *Religion in the Industrial Revolution in South Wales*, 160-161; McLeod, *Religion and Society in England*, 202-203.

that the significance of these 'defining moments' is exaggerated in memory.[28] The tensions and resentments inherent in the day to day relations between employers and workers and between members of different classes, and the problems faced by their clergy in their attempts to hold together a fractured community, may have had an equally significant role. In some parts of later nineteenth-century Europe there was a collapse of involvement in the church by the male working class, and this was sometimes linked with open hostility towards the clergy and others associated with the church. In 'red' Wedding the famous working-class district in north Berlin, Parish Helper Buchholz, himself a worker, claimed that "one is treated as a criminal just because one belongs to the church".[29] Berlin is in some ways an extreme case. But all over Europe at this time, class resentment coloured relations between the working class and the established church of their country. This found expression variously in atheism, in a non-church Christianity, in religious dissent, or in a pious anti-clericalism.[30]

Criticism of the church was most passionate when the critics were inspired by an alternative vision of how the world might be. In early twentieth-century Berlin, that was likely to be some kind of Socialism. The most acute crises faced by the Christian churches in the period from the later eighteenth to the mid-twentieth century were political because political parties and political ideals potentially had the mass appeal that faith in salvation by science or music lacked: the fear that reactionary churches were barring the way to a political utopia could provoke a fanatical hatred which relatively seldom arose from more abstract objections to Christianity.[31]

Government programmes of dechristianisation backed by the law, and where necessary by soldiers and police, were imposed briefly in France between 1793-1794, by the Spanish Republicans during the Civil War, and at greater length by Communist governments after 1945. In the former cases the attack though brief was very violent, including massacres of priests and a general closure of churches. In the latter cases more emphasis was put on atheist education and other forms of propaganda, though this was backed up by infiltration of the churches by police agents and imprisonment of clergy deemed too independent-minded. More limited secularising programmes have been carried out at other times, notably in the French Third Republic, where the objective was to eliminate reli-

28 The communicant statistics in Hölscher, ed, *Datenatlas*, IV (Westen), suggest a gradual long-term decline in the Ruhr mining towns rather than a sudden break in 1905, though in one district (Gelsenkirchen) there was a large drop between 1905 and 1906.

29 McLeod, *Piety and Poverty*, 26.

30 Idem, *Religion and the People of Western Europe*, 118-131.

31 On this theme, see Burleigh, *Earthly Powers*, and Idem, *Sacred Causes*.

gious personnel and symbols from public institutions and to oust practising Catholics from positions of power. This campaign was directed against the Catholic Church rather than against religion as such, and Protestants and Jews were generally strong supporters of the republic, though there were also many freethinkers among the anti-Catholic forces.

The effects of these campaigns were two-edged. They could be counter-productive, and in areas where the church enjoyed a very high level of popular support, or where it could become a focus for resistance to an unpopular government, external attack could reinforce loyalty to the church. On the other hand, where the church had already suffered a significant loss of support, persecution could deliver a fatal blow. It seems that in some parts of France the Catholic Church never fully recovered from the revolutionary dechristianisation.[32] During the Communist era the effects of attacks on the church varied considerably from country to country - failing in Poland, but being much more successful in East Germany and Czechoslovakia.[33] Indeed, staying out of the church seems to have become one of the ways by which the easterners can maintain some degree of identity within the reunited Germany.[34] The Nazi attack on Christianity and the churches was interrupted by the outbreak of the Second World War, but initial results seem to have been favourable from the Nazi viewpoint, as in the years 1937-1939 a million Germans left the Protestant church and the number of Protestant communicants fell by a third.[35]

When a political movement gains power there is the likelihood that it will fail to achieve many or even most of its objectives, and that supporters will become disillusioned. But as long as its opportunities for turning rhetoric into reality all lie in the future, supporters can continue to sustain limitless hopes, with corresponding bitterness towards any institution or movement that seems to be standing in the way. Extremes of disaffection from the church in the later nineteenth and early twentieth centuries were reached in areas where radical politics had become an alternative faith. In some strongholds of rural radicalism, like the Creuse department in central France or the sawmills districts of northern Sweden there were villages where no men, and hardly

32 For the differential legacy of the revolutionary attacks in various French regions, see Cholvy and Hilaire, *Histoire religieuse de la France contemporaine 1800-1880*, 259-300.

33 Lambert, "Religion", 156-157 showed huge differences in religious belief, practice and affiliation between the former Communist countries in 1999. The proportion saying they had a religion was 96% in Poland, but 34% in the Czech Republic.

34 For the effectiveness of atheist propaganda in East Germany, see Schmidt-Lux, *Wissenschaft als Religion*.

35 Hölscher, ed, *Datenatlas*, IV (Westen), 697, 704.

any women, went to church.[36] In towns and cities, or even large villages, there would be more people willing to defy the prevailing local orthodoxy. But for large sections of the population a radical subculture, with its own organisations, meeting places, festivals and even sacred rituals would meet most of the needs that were provided for elsewhere by religion and the churches.[37]

What is new?

What is old and what is new in the present religious crisis? Debates between 'science' and 'religion' continue on lines not very different from those of the mid-nineteenth century. Though new evidence has become available in support of the various positions in this debate, the basic arguments have not changed very much. Political messianism, on the other hand, seems at the moment a spent force, though it enjoyed a major revival in the 1960s and 1970s. And class-divisions clearly play a smaller role in present-day European societies than in the nineteenth century and the first half of the twentieth century - though they remain more important than many people would like to think. There are four areas, however, in which the present crisis is substantially different from those of the period before 1960. First there has been a radical expansion in the range of world views accessible to West Europeans; second, there have been changes in the relationship between religion and gender; third, there is the decline in participation in Christian rites of passage; and fourth changes in the relationship between religion and politics. Even in these areas there are elements of continuity. So, while recognising what is new in the situation emerging since the 1960s, we should not exaggerate the extent of the break with the past.

The 'spiritual market place' which has emerged since the 1960s is not entirely new. In Britain and the Netherlands, especially, there has for long been a huge variety of Christian denominations. And at least in the cities a variety of non-Christian alternatives were becoming available by the latter part of the nineteenth century. In particular, all forms of Spiritualism were flourishing in this period. By the 1880s and 1890s beliefs of Eastern origin were fashionable, and in Germany, according to Nipperdey, there were numerous forms of what he calls "vagrant religion".[38] Nonetheless, it can reasonably be argued that awareness of

36 Pérouas, *Refus d'une religion*, 57-65; Gustafsson, *Socialdemokratien och kyrkan*, 181-183.
37 See Lidtke, *The Alternative Culture*, or (for a more recent period) Bernard, *Paris rouge*.
38 Nipperdey, *Religion im Umbruch*, 143. See also, McLeod, *Secularisation in Western Europe*, 147-170.

these options has greatly increased since the 1960s, and unconventional forms of religion have also become more socially acceptable. For a young person growing up in the 1950s and seeking a systematic world view, the main alternatives were still Christianity, Marxism and scientism, or some mixture of these. Alternatives existed, but were mainly limited to the very adventurous or the willingly idiosyncratic. By the 1990s the possibilities were much wider, and eclecticism, rather than requiring some degree of bravery, had become normal.[39] A trend already well-established was now further accentuated by the internet, where the Pope competed on equal terms with dissident priests and those claiming to have received messages from the Virgin Mary, with Pagans and mystics, with Satanists and users of mind-expanding drugs. While the internet created new possibilities, long-term social changes had already prepared the way, and once again it was in the 1960s that the speed of change accelerated. One important trend was the decline of the kind of tightly-knit mainly working-class communities, often built around a locally-dominant industry, and bound together by common religious or political identities. Mining villages, port districts, textile towns, were all typical examples. Another important aspect of the 1960s was the development of a rebellious youth culture, built round pop music and fashion, open to experiments with sex and drugs, and facilitated both by more permissive styles of parenting and by the availability of relatively well-paid jobs for teenagers.[40] Symptomatic of the connection between youthful rebellion and religious experimentation was the flirtation with Eastern religion by the Beatles. There was also a combination of influences which favoured the widespread adoption of an ethos of individual self-fulfilment and complete freedom of personal choice, and which was correspondingly hostile to any idea that beliefs could be inherited.

A second way in which the current religious crisis is new is that it affects women as much as men. Callum Brown indeed claims that the most important dimension of religious change in the 1960s was the "de-pietisation of femininity and a de-feminisation of piety".[41] In the nineteenth and early twentieth centuries, men were much more likely than women to leave the church, and wherever there was a decline in religious practice, the 'gender gap' grew, because most of those who were giving up were men. There still is a gender gap. In most Christian congregations the majority of worshippers are still women, and a British poll of 1989 suggested that more women than men believe in God, though the difference is not dramatic - 84% as against 67%. Perhaps more surprisingly, research on the

39 Lambert, "Religion", 143-144, 146.

40 The British youth culture emerging in the later 1950s is described at length in Marwick, *The Sixties*, 55-80.

41 Brown, *Death of Christian Britain*, 192.

religious attitudes of teenagers in Britain suggests that a gap opens up between the ages of 13 and 15. By the latter age girls already score higher than boys on most indices of religious belief and practice.[42] In England between 1960 and 1979, the proportion of adolescent girls being confirmed into the Church of England fell by 56%, but the proportion of adolescent boys doing so fell by 62%.[43] The gap between boys and girls was thus actually widening slightly. In France it is estimated that the proportion of women who went to mass regularly fell from about 40% to about 14% between 1960 and 2000, while the rate for men fell from about 20% to about 7%.[44] More significant, however, than the continuing predominance of females among those who remain religiously active is the big drop since the 1960s in the proportion of females who *are* religiously active. By the 1970s, and to an increasing extent thereafter, fewer young women were coming to motherhood from a background of teenage religious involvement. Children are no longer being sent to Sunday School, no longer learning prayers at their mother's knee. Nor are the mothers likely to be setting an example of pious practice. The 'sexual revolution' of the 1960s sometimes played a part here as rejection of the church's sexual teaching could act as a catalyst for a wider revolt[45] - though changing patterns of family life may have had a bigger impact on religious practice. As the full-time mother increasingly gave way to the woman who combined motherhood with a career, many women simply had less time for seeing to the spiritual nurture of their children. Meanwhile, the women's liberation movement as it developed in the 1970s, in searching for explanations for women's subordination, tended to see the churches as among the major culprits. It seemed, at least for a time, that there was a contradiction between being a Christian and a feminist.

Women had often taken the lead in deciding that they would marry in church and in ensuring that their children were baptised. As women were becoming more distanced from the church, levels of participation in the rites of passage often dropped. This rebellion provided explosive material for family conflict. Parents were mortified to learn that their daughter was not going to be married in church, or even worse that she intended to cohabit without any marriage ceremony. Further unhappiness was on the way when they learnt that their grandchild was not going to be christened, and would grow up as a 'heathen'.

42 Davie, *Religion in Britain*, 119; Kay and Francis, *Drift from the Churches*, 10-21.

43 Brown, *Death of Christian Britain*, 191.

44 Diébolt, "Les femmes catholiques", 220.

45 The impact of the 'sexual revolution' is emphasised in Brown, *Religion and Society*, 240-253, while McLeod, *Religious Crisis*, 161-187, and passim, puts more stress on other reasons for the distancing of women from the church.

Again, the novelty of this situation should not be exaggerated. During the period between about 1800 and 1960 the popularity of the various rites of passage oscillated, as well as varying between religious traditions. There are many example of their neglect or rejection at particular times and places. Sometimes, as in France during the Third Republic refusal of Catholic rites was quite common in republican families, and was driven by a hostility to the church that was mainly politically motivated. In particular secular funerals were quite frequent.[46] More often the motives for neglect were less ideological. Civil weddings were common in Berlin in the Weimar period, the desire to save money being apparently a major consideration, since the civil ceremony was legally required and the religious ceremony was thus seen as an expensive duplication. Civil weddings were also common in some parts of England and Wales in the nineteenth century, but seem to have had nothing to do with secularism. In London, where many babies were unbaptised in the middle years of the nineteenth century, the rising baptismal rate in the later nineteenth century seems to have been associated with the establishment of more stable working-class communities, with large number of kin living in the same area, and with links being established between families and particular churches.[47] For reasons that do not seem to be known, the proportion of religious funerals in Germany rose from quite a low level in the mid-nineteenth century to a very high level in the early twentieth century.[48]

But rejection of the rites of passage in the nineteenth and early twentieth century was generally selective, or at least highly localised. Outside a few secularist strongholds, like the Creuse department, those who did without a church wedding would still baptise their children; and those who did not baptise their children would still want to give their loved ones a Christian burial. Participation in the rites of passage was a basis for Christian identity, and one of the chief means through which the mass of the population remained in contact with the church - though in some urban parishes, baptisms, weddings and funeral were so numerous, that the resulting contact may often have been rather superficial.[49] What is new in the present situation is the number of those rejecting all of the various rites - though selective rejection still persists. In Belgium, for instance, between 1967 and 1993 the proportion of babies being baptised fell from 94% to 73%, and the proportion of religious marriages fell from 86% to 57%, while

46 McLeod, *Secularisation in Western Europe*, 261-263.

47 Idem, *Piety and Poverty*, 183; Anderson, "The incidence of civil marriage in Victorian England and Wales"; Bartlett, *The Churches in Bermondsey*, 182-188.

48 Hölscher, ed, *Datenatlas*, I (Norden), 16-17.

49 McLeod, *Piety and Poverty*, 7.

the drop in religious funerals was only from 84% to 80%.[50] In England, too, there has been a sharp drop in the proportion of babies being baptised, but the proportion of Christian funerals remains very high - though in keeping with the eclectic spirit of the age, it is becoming common to mix Christian liturgies with readings and music from other sources.[51] However there are big differences between European countries both in the overall level of participation in the rites of passage and in the relative popularity of the various rites. The decline has been greatest in France, Belgium, the Netherlands and Britain, whereas the overall level remains high further south in Spain and Italy, further north in Finland and the Scandinavian countries, and further west in Ireland.[52]

A fourth area of changes lies in the loosening of the links between religion and politics. In the later nineteenth century, there were high levels of correlation between people's denominational affiliation or level of religious practice and their voting; religious issues featured prominently in party programmes; religious or anticlerical rhetoric played a big part in political propaganda; clergymen often had close links with particular parties, and sometimes offered their congregations guidance on how they should vote.[53] In Britain it was as early as 1918 that class replaced religion as the principal influence on voting.[54] Crucial here was the fact that the British Labour Party was not anticlerical or antireligious in the manner of many of its continental counterparts, so the church-going worker could vote Labour for class reasons, and opposition to Labour was mainly based on economic rather than religious arguments. At the same time, the Church of England was moving away from its historic identification with the Conservative Party, and trying to establish a position of political neutrality: in 1920, nine bishops were declared Conservatives, but by 1930 there was only one.[55] However, in much of Europe, religious affiliation and practice still in the 1960s provided the best predictors of how a person would vote.[56] Since the later 1960s the political significance of religion has generally diminished.[57] This is partly, but only partly, a consequence of declining levels of religious commitment: in earlier periods those who left the church often joined anticlerical radical movements, but now this is rare. A great number of other factors have played a role.

50 Voyé, "Belgique", 204.
51 Gill, *Myth of the Empty Church*, 218; Wolffe, *Great Deaths*, 272-273.
52 Davie, *Religion in Modern Europe*, 72-78.
53 See, for example, Wald, *Crosses on the Ballot*; Sperber, *The Kaiser's Voters*; Ormières, "Les rouges et les blancs".
54 Wald, *Crosses on the Ballot*.
55 Catterall, "The Conservative Party and Religion", 644-647.
56 Madeley, "Politics and Religion in Western Europe", 30.
57 Dogan, "Class, Religion, Party".

The generally more volatile electoral situation, and the weakening of party loyalty has weakened all the large old-established parties, including Social Democrats and Communists, as well as Christian Democrats. The period from the late 1950s onwards saw parties of the Left gradually dropping a large part of their anticlerical traditions, at the same time that the Second Vatican Council and a variety of radical movements within the Protestant churches were undermining the idea that Christians should also be conservatives. By the 1980s both believers and unbelievers were to be found at most points on the political spectrum. Though correlations still existed between particular kinds of religion and support for a particular party, the differences were not large enough to make a major electoral impact.[58] At the individual level the connections between religious and political beliefs often remained very important[59], but these connections were made in such varied ways that the political impact of religion has become diffused. In the nineteenth century hatred of the church was rooted in politics, but politics was also a source of loyalty to the church. As going to church ceases to have a clear and consistent political meaning, indifference has become easier.

Conclusion

The Christian churches in Western Europe recovered from earlier crises which were, in particular places, as severe as that experienced at the present day. However, these earlier crises were more localised. Catastrophic decline in one place was always matched by continuing, or increasing strength elsewhere. The present crisis is uniquely wide-ranging, in that all countries and regions are in greater or lesser degree affected, all classes, women as well as men. In the Western Europe of the nineteenth and early twentieth centuries there were deep cultural divides between countries, regions, classes: the churches became deeply identified with some groups and communities and deeply alienated from others. With the increasing homogenisation of European societies in the later twentieth century, both commitment and alienation have become mainly individual phenomena, no longer deeply rooted in the life of particular communities. For European Christians this presents a new and unfamiliar situation, though also one which offers new opportunities. Madeley suggests that

58 Cautres, "Religion et comportement électoral en Grande-Bretagne". The maps of voting in the French presidential elections of 1988 and 1995 in Ormières, "Rouges et blancs" graphically illustrate the tendencies towards homogenisation and the weakening of old religiously based regional patterns.

59 A survey of members of the UK Parliament in 1994 found that 65% of Conservative MPs and 49% of Labour MPs claimed that religion had been a significant factor in shaping their political views. McLeod, *Religion and the People of Western Europe*, 150-151.

"religion's contribution to political life" has changed from being "a straightjacket" to "a coat-of-many-colours".[60] The weakening of historic links with particular political parties or social classes leaves more space for the experimental and the unconventional.

60 Madeley, "Politics and Religion in Western Europe", 64.

Feu la "nouvelle chrétienté"?

Étienne Fouilloux

Deux sondages grandeur nature, en guise d'introduction. Dans la riche production sur l'histoire des intellectuels au XXe siècle, les catholiques d'expression française ont enfin reçu l'attention qu'ils méritaient. S'il n'existe pas d'étude équivalente pour la Suisse romande[1], leur activité en Wallonie et en France a récemment fait l'objet de recherches approfondies.

La thèse de Jean-Louis Jadoulle, soutenue à Louvain-la-Neuve le 8 octobre 1999, explore le parcours et les positions de quatre vecteurs intellectuels wallons entre 1945 et 1958: *La Relève*, publication de l'aile rénovatrice du Parti social-chrétien; sa consoeur bien connue *La Revue nouvelle*, autour du chanoine Jacques Leclercq et de ses jeunes disciples; le supplément belge à l'hebdomadaire parisien *Témoignage chrétien*; les groupes "Esprit" de Belgique. Il ne s'agit certes là que de périodiques et de cercles qualifiés par l'auteur, de "modernes" ou de "progressistes", à l'exclusion de personnalités et de milieux plus modérés, voire franchement conservateurs ou traditionalistes.[2] Malgré cette incontestable limite, les résultats de l'enquête se révèlent fort instructifs pour notre propos. Les quatre courants décrits acceptent, pour l'essentiel, le diagnostic venu de France quant au détachement religieux d'une partie de la population wallonne, spécialement dans le monde ouvrier. Ils en acceptent aussi le corollaire sur l'urgence du "retour des masses au Christ", sur la nécessité d'une "reconquête chrétienne" ou d'une "rechristianisation de notre époque", toutes expressions relevées dans *La Revue nouvelle*.[3] Mais un tel désir

1 Signalons malgré tout *De l'amitié. Hommage à Albert Béguin*, textes réunis par Martine Noirjean de Ceuninck sous la direction de Jean Borie.
2 Jadoulle, *Chrétiens modernes?*
3 Ibidem, 357.

s'accompagne rarement de la volonté de "rebâtir une chrétienté"[4], même une "chrétienté nouvelle" sans nostalgie vis-à-vis de la chrétienté médiévale, pour peu qu'elle ait vraiment existé.[5]

Jacques Maritain n'est pas oublié, mais certaines appréciations portées sur son œuvre critiquent sa trop rigide orthodoxie thomiste.[6] Quand elle est évoquée, la "chrétienté future" lui doit pourtant beaucoup, bien que dilatée aux dimensions d'"une unité d'inspiration de toutes les bonnes volontés - dont les chrétiens doivent d'ailleurs être les animateurs - à la poursuite des valeurs humaines manifestées dans l'Évangile et que nous traduisons habituellement par l'expression 'droits et devoirs des personnes'", selon le dominicain Paul Bourgy, dans le supplément belge de *Témoignage chrétien*.[7] Significative, d'un tel point de vue, apparaît la distance prise par rapport à la thèse de l'État chrétien en honneur dans l'Espagne du général Franco.[8] Seuls quelques animateurs des groupes "Esprit", comme Jean Ladrière, consomment toutefois la rupture avec l'hypothèse de la tolérance pour les non-catholiques et appellent de leurs voeux une pleine liberté religieuse.

D'ailleurs, souligne Jean-Louis Jadoulle, "le terme de 'chrétienté' est très rarement utilisé" dans le matériau qu'il a dépouillé. On y va même jusqu'à mettre en doute l'existence d'un modèle catholique de société: "il n'y a pas de doctrine sociale de l'Église, écrit Paul Bourgy dans *Témoignage chrétien* dès 1949, mais une doctrine morale de l'Église en matière sociale".[9] À l'évidence, l'instauration ou la restauration d'une chrétienté, fût-elle nouvelle, n'est plus une priorité pour ces intellectuels belges au lendemain de la Seconde Guerre mondiale. *La Cité chrétienne* de Jacques Leclercq ne s'est-elle pas transformée, au prix d'un certain nombre de modifications éclairantes, en *Revue nouvelle*?[10]

La lecture de la thèse de Claire Toupin-Guyot sur le Centre catholique des intellectuels français, soutenue à Lyon le 1er juillet 2000, conduit à des conclusions voisines.[11] D'autant que le C.C.I.F., du fait de son souci de dialogue tous

4 Jadoulle, *Chrétiens modernes?*, 358 (*Témoignage chrétien belge*, 2 juin 1950).
5 Ibidem, 362 (Jacques Leclercq dans *La Revue nouvelle*, 15 novembre 1952).
6 Ibidem, 751.
7 Ibidem, 400 (5 janvier 1951).
8 Voir les références données dans Ibidem, 362, note 101.
9 Ibidem, 376 (25 février). Ou encore, du même: "Les principes généraux de la doctrine sociale de l'Église sont compatibles avec des conclusions et des applications très divergentes", Ibidem, 374 (29 juillet).
10 Sauvage, "*La Cité Chrétienne*", 222-225; Ibidem, *Jacques Leclercq*, 187-276.
11 Elle a bénéficié d'une large publication sous le titre: *Les intellectuels catholiques dans la société française*.

azimuts, est plus représentatif du monde intellectuel catholique français que l'échantillon de Jean-Louis Jadoulle, marqué à gauche et au centre-gauche. Sur "Ordre temporel et vérité religieuse", l'intransigeant abbé André Richard débat ainsi avec les pères Bouillard et Congar, en 1950.[12] L'année suivante, le Centre finit par publier, non sans retouches, la réponse de Louis Salleron, affirmative jusqu'à la polémique[13], à la question: "Les chrétiens ont-ils un espoir temporel?" En difficulté avec le Saint-Office pour avoir donné la parole à des auteurs suspects, les animateurs de la rue Madame cherchent à élargir leur palette sur la droite: Gustave Thibon est invité à la Semaine des intellectuels 1956; Jacques Chevalier, et l'Italien Luigi Gedda, à celle de 1957.[14] Un tel dosage non dépourvu de signification "politique" ne doit cependant pas tromper: à partir de 1952, les prises de position du Centre contre la répression au Maroc, puis contre la torture en Algérie, lui aliènent de façon durable, et parfois violente, l'aile conservatrice du catholicisme français.[15] Au total, il a d'ailleurs éprouvé plus de difficultés pour instaurer un dialogue entre les diverses tendances de celui-ci que pour établir des liens avec nombre de penseurs extérieurs à la foi. Et sa tentative avouée de synthèse chrétienne a vite trouvé des limites sur sa droite.

Le thème de la chrétienté en fournit un bon exemple, tant par sa rareté dans les travaux du Centre que par la manière dont il y est traité, de façon incidente le plus souvent. Rareté? Un minutieux relevé des différentes manifestations organisées par le C.C.I.F. la met en évidence. En outre, le thème n'est presque jamais abordé de front, mais à titre de comparaison, sinon de repoussoir: éviter le ghetto de la chrétienté afin de mieux servir les "réalités terrestres et humaines telles qu'elles sont vécues dans la culture actuelle".[16]

Traitement? Plusieurs des orateurs invités par le Centre ne craignent pas de critiquer vertement les attitudes, comportements et programmes de chrétienté. Lors de la première Semaine des intellectuels catholiques, le 16 avril 1948, un jeune historien alors peu connu déclare: "Il me semble que l'expression 'doctrine sociale de l'Église' n'est pas heureuse; prêtant à confusion, elle fait équivoque [...] Pas plus qu'il n'y a de régime politique ou juridique qui puisse se dire le régime catholique, il n'existe d'ordre social qui soit l'ordre

12 Toupin-Guyot, *Les intellectuels catholiques*, 72.
13 Ibidem, 44.
14 Sur les difficultés du Centre avec Rome à cette époque, Ibidem, 170-176.
15 Guyot, "Entre morale et politique".
16 Citation de l'article "Monde" dans l'encyclopédie *Catholicisme*, t. 9, 558, reprise par Toupin-Guyot, *Les intellectuels catholiques*, 75.

social chrétien".[17] Ces propos qui invoquent la caution de Maritain font scandale, et René Rémond, puisqu'il s'agit de lui, doit rectifier le tir dans un article de *La Vie intellectuelle* en octobre suivant.[18] Quelques mois après cette Semaine, l'abbé Émile Berrar, conseiller ecclésiastique du C.C.I.F., participe aux Conversations catholiques internationales de Saint-Sébastien pour la rédaction d'une déclaration sur "les droits et les devoirs de la personne humaine dans la société civile selon la doctrine de l'Église catholique". Il y prend nettement ses distances avec la thèse de l'État chrétien, en se référant aux dernières interventions pontificales pour nuancer les abruptes déclarations antimodernes de Rome au XIXe siècle.[19] Au printemps de 1949, Emmanuel Mounier présente à la deuxième Semaine des intellectuels catholiques un exposé primitivement intitulé "Foi chrétienne et civilisation" qui est repris, peu après sa mort, sous le titre sans équivoque "Feu la chrétienté", étendu à l'ensemble du recueil de ses récents écrits à caractère religieux.[20] La Semaine 1955 a pour thème général "L'Église et les civilisations". Dès sa première séance, le père Daniélou et François Mauriac contestent la pertinence du concept de "civilisation chrétienne".[21] Ils reçoivent aussitôt le renfort des historiens Henri-Irénée Marrou et René Rémond, ainsi que de l'abbé Berrar lui-même, sur le thème "L'Église n'est pas cléricale". De *Carrefour* à *Rivarol* et de Louis Salleron à Jean Madiran, tout un catholicisme traditionaliste s'indigne.[22] Même *Tala-Sorbonne*, organe des étudiants du Centre Richelieu, s'inquiète.[23] Et encore n'a-t-on retenu ici que les péripéties les plus saillantes d'une chronique agitée, parmi bien d'autres.

Non sans courage, le C.C.I.F. organise le 10 décembre 1956 un hommage public à Jacques Maritain et publie l'année suivante un cahier *Recherches et débats* qui lui est entièrement consacré; ceci au moment précis où le philosophe thomiste est violemment attaqué sur sa droite, à Rome et ailleurs.[24] L'un de ses disciples dominicains y défend son "humanisme intégral" "que d'aucuns, on se demande par quelles méprises, ont qualifié de 'naturalisme

17 *Les intellectuels devant la charité du Christ*, 148.
18 Rémond, "Bonne volonté et réalités politiques".
19 Berrar, "Caractères d'une déclaration catholique".
20 Mounier, *Carnets de route*. 1: *Feu la chrétienté*.
21 Séance intitulée "Vérités et équivoques de la civilisation chrétienne".
22 Voir le témoignage de René Rémond, *Le catholicisme français*, 145, et le commentaire de Toupin-Guyot, *Les intellectuels catholiques*, 166-170.
23 Dans son numéro de décembre 1955. Voir Pruvot, *Monseigneur Charles*.
24 Durand, "La grande attaque de 1956".

intégral".[25] C'est en 1957 aussi qu'Olivier Lacombe, maritainien de longue date, accède à la présidence du Centre.[26] Ces preuves d'attachement, qui touchent beaucoup le philosophe, ne s'accompagnent pourtant pas d'une prise de position nette en faveur de sa "nouvelle chrétienté".

La ligne directrice du Centre en la matière, adoptée au début des années 1950, est plus modeste. Dans un univers de pensée fondé sur le pluralisme structurel des opinions et sur la libre circulation des idées, double acquis jamais remis en question, il s'agit de fédérer les diverses tendances d'un humanisme chrétien suffisamment ouvert aux grandes tendances intellectuelles, scientifiques et artistiques de son temps pour pouvoir entrer en dialogue constructif avec elles, sans concession, mais sans impérialisme non plus. L'humanisme existentialisme et l'humanisme marxiste sont ainsi les principaux défis, et aussi les principaux interlocuteurs, du C.C.I.F. dans les années 1950 et 1960. La confrontation avec eux fait, d'une certaine manière, la fortune du Centre, qui entre en crise avec eux quand leur commun humanisme subit la contestation radicale de Louis Althusser, de Michel Foucault ou de Jacques Lacan.[27] Une telle fringale de dialogue se situe très en deçà du projet d'une chrétienté, fût-elle nouvelle. Et les chevaliers de la chrétienté n'ont pas manqué de la reprocher au C.C.I.F.

Une diffusion internationale

Alors, "nouvelle chrétienté" introuvable? Pas vraiment si on la cherche du côté de certains de ses inventeurs, et plutôt hors de France, où ils ne semblent pas avoir eu, sur ce point à tout le moins, de riche postérité.

Dans son livre consacré aux sources catholiques de l'unité européenne, Philippe Chenaux a attiré l'attention avec raison sur le Mouvement international des intellectuels catholiques, dont le congrès fondateur s'est déroulé à Rome du 9 au 14 avril 1947 autour d'un thème qui ne saurait laisser indifférent ici: "Les intellectuels catholiques dans la chrétienté".[28] Deux des conférences majeures y furent en effet prononcées par deux des créateurs du concept de

25 Kaelin, "L'inspiration évangélique dans la pensée de Jacques Maritain", 193 (l'expression dénoncée vient de l'article du jésuite Antonio Messineo, dans *La Civiltà cattolica*); voir aussi la contribution du prêtre suisse Charles Journet, "Le philosophe de la cité".

26 Pour ces épisodes, Toupin-Guyot, *Les intellectuels catholiques*, 174-175.

27 Sur une telle crise voir, outre Toupin-Guyot, *Les intellectuels catholique*, 213-217; Pelletier, *La crise catholique*, 252-256.

28 Chenaux, *Une Europe vaticane?*, 66-73.

"nouvelle chrétienté". Jacques Maritain se prépare alors à rééditer *Humanisme intégral. Problèmes temporels et spirituels d'une nouvelle chrétienté*, avec seulement "un petit nombre de corrections de détail, préférant le laisser tel qu'il a été écrit avant des événements qui sont loin [...] d'infirmer les vues philosophiques proposées dans cet ouvrage".[29] Celles-ci ont d'ailleurs reçu entre temps l'aval de son grand ami et conseiller théologique l'abbé Charles Journet, dans le premier tome de *L'Église du Verbe incarné*, paru en 1941.[30] Aussi le philosophe, devenu ambassadeur de France près le Saint-Siège, ne peut-il que persister et signer. Face au danger totalitaire, "c'est vers l'idéal d'une nouvelle chrétienté, d'une civilisation vraiment chrétienne que les catholiques conscients de leur mission auront à orienter leurs énergies: je dis vers l'idéal d'une civilisation chrétienne dans son inspiration et dans sa réalité, chrétienne évangéliquement, et qui corresponde au climat historique de notre temps".[31]

Le second exposé clé du congrès a été confié à Étienne Gilson, auteur en 1934 de *Pour un ordre catholique*, ouvrage rassemblant des articles parus dans l'hebdomadaire dominicain *Sept*. Il y proposait, comme première étape d'une nécessaire reconquête[32], "l'instauration par les catholiques eux-mêmes, d'un ordre social catholique" (ou "chrétien indifféremment"), c'est-à-dire d'une sorte de pilier réunissant "l'ensemble des organisations sociales indispensables à l'exercice de notre vie chrétienne, dans un État qui n'est pas chrétien".[33] À Rome en 1947, le propos du philosophe est autrement plus ambitieux. En s'appuyant sur un récent discours de Pie XII et sur l'"humanisme intégral" de son ami Maritain, il prône l'extension à l'ensemble de la planète de la chrétienté, définie comme une "civilisation chrétienne" animée par une "pensée chrétienne": "ce n'est pas derrière nous que nous chercherons la Chrétienté, mais devant; non dans un passé si admirable soit-il, mais dans un avenir que nous voulons plus admirable encore. Nous ne nous sommes certainement pas réunis dans la Ville Éternelle pour y constater le décès de la Chrétienté, mais pour annoncer au monde qu'elle n'est jamais morte et que nous ne la

29 P.S. du 31 mai 1946, dix ans après la sortie du livre en 1936 ... et après la Seconde Guerre mondiale. Maritain, *Humanisme intégral*, 7.

30 Journet, "Le régime de la chrétienté profane".

31 Maritain, "Les civilisations humaines et le rôle des chrétiens", 105 (conférence du 11 avril 1947).

32 "Tout se passe comme si l'œuvre de plusieurs siècles se défaisait sous nos yeux. Que nous reste-t-il à faire? Rien, sinon de la recommencer". Gilson, *Pour un ordre catholique*, 21.

33 Ou encore "un ordre d'institutions créées par les catholiques pour assurer la réalisation des fins catholiques dont l'État n'assume pas la responsabilité". Ibidem, 11, 13 et 103.

voyons pas aujourd'hui dans la décrépitude de sa vieillesse, mais dans la fleur de sa jeunesse", déclare-t-il dans un élan qui se veut prophétique.[34]

Or ces positions, dont le C.C.I.F, branche française du M.I.I.C., ne va pas tarder à s'éloigner, sont adoptées comme références par le congrès de Rome. Le ralliement le plus significatif à la "nouvelle chrétienté" y est sans doute celui de Mgr Bernareggi, évêque de Bergame et aumônier du Movimento Laureati di azione cattolica italiana, dans son rapport sur les "principes fondamentaux pour l'action des intellectuels catholiques dans le monde". Il y défend le projet d'une "Civitas christiana" dans la vie civile, d'ambition plus modeste que la "Civitas Dei" de saint Augustin ou que le "Regnum Dei" de Pie XI. Et il assimile explicitement cette "Civitas christiana" à la "nouvelle chrétienté" maritainienne qui lui paraît en effet "répondre à la vérité historique de notre temps, ainsi que, par ailleurs, à la saine doctrine catholique".[35] Forts d'un tel soutien, les dirigeants du M.I.I.C., le Français Roger Millot et le Catalan Ramón Sugranyes de Franch, lui fixent pour tâche "l'établissement de la chrétienté nouvelle; de la *civitas christiana* - qui n'est pas une cité mystique, comme la Civitas Dei de S. Augustin [...] mais une *civitas humana*, plongeant ses racines dans le temporel", selon la direction indiquée par Maritain.[36] Le décalage entre l'ampleur mondiale d'un tel programme et la discrétion relative de ses échos au sein de l'intelligentsia catholique francophone saute au yeux.

"Nouvelle chrétienté" ou chrétienté tout court?

Ce décalage est encore plus flagrant si l'on intègre à l'épure la lettre de présentation des actes du congrès de Rome, signée par le cardinal Pizzardo, "protecteur" de Pax Romana[37] et préfet de la Congrégation romaine des séminaires et universités. "Le programme de Pax Romana peut donc se résumer ainsi, écrit-il: collaborer avec la Hiérarchie pour l'extension et pour la défense du Règne de Notre Seigneur Jésus-Christ".[38]

Une telle définition renvoie moins à Gilson ou à Maritain qu'au premier Pie XI; et elle oblige à revenir sur le regain d'intérêt ambigu pour la chrétienté depuis la fin de la Première Guerre mondiale au sein de l'Église. Tout au long de sa montée en puissance durant le XIXe siècle, le catholicisme intransigeant

34 *Les intellectuels dans la chrétienté*, 166 (conférence du 12 avril).
35 Ibidem, 45.
36 Préface datée du 15 juillet 1948. Ibidem, 15.
37 Qui unit désormais le M.I.I.C. au Mouvement international des étudiants catholiques.
38 *Les intellectuels dans la chrétienté*, 7.

n'a certes cessé d'opposer au libéralisme triomphant l'utopie d'une chrétienté idéalisée. Mais la Grande Guerre, qu'il interprète comme la faillite de la modernité libérale, semble lui fournir l'occasion de donner enfin corps à cette utopie. Pie XI, qui a pris pour devise "Pax Christi in Regno Christi", dresse le diagnostic de fin d'un monde et de retour à la barbarie, dans son encyclique inaugurale *Ubi arcano Dei*, du 23 décembre 1922. Trois ans plus tard, il fournit le remède dans *Quas primas*, nouvelle encyclique instaurant la fête du Christ-Roi: construire la royauté sociale de Jésus-Christ, non pas dans un au-delà spirituel, mais bien sur cette terre, sous la forme d'un ordre que précisera en 1931 une troisième encyclique, *Quadragesimo anno*.[39]

Ce thème de la royauté sociale, dont Daniele Menozzi a scruté l'apparition et le développement depuis le milieu du XIXe siècle[40], inspire la réforme de l'Action catholique du même pape, la fête du Christ-Roi devenant ainsi la "journée du mandat" confié à celle-ci pour rechristianiser la société. Un tel projet à caractère théocratique, puisqu'il subordonne nettement le pouvoir temporel au pouvoir spirituel[41], ne prétend pourtant pas restaurer la chrétienté médiévale, ni même bâtir un "nouveau Moyen âge" du type de celui que préconise Nicolas Berdiaev après la révolution russe. Il comporte néanmoins une certaine nostalgie de cette époque mythique et lui emprunte nombre de traits, à commencer par le corporatisme, au prix il est vrai d'une indispensable transposition. Avec la condamnation de l'Action française, c'est-à-dire d'un projet politique susceptible d'entraîner une confusion avec ce projet social et religieux, les découvreurs de la "nouvelle chrétienté" prennent leurs distances avec la chrétienté tout court, mais sans pouvoir le faire franchement, ce qui ne manquerait pas de heurter Pie XI, auquel ils apportent un soutien explicitement sollicité contre Maurras et les siens.

Certains s'en tirent par un coup de chapeau à la chrétienté médiévale qui ne cache pas ses limites. "Je me suis souvent référé à la cité médiévale, parce qu'elle est un exemple commode d'une part de ce qui peut être une civilisation saine, d'autre part une civilisation chrétienne, mais je n'en retiens que les principes non les réalisations. Il ne me coûte pas de dire que le Moyen âge

39 Bouthillon, "D'une théologie à l'autre".
40 Menozzi, *Sacro Cuore*.
41 En effet, "les chefs d'État ne sauraient [...] refuser de rendre, en leur nom personnel, et avec tout leur peuple, des hommages publics de respect et de soumission à la souveraineté du Christ" ("*Quas primas*", 76).

est un échec", affirme ainsi le jeune Henri-Irénée Marrou en 1934.[42] Quant à Jacques Maritain, il oppose trait pour trait sa nouvelle chrétienté profane à la chrétienté sacrale médiévale. Unité minimale d'un pluralisme relatif contre unité maximale de type organique; autonomie, elle aussi relative, du temporel contre subordination de celui-ci au spirituel; liberté des personnes ou personnalisme chrétien interdisant l'utilisation de la force publique à des fins spirituelles; démocratie organique de type dominicain contre hiérarchisation et séparation des catégories sociales; œuvre commune d'ordre humain à concrétiser historiquement et non "empire du Christ" dès ici-bas.[43] La distinction des deux projets paraît donc nette.

L'impossibilité où se trouvent les tenants de la "nouvelle chrétienté" de renier l'héritage de *Quas primas* et l'utilisation par eux des mêmes mots que Pie XI, à commencer par celui de chrétienté, quoique dans un sens différent, se révèlent pourtant riches en amalgames et en confusions, involontaires ou délibérées. Exemple? Comme Émile Poulat l'a bien montré naguère[44], la brochure du père Chenu, *Dimension nouvelle de la chrétienté*, qui insiste en 1937 sur la nécessité de réintégrer le monde ouvrier dans l'espace catholique, est incontestablement d'obédience maritainienne.[45] En revanche, la préface de l'abbé Cardijn, fondateur de la Jeunesse ouvrière chrétienne, paraît plus proche du projet primitif de Pie XI: "S'agit-il d'une 'nouvelle' dimension de la chrétienté, ou plutôt d'une mise au point et d'une restauration 'intégrale et totale' de la véritable chrétienté?" Et encore: "L'Action catholique [...] vise à la rechristianisation de *toute* la vie laïque, de *tous* les milieux laïques, de *toutes* les institutions laïques, privées ou publiques; elle veut ramener tout le monde laïc à sa destination providentielle".[46] Dans une telle perspective, le côté profane de la chrétienté souhaitée est réduit à sa plus simple expression. Aussi Bernard Besret était-il fondé à appeler de ses voeux une enquête fine portant "sur le

42 Sous son nom de plume Henri Davenson, *Fondements d'une culture chrétienne*, 127. Ce livre a été écrit pour les cadres de la Jeunesse étudiante chrétienne deux ans auparavant. Il répond bien à leurs préoccupations qu'exprimait clairement l'un d'entre eux: "Pas à pas, nous referons une atmosphère chrétienne, où des institutions chrétiennes puissent surgir". La tâche prioritaire: instaurer "un ordre de chrétienté" (Marc Schérer, "À pied d'œuvre", éditorial du premier numéro de *Chantiers*, janvier 1932, cité par Prévotat, "Fondements d'une culture chrétienne").

43 "L'idéal historique d'une nouvelle chrétienté", chapitres IV et V du livre Maritain, *Humanisme intégral*, dont la dernière réédition, avec une préface de René Rémond, date de 2000, toujours chez Aubier.

44 Poulat, "*Humanisme intégral*", 155.

45 "Nous résumons et citons le chap. VI d'*Humanisme intégral*: 'Des chances historiques d'une nouvelle chrétienté'", précise en note le théologien (Chenu, *Dimension nouvelle de la chrétienté*, 28).

46 Ibidem, 1 et 2, avec les italiques de Cardijn.

sens précis accordé alors au mot 'chrétienté'", terme proche du concept d'incarnation qu'il avait choisi d'éclairer.[47] Malheureusement, son appel n'a pas vraiment été entendu; et les quiproquos demeurent.[48]

La tenaille

En dépit de son ambiguïté congénitale, ou à cause d'elle, l'"idéal historique concret" de la "nouvelle chrétienté" a fait florès au cours des années 1930, comme réponse catholique à la grande crise et à ses issues totalitaires qui confirmaient la déroute du libéralisme. Il a fourni une armature intellectuelle aux mouvements d'Action catholique spécialisée dès leur naissance. Il a produit pour ce faire une littérature abondante, mais de qualité variable, qu'Yvon Tranvouez estime à une trentaine de titres, français pour la plupart.[49] Il n'a pourtant pas tardé à être pris sous le feu croisé de critiques antagonistes, venues de sa droite comme de sa gauche.

Les combattants du Christ-Roi

Des Cristeros mexicains résistant à la persécution sanglante de l'État, entre 1926 et 1929, aux cris de "Viva Cristo Rey" jusqu'aux Guerilleros du Christ-Roi nostalgiques du franquisme espagnol, en passant par les premiers apôtres du rexisme wallon ou par certains défenseurs de l'Algérie française, ils n'ont pas manqué. Mais l'institution Église a toujours su se démarquer de leur radicalité. Elle préférait une dévotion plus officielle et moins risquée: celle de la Colombie, par exemple, élevant en 1929 la solennité du Christ-Roi au rang de fête nationale.[50] Aussi cette dévotion et le projet de restauration qu'elle entendait promouvoir se sont-ils trouvés déportés vers la droite au fur et à mesure de l'évolution du mouvement catholique dans son ensemble, et de la papauté elle-même. On en veut pour preuve, en France, des foyers tels que les Coopérateurs paroissiaux du Christ-Roi du père Vallet, à Chabeuil dans la Drôme, ou la Cité catholique de Jean Ousset, dont le manuel s'intitule *Pour qu'Il règne*.[51] Aujourd'hui encore, quelques cercles traditionalistes font de la "réactualisa-

47 Besret, *Incarnation ou eschatologie?*, 39.

48 Ainsi Jacques Prévotat se montre-t-il, à tort, "un peu surpris de la place considérable accordée au Moyen âge" par le jeune Marrou (Prévotat, "Fondements d'une culture chrétienne", 127). Comment évoquer la chrétienté, en 1934, sans se référer à cette époque de référence?

49 Voir sa liste dans Tranvouez, *Catholiques d'abord*, 122-124.

50 Menozzi, "Rinnovamento dottrinale e storiografia", 267.

51 De Neuville, *Jean Ousset*.

tion de la doctrine du Christ-Roi" un moyen de sortir l'Église d'une crise qu'ils déplorent.[52]

Les intellectuels de cette tendance n'ont jamais accepté la "nouvelle chrétienté" de Maritain. Pour se protéger sur sa droite, celui-ci avait pourtant multiplié les précautions en forme de ni ... ni. Pas de retour au modèle médiéval, mais pas de concession non plus au libéralisme philosophique, culturel, social ou politique. Et tous les commentateurs de bonne foi ont souligné ensuite qu'il n'y bradait aucunement son thomisme "antimoderne".[53] Pourtant, les partisans de la chrétienté sans adjectif ont tout de suite bronché sur l'autonomie du temporel, la liberté des personnes ou la démocratie. Ils ont accusé Maritain de trahison en faveur du libéralisme honni. Certes, les attaques les plus virulentes sont moins venues du traditionalisme francophone que de son homologue hispanique, espagnol ou latino-américain, ainis que le montre, entre autres, le succès madrilène du livre de Leopoldo Palacios, *El mito de la nueva Cristiandad* (publié en 1951 et réédité l'année suivante).[54] La polémique contre Maritain est toutefois relayée en France par des organes comme *La Pensée catholique*. Aux Conversations catholiques internationales de Saint-Sébastien 1949, son directeur l'abbé Luc J. Lefèvre s'en prend frontalement à *Humanisme intégral* dans son analyse sur "Les droits de l'homme et la chrétienté".[55]

Ainsi que le suggérait la discordance Pizzardo-Bernareggi à propos du Mouvement international des intellectuels catholiques, le débat entre chrétienté sacrale et "nouvelle chrétienté" n'épargne pas les sommets de la hiérarchie ecclésiale. Le "parti romain" mis en valeur par Andrea Riccardi[56] tient ferme pour la première, avec des appuis aussi solides que l'athénée du Latran, les jésuites de *La Civiltà cattolica* et bien sûr le Saint-Office d'Alfredo Ottaviani. Proches de Mgr Montini, substitut de la Secrétairerie d'État, Mgr Bernareggi ou le laïc Vittorino Veronese sont, quant à eux, gagnés aux thèse maritainiennes.[57] La disgrâce-promotion de Montini à l'archevêché de Milan, fin 1954, manque de sceller le sort de la "nouvelle chrétienté", comme semble l'annoncer la "grande attaque" du père Messineo dans *La Civiltà cattolica* deux ans

52 Titre d'un article de Claude Barthe dans *Catholica*, 36 (1993), 9-24.

53 René Rémond entre autres, dans sa préface à la récente réédition de Maritain, *Humanisme intégral*, VI-VII.

54 L'influence du philosophe thomiste a aussi joué en sens inverse, comme l'a prouvé la thèse d'Olivier Compagnon, *Jacques Maritain et l'Amérique du sud*.

55 *Documentos*, (1950) 4, 107-121.

56 Riccardi, *Il "partito romano"*.

57 Chenaux, *Les rapports du "montinianisme" et du "maritanisme"*.

plus tard.[58] Les réactions que suscite celle-ci et la mort de Pie XII suspendent toutefois *sine die* un procès qui ne sera pas repris en cour de Rome. Le pape Pacelli d'ailleurs, malgré sa sympathie pour les États chrétiens ou supposés tels (Espagne, Argentine, Colombie, Équateur), ne s'est pas résolu à trancher clairement pour la chrétienté sacrale au détriment de la "nouvelle chrétienté".[59]

"Chrétienté ou mission?"

Assez loin de son plaidoyer de 1937 pour une "dimension nouvelle de la chrétienté", le père Chenu choisit nettement la mission dans cette intervention de 1950 qui justifie la signature par des catholiques de l'appel de Stockholm contre l'arme atomique: il s'agit d'une attitude missionnaire, alors qu'un refus en resterait au réflexe de chrétienté.[60] Et il n'est pas le seul!

Certes, dans la France et plus encore dans la Belgique d'après 1945, la logique d'incarnation qui vise à "la christianisation du monde moderne par un engagement dans l'action temporelle"[61], demeure d'actualité, sans pour autant utiliser un vocabulaire ni des méthodes de chrétienté. Elle reste la ligne directrice de l'Action catholique, appuyée sur des références intellectuelles comme *La théologie des réalités terrestres* et *La théologie de l'histoire* du professeur de Louvain Gustave Thils. Elle a d'ailleurs mieux réussi en Belgique qu'en France et y sera contestée plus tardivement.[62]

En France, les bouleversements introduits par la Seconde Guerre mondiale entraînent une contestation précoce et plus ou moins radicale, non pas de la "nouvelle chrétienté" maritainienne, mais de la chrétienté elle-même, pour le présent comme pour l'avenir. Les diverses composantes d'une telle contestation partagent toutes le diagnostic du livre-culte que fut, pour le catholicisme hexagonal, *La France, pays de mission?* D'après les abbés Henri Godin et Yvan Daniel, celle-ci n'est plus un pays de chrétienté, bien qu'elle "comporte des paroisses de chrétienté vivantes et très actives, mais minées par le dedans".[63]

58 Durand, "La grande attaque de 1956"; mais aussi, dans la même conjoncture, Komonchak, "The silencing of John Courtney Murray".

59 Voir son discours sur la tolérance du 6 décembre 1953, souvent interprété comme un correctif aux propos abrupts du cardinal Ottaviani, le 2 mars précédent au Latran.

60 Chenu, "À propos des 'Mouvements de paix'". On sait qu'il ira jusqu'à nier l'utilité d'une doctrine sociale de l'Église (Chenu, *La 'doctrine sociale' de l'Église comme idéologie*).

61 Besret, *Incarnation ou eschatologie?*, 55.

62 Comblin, *Échec de l'Action catholique?*

63 Godin et Daniel, *La France, pays de mission?*, 12.

Elle est aussi, dans quelques-unes de ses zones rurales et surtout dans ses grandes agglomérations, un pays de mission que l'Action catholique spécialisée est impuissante à rechristianiser. Pour "refaire chrétienne" la classe ouvrière, pour "bâtir une chrétienté en plein dans le milieu populaire", il faut employer des méthodes proprement missionnaires.[64] Autre document-culte, la lettre pastorale pour le carême 1947 du cardinal de Paris Suhard, *Essor ou déclin de l'Église*, est moins pessimiste. Tout en se plaçant dans une perspective apostolique et en insistant sur l'urgence d'une intervention des fidèles dans la cité[65], elle récuse toute "confusion entre 'Église' et 'chrétienté' ou entre 'Christianisme' et 'chrétienté'", c'est-à-dire entre le message évangélique et ses incarnations historiques successives.[66] Dans une Église désormais "en état de mission", selon la formule inventée par le père Chenu et reprise à son compte par Suhard[67], l'heure de la chrétienté, même nouvelle, est passée. De façon convergente et quasi simultanée, deux recueils importants viennent d'ailleurs de constater l'extériorité de l'Église par rapport aux forces les plus dynamiques de son environnement: "La crise de la civilisation chrétienne", cinquième cahier de Jeunesse de l'Église en décembre 1945 et "Monde chrétien, monde moderne", enquête d'*Esprit* publiée en juillet-août 1946.

Trois des courants intellectuels majeurs du catholicisme français affirment alors la transcendance du message chrétien à l'égard de ses différents avatars, affichent leur pessimisme sur son incarnation présente, voire manifestent leur scepticisme quant à la "logique de l'incarnation".[68] Emmanuel Mounier promet le pire, dès mai 1946 dans la revue *Esprit*, au "corps malade de la chrétienté": un "Sedan spirituel", "une agonie, cette fois sans métaphore ni échappatoire".[69] D'où le titre du recueil posthume qui reprend un tel brûlot: *Feu la chrétienté*. Certes, il ne s'agit pas de "la mort du christianisme, mais de la mort de la chrétienté occidentale, féodale et bourgeoise. Une chrétienté nouvelle naîtra demain, ou après-demain, de nouvelles couches sociales et de nouvel-

64 Ibidem, 99 et 182 (préface originelle de l'abbé Georges Guérin, fondateur de la J.O.C. en France).

65 "De quoi s'agit-il en effet? De construire un monde nouveau, de définir et préparer les structures qui permettent d'être pleinement homme, dans une cité digne de lui; de transformer toutes choses pour en faire un monde chrétien" (Suhard, *Essor ou déclin de l'Église*, 155).

66 Ibidem, 63, note 1.

67 Chenu, "L'Église en état de mission", témoignage (signé Testis) du théologien dominicain, qui fait remonter cette invention à la session de la Mission de France tenue à Lisieux en juillet 1947.

68 "Logique qui couvre de plus en plus fréquemment un tour de passe-passe qu'il nous faut une fois pour toutes récuser, que ses conclusions soient blanches ou rouges". Mounier, "L'agonie du christianisme", 727.

69 Ibidem, 717-718.

les greffes extra-européennes. Encore faut-il que nous ne l'étouffions pas avec le cadavre de l'autre".[70] Mounier ne fournit toutefois ni programme ni calendrier. Pour l'heure, il maintient le cap fixé aux origines de sa revue: dans un monde accepté comme pluraliste, travailler avec toutes les bonnes volontés disponibles à la construction d'une cité pleinement humaine, respectueuse des personnes et des communautés, pas d'une cité chrétienne. Telle est la logique de l'engagement.

Le dominicain Maurice Montuclard et son mouvement "Jeunesse de l'Église" sont aussi réticents, bien que dans un sens quelque peu différent. Retraçant leur itinéraire intellectuel et militant, Gilles Ferry retient comme particulièrement importantes, la dénonciation de "la crise de la civilisation chrétienne" (cahier 5) et la récusation des "méthodes d'évangélisation qu'on peut appeler 'chrétienté'" pour s'y substituer.[71] À la différence de tout le courant issu de *La France, pays de mission?*, "Jeunesse de l'Église" ne propose aucun plan de conquête ni de reconquête, du monde ouvrier en particulier: "il est impossible d'annoncer présentement la Bonne Nouvelle à ce monde", ne craint pas d'écrire Montuclard.[72] La seule attitude envisageable est celle de Jean-Baptiste: "Nous tracerons des plans, nous ferons des maquettes: nous ne bâtirons pas la cathédrale".[73] Dans l'immédiat, il est urgent de se taire[74] pour mieux s'immerger dans les milieux non chrétiens afin d'en comprendre et accepter les structures, marxisme compris, quitte à troquer la logique d'incarnation typique d'une chrétienté défunte pour une logique d'assomption du réel tel qu'il est: "on le laisse pénétrer en soi, assimiler par l'énergie vitale de la charité qui veut le présenter à Dieu, et, grâce à la charité, une décantation s'opère qui met à part, dans le réel, ses authentiques valeurs".[75] Plus encore que Mounier, Montuclard fait des "événements", c'est-à-dire de l'histoire humaine, le seul terrain d'une action dont la finalité religieuse est suspendue à une mutation substantielle des sociétés occidentales.

Au rebours des deux courants précédents, celui qui s'exprime entre 1945 et 1955 dans les cahiers *Dieu vivant* professe un pessimisme plus ou moins

70 Mounier, "L'agonie du christianisme", 730.

71 "Lettre à un ami sur Jeunesse de l'Église, 1940-1951" (*Les événements et la foi*, 110).

72 "L'Église et le mouvement ouvrier" (Ibidem, 59). Et encore: "Nous avons même renoncé à l'intention de convertir" (Ibidem, 60).

73 Ibidem, 53.

74 "Il n'y a pour nous qu'une attitude possible et vraie: nous taire; nous taire longtemps, nous taire des années durant; et participer à toute la vie, à tous les combats, à toute la culture latente des populations ouvrières" (Ibidem, 59-60).

75 Ibidem, 162 ("La logique d'assomption", texte extrait du cahier n°5 sur "La crise de la civilisation chrétienne").

accentué à l'encontre du monde moderne, dans ses composantes historique et scientifique notamment, pessimisme incompréhensible sans Auschwitz et Hiroshima.[76] Comme ceux qui l'ont précédé, et même plus qu'eux, ce monde est marqué par le péché et par la croix dont un chrétien ne saurait faire l'économie. Pour ce dernier, "le monde de la vie naturelle et de la science, le monde de la cité temporelle et de la vie économique a quelque chose d'essentiellement anachronique", écrit ainsi le jésuite Jean Daniélou. "Il est dépassé radicalement par le monde de l'Église qui est son avenir déjà présent".[77] Dans cette perspective, seules importent l'histoire du salut et une rédemption qui ne saurait être intramondaine, mais toute entière tendue vers la parousie. D'où l'affirmation plus ou moins abrupte d'une position eschatologique refusant d'un même mouvement les logiques d'incarnation, d'engagement et d'assomption. "Il reste toujours au fond du coeur du chrétien un penchant au 'constantinisme'. On le voit trop souvent espérer dans le salut par les institutions sociales, aspirer à la paix et au bonheur dès ici-bas, identifier la victoire de l'Agneau avec le concept de 'civilisation chrétienne', penser et agir enfin comme si les lois de la société pouvaient le protéger contre le 'Voleur'", lit-on par exemple dans le second liminaire de *Dieu vivant*.[78] Une telle volonté de rupture, est autrement radicale que celles de Mounier et de Montuclard. Ils annoncent la mort de la chrétienté; *Dieu vivant* conteste jusqu'à la possibilité d'une chrétienté: pour son équipe, le Royaume n'est décidément pas de ce monde. Peu importent ici les débats, souvent vifs, entre ces trois tendances, autour du sens et de la valeur de l'histoire des hommes notamment. Il suffisait de signaler leur convergence dans le refus de l'hypothèse nommée chrétienté.

Sous sa forme maritainienne de "nouvelle chrétienté", cette hypothèse a sans doute connu un sort meilleur en Belgique et en Suisse qu'en France, mais aussi dans l'action des mouvements catholiques que dans l'esprit des intellectuels. Force est d'admettre pourtant que ses inventeurs, à l'image de Gilson ou de Maritain lui-même, n'ont guère eu de continuateurs. Les partisans d'une chrétienté sans adjectif, un Marcel de Corte en Belgique, un Gonzague de Reynold en Suisse[79], un Louis Salleron ou un Gustave Thibon en France, ont refusé la distance qu'elle prenait avec l'instauration ou la restauration d'un ordre social intégralement chrétien. Quant aux partisans de l'engagement

76 Besret, *Incarnation ou eschatologie?*, 107-144 et Fouilloux, "Une vision eschatologique du christianisme".

77 Daniélou, "Christianisme et Histoire", 183.

78 *Dieu vivant,* (1945) 2, 10.

79 Mattioli, *Gonzague de Reynol*, 255-263.

pluraliste, de l'assomption des valeurs mondaines ou de la tension eschatologique, ils ont discuté le bien-fondé, non pas d'une "nouvelle chrétienté", mais de la chrétienté tout court. Aussi la naissance et la fortune du concept de "nouvelle chrétienté" au cours des années 1930 font-elles figure en dernière analyse de phase transitoire, chez les intellectuels catholiques de langue française, entre les espoirs de retour en chrétienté nés de la Première Guerre mondiale et la ruine de tels espoirs dans l'apocalypse de la Seconde. Cette phase a permis de passer, non sans affrontements croisés, du rêve d'un ordre social chrétien à la réalité du libre échange des idées dans nos sociétés pluralistes et sécularisées, où l'annonce de l'Évangile se veut modeste plutôt que conquérante. Un symbole? Chrétienté ne fait pas partie du vocabulaire de Vatican II.[80]

80 D'après Delhaye, Guéret et Tombeur, *Concilium Vaticanum II.*

Restoration and Erosion of Pillarised Catholicism in Western Europe

Wilhelm Damberg & Patrick Pasture

To discuss the question of the continuities and discontinuities in the position of Christendom before and after the Second World War, we must adopt a long-term perspective, in particular because the history of modern Christendom is often still seen within the framework of modernisation and secularisation discourses that assume that the influence of religion in society gradually declined since a mythical 'age of faith', usually situated in the Middle Ages or the Ancien Régime, and even up to the blurb of this conference.[1] As we shall see, secularisation theories do have their merit, but that must be limited to Europe since the 1960s; if they were right about the long term, we obviously would not have much to talk about today...

Christendom in the Modern World: The Formation of Pillarised Catholicism

There is no doubt that the Catholic Church in Western Europe in the late eighteenth century entered a crisis perhaps even more profound than the one that gave way to the Protestant and later to the Catholic or Counter-Reformation.[2] It culminated in the *déchristianisation* of the French Revolution. There is no doubt either that industrialisation, urbanisation, and

* This chapter has been written for the international conference *The Transformation of the Christian Churches in Western Europe 1945-2000*, KADOC, Leuven, 18-21 September 2002. References have been updated.

1 The standard accounts of the secularisation thesis as a long term development are now the two volumes of Steve Bruce, *God is Dead* and *Religion in the Modern World*.

2 On the latter terminology see O'Malley, *Trent and All That*; von Greyerz, *Religion and Culture in Early Modern Europe*, 40-69.

political democratisation in the nineteenth century also presented tremendous challenges. Among some social groups and in certain regions the Church would never recover.[3]

However, around the 1840s the Catholic Church, at least in some major parts of Europe, had already started to redress itself (admittedly, its position was undermined beyond repair in some regions and in particular among industrial workers and some liberal bourgeois). It found a new language to address the issues of the time, focusing on a sentimentalist discourse and introducing 'modern' features such as centralisation, bureaucratisation, and an original use of modern media techniques and 'invented' traditions. With the 'culture wars' in the 1870s and 1880s, the Church learned to organise the Catholic masses and, in the 1900s, adapted effectively to mass society. Far from disappearing, the Church once more, and in some respects more than ever, became in nineteenth-century Europe a dominant force in society as is demonstrated paradoxically in the bitter fights between Catholics and the new secular and often anticlerical and antireligious forces.[4] This ideological fault line became the most salient political divide in continental Western Europe until the late twentieth century, arguably even more than the region and class divides which are more commonly associated with the Modern Age.[5] After the 'secularisation' of the French Revolution, Europe entered a phase of *Fundamentalpolarisiering* (Benjamin Ziemann), in which confession, as Olaf Blaschke argues, became a major dimension.[6]

The Catholic Church indeed succeeded in appealing to the modern man, though in first instance mainly to the 'modern' woman. Indeed, after Protes-

3 The best assessment of the challenges to the churches in Europe from a secularisation perspective in McLeod, *Religion and the People of Western Europe* and Idem, *Secularisation in Western Europe*.

4 Cf. Hellemans, "How Modern is Religion in Modernity?"; Anderson, "The Limits of Secularization"; De Maeyer and Hellemans, "Katholiek reveil"; Nash, "Reconnecting Religion with Social and Cultural History". A critical assessment of the recent criticism of the secularisation in the 19th century in Ziemann, "Säkularisierung, Konfessionalisierung, Organisationsbildung". On the culture wars see Clark and Kaiser, eds., *Culture wars*.

5 Lipset and Rokkan, eds., *Party Systems*; Broughton and ten Napel, eds., *Religion and Electoral Behaviour in Europe*; Hellemans, *Strijd om de moderniteit*.

6 Ziemann, "Säkularisierung, Konfessionalisierung, Organisationsbildung", 485-508. Ziemann nevertheless severely criticises the concept of a "second confessional age" introduced by Blaschke. Compare Blaschke, ed., *Konfessionen im Konflikt* as well as, but from a different perspective, Hölscher, "Konfessionspolitik in Deutschland zwischen Glaubensstreit und Koexistenz"; Bennette, "Threatened Protestants". Other critical overviews of the idea of the 19th century as a "second confessional age", are, among others, Steinhoff, "Ein zweites konfessionelles Zeitalter?"; Kretschmann and Pahl, "Ein 'zweites Konfessionelles Zeitalter'?" and Dietrich, *Konfession im Dorf*.

tantism, Catholic piety also became sentimental in the nineteenth century. A profound differentiation of gender roles was one of the defining features of Modernity in the nineteenth and twentieth centuries, and the Church used it perfectly to its advantage. To reiterate the seminal expression of Ralph Gibson popular Catholicism since the mid-nineteenth century has 'appealed to the heart' rather than to the 'head'.[7] Within Catholicism, this reorientation expressed itself most clearly in a new appreciation of popular religion, particularly of apparitions, the cult of Mary and the Sacred Heart, the return of magic, miracles and wonder (Lourdes!), and of processions and pilgrimages.[8] To be sure, the Catholic Church knew the power of the (re-)'invention of tradition', which, as Eric Hobsbawm and Terence Ranger in their seminal volume demonstrated regarding nationalism, is a profoundly 'modern' feature.[9]

Therefore, in the late nineteenth century, in most continental European countries, relatively 'closed', exclusive political communities were formed called *zuilen* (pillars) in Belgium and the Netherlands, *Milieus* or *Subgesellschaften* in Germany and Switzerland, and *Lager* in Austria. They consisted of large networks of interrelated organisations with a common political perspective, represented collectively by one integrating political party, and sharing a large number of common values, practices and ideals. In other words, sharing a common culture that appealed both to men (who found there a terrain in which they could develop a masculine religiosity in the public sphere) and to women.[10] Particularly Socialists, Calvinists and Catholics developed such 'pillarised' communities (quite more so than Liberals and Lutherans), although

7 Gibson, *Social History of French Catholicism*.

8 See the overviews of Pasture, "Beyond the Feminisation Thesis"; Van Osselaer and Buerman, "Feminization Thesis. A Survey of International Historiography and a Probing on Belgian Grounds"; Schneider, "Feminisierung der Religion im 19. Jahrhundert"; Götz von Olenhusen, "Die Feminisierung der Religion und Kirche im 19. und 20. Jahrhundert"; Ford, "Religion and Popular Culture"; Anderson, "Piety and Politics"; and Blackbourn, "The Catholic Church in Europe". On Lourdes see Harris, *Lourdes*.

9 Hobsbawm and Ranger, eds., *The Invention of Tradition*. The classical socio-anthropologic view since Max Weber, which views tradition as essentially premodern, from an historical perspective is fundamentally flawed.

10 The literature on pillarisation is particularly well developed in Belgium and the Netherlands. The best comparative study is Hellemans, *Strijd om de moderniteit* (see also Hellemans's comparative article "Zuilen en verzuiling in Europa"). See also Blom and Talsma, eds., *De verzuiling voorbij*; Billiet, ed., *Tussen bescherming en verovering;* and Righart, *De katholieke zuil in Europa*. Two recent overviews of the pillarisation debate are Wintle, "Pillarisation, Consociation, and Vertical Pluralism" and Blom, "Pillarisation in Perspective". Still, al these studies are particularly gender blind. They hardly note the existence of women's movements, and if so, without properly assessing their significance, let alone any understanding of the role of men in the pillars. At most, more detailed studies about women's movements point at some tensions between masculine and feminine perspectives.

the Catholic hierarchy was very reluctant to tolerate an alternative political power centre beside it. It only did so as long as it offered the most effective strategy against the attacks of the political secularists and when no real alternative existed.[11]

Within such political communities (secular or Christian) a particular subculture developed, where, particularly in the interwar period, emphasis was put on isolation and education of the faithful. Among Catholics a *civilisation paroissiale* (a 'parochial' civilisation) came into being, focused on the parish life and in which the life of the faithful, from the cradle to the grave, stood under the sign of Christ, and the Church had its say about virtually every single activity. It is this combination of popular Catholicism and politically inspired mass organisation that we label 'pillarised Catholicism', referring to the Belgian and the Dutch concept of *verzuiling* or pillarisation.[12] While the term definitely evokes the compelling character of this subculture, one should realise that some domains - such as the high arts - were never integrated in these networks , that the dynamics of pillarisation could diverge locally, that individuals certainly could find ways to escape or 'negotiate' personal exceptions, and that it always was contested.[13]

Catholic Action and the Challenges of Fascism in Interbellum Europe

Pillarised Catholicisms were formed in the nineteenth century and boomed after the First Word War, but they were challenged, from both the internal and from the external world.

During the 1920s Popes Pius XI and Pius XII frequently called upon Catholics to fight secularism in the so-called Catholic Action (*Azione Catto-lica*). Due to the vagueness of the popes' statements however, the contemporary and historical interpretations of Catholic Action, are far from unanimous. Never-

11 On the political strategies of the Church see Kalyvas, *The Rise of Christian Democracy*.

12 For references see note 10. Other concepts are less adequate. The term *milieu* in German and French has quite divergent meanings and connotations, while the concept of *Volkskirche* - which has its roots in German Protestantism of the 1920s - is more focused on pastoral activities than on social networks. In the German language the sole word *Katholizismus* fits our subject very well, but it cannot be used as such in an English translation, since Catholicism refers to the religion itself.

13 Cf. Walser Smith and Clark, "The Fate of Nathan", esp. 10; Blom and Talsma, eds., *De verzuiling voorbij*; Luykx, *Andere katholieken*.

theless, some principles can be found. First of all, Catholic Action made an appeal to the laity (both men and women, though the discourse definitely was rather masculine) to realise their individual responsibility in the apostolate of the Church and to fight the secularisation of society wherever they lived and worked. This principle clearly differed from the traditions of pillarised Catholicism, which emphasised collective responsibility in associations, unions and parties. Secondly, since the popes did not want the flock to go astray the hierarchy emphasised a systematic religious education of the faithful, and ordered the organisation of special committees run by the clergy for supervising the laity's activities. According to the teaching of the popes, the strict subordination of the laity to the control of the hierarchy in Catholic Action was essential. Only that way was the Church, under the banner of Catholic Action, as an *acies bene ordinata*, a well-organised battle line, to march for the kingdom of Christ.[14]

It is no wonder that the leaders of the Catholic social associations could hardly hide their contempt for these new ideas. Moreover, since in Italy Catholic Action was part of Pius XI's 'deal' with Mussolini and was used as a pretext to abandon the Christian Democratic *Partito populare* of Don Sturzo and the Catholic 'white' unions, Christian Democrats in Europe understandably regarded Catholic Action with much distrust. Sometimes Catholic Action organisations even allied with the fascists or became fascist themselves, as did Rex in Belgium.[15] In Germany, as well as in Belgium and the Netherlands (although there was little 'real' Catholic Action in the latter country)[16], the leaders of the Catholic pillars simply declared that there was no need to introduce Catholic Action because its objectives were already being met in their own organisations. Catholic Action, however, opposed separate organisations for different classes, in particular workers. Different organisations for different classes would undermine the spirit of social cohesion and harmony among

14 From 1922 up to the years after the Second World War the papal call for Catholic Action was as popular in the Catholic world as it nowadays has fallen into oblivion. As Heinz Hürten in his opus magnum on German Catholicism 1918-1945 has observed, historical research has not yet realised the enormous impact of this program on the internal change of the Catholic Church up to the Second Vatican Council: Hürten, *Deutsche Katholiken* (see also Idem, *Kurze Geschichte des deutschen Katholizismus*). Not surprisingly, there is no comprehensive comparative study on the subject either. As a German case study see Damberg, *Abschied vom Milieu*, esp. 73-172; Idem, "Radikal katholische Laien an die Front!". On the Netherlands: De Haan, *Van volgzame elitestrijder tot kritische gelovige*; on Belgium Van Osselaer, "Christening Masculinity?"; Vos, "Het dubbelspoor van de Katholieke Actie".

15 Conway, *Collaboration in Belgium*; Idem, "Introduction", esp. 22-23.

16 See Patrick Pasture's review of De Haan, *Van volgzame elitestrijder tot kritische gelovige*, in *Trajecta*, 4 (1995) 3, 274-275.

Catholics, and would introduce class struggle into the heart of the Church. Nevertheless, there was a compromise between the two opposing visions on the organisation of Catholic society to be found. Father Joseph Cardijn and his 'Katholieke Arbeidersjeugd/Jeunesse Ouvrière Chrétienne' (KAJ/JOC) showed the way towards a common ground. Catholic Action would be most effective, Cardijn argued, if tailored to the needs and languages of the different social groups and classes. In doing so, it could concentrate its work on educating a small elite group. In a second step, this militant elite group would take social action within a certain 'milieu' and generate support from the 'masses'.[17] In this way, the oppositions could be overcome and Catholic Action, as happened most clearly in Flanders, turned into a constituent part of the Catholic pillar. Still, Catholic Action eroded the basis of the political segregation of Catholics and contributed to the erosion of the Catholic pillar from within.[18]

Obviously, the most severe challenge for the pillarised Catholic societies was fascism. Fascism primarily targeted political parties and movements, and secondarily, socio-economic pressure groups and in particular the Christian trade unions. Wherever the fascist regimes came to power, before or after the outbreak of the Second World War, Catholic Action emphasised being strictly spiritual and apolitical. In doing so, it offered Catholic activists (albeit under hierarchical control) a safe haven. However, the Nazis, notwithstanding the guaranties of the concordats in Germany and Austria, after some time extended their grip on society and suppressed all non-liturgical activities of the Church, including Catholic Action. This was much less the case in Italy and Spain, however. After the Civil War, Franco even drew strong support from the Church and the two became allies for a long time.[19]

17 Gerard, "Adaptation en temps de crise"; Idem, *Église et mouvement ouvrier chrétien en Belgique*; Hellemans, *Strijd om de moderniteit*, 174-221; Mayeur, *Catholicisme social et Démocratie chrétienne*, 71 and 103; Milza and Bernstein, *Le fascisme italien*, 158-172.

18 See in particular the publications of Emmanuel Gerard on the interwar period, esp. "Adaptation en temps de crise" and *De Katholieke Partij in crisis*, and Pasture on the post-war period: *Kerk, politiek en sociale actie* and "Modèles internationaux d'action ouvrière catholique". On the KAJ in Flanders see Alaerts, *Door eigen werk sterk*.

19 Cf. Wolff and Hoensch, eds., *Catholics, the State and the European Radical Right*; Hürten, *Deutsche Katholiken*.

Restoration and Modernisation of Pillarised Catholicism after the Second World War

Under these circumstances, after the end of the occupation and the defeat of Nazi Germany, in many cases, the Church had to make a strategic choice. Should it allow the Catholic pillars to simply be restored as they originated in the nineteenth century and continued to blossom during the first years of the interbellum, or should it impose upon the laity the principles of Catholic Action, which had helped to arrange a sort of a status quo with the fascist regimes? The answer was not only its own, however. Society after the war in many ways appeared quite different from the 1930s.

It is often argued that the Second World War opened a 'window of opportunities' to a fundamental modification of the pre-war political divisions and to a political realignment on the basis of the socio-economic class divide. After the war, many believed that pre-war divisions among labour had weakened the response to fascism, and mutual experiences in the resistance had created a sense of solidarity and unity. Such ideas fitted well into the new views on apostolate among Catholics, as they called upon both laity and clergy not to hide behind walls, but to 'enter the world', to act as leaven in the midst of the secular, and to focus on the de-Christianized masses of the proletariat. So, a wave of unitary initiatives resulted in the creation of 'left Catholic' parties, unitary trade unions, and new forms of apostolate, such as the worker priests and the 'Mouvement Populaire des Familles' (MPF) in France, Belgium and Switzerland.[20]

Hence, it seemed that pre-war 'pillarised' societies, with their politically integrated networks of associations and organisations isolating the faithful, would not be restored. However, this perception was flawed on several points. Suffice it to say that if war and occupation sometimes indeed initiated solidarities, they more often also created new rifts between social groups and communities or confirmed and deepened old divisions.[21] As far as the position of the Catholic Church is concerned, one should moreover observe that the war finally was far from a 'secularising event'. On the contrary, it enhanced

20 See Horn and Gerard, eds., *Left Catholicism*.

21 For a provocative and revisionist reappraisal of the effects of war and occupation on post-war solidarities and divisions (albeit from a labour history perspective) see Pasture, "Window of Opportunities".

the influence of the Church in society and heralded a restoration and renewal rather than a crisis.[22] Furthermore, some of the new apostolic movements soon drifted away from the spiritual quest and their original apolitical perspective, and turned into leftist political movements. The evolution of the French Catholic Action movement 'Mouvement Populaire des Familles' (MPF) to the 'Mouvement de Libération du Peuple' (MPL) is emblematic for this most remarkable development.[23] In doing so, they actually cleared the way for the hierarchy to intervene and regain authority in politics and society.

More importantly even, the major political event in continental Western Europe was the breakthrough of Christian Democracy. As a modern political movement, which proposed a general political program and a genuine ideology, and (at least in theory) appealed to a wider electorate than the community of believers, Christian Democracy constituted a perfect mix of continuity, renewal and flexibility.[24] Christian Democratic parties defined themselves as independent from clerical tutelage, but maintained variable and flexible relations with the Catholic social and cultural organisations of the former 'Catholic pillars', even in the Axis countries where apparently confessional parties and cultures had been destroyed by Fascism.[25] Although they certainly were not puppets of the Catholic Church, and of any other denomination, Christian Democratic parties nevertheless promoted policies that were compliant with

22 Conway, "The Age of Christian Democracy", esp. 48-53. Note some qualifications in Pasture, "Window of Opportunities" though.

23 Duriez, "Left Wing Catholicism in France".

24 Much attention has recently been devoted to post-war Christian Democracy. An overview of the most recent general literature in Kaiser, "Review Article: Christian Democracy in Twentieth Century Europe". The latest title is the double volume of Kaiser and Wohnout, eds., *Political Catholicism in Europe* and Gehler and Kaiser, eds., *Christian Democracy in Europe*.

25 See Pasture, "Window of Opportunities". Even if in the Netherlands the Roman Catholic Party formally opened its ranks to non-Catholics and changed its name into Catholic People's Party (KVP), the Dutch Catholic pillar, however, was restored more or less intact. In Germany, by contrast, the Christian Democratic party CDU/CSU did not define itself as confessional and effectively unified Catholics and Protestants (even if Catholics remained largely majoritary). Hence the Catholic world was fundamentally reorganised rather than simply restored. Still, post-war Germany remained characterised by a pillarised, albeit not confessional, subculture. Damberg, *Abschied von Milieu?*; Idem, "Van voorbeelden en schrikbeelden". To emphasise the impact of Catholics in the CDU/CSU and on the post-war Federal Republic of Germany Martin Conway even goes as far as to describe the Bundesrepublik as "the first Catholic national state on German soil". Conway, "The Age of Christian Democracy", 51. For Belgium see Pasture, "Entre Église et citoyen". More examples in Gehler and Kaiser, eds., *Christian Democracy in Europe*; Conway and Buchanan, eds., *Political Catholicism in Europe;* and Lamberts, ed., *Christian Democracy in the European Union*.

its social views (e.g. regarding family and education).[26] The Cold War further enhanced these types of political cultures, also in Italy and Germany, where previously no real pillars had existed.

In the new post-war social and political order, the Church, albeit reluctantly[27], had to accept the political rules of democracy and pluralism. This also implied that it had to consent to the primary role of the laity in politics. However, it was not prepared to submit itself to democratic and laic rule. Hence, the Church again turned to the ideas of Catholic Action. The clerics had to reduce their direct entanglement in the realm of the temporal and concentrate their work on the spiritual 'core business' of the Church: liturgy and religious education. Similarly, the hierarchy emphasised the importance of educational social organisations, which would give the militants guidance in their daily life and in particular politics and which would build up a reliable political elite.

The theory sounded convincing, but, as Giovanni Guareschi's archetypical Italian village priest Don Camillo (immortalized by the French actor Fernandel) epitomised, in practical life the realms of the spiritual and the temporal were not that easy to separate. In Italy, Belgium and, particularly, the Netherlands, the hierarchy explicitly limited the freedom of the faithful in politics and society: Catholics were not allowed to affiliate to other non-Catholic organisations or cast their vote to parties other than the Catholic or Christian Democratic ones.[28]

Aggiornamento in the 1960s?

Notwithstanding the restoration and modernisation of pillarised Catholicism after the Second World War, a profound transformation of Catholic practice and an unparalleled decline in religious participation characterised the 1960s.

Signs of these developments could be detected as early as the 1950s. In fact, popular Catholicism after 1945 did not reach the heights of the 1920s and 1930s, and vocations started to decline.[29] Migration from the countryside into rapidly expanding suburbs, commuting as a mass phenomenon, shrinking working hours and individual mobility during the longer 'weekend', a pros-

26 See the literature quoted in note 25, in particular the essay of Conway, "The Age of Christian Democracy".
27 Conway, "The Age of Christian Democracy".
28 See for an overview Ibidem.
29 Dellepoort, ed., *Die europäische Priesterfrage.*

pering market of information and leisure industries, contributed to fundamentally modified lifestyles, as a result of which the local life in the *civilisation paroissale* evaporated. In particular, the religious socialisation of young people changed.[30] Indeed, the teenagers of the late 1950s took a significantly more distanced attitude towards the Church than their parents. The results of religious education in schools were disastrous and apostolic youth organisations lost their appeal. The fight of the clergy against the new popular culture of rock 'n' roll, movies and the black box was lost. The Church did try to control the modern media, but in contrast to what happened in the United States (or a century earlier with the printed mass media), it did not find ways to use them to its advantage. In the 1960s then, the reins were loosened and the youth, especially young women, escaped from ecclesiastical tutelage. Since women played a crucial role in family life and in the transmission of religious beliefs and practices, also in the daily operation of the Church (in the parishes as in many religious institutions), the importance of this development can hardly be overstated.[31] Catholic sociologists soon realised that pastoral problems of unknown dimensions loomed large. Indeed, in most European countries, the Church entered into a deep and lasting crisis.

It is in this context that the Second Vatican Council came to renew the Catholic Church. The issue was indeed, in the words of Pope John XXIII, to open the doors and windows of the Church, and to realise an *aggiornamento*, to bring the Church 'up to date'.

Aggiornamento in Rome: The Second Vatican Council

Before discussing the innovations of the Council, we should emphasise that the Second Vatican Council in the first place profoundly modified the process of communication in the Catholic world. Indeed, since the nineteenth century in particular, Catholics were used to following the sole decisions of the hierarchy, safely guided by the Holy Spirit. *Roma locuta, causa finita*, when the highest authorities spoke out, the case was closed. However, in 1962, when even cardinals and bishops started to use arguments and votes, discussions soon followed in every parish council. Incidentally, the cardinals and bishops prompted this breakthrough themselves when they refused to act as a mere

30 For a Dutch case study, see Pennings, "Jongeren en ontzuiling"; for Germany, Damberg, *Abschied vom Milieu?*, 339-348; Idem, "Religiöser Wandel im Generationenwechsel"; for the French countryside, Lambert, *Dieu change en Bretagne*.

31 Cf. Brown, *The Death of Christian Britain*; Ziemann, "Das Ende der Milieukoalition"; McLeod, *The Sixties*.

voting machine for the prepared papers of the papal administration. Secondly, the media discovered the Council as a media event and presented the to and fro of the discussions to the eyes and ears of a worldwide audience.[32]

Arguably, one of the most important decisions of the Council was the acceptance of historical thinking. In 'ultramontane' theology this was *anathema*. The pope and the bishops only had to repeat truths which were valid once and for all. Now, in striking contrast, the Council accepted the need for a reassessment of the 'state of the Church' and its theology. This was the condition of coping with an ever-changing world.[33]

The acceptance of the historical nature of theology was part of a wider recognition, as it was viewed at the time, of the values of 'the modern world'. From a similar perspective, the Council recognised the importance of the state, established the plurality of modern society (which led to a fundamental change in the relations of the Catholic Church with other faiths) and came out with a powerful new concept of the Church itself, viewed as the 'People of God', and of the relations between the laity, the clergy, and the sacred. Hence, laypersons were also given a voice in the Church through parochial and episcopal councils. Moreover, the Council fundamentally renewed the liturgy, establishing the use of the vernacular language, surely the most tangible change for the ordinary faithful. These increasingly made their mark on the liturgy and rites, particularly since the 1980s.[34]

In many respects, the Second Vatican Council fitted in perfectly with the spirit of the 1960s. During those years, all over the Western industrialised world, there was an optimistic outlook for the future, and there were 'grand expectations', as Patterson's famous book on the United States phrases it.[35] The Council fostered those 'grand expectations', and in some ways, it even anticipated the discussions about globalisation that were not yet on the agenda then. However, the optimistic mood of the 1960s soon evaporated. At last, during the 1970s, the social landscape was marked by economic troubles, shrinking budgets and political quarrels and polarisation between conservative groups

32 Giuseppe Alberigo as the leading editor of the voluminous *Storia del concilio Vaticano II* has especially stressed the character of the Council as an 'event', whose impact reaches far beyond the theological declarations. See Fattori and Melloni, eds., *L'evento e le decisioni*; Alberigo, "Criteri ermeneutici".

33 *In nuce* this was made perfectly clear by Pope John XXIII in his famous opening speech.

34 This de-clericalisation and individualisation is nicely analysed with regard to Catholic death rituals in Flanders by Bleyen, *Het taboe voorbij?*, and Idem, *De dood in Vlaanderen*.

35 Patterson, *Grand Expectations*.

mobilising against the political trend of the 1960s and radicals who wanted to push reforms even further.[36]

Since the Council, the radical character of many innovations has been emphasised and often contrasted with a perceived 'regression' afterwards. No doubt the vast majority of the faithful welcomed most of the changes introduced by and after the Council, especially those in the liturgy. Nevertheless, some scholars, most notably the French historian Denis Pelletier, have proposed a different, and far more critical appreciation of the Second Vatican Council.

A Revisionist Approach to the Second Vatican Council

Indeed, the Council did not end the crisis of the Church. On the contrary, religious participation in all Western European countries declined even further. Perhaps the most significant notice was the crisis in the clergy. Not only did vocations in the late 1960s plummet, but numerous clerics also threw off the cowl, and not always quietly as in the past, but often publicly, with slamming doors.

Furthermore, the innovations after the Council, particularly regarding internal democratisation and birth control, fell short of the expectations. Particularly, the encyclical *Humanae vitae* in 1968 provoked a short circuit between the Church and the ordinary faithful, because of the authoritarian way it was proclaimed. It was symptomatic of the crisis the Catholic hierarchy faced.

The alternative interpretation states that the *aggiornamento* may have concerned fundamental and long-standing issues regarding the relationship between the Church and the modern world, but that these in fact were becoming out of date already, and that it surely did not anticipate the cultural revolution of the 1960s. In a thought-provoking essay, Denis Pelletier has argued that the Council was dramatically out of tune with the new intellectual and cultural climate that prevailed in France and, albeit less pronounced, throughout the rest of Europe. The neo-Thomist Christian humanism that finally triumphed at the Council, even when it was already quite over the heads of many less theologically trained bishops, was superseded in intellectual circles by new and fundamentally different philosophies: structuralism, soon giving way to even more radical forms of thinking about modernity

36 On the complex relations between shifts in political life and the pontificates of the last popes, see Damberg, "Pontifikate und politische Konjunkturen".

than the venerated prelates could ever imagine, post-structuralism and post-modernity. There is a world of difference between a Marie-Dominique Chenu or a Henri de Lubac, and a Claude Lévi-Strauss, a Roland Barthes, a Jacques Lacan, or a Michel Foucault, let alone the Derridas, Baudrillards and Lyotards who would soon follow suit.[37] Moreover, the Catholic social activism that the Council prophesied differed considerably from the one of the protest generation of the students and workers of '1968'. The latter gave way to a radical New Left Catholicism that also directed its social and political criticism towards the Church itself. In the same wake, the Church was losing touch with social emancipation movements, in particular with feminism, although in the past it had often encouraged women to be involved in the public sphere. More important, perhaps, was that the Council did not properly address the problems arising from the breakthrough of the consumer society.[38]

Witnessing the success of fundamentalist denominations and religious sects and movements since the 1950s in their own country, American scholars also argued that the Council impoverished the spiritual dimension of the Church, precisely at a moment when emotion and interest in spirituality in society were on the rise. After all, the times since the 1960s were labeled the 'Age of Aquarius', while the students revolting in Paris and Berlin called for "l'imagination au pouvoir". The new Catholic liturgy, in contrast, privileged the Word above ritual and sentiment, and reduced ecclesiastical decorum to a minimum.[39]

Furthermore, from a market-oriented perspective, it has been argued that religions actually have to raise their bids (i.e. they have to be sufficiently other-worldly and demanding) and not act too softly on rewards or sanctions after life. In this perspective, the post-Vatican II Catholic Church, in the words of one scholar, combined the worst of both worlds: "discarding cherished distinctiveness in the areas of liturgy, theology, and life-style, while at the same time maintaining the very demands that its members and clergy are the least

37 One of the rare figures who perceived the gulf that separated the so-called *aggiornamento* of the Second Vatican Council from the real world was Mgr Matagrin, auxiliary bishop of Lyon (France), who admitted he would not be able to speak about the new Christian-humanist concept of human person with students because the texts of the Council spoke "in categories that they considered outdated". "Là, j'ai pris conscience que le Concile était en train de décrire un monde au moment même où celui-ci devenait autre". Quoted in Pelletier, *La crise catholique*, 23.

38 Pelletier, *La crise catholique*.

39 See esp. Ellwood, *The Sixties Spiritual Awakening*. For a general discussion of the 1960s encompassing a European and an American perspective, see Pasture, "Christendom and the Legacy of the Sixties", as well as McLeod, *The Sixties*.

willing to accept".[40] However, other scholars have emphasised the dynamics that the Council unleashed and its contribution to the most recent religious 'Awakening' in the United States.[41]

The reappraisal of the Second Vatican Council remains controversial, however. One is certainly entitled to ask if there really was a spiritual awakening in the society of the 1960s. Rational thinking, planning and the organising of the welfare state to distribute the increasing wealth of the post-war economic boom dominated Europe's 'golden sixties' even more, as did the demands for greater participation of ordinary people in public affairs, for higher standards of health care, education and so on. From this perspective, the so-called 'revolution of the sixties' could be seen as a marginal and counter-cultural phenomenon. Moreover, political activism tended to prevail, and as far as religions are concerned, the new religious movements have only gathered some attention since the 1970s, and research has stressed that their reach should not be overestimated.[42] However, the issue remains unsettled.

Ambiguities beyond the Second Vatican Council

From the viewpoint of pillarised Catholicism, however, more definite yet complex conclusions can be formulated. The view that the Church had to stand within the world and not isolated from it, could be interpreted as undermining the basis of the pillarisation strategy[43], but, in practice, the conclusions of the Council did not speak out exclusively in favour of one pastoral strategy, and its concrete effects in that respect were limited. But the Council did legitimise an evolution by which Christian social organisations emphasised their secular objectives above their confessional identity.[44] This contributed to an increased pluralism within the Church and arguably might be considered one form of secularisation.

40 Laurence R. Iannaccone quoted in Finke and Stark, *The Churching of America*, 261.

41 E.g. Porterfield, *The Transformation of American Religion*, 70-75. A nuanced assessment in Isserman and Kazin, *America Divided*, esp. 248-252.

42 Pollack, "Wiederkehr des Religiösen?", esp. 22; Wilson and Cresswell, eds., *New Religious Movements*; Clarke, "Introduction".

43 Pasture, "Modèles internationaux".

44 Idem, *Kerk, politiek en sociale actie*, chapter 4.

Public Appearance and 'Professional' Christendom

In the 1950s, Christian Democratic parties prospered and played a predominant role in Western European politics. In addition, because there were fewer formal ties between the Church and the parties, the Catholic Church got involved more directly in the public sphere by issuing statements on different social issues, especially after the 1960s.

Moreover, notwithstanding their reservations about state intervention, Catholic as well as Reformed social and economic (even cultural) organisations were integrated in the development of the welfare states. The range and limits of the process depended on national legislation, which in Germany, Austria, Switzerland, Italy, Luxemburg, Belgium and the Netherlands was partly inspired by Christian Democrats.[45] Apart from the Netherlands, this integration allowed confessional organised welfare and cultural activities to expand enormously. In Germany, for example, the Catholic welfare organisation Caritas became the biggest non-governmental employer in Europe with nearly 500,000 employees on their payroll.[46] Moreover, the Second Vatican Council even gave a new impetus to further involvement of the parishes in secular activities, either to protect the faithful from outside influences (the traditional pillarisation perspective) or to be present in the secular world and to act together with people outside of the Church. In many Flemish towns, for example, the Council aroused a new interest in the construction of parochial centres.[47] In Germany, Catholic youth work was completely reorganised. The traditional associations obtained a professional staff and improved training opportunities for the volunteers. Also, the dioceses promoted local youth centres with professional services. Today, the demand for such activities remains high, as does the strong demand for admission to in the numerous Catholic schools run by the diocese or by religious orders.[48] Similar develop-

45 Idem, "Building the Social Security State"; Idem, "Diverging Paths"; Frie, "Zwischen Katholizismus und Wohlfahrtsstaat".

46 On 1 January 2001 the statistics of the *Deutsche Caritasverband* counted exactly 495,219 employees, not inclusive the trainees, part-time volunteers or *Zivildienstleistenden* (conscientious objector). <www.caritas.de> (06.02.2003). The protestant equivalent in Germany, the *Diakonie*, has an additional 402,000 employees. <www.diakonie.de> (06.02.2003). In the Netherlands the public sector expanded far more than the private confessional sector.

47 Soen, "Ieder huisje heeft zijn kruisje".

48 Damberg, *Abschied vom Milieu?*, 417-421, 496-503. In Germany, the system of *Kirchensteuer* allowed the churches to develop their social services with a high level of professionalisation. Damberg, *Abschied vom Milieu?*, and Idem, "Van voorbeelden en schrikbeelden". For Belgium, see Pasture, "Divergent Developments". See also Hellemans, *Strijd om de moderniteit*, 248-251.

ments occurred in Belgium. In contrast to the Netherlands, where the Catholic pillar disintegrated, their integration in the welfare state has saved the pillars in the other countries.

But the decision to engage itself in the emerging welfare state did not leave the Church unchanged. This coin had two sides. At the very least, it led to a professionalisation of Catholic social services, to some extent at the expense of religious engagement (if only because low-skilled nurses and nuns were to be replaced by high-skilled professionals). Moreover, in exchange for public subsidies, the state obtained quality control rights and thus intervened in the confessional organisations. Paradoxically, the social demands of the churches increased the role of the (secular) state and thus contributed to a certain secularisation of social welfare.[49] Apart from the Netherlands, however, Catholic social services managed quite well in using state subsidies to their advantage. However, they paid a price: the Catholic identity gradually evaporated into what Karel Dobbelaere and Jaak Billiet, speaking about Belgium, in the 1970s baptised a 'socio-cultural Christianity', characterised by a number of humanist, *gemeinschaftliche* values (including, incidentally, the search for 'quality' and efficiency).[50] Increasingly, these organisations adopted a secular, domain-specific logic (incidentally an evolution that was explicitly sanctioned by the Council). The result, however, was a deep transformation. In general, the pillars gradually lost their ideological distinctiveness, which in the long term could have meant their over all disintegration. Some organisations or pillars in the 1980s and 1990s turned into 'political concerns' (as they were aptly coined by Luc Huyse) that adopted the logic of the economic and political market and power relations. Christian workers' and farmers' cooperatives in Belgium even split off from the pillarised community they originated in, to become purely commercial enterprises.[51]

49 Pasture, "Building the Social Security State". A similar observation on the USA in Wuthnow, *The Restructuring of American Religion*, 321.

50 International references to this 'socio-cultural Christianity' (repeated in uncountable articles elsewhere) include Voyé, "From Institutional Catholicism to 'Christian Inspiration'"; Dobbelaere, "Professionalization and Secularization"; Dobbelaere and Billiet, "Les changements internes". We believe these observations can be applied to other countries as well, particularly to Germany, Switzerland and Austria, as well as to Italy. See also Hellemans, *Strijd om de moderniteit*; Damberg, *Abschied vom Milieu*; Idem, "Van voorbeelden en schrikbeelden".

51 The process has been analysed by Luc Huyse in *De verzuiling voorbij*. Compare Hellemans, *Strijd om de moderniteit*, who speaks of "neo-zuilen" ('neo-pillars'). On the Belgian cooperatives see Van Dijck, *Entreprendre avec du capital coopératif*; Buyst et al., *CERA*; Gerard et al., *Van arbeiderscoöperatie tot bank*.

Social Criticism and Pluralism

We have just argued that the decisions of the Second Vatican Council did not necessarily herald the demise of pillarised Catholicism. That may be true, but the concept of pillarisation implies a sense of unity within the Church that was definitely lost after the 1960s. To be sure, this resulted, in the first place, from a larger process of individualisation since the 1950s, which affected more than just the Church. Indeed, the mental frameworks that were established since the early nineteenth century started to crumble. Paradoxically, pillarised Catholicism had played a part in this development. Its social and political activities and structures had contributed to increased prosperity, and its educational activities, not only in the schools but also, and maybe even particularly, through Catholic Action, had helped to empower people, particularly the weak.

Furthermore, as already mentioned, the Council provoked diverse and even conflicting reactions. The decisions of the Council were widely debated in Catholic milieus and beyond, but debate implies opposition. This increased with the implementation of the Council. Paul VI, indeed one of the architects of the *aggiornamento*, once on Peter's throne felt stuck and tried to re-establish his authority by putting the brakes on an uncontrollable acceleration of the reform of the Church. Some believers followed him, but many also felt he had betrayed the Council. Finally, some even rejected the Council and split away in the schism of Mgr Lefebvre.

Catechism and the Spiritual and Theological 'Amnesia'

Paradoxically, perhaps, debates about the Council illustrate that despite the structural crisis that the Catholic Church faced, and the deceptions that Paul VI provoked, the Council did raise enthusiasm and inspired new initiatives (and not all of these were suffocated afterwards). At the local level, spiritual initiatives were taken, and young people were inspired by new (or newly recognised) prophets, such as (the Protestant) Father Schutz in Taizé, or movements such as *Comunione e liberazione*.[52] The fate of the majority of religious practices in the 1970s and 1980s showed how the ordinary flock drifted away from the objectives and aspirations of the Church. The most significant development in our view, however, was the loss of religious insight and knowledge.[53]

52 Jenkins, *God's Continent*, 93-102.

53 The following observations are inspired by the work of Hervieu-Léger, *Religion as a Chain of Memory* (orig. *La religion pour mémoire*), but push her arguments somewhat beyond their initial intent. They do have a largely hypothetical character.

After the Council, the traditional view of the catechism as transmission of belief was generally abandoned for a more 'life-oriented' approach that started from the experiences of the people. It was an approach that also took into account the increasingly secularised context in which the faithful lived. A famous example of this change was the Dutch *Nieuwe Catechismus*, which was widely distributed outside the Netherlands as well. But when the new methods of teaching were introduced, they did not turn the tide, and they may even have accelerated de-Christianisation. When the abstract 'simple truths' of the traditional catechism, quite alien indeed to daily experience, were replaced by what was later labelled a vague and this-worldly theology, the immediate, if unintended, result apparently was that religious education, in whatever form and place, became all but redundant. To be sure, to a certain extent this development can be related to changes in the structure of education itself, such as the promotion of higher education levels in centralised school centres in Germany. The latter destroyed the historical relations between the parish and the small local schools, another blow to the *civilisation paroissiale*.

In the end (in the 1980s and 1990s), the body of traditional religious knowledge of the ordinary faithful collapsed. As the subsequent European Values Studies show, basic concepts of the Catholic doctrine such as belief in hell, the devil and angels are less and less often believed or even understood. Similarly, liturgical practices sometimes show an astounding lack of consistency.[54] Furthermore, in practice, the differences between mainstream Protestantism and Catholicism tended to fade away. This blurring of boundaries went far beyond the formal achievements of the ecumenical movement, let alone what was formally 'allowed' in the eyes of the Holy See. Olaf Blaschke therefore diagnoses the 1970s as "the end of the confessional era".[55]

Rather than just the 'failure' of the Council and post-Conciliar catechism, these observations illustrate the advent of what we call, with Danièle Hervieu-Léger, an amnesiac society, in which basic knowledge and understanding of the religious 'traditions' has been lost. This is also illustrated by the self-evidence by which people since the 1980s construct their own religious worldview and

54 Examples include the reference to Tolkien's *Lord of the Rings* in a Christian funeral (referred to in Bleyen, *De dood in Vlaanderen*, 82-83). See also the results of the EVS and the contribution of Karel Dobbelaere and Jaak Billiet elsewhere in this volume.

55 Blaschke, ed., *Konfessionen im Konflikt*; Pasture, "Christendom since the Sixties".

practices (religious 'bricolage' or 'religion à la carte').[56] Hence mixed marriages in the eyes of the ordinary flock are no longer considered a problem (though they still are for the Congregation for the doctrine of the faith).[57] Equally important and illustrative for this new type of society is the increasing number of people who refuse any religious affiliation and who consider themselves without religion.[58] The amnesiac society nevertheless also opens space for new religious initiatives or utopias. As Grace Davie argued, however, in contrast to North America, there was little opportunity for such initiatives to materialise in the European societies of the 1960s and 1970s, when public broadcasting companies monopolised the air for radio and television. Neo-Pentecostalism and the Charismatic Movement, for example, which since the 1960s has skyrocketed in North and South America, Africa and Asia, have hardly been able to get a foothold in the Old Continent.[59] Many individuals then remain, in the apt formulation of Staf Hellemans, "longing without belonging".[60]

Conclusion

To conclude, let us first of all emphasise that pillarised Catholicism originated in the nineteenth century as a quintessentially modern phenomenon, that it was the result of a combination of different and sometimes conflicting strategies (Catholic Action should be considered originally as an alternative, even opposing strategy to the pillars, even if in Flanders it ultimately contributed to its reinforcement)[61], and that it was continu-

56 Dobbelaere, *Secularization*. Hervieu-Léger correctly observes how this is a general feature of contemporary society, not particular to Catholicism: Hervieu-Léger, *Religion*, 127-130.

57 Bendikowski, "Eine Fackel der Zwiedracht".

58 In the Netherlands this was already 23,6 percent in 1971, and 44,2 percent in 1980. Laeyendecker, "The Case of the Netherlands", 132. The high number of unchurched in the Netherlands, however, is exceptional even for Western Europe. This situation was anticipated in 1966 by François Roustang, editor-in-chief of the review *Christus*: arguing against the humanist perspective of the Second Vatican Council, Roustang detected the birth of a Third Man who found no relevance in the teaching of the Church. Roustang, "Le troisième homme" (referred to in Pelletier, *Crise catholique*, 25-26). It surely is no accident that Roustang was close to Michel de Certeau, who also influenced Hervieu-Léger.

59 Davie, *Religion in Modern Europe*, esp. 98-114. On the world-wide spread of Pentecostalism see Martin, *Pentecostalism*.

60 Hellemans, "From 'Catholicism Against Modernity' to the Problematic 'Modernity of Catholicism'", 124.

61 Compare Pasture, *Kerk, politiek en sociale actie,* to Laermans, *In de greep van de Moderne Tijd*. The latter author emphasises the contribution of the Catholic Action to the growth of Catholic social organisations (hence of pillarisation) in Flanders, without noticing Catholic Action originally was designed as an alternative to them.

ously modified and modernised. In this process, pillarised Catholicism had to permanently cope not only with secularising forces, which partly originated from within, but also with a growing tendency within the Church towards a *Verkirchli-chung* of social action, by which a centralising hierarchy tried to regain control over the laity.[62]

Already in the 1950s, but particularly in the 1960s, new patterns in industrial production, living (migration) and consumption, leading among other things, to a fundamentally new and different restatement of gender roles, undermined the pillars. The Council tried to bring the Church up to date, but despite its 'revolutionary' new practices and visions, it remained trapped in debates about 'modern' society that already belonged to a world that was disappearing fast. It could not prevent the Catholic Church coming close to a watershed in Europe in the second half of the 1960s (in contrast to the United States).

The demise of Christian practices provoked sociologists to take up an old theme in social sciences: secularisation of society as the inevitable result of modernisation.[63] From a historical perspective, this theory has fallen into oblivion.[64] The closest thing to the mythical 'age of faith' might well be pillarised Catholicism as it developed in the nineteenth and twentieth centuries, but the 1960s in Western Europe do fit quite well into the model. Let us then apply the seminal, threefold definition of secularisation proposed by Karel Dobbelaere, albeit in a simplified form: fewer people practiced, the influence of the churches on society declined, and even the beliefs evaporated into vague, inconsistent and this-worldly opinions.[65] As a result of functional differentiation and individualisation, religion increasingly became a private matter, and the model of pillarised Catholicism was about to expire sooner or later.

62 The concept of *Verkirchlichung* has been introduced in Germany by Kaufmann, *Kirche begreifen,* and Hürten, "Zukunftperspektiven kirchlicher Zeitgeschichtsforschung", esp. 110 ff. From a different perspective see also Pasture, "Modèles internationaux d'action ouvrière catholique".

63 The process was described and analysed by authors such as Sabino S. Acquaviva (*L'Eclissi del sacro nella civiltà industriale*), Bryan R. Wilson (*Religion in a Secular Society*), Peter L. Berger (*The Sacred Canopy*), Thomas Luckmann (*The Invisible Religion*), David Martin (*The Religious and the Secular*), Robert N. Bellah (*Beyond Belief*). See for overviews Dobbelaere, *Secularization,* and Tschannen, *Les théories de la sécularisation*.

64 Nash, "Reconnecting Religion with Social and Cultural History".

65 Dobbelaere, *Secularization*.

However, notwithstanding the depth of the crisis, the pillars were not as easily destroyed as some contemporaries suspected. After all, the disintegration of the Catholic pillar in the Netherlands turned out to be the exception rather than the rule. A pillarised Catholic network survived in Germany, Italy, Austria, Switzerland, and Belgium in the 1970s and 1980s. To do so, many confessional organisations emphasised their secular objectives at the expense of their confessional identities and ties to the Church. Advocates of the secularisation theory are correct to consider this development an argument in favour of rather than as a refutation of secularisation. Religion indeed became a private issue, and was further undermined by rationalisation as well. Hence, the survival of pillarised Christian subcultures did not prevent religious practice from sliding.[66]

However, religion, even Catholicism, did not disappear from the public scene. On the contrary, although it would be exaggerating to speak of a return of religion in politics (at least in Western Europe)[67], the churches, particularly since the 1960s, did raise their voice again as guardians of social ethics. Pushing an observation made by Denis Pelletier somewhat beyond its initial intent[68], we may conclude that while secularisation, both as an abstract sociological pro-cess and as a political objective, tried to encapsulate religion into the private sphere, the Catholic Church completely lost its authority there, whereas when it spoke out about social and political issues, its voice (although stripped of its magisterial authority) was heard once again (although one should not overestimate its impact either). With the late Pope John Paul II, Catholicism became once more an important political actor on the world stage.[69]

In the 1980s and 1990s, while virtually all available statistics and sources in Western Europe indicated a continuous decline and crisis, pillarised Catholicism was replaced by the emergence of a pluralised Catholicism,

66 Dobbelaere and Voyé, "Europäische Katholiken und die katholische Kirche".

67 It needs no further comment that since these lines first were written in 2003, the debate about a 'clash of civilisations', with religion as a central issue, only has increased. Likewise, it is evident enough that the influence of religion on politics and society in the post-war USA since the 1950s gradually increased up to becoming a dominant force.

68 "Autrement dit, par un étrange retournement des choses, cette Église que la République laïcisatrice avait cherché à contenir dans les limites du for privé pendant un siècle, se voit alors privée de toute influence en ce domaine, au moment même où sa voix redevient audible dans la vie publique, moyennant l'acceptation du fait qu'elle n'y soit plus en situation de magistère privilégié". Pelletier, *Crise catholique*, 277. See also the discussion in Voyé, "From Institutional Catholicism to 'Christian Inspiration'", esp. 204-206.

69 Casanova, *Public Religions.*

which is characterised by the more or less autonomous development of parts (*Sektoren*) of the old pillars. With Karl Gabriel we can trace back some of them, in different proportions and relations, in different European countries: (1) a small fundamentalist sector; (2) a traditional, 'explicit' or 'interactive' Catholicism, concentrated around parochial life; (3) a diffuse Catholicism, strongly individualistic, but with a strong social orientation; (4) organised Catholicism, i.e. the pastoral and the welfare system; and (5) the realm of the social movements, fostering individual religious and group experiences, with very different objectives.[70] In this perspective, as has been the case in Germany already since 1945, Christian Democracy constitutes one part of the former pillars that has become autonomous from the Catholic Church. Hence, it follows its own course, but far less predictably than the prophets of the 1960s and 1970s had assumed. In addition, the meaning of believing and religious participation has changed. But that was not the subject of this chapter.

70 Gabriel, *Christentum zwischen Tradition und Postmoderne.*

Left Catholicism in Western Europe
A Brief Survey

Gerd-Rainer Horn

No sequence of events shook up modern European societies as much as the Second World War, the Nazi occupation of vast portions of the continent and the ensuing antifascist resistance efforts. The experience of occupation, resistance and liberation turned European societies upside down. Previous certainties oftentimes dissolved into distant memories, and new conceptions of society, politics and culture began to agitate the hearts and minds of those Europeans who were fortunate enough to survive. When the moment of liberation eventually arrived, significant numbers of Europeans were no longer willing to return to the status quo ante. They instead hoped for a thorough renewal of their societies and polities. Politically, this manifested itself in a massive leftward shift, and the years 1944-1947 must be regarded as the historic low point of popular acceptance of capitalism on a continental scale. This observation holds just as true for Western as for Eastern Europe.

It would have been wholly surprising if this major shift in popular attitudes would not have affected the world of Catholicism like everything else. After all, literally all of Catholic Europe experienced the loss of democracy firsthand, whether imposed by domestic reaction, by foreign conquest, or both. And indeed, the most significant case of an antifascist resistance movement to arise west of the line from Trieste to Poznan, the Italian *resistenza*, directly affected the heartland of Catholicism. Catholics thus fought side-by-side with co-religionists of other faiths, as well as secular Marxists and others, in both the civilian and the military resistance to the Nazi empire - and not just in Italy. It is the commonplace of resistance literature that the experience of joint suffering and struggle brought about a loosening of pre-existent mental and physical barriers which previously separated the various ideological camps. In the antifascist underground, some Catholics and communists suddenly found themselves, in some cases for the first time ever, on the same side of the literal and proverbial barricades.

Catholic Political Parties

Perhaps the most visible manifestation of this shift to the political Left within the ranks of European Catholicism was the sudden prominence of left currents and tendencies within traditional Catholic parties, or the creation of novel Catholic parties belonging to the spectrum of the moderate or even the radical Left. In what was to become West Germany, 'Christian socialism' became the watchword of the day, influencing the early history of the Christian Democratic Union, with the distinctly Left Catholic *Frankfurter Hefte* receiving more than two hundred thousand subscription requests in the immediate post-war era.[1]

In neighbouring Belgium, the revamped *Parti Social Chrétien/Christelijke Volkspartij* (PSC/CVP) likewise emphasised its 'progressive' side in the immediate post-war era. But, if on the surface level, leftward shifts within the PSC/CVP were less clear and distinct than the corresponding movements within German Christian Democratic politics, this was not the result of greater moderation to the west of Aachen. In Belgium, the efforts of Left Catholic reformers were initially focussed on the construction of a new party independent of the PSC/CVP. The activists of the *Union Démocratique Belge* (UDB) attempted to crystallise the Belgian Catholic (but not exclusively Catholic) resistance legacy in a new formation which attracted much of the Belgian Catholic Left with its daily paper, *La Cité Nouvelle*, boasting a circulation of 100,000 copies.[2]

Political Catholicism in France underwent a major evolution in the mid-1940s as well. Of the two Catholic parties operating in pre-war France, only the smaller one, *Jeune République* (JR), survived. Allied to a new political formation which also included sections of the French Catholic Left, the *Union Démocratique et Socialiste de la Resistance* (UDSR), the joint slate for the October 1945 Constituent Assembly elections obtained 25 MPs, and JR's popular and influ-

1 Lienkamp, "Socialism out of Christian Responsibility", 220. The two standard monographs on this topic remain Focke, *Sozialismus aus christlicher Verantwortung* and Uertz, *Christentum und Sozialismus in der frühen CDU*.

2 Beerten, *Le rêve travailliste en Belgique*, 29.

ential president of the Liberation Committee in the Savoie, Lucien Rose, became the first speaker of France's post-war Constituent Assembly.[3]

The somewhat more moderate but nonetheless (in comparison to pre-war French Catholic politics) profoundly radicalised, newly formed *Mouvement Républicain Populaire* (MRP) soon became the largest Catholic party in France. Exceeding even its wildest pre-election hopes, the MRP obtained 24,9% of the vote for the Constituent Assembly and formed part of most initial post-war governments, together with the Socialist and Communist parties. Originally much closer to the spirit of the Belgian UDB than the PSC/CVP, the MRP must be regarded, until 1947, as a party of the Left.[4]

In Italy, Left Catholicism underwent a different evolution than in Belgium and France. In the mass movement phase of the resistance after 1943, three competing Catholic currents operated in the underground: *Democrazia Cristiana* (DC), the *Partito Cristiano-Sociale* (PCS) and the *Partito della Sinistra Cristiana* (PSC). While DC was, on the whole, the numerically most influential tendency, in some parts of the country its two competitors far outnumbered DC activists. In the important industrial port city of Livorno, for instance, the sole Catholic representative on the influential provincial Liberation Committee was a member of the PCS, which can be classified as a moderate (Catholic) socialist organisation. The PSC, at one point adopting the unequivocal label *Partito Comunista Cristiano*, constituted, after the Italian Communist Party (PCI), one of the most important of all underground organisations in the capital city of Rome.[5] But when liberation came in April 1945, DC indeed emerged as by far the most popular Catholic party in the Italian state.

Perhaps due to the early organisational independence of the more radical tendencies within Italian Left Catholicism, the PSC and PCS, it took approximately two years before a clearly recognisable left opposition began to arise within the post-Liberation DC. Led by three of the most important Italian Catholic intellectuals in the postwar era, Giuseppe Dossetti, Giorgio La Pira and Giuseppe Lazzatti, this *corrente dossettiani*, after 1946, agitated for far-reaching, progressive, socio-economic, structural reforms as well as the rejec-

3 Guerrier, *La Jeune République de 1912 à 1945*, 752-755. On the UDSR in particular, see Duhamel, *L'Union démocratique et socialiste de la résistance*.

4 Letamendia, *Le Mouvement Républicain Populaire*, is the standard reference work. For a lucid analysis of the entire spectrum of the French Catholic Left at mid-century, see Delbreil, "The French Catholic Left and the Political Parties".

5 For the PCS, see, above all, Parisella, ed, *Gerardo Bruni e i cristiano-sociali*; for the PSC, see Malgeri, *La Sinistra cristiana*, and Casula, *Cattolici-comunisti e sinistra cristiana*.

tion of NATO membership while demanding more central attention to the social gospel of the church. At the highpoint of their influence, at the occasion of the June 1949 Venice DC congress, their chief motion garnered 35% of the assembled DC delegates. And, for a while, even after the demise of this distinctly Left Catholic current in 1951, leading figures, above all Dossetti himself, continued their efforts to fashion a Catholic Left which now had the active support of prominent figures such as Felice Balbo, a former member of the PSC who had, in 1944, together with most PSC members, joined the PCI but then separated from it just before linking up with Dossetti.[6]

Giorgio La Pira, for his part, concentrated his efforts on the construction of what must be regarded as a form of 'municipal socialism' in Florence. Starting in 1951, as a (nominally DC) mayor of this key Italian city, La Pira, for more than a decade, attempted not only to transform Florence into a showcase for people-oriented Catholic municipal politics, but also organised a series of high-level, East-West, international peace conferences which flew in the face of the staunchly pro-Nato official DC course.[7]

Theological Shifts and Apostolic Social Movements

Such unprecedented new departures in the realm of Catholic party politics were part and parcel of an extensive reconfiguration of Western European Catholicism in the 1940s. Catholic philosophy and theology were indeed deeply affected by the horrors of fascism and the Second World War. And, just as the war must be seen as the climax of, what Arno Mayer called, "The Second Thirty Years War", it became clear that the first openings within the Catholic universe towards the Left predated the 1940s. Thus, the undisputedly major figure in this development of Western European Left Catholic theology, Jacques Maritain, had already published his *Humanisme intégral* in 1936. But this prescient work, published in the heady days of exper-

6 On the experience of the *corrente dossettiani*, indispensable reference works are, above all, Pombeni, *Le 'Cronache Sociali' di Dossetti*, and Idem, *Il gruppo dossettiano e la fondazione della democrazia italiana*. But note also the more recent anthologies by Alberigo, ed, *Giuseppe Dossetti*, and Mason and Villa, eds, *Giuseppe Dossetti*. Some insights into the political designs behind the episode of cooperation between Dossetti and Balbo can be gleaned in the collection of documents, entitled 'Post-Rossena', Fondo Cronache Sociali C 24 260, Istituto Superiore di Scienze Religiose, Bologna.

7 Balducci, *Giorgio La Pira*, and De Giuseppe, *Giorgio La Pira*, are solid introductions to the life and work of this Sicilian-born Left Catholic populist. On the whole complex of Italian Left Catholic politics at mid-century, within and outside of *Democrazia Cristiana*, see also Parisella, "Christian Movements and Parties of the Left in Italy".

imentation with united and popular fronts, obtained its widest audience in the course of the deprivations of Nazi occupation policies rather than in the earlier pre-war era. Whereas the second half of the 1930s witnessed important moves towards the acceptance of the political Left as an important partner for some Catholics, it was the collapse of old certainties in all walks of life during the Second World War which opened the floodgates of popular interest in such groundbreaking works as *Humanisme intégral*.[8]

Elsewhere, I have outlined the overall contours of this emerging Left Catholicism in the field of philosophy and theology.[9] Here it may suffice to draw attention to their contemporaneous discovery of Marx as an interlocutor rather than as an enemy to be caricatured and then destroyed. Emmanuel Mounier may stand as one of many representatives of this particular intellectual trend. Reflecting this growing recognition of the positive accomplishments of the secular Left, Left Catholic theologians, for instance, soon began to produce various thematically overlapping 'theologies of labour'. The titles of two calls to action, written between 1943 and 1945 by two locally influential priests in northern Italy, *The Social Revolution of Jesus Christ* by Don Zeno Saltini and *Christian Revolution* by Don Primo Mazzolari, may stand as a symbolic testimony to the sudden spread of Left Catholic theory and practice at the point of liberation in Western Europe.[10]

But the spirit and the message of this wave of Left Catholicism can be gauged most visibly neither in the growth rates of Left Catholic political currents and parties, nor in the publication of their theological handbooks. The key to understanding the impact of such reflective practices lies in the trajectory of corresponding apostolic social movements at that time.

In francophone Europe, the most internationally prominent manifestation of such ferment was the experience of the worker priests. These ordained priests, choosing to take up full-time industrial labour, were initially motivated by their desire to missionise what they had come to regard as the increasingly secularised world of industrial labour. In the process of their apostolic work,

8 Mayer, *Why Did The Heavens Not Darken?* Jacques Maritain's *Humanisme intégral* has most recently been reissued with a foreword by René Rémond (2000).

9 My first attempt at providing an initial survey of Left Catholic theological and philosophical innovations at that time was published as "Left Catholicism in Western Europe in the 1940s". But see now my *Western European Liberation Theology. 1924-1959. The First Wave.*

10 Saltini, *La Rivoluzione Sociale di Gesù Cristo* and Mazzolari, *Rivoluzione Cristiana*. The most prominent contemporaneous 'theology of labor' was Marie-Dominique Chenu's *Pour une théologie du travail.*

they adapted to their new political, social and cultural environment they had entered in various contradictory but fundamental ways, oftentimes becoming influential spokespersons for the concerns of the blue collar communities they had originally chosen to missionise.[11]

Yet there existed never more than one hundred worker priests prior to their brutal interdiction by the Catholic church hierarchy in 1954 (France) and 1955 (Belgium). The quantitatively, incomparably more firmly implanted *Mouvement Populaire des Familles* (MPF) remains, in curious contrast, far less well-known. The MPF had evolved into a social movement in the closing years of the Nazi occupation in both francophone Belgium and France. The MPF became the quintessential Catholic social advocacy group in the immediate post-war era, employing mass mobilisation strategies already prior to the moment of liberation, the latter making such actions less inherently dangerous. Focusing on the needs of neglected working class neighbourhoods in francophone Europe, the more than 100,000 members of the MPF had recourse to direct action tactics such as squatting in response to shortages of affordable housing, or mass demonstrations demanding immediate attention to the lack of blue collar neighbourhood infrastructures or the lack of adequate nutrition for the children of the working poor.[12]

MPF activists knew few taboos. Legal under Vichy, they openly attacked the prefects of Vichy France for lack of attention to the needs and desires of their constituency. After Liberation, they attacked with equal fervour the post-Liberation prefects' procrastinations. The spirit of MPF activism is reflected in an exemplary fashion in the following brief sentence, penned in the heat of struggle, by the spiritual advisor of the Belgian MPF, Philippe de Soignie: "Born out of the needs of the working class, led by the workers themselves, the MPF draws its program and its action from the powerful current of working class emancipation which is gripping the popular masses today."[13]

11 The classic study of this phenomenon has in 1999 been republished with a new and controversial title: Poulat, *Les prêtres-ouvriers: Naissance et fin*. But see also Arnal, *Priests in Working-Class Blue*, and Margotti, *Preti e operai*. The superior study of the Belgian worker priest phenomenon remains Gaëlle, *Jalons pour une histoire des prêtres-ouvriers en Belgique*.

12 On the MPF, see Debès, *Naissance de l'Action catholique ouvrière*, but above all the fourteen *Cahiers du G.R.M.F.* published between 1983 and 2006. Duriez, "Left Wing Catholicism in France", is a comprehensive introduction to this understudied phenomenon.

13 de Soignie, *Mystique chrétienne et ascension ouvrière*, 67.

The Italian Crucible

Italy never produced the equivalent of the MPF, mostly because the Catholic hierarchy usually intervened much more quickly to stamp out unorthodox developments on the activist-oriented Catholic Left. But a closer look at the regional and/or local patchwork of Left Catholic activism in Italy suggests that the sentiment which gave rise to the nationally organised MPF in francophone Europe was equally present, if not more prominently, south of the Alps. I will focus on two specific, powerful local manifestations of Italian Left Catholicism in the Po Valley of northern Italy.

It is characteristic of the Italian context of the first post-war decade that most instances of radical Left Catholic ferment were restricted to, at best, a local level, not necessarily by choice but because of the repressive actions of the Catholic Church hierarchy combined with the constraining presence of moderate DC on a local, regional and national level. Mainstream DC had nothing to lose and everything to gain from an enforced marginalisation of Left Catholic activism, which could only threaten DC's rapid accommodation to the new cold war consensus on the western side. The Church hierarchy itself had little interest in tolerating Italian variants of the rising tide of unorthodox Gallic challenges to the hegemony of the theological status quo defended by Rome.

If the most internationally and prominent representatives of unorthodox theological trends (Maritain, Mounier, Chenu) emanated from francophone portions of Catholic Europe, this should not mislead observers to automatically assume that this fertile theological imagination was a direct reflection of French Left Catholic activism outdistancing the Catholic clergy and laity everywhere else. France and francophone Belgium were home to the worker priest phenomenon, but Italy's *capellani del lavoro* in some centres of Italian industry performed a role not very different from that of their colleagues who had taken up full-time industrial labour between Marseille and Liège.[14] The MPF was, by all accounts, the largest Left Catholic social movement anywhere in Western Europe, but for the most part even the MPF operated more as a loose association of powerful local and/or regional activist centres

14 One of the few studies of this phenomenon is Bertini and Casadio, *Clero e industria a Torino*. For some interesting hints with regard to some unorthodox practices amongst the multitude of efforts by the Italian Catholic hierarchy to missionise Italy's working class, see the section on "Rechristianiser le monde ouvrier" in Durand, *L'Église catholique dans la crise de l'Italie*, 471-497.

in certain towns of provincial France rather than as a coherent, nationally coordinated challenge to the status quo.

In short, one should be careful not to regard the Italian cases briefly presented below, though mostly local initiatives with little more than a regional echo, as a disconnected and contingent set of experiments with little meaning for the larger political landscape of Italian Catholicism as a whole. Other towns and regions saw similar local experiments.[15] The open challenge by Italy's most well-known Left Catholic activists (Lazzati, Dossetti and La Pira) to the hegemony of DC politics by De Gasperi was equally short-lived and yet another prominent indicator of the volatility of Italian Catholic politics. When compared to French productions further west, one probable reason for the relative marginalisation of Italian Left Catholic accomplishments on both a theoretical (theological) and practical plane in the eyes of non-Italian Catholics and academics, is the perennial relative neglect on the part of Western anglophone and francophone observers of Mediterranean Europe in general and its cultural products in particular.

What, then, did Italian Left Catholics do when they attempted to translate their interpretations of the social gospel of Jesus Christ into practice? In the traditional 'red' province of Emilia Romagna, for instance, the aforementioned Don Zeno Saltini devoted his efforts not only to the creation of an orphanage, which eventually became home to 1,500 children, but, for a while, also intended this social activism to become a building block for his more all-encompassing social revolutionary project. Soon after Liberation, Don Zeno embarked on a ceaseless bout of activism, giving countless speeches in many locations throughout the region on a topic that he had just addressed in writing *The Social Revolution of Jesus Christ*. A collection of various letters inviting Don Zeno to address local audiences throughout the region and subsequent expressions of gratitude for his performances, penned by deeply-moved and appreciative audiences, including local Liberation Committees, resistance formations and entire Communist Party branches, provide moving testimony of the impact of Don Zeno Saltini's social revolutionary gospel. Using his *Opera Piccoli Apostoli* and, subsequently, the *Unione Padri di Famiglia Piccoli Apostoli* as his power base, Don Zeno's ultimate plans remain obscure, for his ecclesiastical superiors forced him to abandon his efforts shortly after the successful February 1946 congress in San Giacomo Rondole di Mirandola.

15 This clear and present picture of countless viable, if localised, Left Catholic initiatives in various corners of Italy emerges unmistakably from Giorgio Vecchio's stimulating "'Left Catholicism' and the Experiences 'On the Frontier' of the Church and Italian Society".

The mass gathering had openly proclaimed the need to leave behind the bourgeois social order, its intention to create a movement labelled *Pionieri della Fraternità Sociale*, and expressed the hope that this initiative, started in the Province of Modena, would be emulated elsewhere in the Italian state.[16]

A few years later, Don Zeno Saltini, after providing a more permanent and suitable home for his orphanage on the grounds of the former Nazi transit camp of Fossoli, which he obtained for his project by means of an illegal squatting operation, returned to broader social revolutionary activism. His copious letters impressively chronicle the reappearance of this quasi-millenarian desire prior to the official launching of a *Movimento della Fraternità Humana* in the course of 1950. This time the *Movimento* took on more of a concrete organisational shape and cast a wider net. Its steering committee, though firmly in the hands of ardent Catholic believers, included at least one secular anarchist, Leon Victor Roto. Don Zeno once again embarked upon a whirlwind tour of the region spreading his popular message in his native regional dialect. A public conference in October 1950 in Modena was followed by further efforts to consolidate this grassroots social movement. Yet, once again, his efforts were brutally cut short by the combined powers of the upper hierarchies of both the Church and *Democrazia Cristiana* in the course of 1951, ultimately leading to the forcible dissolution not only of the *Movimento* but the orphanage as well.

Approximately seventy kilometres to the northwest of Don Zeno Saltini's power base, across the provincial boundary in Lombardy, on the northern side of the River Po, another parish priest pursued very similar ideas. The publication of extracts from Don Primo Mazzolari's *Rivoluzione Cristiane* in 1945, edited by the local branch of *Democrazia Cristiana* in Mantova, had already netted the parish priest in Bozzolo the official condemnation of the Holy See. On 20 February 1946, Don Mazzolari was ordered to remove the contested publication from public circulation, to subject himself to 'five days of spiritual exercises', and was temporarily forbidden to say Mass.

In January 1949, Don Primo Mazzolari, once again closely paralleling the spiritual and political trajectory of Don Zeno Saltini, launched a new publication, *Adesso*, which became a leading journalistic mouthpiece of Left Catholic

16 The documentation concerning the subject matter mentioned in this and the following paragraph can be found in the excellently organised and well-maintained Archivio di Nomadelfia (Grosseto), a treasure trove for audio-visual material in addition to its copious printed documentation (see <www.nomadelfia.it>). A recent multi-author assessment of Don Zeno Saltini's oeuvre is Guasco and Trionfini, eds, *Don Zeno e Nomadelfia*.

theory and practice in the Italian state. In the course of 1950, with the storm clouds of war gathering international force, Don Primo devoted further energies to the creation of an organisation, *Avanguardie Cristiane*, which was initially devoted, above all else, to the pacifist cause. But by the time these Christian Vanguards met for their first convention in Modena on 7 January 1951, the range of topics had broadened to include the whole gamut of questions that were of interest to the Christian Left.[17]

At first sight, the lack of any coordination between the efforts of the two priests operating within one hour's travel time of each other may appear surprising to the outside observer and historian. Yet, upon closer investigation and reflection, this lack of direct communication between Saltini and Mazzolari is in fact a powerful indicator of the spirit of that time. The movements spawned by these two politico-spiritual activists thrived not because of close cooperation, but because they reflected a much more powerful and widespread sentiment within Italian Catholic communities at that time. Left Catholicism was 'in the air', so to speak.

Differing political strategies may have prompted the two priests to work on their own. Whereas the *Movimento della Fraternità Humana* placed its bets on firm, local implantation, the *Avanguardie Cristiane* saw themselves as a nascent, national force from the very beginning. The attendance list of the latter's January 1951 meeting reads like a 'who's who' of the entire Italian Catholic Left, whereas the October 1950 gathering of the *Movimento*, also in Modena, primarily assembled local activists with virtually no overlap between the two.

Yet, however different the strategies of these two exemplary cases of Italian grassroots Left Catholic activism, in the end they suffered a very similar fate. In February 1952, the Holy See temporarily suspended the publication of *Adesso* and forbade Mazzolari to preach beyond the borders of his diocese. For Mazzolari, just like Saltini, had earned a reputation as a powerful and popular speaker not only from the pulpit but in the central squares of the

17 This section draws heavily on documentation in the Fondazione Mazzolari, Bozzolo (Mantova), another treasure trove of material for the reconstruction of the social and intellectual history of postwar Italian Left Catholicism. An overall survey of Mazzolari's politico-religious life can be found in Campanini, *Don Primo Mazzolari fra religione e politica*. The last ten years of Mazzolari's life, which coincided with the publication of the controversial newspaper *Adesso*, has been relatively well-analysed in Italian language publications; see Maraviglia, *Chiesa e storia in 'Adesso'*; Bedeschi, *L'ultima battaglia di Don Mazzolari: 'Adesso'*; and Campanini and Truffelli, eds, *Mazzolari e 'Adesso'*.

region. Contemporary pictorial evidence, written documentation and oral testimonies uniformly highlight the impact of Mazzolari and Saltini as speakers able to captivate large audiences. There was, for instance, an unmistakable gleam in the eyes of an elderly man in Bozzolo that this author spoke with in April 2002, when he recounted how, in the main square in Mantova, sometime in the second half of the 1940s, Don Primo Mazzolari had engaged in a heated public discussion with Titta Foti, a local anarchist celebrity. The initially less-than-friendly exchange gave way to increasing mutual respect, and the two protagonists ended up embracing each other on the speaker's platform with the throng of onlookers watching with wide-open eyes.[18]

Left Catholicism in the 1960s

Was Western European Left Catholicism only a brief post-Liberation phenomenon, dying a slow and painful death as the Cold War consensus gathered force, the latter propelling the conservative variant of Christian Democracy to the centre stage? Indeed, by the second half of the 1950s, the immediately preceding wave of Left Catholic activism must have appeared to many contemporaries as the superseded product of a bygone age. *Adesso* was allowed to resume publication for much of the 1950s, but the extraordinary dynamic behind the organisation of the Christian Vanguards was broken. Don Zeno Saltini, thanks to a generous donation by a member of the Pirelli family, was eventually able to start up a new community of orphans and their caregivers in the southwest corner of Tuscany. But the extroverted social revolutionary impulse of Saltini's activities in his native 'red' Emilia Romagna now gave way to introverted community building. In France, many remaining activists of the former MPF had severed their ties to the organised Church. Emmanuel Mounier died a premature death in 1950. Perhaps most symbolically, Jacques Maritain, whose *Humanisme intégral* had been the standard reference work of the European Catholic Left, eventually retreated into the private sphere, joined a monastic order and ultimately returned close to his conservative roots with the 1966 publication of his *Le Paysan de la Garonne*.

Still, not everyone followed Maritain's personal and political itinerary. The dynamic of Left Catholicism was broken, but the spirit lived on. Crucially, when the Second Vatican Council re-created an opening for dissident voices on the Catholic Left, many veterans of the battles of the post-Liberation

18 Conversation with Aldo Compagnioni, 8 April 2002, Bozzolo (Mantova).

period re-emerged from their forced obscurity. The Council gave media attention to the new generation of Third World theologians who were soon to make Liberation Theology a household name in the Catholic world. One way, though by far not the only one, in which a generational transference occurred between Western European Left Catholicism of the immediate post-war era and a younger generation of Third World Liberation theologians was a by-product of the deliberations of the Council.

The story of the behind-the-scenes operations of European Left Catholic intellectuals as the spiritual advisors of some Third World bishops assembled in Rome remains to be written. But one might catch a glimpse of what frequently happened in Vatican corridors with the example of the spiritus rector of the surviving core of 'first generation' European Left Catholicism, Marie-Dominique Chenu. Chenu suddenly re-emerged on the centre stage as the theological advisor to the Bishop of Antsirabe in Madagascar, Mgr Claude Rolland. When receiving the invitation to attend the Council, Claude Rolland had immediately approached his former teacher at Saulchoir, the Dominican seminary school where Rolland had been a missionary student in the 1930s, and asked for guidance. Chenu was more than happy to comply. In the process, Chenu not only provided the requested theological advice, but he in effect became the author of the disquisition, *Les Chrétiens, La Lutte Contre la Misère, le Développement Économique*, officially published in the name of the Madagascar bishop as the "Lettre de Son Ex. Mgr. Claude Rolland, Évêque d'Antsirabe" on 1 May 1964, "en la fête de St. Joseph Travailleur".[19]

The ghostwriting by European Left Catholics of important documents emanating in the context of the Second Vatican Council and published in the name of Third World ecclesiastical authorities was by no means the norm. But this anecdote draws attention to the remarkably creative and wholly understudied cooperation between left-leaning Third World bishops and Left Catholic European theologians at the Council. Third World bishops and other non-European Catholics had, of course, undergone their own evolution in the direction of an engagement with the radical social gospel of Jesus Christ, and they needed little prodding from Europeans to move decisively towards the

19 See the various letters and documents in the Fonds Chenu, Correspondance H-Z, "Mgr. Claude Rolland", Bibliothèque de Saulchoir, Paris, which includes Chenu's typewritten manuscript of the text. The 'peculiar' dating of the 'Lettre' can be found on p. 21 of the printed version, *Les Chrétiens*, under Charles Rolland's name. In this context, it is well worth noting that a stimulating glimpse behind the scenes of Vatican II is provided by Marie-Dominique Chenu, *Notes quotidiennes au Concile*, with an important lengthy introduction by Alberto Melloni, who also provided the detailed annotations to Chenu's diary entries.

political left. Third World Liberation Theology is a product *sui generis* of the combustible mix of economic exploitation, political repression and theological ferment in Latin American and other Catholic Third World states.

But it is symptomatic of the transnational radiance of 'first generation' Western European Left Catholicism that these European Catholics' examples had often provided an important inspiration to young Third World theologians even prior to the breakthrough of the Second Vatican Council. In the dark decade of the 1950s, many extra-European Catholics had come to study at world-renowned European centres of Catholic learning, such as Leuven or Lyon. But, once there, they not only assimilated the classic tradition of European Catholicism, but at the same time they came into first-hand contact with European Left Catholic theory and practice. Profoundly influenced by what they saw, experienced and learned, and inspired by the worker priest phenomenon in particular, they returned to their native lands to become the founding fathers of Liberation Theology. One should note, for instance, the personal and theological itinerary of perhaps the most well-known figure in Latin American Liberation Theology, the Peruvian Gustavo Gutiérrez, who studied in Lima, Rome, Leuven and Lyon. He later repeatedly professed his admiration for the worker priest experience, which had profoundly shaped his own theological education.[20]

But it would be one-sided to suggest that the creative spark of Western European Left Catholicism survived and eventually prospered solely on extra-European soil. No serious study of the anti-Franco and anti-Salazar underground struggle for democracy and social justice up to the mid-1970s can ignore the signal contributions by Spanish and Portuguese Left Catholic activism. For the Spanish case, it is incumbent to highlight that the powerful, working-class-based resistance to the Franco dictatorship was by no means composed of exclusively secular Marxist activists. An important constituent element of this underground resistance to Franco was organised by Left Catholics developing new forms of activism within official Catholic structures founded by the conservative Catholic hierarchy in the heyday of Franco's rule in the 1940s.

20 On the worker priests as inspiration for Gutiérrez, see Kaufmann, "Ansätze einer Theologie der Befreiung in Europa?", 280. In this context, it is likewise symbolic and instructive to note that the preface to Marguerite Fiévez and Jacques Meert, *Cardijn*, 7-10, was written by none other than Dom Helder Camara. Joseph Cardijn, of course, never really belonged to the Left Catholic "camp" as such, but his *Jeunesse Ouvrière Chrétienne* (JOC) early on had developed its own dynamic, and elements originating in the JOC merged, for instance, into such "orthodox" Left Catholic movements, such as the MPF.

Finding spiritual and material reinforcement in decisions taken by the Second Vatican Council, the Left Catholic *Acción Sindical de Trabajadores* (AST), one of a variety of Left Catholic organisations rising to prominence in the post-war period, emerged out of various earlier organisational experiments, and from 1964-1969, the AST was a major player in sections of the Spanish underground. Like similar experiences elsewhere in Catholic Europe, from about 1970 onwards, finding new allies in radicalising student movements, the AST underwent an organisational conversion into an increasingly secular political organisation, the *Organización Revolucionaria de Trabajadores* (ORT), though not without suffering a series of splits.[21]

A similar evolution, closely resembling developments in the Spanish Catholic world, occurred in Italy, be it under far more favourable political conditions. Here, too, a Catholic trade union federation (in this case operating legally) began to adopt, in the late 1950s, increasingly unorthodox interpretations of the meaning of the Christian social gospel within the world of industrial relations. Powerfully reinforced by the paradigm shift that emerged from the Second Vatican Council, the *Confederazione italiana sindacati lavoratori* (CISL) by the late 1960s moved closer to the anti-hierarchical, grassroots democratic spirit of Italy's 1969 Hot Autumn than any other Italian trade union federation. Again, similar to Spain, by the late 1960s, this working class Left Catholicism merged with Left Catholic manifestations of the suddenly emerging student movement.[22]

The Catholic University of Milan not only became an early centre of student activism, but along with Left Catholic student activists from elsewhere, such as the University of Trento, the birthplace of the Italian *movimento studentesco*, it produced some of the most well-known spokespersons for the Italian national student movement as a whole. It is testimony to the radiance of Left

21 A brief survey of this understudied phenomenon of anti-Franco Left Catholicism in the 1960s is Laíz, *La lucha final*, 50-63. Some of the most important experiences of progressive Catholicism in Francoist Spain emerged within the fold of Spanish Catholic Action. On the crucial *Hermandad Obrera de Acción Católica* (HOAC), see for instance the study by López García, *Historia de la HOAC*. A relatively extensive literature exists by now on the impact of Left Catholicism within the Spanish JOC. Note, for instance, the study on the Catalan JOC by Martínez Hoyos, *La JOC a Catalunya*.

22 For some insightful comments on internal shifts within the CISL, see Bedani, *Politics and Ideology in the Italian Workers' Movement*, 78-80, 118-126 and passim. A key supporter of such renewed departures towards the political Left within the world of Italian Catholicism was Cardinal Giacomo Lercaro in Bologna. Originally dispatched to "red" Bologna in 1952 to counteract the strong Communist presence there, he developed into a powerful voice for radical change, resulting in his forced retirement in 1968. On Giacomo Lercaro, see, amongst others, Alberigo, ed, *Giacomo Lercaro*.

Catholicism in Italy that the single-most influential document inspiring virtually all (not just Catholic) Italian student activists of the "generation of 1968" was a product of the radical priest Don Lorenzo Milani. It was the 1967 *Lettere a una professoressa*, which he edited together with his students in the Scuola di Barbiana, the latter being an Apennine village to which Don Milani had been exiled ten years earlier by his church superiors.[23]

The equivalent to the Italian CISL in France, the *Confédération Française des Travailleurs Chrétiens* (CFTC) underwent an important transformation in 1964 when becoming the nominally secular *Confédération Française Démocratique du Travail* (CFDT). This voluntary secularisation occurred with few organisational losses, but the CFDT in more ways than one continued to give expression to ideas, which emerged from its original Left Catholic milieu. It is thus wholly unsurprising that the CFDT became the quintessential trade union expression of the self-management oriented spirit of the French experience of "May '68."[24] But, of course, in France too, the spirit of "May '68" affected more than "only" proletarian strata in the Catholic world. French Catholics of all walks of life were affected by the *esprit contestateur* unleashed by the events in Paris and elsewhere. And, even if ultimately, as elsewhere, only a minority of Catholics joined the camp of the insurgents, few individuals lived through this period entirely unaffected. Even the Archbishop of Paris, Msgr. Marty, the *primus inter pares* within the French Catholic upper level church hierarchy, caught up between two hostile camps, began to reflect some subtle changes. From 1973 onwards he refused to take part in the annual great patriotic show of the Bastille Day celebrations in Paris, where he had traditionally been allotted a seat of honour amongst the members of the *grands corps d'État*. Increasingly resentful of traditional displays of pomp and circumstance, he vastly reduced representational costs and other features associated with his high church office; "the image of the bishop himself behind the steering wheel of his 2CV has left a permanent imprint on [Catholic] spirits".[25]

23 General introductory texts on Left Catholic ferment in the post-1965 Italian state include Cuminetti, *Il dissenso cattolico in Italia*; Beretta, *Il lungo autumno*; and Giovagnoli, ed, *1968*.

24 On the CFDT, see, above all, Cours-Saliès, *La CFDT*, and Georgi, *L'invention de la CFDT*.

25 Solid first assessments of the Catholic involvement in the French "May 1968" experience are Barrau, *Le Mai 68 des catholiques*, where the citation can be found on p. 126, and Pelletier, *La crise catholique*.

Left Catholicism: a Balance Sheet?

These snapshots of the Left Catholic presence in France, Italy and Spain in the 1960s only trace the barest of all outlines of Left Catholicism's contributions to post-conciliar European Catholic life. Yet perhaps they may suffice to serve as a platform from which to draw a preliminary balance sheet on Left Catholic accomplishments in the postwar European world. In an important contribution to the first coordinated effort to approach Left Catholicism from a comparative and transnational perspective, Martin Conway drew attention to the fact that "the most durable change in European political life brought about by the war" was not in fact some sort of radicalisation but (and this, of course, had powerful consequences for the realm of Catholic politics in particular) "the establishment of a broad centre-right alliance which, under the title of Christian Democracy, dominated political life in much of Western and Central Europe until the 1960s".[26] Though frequently originating in the periphery of Left Catholic activism at the point of liberation from the Nazi yoke, Christian Democracy, having rapidly shed its youthful engagement with Left Catholicism, became the dominant paradigm in the post-war European Catholic imagination. The political and intellectual hegemony of conservative but pluralist Christian Democratic values and the Catholic acceptance of the liberal bourgeois order constituted the most important historical caesura in the world of modern Catholicism, not the radical innovations of the Second Vatican Council. The latter is, of course, rightfully regarded as standing in a direct line of continuity with the wave of Left Catholicism in the immediate post-war era.

But, as Conway likewise underscores, the Left Catholics' failure "to prevent the evolution of Catholic politics into a centre-right mould" should not obscure "the real significance of Left Catholicism which lay not in its very modest impact on the politics of the age but in what it revealed about the diverse ... currents which coexisted within European Catholicism"[27] during the post-war era. Catholicism in the 1950s, Conway writes, "while presiding politically over the post-war reconstruction of Western Europe, retained within it the intellectual components of a profound critique of the liberal and individualist values" which underpinned European society and culture in the post-war decades.[28]

26 Conway, "Left Catholicism in Europe in the 1940s", 277-278.
27 Ibidem, 278.
28 Ibidem, 281.

Several commentators have misinterpreted Conway's text to suggest that Left Catholicism as such (and not just its medium-term impact on Catholic party politics) "must inevitably appear as something of a historical footnote".[29] There may indeed exist a certain, perhaps unresolved, tension in Conway's text which makes unwarranted wholesale condemnations of the entire Left Catholic project by second-hand observers possible, though not justifiable.[30] Another attempt at a summary of Left Catholic accomplishments may thus be timely and pertinent.

European Left Catholicism played a constituent role in the fashioning of early Christian Democratic political formations at the point of liberation. But this confluence of Catholic renovatory spirits did not last very long. Most importantly, the variants of Christian Democracy which eventually left a lasting imprint on European societies, "mature" Christian Democracy so-to-speak, differed in all but name from its early experiments which had seen Left Catholics not infrequently amongst the co-founders and early grassroots activists. Most Left Catholics, if they remained such, left the ship of Christian Democracy as it embarked upon a wholly different journey. Even Giuseppe Dossetti, for instance, a representative of the most moderate variant within the colourful spectrum of European Left Catholicism in the 1940s, remained a scathing critic of Italian Christian Democracy's practice even and especially after his supposed retirement from party politics in 1951. Note, for instance, the following words written in an untitled and undated document shortly after Dossetti officially retired from DC party politics. While drawing up a fifteen-point action programme, designed to provide guidance for his remaining supporters within and outside the DC, listing "some of the most fundamental characteristics of the current political situation", the very first item prominently heading up his detailed proposals read as follows: "Distrust of DC as a tool for renewal. Impossibility to enter into a dialogue with its leadership team which is responsible for having guided DC into the rut of the current political impasse".[31]

By the early 1950s, the dynamic of the first wave of Western European Left Catholicism was essentially broken. Despite the combined flowering of some experiments (most notably the worker priest phenomenon which peaked

29 See Ibidem, 278, where he clearly limits the relevance of this statement to the realm of straightforward party politics *after* the immediate post-Liberation period.

30 For one such misuse of Conway's text, note the review by Raymond Grew of the anthology in which Conway's piece appeared; see the *American Historical Review*, 2 (2003) 108, 568-569.

31 Fondo Cronache Sociali C.26.260.1, Istituto Superiore di Scienze Religiose, Bologna.

just when it was suppressed by the authoritarian command structure of the Catholic Church) Left Catholics knew full well that the tide had turned against them. Precisely this unfavourable conjuncture (the moment of triumph of conservative Christian Democracy) convinced some of their leading advocates, those who had not already been silenced by their spiritual superiors, to abandon the political plane and to return to the private or monastic sphere. Dossetti and Maritain may exemplify the personal and political itinerary of many in this cohort of "first generation" Left Catholics. In inverse proportion to the rise of Christian Democracy, Left Catholicism underwent a seemingly fatal decline. But the theological elaborations by its leading proponents, the manifold accomplishments of its activist apostolic social movements, its concrete inspiration for subsequent generations of activists in Europe and the non-European world; all these and other products of the fertile Left Catholic imagination are powerful and relevant reminders that Left Catholicism, though politically marginalised, indeed remained ever present in the European and, most certainly, the extra-European Catholic imagination.

My sketch of Western European Left Catholicism's revival after 1965 should further caution against interpretations that relegate European Left Catholicism to the footnotes of immediate post-war Christian Democratic history. Of course, even in the second spring of Left Catholic ventures between, roughly, 1965 and 1975, it nowhere managed to convince a majority of Catholic believers. When Konrad Adenauer and Alcide De Gasperi had given way to Kurt-Georg Kiesinger and Giulio Andreotti, this second generation of Christian Democratic politicians retained the upper hand over their Left Catholic activist contenders. But the continued pre-eminence of conservative Christian Democracy within the world of post-war European Catholicism is not the same as the absence of all tangible and meaningful historical alternatives.

Left Catholicism from the mid-1930s onwards, however contradictory and difficult to define, called for a socio-political and intellectual paradigm shift in modern society. Whatever its vagaries and hesitations, Left Catholicism took the side of those they regarded as the oppressed. Except for some fleeting moments at their point of origin, Christian Democracy, no matter how much its political outlook differed positively from most pre-war varieties of political Catholicism, promoted and defended the continued socio-cultural predominance of the political and economic elites. The contrast between these two Catholic outlooks could not be any sharper.

In 1965, it only stood to reason that Left Catholics, encouraged and strengthened by the Second Vatican Council, saw history on their side. By the 1980s, at the latest, this spirit of optimism had given way to a more pessimistic perception of the relationship of power within the Catholic Church. In the most recent decades, conservative Catholicism has further consolidated its position of political and cultural dominance within the Catholic world. But is it possible to proclaim with any degree of reasonable certainty the supposed irreversibility of the post-conciliar conservative backlash? The unforeseen second wave of Left Catholic activism in 1965-1975, itself encouraged by the equally unpredicted turn of events at the Council, should caution against such complacent views. Given the trend towards secularisation of the Western world (itself not an irreversible trend!) it is of course conceivable that Left Catholicism as a clearly distinguishable tendency in Western European societies has outspent its force. But, then, the same fate could easily befall a Christian Democracy (or what remains of it) which is beginning to lose (and actively loosens) its umbilical cord to the Catholic Church.

Opening Windows or Opening Doors? Catholic Intellectuals as the Bearers of Secularisation in the Netherlands, 1945-1970

Lodewijk Winkeler

In July 1966 the director of the well-known Catholic publishing house De Spaarnestad, Dr H.J.A. de Goeij BSc, published a short letter to the editor in the newspaper *De Tijd* under the provocative title, "The betrayal of the clerks". In his letter he criticised Dutch theologians for questioning the truth of central dogmas of the Catholic Church. Existentialist philosophy, the modern sciences, and the humanities had caused, as he stated, an explosion of modernist thinking. Neo-modernism was, he said, a "freezing storm which has blown in through clerics and seminary professors, even more than through lay people".[1]

De Goeij's letter caused a series of indignant reactions from well-known intellectuals. The priests among them had learned during their studies that modernism was a repository for all heresies, and at the occasion of their ordination they had taken the anti-modernist oath. Having been educated with a very negative image of modernism, it is not surprising that they vehemently rejected the accusation by Dr De Goeij.

Remarkably, the liberal professor Han Fortmann, who taught psychology of religion and culture at the Catholic University of Nijmegen, and who was widely known for his weekly columns (mostly about liturgy and holy days) in the newspaper *De Volkskrant*, in a sense agreed with the conservative De Goeij. His column, published one month later, was entitled, "Please do not burn the heretics", and, among other things, he stated: "There really is a certain relation between the problems of today and those in the years of Pope Pius X. In fact the tragedy is, that the case which the modernists championed was never

1 De Goeij, "Het Verraad der Clercken".

coped with by the Church. They were bluntly dismissed, and on top of resigning of their own accord, were expelled. Their attempts to seriously integrate modern thinking with faith was never taken seriously by the Church in those days [...]. It is foolish to close our eyes to the fact that the Church has been wrestling with this problem for a century - and in fact much longer."[2]

Fortmann was right. From the second half of the 1950s onwards, Dutch Catholicism had been urgently confronted with the modernisation of society and with the development of wealth and welfare after a decade of post-war reconstruction, after ten 'years of discipline and asceticism'.[3] However, the intellectuals who were attacked by De Goeij in 1966 certainly did not aim at a complete subjectivism of faith, which they also saw as the nucleus of modernism. Instead they tried, as they argued, to make faith intelligible for modern man in a modern world.

They felt supported by Pope John XXIII and by what was called 'the spirit of Vatican II'. When John XXIII opened Vatican II in 1962, he said in his opening address: "For the substance of the ancient deposit of faith is one thing, and the way in which it is presented is another". This is a quotation from the original text, spoken in Italian, which may be found in Peter Hebblethwaite's biography of Pope John. When we compare this papal statement with the anti-modernist decree *Lamentabili* (1907), as Hebblethwaite does, the conclusion that the pope was making a modernist statement is almost inevitable. The Roman Curia immediately reached the same conclusion. The official Latin text of this clause appeared to be extended with some conditions that, as Hebblethwaite points out, could have been, and in fact were taken literally from the text of the anti-modernist oath![4] The highly praised 'spirit of the Council' was by no means shared by the Vatican. But in those same years in the Netherlands, the opinion was voiced that 'we are ahead of the Council'.

2 Fortmann, "Gelieve de ketters niet te verbranden".

3 Blom, "Jaren van tucht en ascese". About the conflicts between post-war restoration and modernity in the 1950s see: Luykx and Slot, *Een stille revolutie?*, especially Luykx' evaluation of historiography on Dutch Catholicism in this period ("Erger dan Reformatie?").

4 Hebblethwaite, *John XXIII*, 432.

Intellectual Thinking in the 1950s

There was indeed some truth to that opinion. Before the Council, Dutch intellectuals were already familiar with the thought that the expression and modelling of faith can and may differ according to time and place. This mode of thought will shortly be referred to as the principle of 'dogmatic relativism'. This 'relativism', or the relativity of belief, as McSweeney called it[5], formed the basis for the innovative ideas which intellectuals have been introducing into Dutch Catholicism since the beginning of the 1950s. The relationship of this dogmatic relativism to the spirit of the modern sciences - already deeply embedded in Western culture - is hard to overlook. It is also evident that this relativism created many possibilities for the accommodation of Catholicism to that same modern Western culture.

Analysing a representative selection of publications by Dutch Catholic intellectuals, as was done some years ago, it is possible to see a growing number of phrases expressing dogmatic relativism.[6] Naturally, one cannot expect that the principle was immediately applied to central aspects of faith and morals, but it was in fact applied to themes that were less sensitive, although still sensitive enough. It could be argued that the principle of dogmatic relativism was tested and verified in the 1950s, and was then extended to its full scope in the 1960s. Three themes that were topical in the 1950s will now be discussed briefly, after which one other theme will be dealt with more extensively.

First there were the slumbering remnants of the post-war breakthrough movement. As in other European countries during and immediately after World War II, there was a short-lived movement in the Netherlands towards breaking through the static structures of society and establishing a progressive movement, based on socialist and Roman Catholic varieties of personalism.[7] The bishops and the pre-war establishment needed only a few years to stop this movement short. However, its spirit remained alive among intellectuals, for instance in the magazine *Te Elfder Ure*[8], but also among younger seminary professors. In fact, the episcopacy felt the need to publish a letter in 1954 entitled "Catholics in modern public life", in which they propagated a

5 Cf. McSweeney, *Roman Catholicism*; Van Melsen, *Geloof, wetenschap en maatschappelijke omwentelingen.*

6 This analysis, including a discussion of the method used, may be found in Simons and Winkeler, *Het Verraad der Clercken*, ch 6.

7 Bank, *Opkomst en ondergang van de Nederlandse Volks Beweging (NVB)*; Horn and Gerard, *Left Catholicism*.

8 Dierick, "De Christofoorgroep".

Catholicism that should be organised within its *own* structures and organisations. Catholics were instructed not to listen to socialist radio programmes, not to be members of the socialist trade union, nor, preferably, of the Labour Party - of which many still were members as a result of the breakthrough movement.[9]

The episcopal letter did not end the discussion, but instead gave it a new incentive. However, thinking about an open form of Catholicism was only possible by recognising some truth in the views of other groups of the Dutch population, i.e. socialists and Protestants. Therefore, thinking about open Catholicism demanded that the idea that the Catholic community was a kind of self-supporting *societas perfecta* be put into perspective.

No more than a year after the famous episcopal letter, the priest and professor of law J.J. Loeff, who first and fore most was the legal secretary of the Roman Catholic Church Province, could state that the traditional Thomistic political science was a *product of its time* and was outdated now.[10] Two years later, in 1957, the chairman of Catholic Action, Professor F. Tellegen, noted that compartmentalisation had been unmistakably functional *in former days*, but that these structures of isolation were in fact anachronistic nowadays.[11] Mind the factor of historical relativism in both statements! This relativism appeared to be fundamental to the renewal movement in Dutch Catholicism during the 1960s.

The discussion reached a climax in that same year, when a report appeared by the respectable Catholic society for ecumenism, the *Sint Willibrord Vereniging*, entitled "Openness and closedness of Dutch Catholics". In this report the anonymous authors, including, undoubtedly, theologians, politely, but sharply criticised the three-year old episcopal letter.[12]

Second, theologians played an important role in those years. German and French theology - *Verkündigungtheologie* in Germany and *nouvelle théologie* in France - gained influence within Dutch theology. In the Netherlands at that time, everything still happened some decades later than abroad. While traditional neo-Thomistic manuals were still officially used, seminary professors introduced the new theologies in their lessons as more relevant to pastoral

9 D'Haens, "De Katholieke Werkgemeenschap in de Partij van de Arbeid".
10 Loeff, *Verhouding staat en rechtsgemeenschap*.
11 Tellegen, "Verdraagzaamheid en verzuiling".
12 "Openheid en geslotenheid van de katholieken in Nederland".

care. The *nouvelle théologie* in particular was based on thorough historical research into patristic and medieval theology, but it was just this historical aspect that brought about the notion of relativism. To give one example, in 1937 M.-D. Chenu gave his famous speech, entitled "Une école de théologie. Le Saulchoir", a speech which cost him a condemnation, although for the essentials of his thinking he could refer to Thomas Aquinas: "Cognita sunt in cognoscente ad modum cognoscentis": "What is known is in the one who knows in the way he is knowing".[13] We are here reminded of the citation from the opening speech of Pope John.

The *nouvelle théologie* was scholarly, but certainly not other-worldly. Congar's *Chrétiens desunis* (1937) was as influential in ecumenical circles, as was his *Jalons pour une théologie du laicat* (1953) in seminary theology. The professors in dogmatics of the two northern and most urbanised Dutch dioceses, Klaas Steur and Herman Fortmann, taught *nouvelle théologie* between the lines of the neo-Thomistic manuals. Steur, young and promising, quickly became popular through his books for engaged and recently married couples, and he also wrote a pamphlet for Catholic Action about the universal priesthood of the faithful in the light of the *nouvelle théologie*, a popularisation of Congar.[14] Fortmann, the elder brother of the aforementioned Nijmegen professor, was professor in dogmatics at the seminary of the archdiocese of Utrecht. He was editor-in-chief of the journal *Nederlandse Katholieke Stemmen*, a professional journal for priests, which characteristically switched to Latin whenever it dealt with sex. He was certainly not progressive, but still increasingly influenced by the new theology.

Third, an interesting development from our point of view was the growing influence of the Dutch Catholic ecumenical movement. It started in the years of World War II with private conversations between Catholic and Protestant theologians, and after the war quickly proliferated in the form of multiple discussion groups consisting of Protestant ministers and Catholic priests. Members of the most important group, the Laren Circle (named after the place were the members met), were Chaplain Frans Thijssen and the seminary professor Jo Willebrands. Through them, a straight line may be drawn between this informal discussion group, via the also informal Catholic Conference for Ecumenical Questions, to the Vatican Secretary for the Christian Unity.[15] For Dutch Catholicism, however, the discussion groups were impor-

13 Chenu, *Une école de theologie: Le Saulchoir*.
14 Steur, *Liefdesstreven*; Idem, *Liefdesleven*; Idem, *Algemeen priesterschap der gelovigen*.
15 Simons and Winkeler, *Het Verraad der Clercken*, 244-247; Jacobs, *'Naar één oecumenische beweging'*.

tant. They were not meant to reach agreements - that was still beyond reach in those years -, but to discuss each other's beliefs and those of each other's churches openly and without prejudice. During the 1950s, many influential Catholic intellectuals were members of one or more of the discussion groups. This development, as well as the following topic I will discuss, are examples of the beginning of the distribution of new ideas through networking, at a time when the fundamental principles of new ideas had to a certain extent been established.[16]

The last example is that of the mental health movement in the Netherlands in the fifties and early 1960s.[17] Catholic psychologists, psychiatrists and educationalists in the 1950s certainly had no intention to undermine Catholic morals. One just has to read what the leading Catholic psychiatrist Cees Trimbos still wrote in 1961 about for instance masturbation to make sure of that.[18] Nevertheless, they became increasingly convinced that the rigid Catholic morals could not be made fully obligatory under all circumstances. As early as 1948, the psychiatrist M. Vaessen published an article in the orthodox Catholic medical journal *R.K. Artsenblad*, discussing the possibility of so-called pubertal onanism as a phenomenon when coming of age. The article gave the Catholic society of doctors (*R.K. Artsenvereniging*) cause to organise a workshop that later became known as the 'onanists conference'.[19] In the same period, in 1951, Han Fortmann wrote an article entitled "New ideas about the psychology and the pedagogy of the will", pleading for reduced pressure of Catholic moral teaching on children and adolescents, arguing that morality is something that has to be learned.[20]

The basic philosophy behind the ideas was phenomenology, emerging from various sources: straight from abroad, such as the phenomenology of Merleau-Ponty and Gabriel Marcel, the psychology of Germans like von Gebsattel and Binswanger, and in the Netherlands, of course, the 'Utrecht

16 Networking by intellectuals was one of the main subjects of research with regard to *Het Verraad der Clercken*.

17 Westhoff, *Geestelijke bevrijders*; Westhoff and Roes, "Seelische versus geistliche Fürsorge".

18 Trimbos, *Gehuwd en ongehuwd*.

19 Papers published in *R.K. Artsenblad*, 28 (1949). The papers were introduced with the explicit editorial remark that "an onanistic act, also by children, is a morally bad act *ex objecto*, a *malum intrinsecum*, and therefore always and under all circumstances prohibited" (p 92).

20 Fortmann, "Nieuwe opvattingen omtrent de psychologie en de paedagogiek van de wil".

School' of phenomenology, led by the internationally renowned Utrecht professor of psychology, Frits J.J. Buytendijk.[21]

Interestingly enough, there was another line of thinking, more or less concentrated in Nijmegen, which did not start from developmental psychology, but from neo-Thomistic, 'rational psychology', arguing from the scholastic psychology of free will. The psychiatrist Anna Terruwe had focused her Ph D research on "The neurosis in the light of rational psychology", based on thoughts which the Nijmegen professor of law W. Duynstee CssR had developed in the 1930s as a neo-Thomist answer to Freudian thinking.[22] Several professors at the Nijmegen Catholic University preferred the traditional lines of thinking of Duynstee and Terruwe to the Utrecht phenomenology. From the point of view of network analysis it may be noted that both groups had but limited contact with each other through Catholic groups and organisations.[23] The written discussion between these two 'schools' therefore was not so much the domain of colleagues in the humanities, as that of moral theologians.[24] Having hardly any experience in mixing neo-Thomism with phenomenology, they leaned heavily on the Louvain tradition in this respect, especially on the psychologist J. Nuttin and moral theologians like A. Snoeck SJ, R. Hostie SJ, P.M.Th. Anciaux and L. Janssens.[25]

The intellectuals in this 'mental health movement' initially felt that exceptions would help to reinforce moral rules. In fact their ideas implied an attitude to morality that was fundamentally new.

As usual, Rome was quick to see the dangers. In 1950, the encyclical *Humani generis* condemned the *nouvelle théologie*, and in 1952 Pius XII also condemned what he called 'situation ethics'.[26]

21 Simons and Winkeler, *Het Verraad der Clercken*, 163-167, 174-175, 180-184. Buytendijk was a Catholic, but a convert, and noticeably not brought up with the voluntarism of a traditional Catholic moral education.

22 Terruwe, *De neurose in het licht van de rationele psychologie* (*The Neurosis in the Light of Rational Psychology*); Duynstee, "De verdringingstheorie".

23 Simons and Winkeler, *Verraad der Clercken*, 122-127.

24 Winkeler, "Verdringing van de moraal".

25 Simons and Winkeler, *Verraad der Clercken*, 183-184. For the Belgian context see Jadoulle, "Les visages de l'Église de Belgique"; Remy and Voyé, "L'Église catholique de Belgique et la transaction avec la modernité".

26 After some addresses of Pius XII (March 23 and April 18, 1952), an Instruction of the Holy Office *De ethica situationis* followed in 1956 (Denzinger and Schönmetzer, *Enchiridion Symbolorum*, 787, No. 3918-3921).

Those condemnations, however, hardly affected theological and moral thinking in the Netherlands, although the personal consequences for some individuals were considerable. Religious orders practised self-censorship for a few years, with consequences for, among others, the Jesuit Piet Schoonenberg, a brilliant theologian, who had to wait until 1964 to receive his professorship.[27] Furthermore, the Dutch Jesuit Sebastian Tromp, working at the Holy Office, made an inquisitorial visit to his homeland in 1954, after which Professor Steur was transferred to a country parish, the psychiatric practice of Anna Terruwe was forbidden for priests and nuns, and Professor Duynstee was exiled to Rome.[28] Nevertheless, Steur's colleague at the seminary, Professor J.C. Groot, published on 'new tendencies in modern theology' no more than a year later.[29]

The Influence of the Intellectuals in the 1960s

It is generally assumed that intellectuals strongly influenced the developments in Dutch Catholicism in the 1960s. The question is, however, *how* they did it. This question is even more intriguing when we consider the speed with which the new ideas became widely accepted by most Dutch Catholics. The development from a strict and closed type of Catholicism towards an open one, in which dogmatic relativism dominated thinking about faith, church, humanity and world, took place in only two decades. One almost gets the impression that introducing new ideas was the work of a well-oiled machine. J. Bots, historian and Jesuit, stated that Catholic intellectuals, or rather, that the whole upper middle class of Dutch Catholicism gradually succeeded in taking over power in the Dutch church.[30] He does not make clear, however, which ingenious strategy they invented to do so.

The answer is relatively simple. The intellectuals just happened to stumble across this well-oiled machine. By this we mean the Catholic pillar, that systematically built whole of class-based organisations, professional organisations, associations and institutes that intended to shape the ideal of the popular church, the Catholic *societas perfecta*, not for the religiously mixed Netherlands as a whole, but for the Catholic part of its population at least.

27 This and other examples in Winkeler, "Ten dienste der seminaristen", 38-39.
28 Idem, "Verdringing van de moraal", 131-132.
29 Groot, "Nieuwe tendenzen in de hedendaagse theologie".
30 Bots, *Kirche in Holland*; Idem, *Zestig jaar katholicisme in Nederland*.

In the Netherlands, intellectuals (priests as well as lay people) had always taken an important place in this. Economists and lawyers participated in the boards and councils. They were supported by neo-Thomistic philosophers who spoke at their meetings, by preliminary advice by their own organisations such as the *Thijmgenootschap*, and lastly they had reluctantly joined forces in their own class organisation *Sint-Adelbert*, 'for gentlemen of the leading class'.[31] Workers moved up in the unions, supported by the courses which that same union organised to get itself a professional staff. Priests, preferably seminary professors, had additional functions as spiritual advisors of organisations, or held edifying talks for the Catholic broadcasting company KRO.

The same channels that were designed to stimulate, if not enforce, Catholic orthodoxy and orthopraxy, turned out to be excellent channels to introduce new ideas to the staffs of many organisations and through them across all levels of Dutch Catholicism, from deacons to workmen. I will give just one example, which is perhaps the most striking.[32]

Until halfway through the 1950s Catholic ambulant mental health care - as we nowadays call it - was largely undertaken by confessors and family doctors. Furthermore, there were only a few Medical Pedagogical Centres (*Medisch Opvoedkundig Bureaus, MOB*) and Services for Psychiatric Prevention and Aftercare (*Psychiatrische Voor- en Nazorgdiensten*). Stretching the point a little, one could add to these the local courses for the engaged, and courses entitled "Introduction to real life".

Nevertheless, the society for Catholic doctors (*RK Artsenvereniging*), anxious about the growing influence of neo-Malthusianism, had already pleaded with the bishops before the war to set up marriage counselling centres. Such offices were established reluctantly in the 1940s and 1950s and were staffed by a priest and a family doctor 'with experience of life'. So problems concerning mental health were regarded in those days either as medical problems - psychiatric problems if they were serious - or as moral problems. This was not typically Catholic, however.[33]

The idea of improving ambulatory mental health care, however, also existed in the Catholic Society for Mental Hygiene (*Katholieke Centrale Vereniging*

31 Winkeler, "Neothomisme en emancipatie".

32 For the following see: Simons and Winkeler, *Verraad der Clercken*, 63-71; Westhoff, *Geestelijke bevrijders*, passim.

33 De Goei, *De psychohygiënisten*.

voor Geestelijke Volksgezondheid, KCV), which had been re-established in 1948 under the energetic leadership of the aforementioned Professor Buytendijk. The idea of establishing Catholic mental health care was not strange in those days. In the beginning of the 1950s the Catholic base was still expanding, and the extending mental health care combined organisation and the rise of the welfare state wonderfully well. Therefore, in 1952, the Catholic National Centre for Mental Health Care (*Katholiek Nationaal Bureau voor Geestelijke Gezondheid-zorg, KNBGG*) was established to co-ordinate existing services and to expand the network of ambulatory care. The centre was staffed by the economist A. Bartels, who later became State Secretary of Social Affairs, and the psychiatrist Cees Trimbos. Together they quickly built an extensive network of mental health care. Within a few years, the existing marriage counselling centres, the courses for engaged couples, the courses entitled "Introduction to real life" and last but not least many visits to the confessional or to the family doctor all over the country were replaced by Catholic marriage counselling centres staffed by social workers, psychologists and psychiatrists instead of priests and doctors.

Trimbos and Bartels, however, not only organised the *structure* of mental health care, they also organised the development of *ideas* about mental hygiene, together with the already mentioned Catholic Society and Buytendijk. The Centre organised working committees, the Society arranged workshops where Catholic psychologists, psychiatrists, educationalists, theologians and doctors met to exchange views about masturbation, modern education, marriage and sexual problems, and so on.

It would be going too far to sum up the numerous study groups in the 1950s and the beginning of the 1960s, that often turned out to be very influential. I will make one exception, however, by discussing the famous Committee for Pastoral Care and Mental Hygiene (*Commissie Pastoraal en Psychohygiëne*), because this committee is a relevant illustration of the strategy - if one may call it that - on the part of the intellectuals.

The Committee was set up by the Catholic Society in 1954. The initiative had been taken by the Utrecht University chaplain N. Vendrik and the seminary professor H. Ruygers, a teacher of philosophy, who was also staff assistant of the National Centre. They were inspired by Buytendijk's pleas for a better integration of modern psychological concepts into pastoral care. The committee had a membership of no less than forty to fifty individuals: not only experts in the field of psychology and, later on, sociologists, but also theologians, carefully selected from the major Dutch seminaries, and editors or journalists of some influential Catholic weeklies! The Committee remained in existence for thirteen years and never hesitated to take on the most burning issues, like psychotherapy for priests and nuns, marriage, engagement and sexuality, homosexuality, and, ahead of its time, the crisis in priesthood which hit in the early 1960s.

It was a rather informal group (its members even preferred to think of it as half secret), which never came forward itself. However, the ideas that were discussed and that matured within the Committee nevertheless reached the public. Almost all editors of the widely read journal *Dux*, for instance, the organ of the Catholic Youth Council (*Katholieke Jeugdraad*), were members of the Committee, which sometimes made the journal appear to be the in-house magazine of the Committee. Other members were editors of the magazine for Catholic soldiers *G-3*, the journal of the breakthrough Catholics *Te Elfder Ure*, and the editor-in-chief of the liberal Catholic weekly *De Bazuin*. However, there were also other ways to exert influence. The secretary of the Committee, the priest H. Bless, who was pastor in a psychiatric hospital, wrote several pastoral-psychological manuals; the Jesuit N. Perquin, Professor of pedagogy at Utrecht University, wrote a column in the women's magazine *Beatrijs*; and Trimbos, of course a member himself, being more or less a member of everything, had his radio talks, which were as popular among listeners as among readers when they were collected and published afterwards.

Along these and other lines the Committee inspired or legitimised the broad-minded views that became widely accepted among Dutch Catholics at the beginning of the 1960s. The work of the Committee was strikingly recognised in an indirect way in 1963 by Bishop W. Bekkers of the diocese 's-Hertogenbosch. The bishop had been a guest of the Committee several times. He dedicated one of his regular television talks (with the Catholic broadcasting company, of course) to birth control. He stated that this was the responsibility of the married couple first and foremost. Consequently, many ordinary believers concluded that artificial birth control was now allowed.

The end of the story, a typical one for Dutch Catholicism, followed only a year later. It was the Catholic National Centre that took the initiative to 'de-pillarise' mental health care, and set up a proposal to organise mental health care on a regional instead of confessional basis. And that was in fact what happened.[34]

34 Van der Grinten, *De vorming van de ambulante geestelijke gezondheidszorg*.

This example of the development of mental health care and the ideas surrounding it shows us the various aspects of 'pillarisation' that could play a part in the influence of intellectuals. First of all, there was the organisational side: the participation of intellectuals as staff members or consultants in institutions and organisations. In the same way as in the field of mental health care, ideas could be spread through labour unions, physical health care, education, ecumenism and so on.

The example quoted, however, is all the more striking because it shows us other important factors of influence, such as grouping and mutual relations, interested grassroots and enthusiastic 'translators': priests, journalists, doctors; and related to that, the possibilities to propagate views in popular journals and magazines, and on radio and television.

In summary, the influence of the intellectuals was made possible by the existing formal and informal structures that Dutch Catholicism abounded in during those decades. The fact that the intellectuals were accepted as leaders within those structures was based on their traditional leading role, or as Gramsci has called it, their 'organic solidarity' with Dutch Catholicism.[35]

The Way to Secularisation

After the developments in the 1950s and first half of the 1960s, the usual picture of the second half of the 1960s is of a still increasing influence from the intellectuals. Judging from their actual participation in Dutch Catholicism, this picture is certainly correct. The Second Vatican Council and the Pastoral Council of the Dutch Church Province (1966-1970) played an important role in this. After 1970, the intellectuals withdrew en masse from religion related activities, on the one hand because they were disappointed by the nomination of conservative bishops, and on the other hand because they were pushed aside not just by those bishops, but by the episcopal conference as a whole.

The characterisation of this period certainly makes sense. One only has to browse through the newspapers from those days to agree. However, this division is based on *structural* participation, and it excludes the intellectuals from the line of fire. Particularly during the first years after the nomination of the conservative bishops Simonis (diocese of Rotterdam) and Gijsen (diocese of

35 Gramsci, "The Intellectuals".

Roermond), the general opinion prevailed that without intervention from Rome, Dutch bishops and intellectuals could jointly have created a kind of Dutch, liberal Catholic utopia.[36] However, other reasons may account for their withdrawal, starting with the common sense, but often overlooked reason J. Thurlings refers to in his famous study about the 'unstable pillar': "For the time being, even an elitist Catholic has not proved that one musters the courage [to be a critical activist] for much longer than a few seasons."[37]

I will first examine the structural side. For the intellectuals, the channels of influence unmistakably widened after 1960. Vatican II appeared to offer more possibilities for episcopal participation than expected, so the bishops soon felt the need for more and different advisors than the usual ones, i.e. the professors from their own diocesan seminaries. Moreover, they realised that they could no longer do without professional advice in a time of growing influence from the social sciences. They made a first, but not very successful attempt as early as 1958, by establishing a Dutch Pastoral Institute (*Nederlands Pastoraal Instituut, NPI*), which was related to Catholic Action.[38] In 1964 it was replaced by the Pastoral Institute of the Dutch Church Province (*Pastoraal Instituut van de Nederlandse Kerkprovincie, PINK*), well-known by its abbreviation PINK.[39] The energetic manager of the PINK was the Franciscan friar Walter Goddijn, a sociologist, who within a year created an impressive number of study groups. In this way he also created many possibilities for intellectuals to propagate their views. As Goddijn himself once said in an interview: "ideas are born at the top". In 1967, for instance, the bishops published a memorandum entitled "Lines of Pastoral Policy for the Practice of the Priestly Office". It was drafted under the auspices of the PINK Institute, and six study groups were involved, as well as the National Council for Vocations and the sociological institute KASKI, which altogether amounted to around a hundred advisors.

36 This is the hardly hidden tendency of the analysis of the sociologist Goddijn, *The Deferred Revolution*, presented with much more nuance in the relevant chapters of the recent history of post-war Dutch Catholicism, with its nevertheless revealing title *Called to Freedom*: Goddijn, Jacobs and Van Tillo, *Tot vrijheid geroepen*. More critical to the intellectuals and Catholic upper middle class in general: Schreuder, "Die deprievierte Mitte".

37 Thurlings, *De wankele zuil*, 181; for his theory on 'depillarisation' see also "Pluralism and Assimilation in the Netherlands".

38 De Haan, *Van volgzame elitestrijder tot kritische gelovige*, 247-272.

39 From episcopal decisions like these one could argue that not only the intellectuals, but also the Dutch bishops played their role in the developments of Dutch Catholicism, or even that the bishops were the most important agents of change, as Coleman does in his *The Evolution of Dutch Catholicism*.

In 1966 the PINK Institute was put in charge of the organisation of the well-known Pastoral Council of the Dutch Church Province, the plenary sessions of which took place between 1967 and 1970. Again, numerous experts and intellectuals were involved. One could see them, hear them and read them almost daily in the mass media.

However, does that also imply that the content of their views had increasing influence? That remains doubtful. The ideas the intellectuals put forward at the time were already shared by a large part of the Dutch Catholic population, as one can see from surveys held during those years. For instance, from the results of the national survey "God in the Netherlands", initiated by the women's magazine *Margriet*, one may draw the conclusion that Dutch Catholics were already on their way to denominationalism and dogmatic relativity. The same can be said about the Pastoral Council. Catholics appeared to be almost unanimous about the views that the experts and intellectuals had put down in their reports, at least in general terms. In other words: insofar as the intellectuals had been influential, this influence must be dated to before 1966.

This raises the question why the intellectuals' influence decreased after 1965. In my opinion there are two causes. In the first place, they no longer had anything to say that was fundamentally new. Secondly, they became alienated from the institutional Church and ordinary believers, because a part of them radicalised their views.

As far as the first cause is concerned: to have no leading and creative ideas and views is of course fatal for being an intellectual. An intellectual is preferably, if not by nature, critical of the status quo. However, from our analysis one may draw the conclusion that the idea of 'dogmatic relativism', which brought about an ideological revolution in the 1950s, had become so popular after 1965 that it constituted the background theme of all public discussion.[40] One can therefore hardly call 'dogmatic relativism' a new and leading point of view. Another example, from my personal experience: after reading so many publications by intellectuals from the 1950s and early 1960s, reading the reports of the Pastoral Council gives one a feeling of *déjà vu*. A closer view of the history of those reports confirms this feeling.[41] Some examples: the report of the study group on "Authority in the Church" was mainly formulated by Professor Loeff - who was already active in the 1950s. The report captured

40 In a random set of publications on certain chosen hot items it was the theme of 30% of the paragraphs (Simons and Winkeler, *Het Verraad der Clercken*, 194-231).

41 Simons and Winkeler, *Het Verraad der Clercken*, 279-284.

the atmosphere of the open social philosophy of the Catholic University of Tilburg. The study groups' report "Marriage and Family", then, was based on an earlier report by Catholic Action, and on the views of moral theologians that had been active in the discussion at an earlier stage. Next, the report of the ecumenical study group was drawn up by staff members of the Catholic Saint Willibrord Society for ecumenism (*Sint Willibrord Vereniging*), and contained hardly any news for the many insiders - the Society had ten thousands of members in those days.

One can see that the intellectuals reached the same conclusion, as they withdrew themselves from public debate in the Church at the end of the 1960s.

But there is more. For a smaller group of still engaged intellectuals, their views after Vatican II were not simply a repetition of what had been said earlier. They increasingly applied 'dogmatic relativism' to the most burning issues in the central aspects of Catholicism. Perhaps inspired by the successes of the past years, a radicalisation of their views took place. At the Pastoral Council they advocated the abolition of celibacy, the ordination of women to the priesthood, and the ecumenical study group recommended far-reaching ecumenical experiments. In their report, the pope was called a kind of 'secretary-general of the united Catholic churches'.

This radicalisation, apart from the serious conflicts with Rome that it caused, also led to the alienation between the intellectuals and their roots in the 'humble faithful'. One indication of this is an opinion poll, carried out at the end of the 1960s by the ecumenical Council of Churches. Offered a choice between long-term ecumenical development or enforcing unity by radical experiments, members of the local councils of churches appeared to prefer a prudent way.

A second indication of the alienation between intellectuals and other believers may be found in the Pastoral Council itself. Despite the predominate unanimity between the study committees and the chosen delegates, some reports were criticised. The criticism took different forms. Some reports showed a lack of a biblical-theological foundation, whereas other reports were judged to be more scientific than pastoral. H. Ruygers, one of the intellectual leaders of the mental health movement and later appointed vicar-general of the Breda diocese, was very clear about this. He characterised one report on "the Church in a secularised society" as one that would perhaps be suitable for an academic society such as the *Thijmgenootschap*, but not for a *pastoral* council. "Be silent, be patient, all will be new", he cited a then popular, sentimental church hymn, adding: "by the god of science".

How to interpret these varying critiques? Given the revival of spirituality that has taken place since the 1990s, I would suggest that in those days, there already existed a mostly hidden need for a more explicit religious approach to the world. Of course this need may have been inspired by a certain nostalgia for religious clarity which had been gone for only a decade. But I would like to suggest the hypothesis that there already was an unconscious feeling that simply embracing the modernised and secularised society was too poor to be a religious approach to the world. Secularisation had just begun to be a part of the theological vocabulary when the limits came into view: how to be religious in a secularised society? At the beginning of the 1960s most intellectuals had no answer to this question. Much later, in 1985, the philosopher H. van Luyk published an extremely sharp article, in which he stated that during the years of the Pastoral Council, Dutch Catholics collectively talked to the side of the basic intuitions of faith. "Of course they talked, even unstoppably so. Dutch Catholics cackled so that it could be heard far abroad, but they did not talk about God. Instead, they talked all the more about the question 'how to talk about God'. The theme was how to pass on faith, not faith itself. Holland made the front pages with the *New Catechism*, a new way of talking about faith. Faith itself attracted considerably less attention."[42]

42 Van Luijk, "De ontreddering van katholiek Nederland". His witticism did not provoke a public discussion in the way that Sheenan did in the United States with two comparable articles: "Revolution in the Church" and "On Satan & Catholic Liberals". It should be noted that neo-conservative views easily, but not necessarily, flow from such an analysis.

Conclusion

In the second half of the twentieth century, a strict and orthodox Dutch Catholicism quickly evolved to a remarkably liberal one. Once the social pressure of organised Catholicism had been shaken off, most Catholics dropped the strict structures and detailed moral rules of traditional religion.

Dutch Catholic intellectuals had a considerable influence on these developments. They found support in the double authority they had in Dutch Catholicism at that time: their traditional authority as the leaders of emancipated Catholicism as well as their post-war authority founded on the increasing status of the social sciences in a modern welfare state. The channels of the highly organised Catholic structure opened the way to spreading such views.

During the two post-war decades, and especially in the 1950s, their most important merits were that so many looked for ways to model a religious life that would fit in the modern world and for an acceptable relationship between religious and scientific thinking. Their own religious background from that same emancipated Catholicism also motivated them to engage in public discussion. They earnestly tried to open the windows of the closed Catholic building to a new and more fundamental religious experience. In fact, they promoted secularisation for many ordinary believers, who did not leave the Church, but 'simply faded away'. The theologian Schoonenberg, for instance, started to publish the first part of a modern dogmatic manual in 1955: "The Faith of our Baptism" (*Het geloof van ons doopsel*), leaving it unfinished after part four in 1964. When asked why he had started such an immense project, he answered somewhat cynically: "They will know from which faith they drop away". The intellectuals, however, did not only legitimise secularisation. They also showed the way for a group of faithful people, albeit a much smaller one, to remain religious in a secularised society.[43]

43 Winkeler, *Stromingen in katholiek Nederland*.

Late 20th-Century Trends in Catholic Religiousness
Belgium Compared with Western and Central European Nations

Karel Dobbelaere & Jaak Billiet

In this article, we discuss trends in Catholic religiousness in Belgium and compare them with similar data from Western Europe at large. Is Belgium a unique case or does it represent a more general trend? Next, we analyse recent data from Western and Central European countries collected through the European RAMP-survey[1] which confronts two theoretical approaches on religious pluralism: Rational Choice Theory (RCT)[2] and Secularisation Theory (ST).[3] The outcome of this confrontation will lead us to our theoretical explanation. Finally, we evaluate a possible development of the current trends.

Belgium Compared with Other West European Countries

In his seminal work on religion, Durkheim emphasised the importance of rituals as a constituent element of religion, together with beliefs. It seems to us that religions of the book, such as Judaism, Christianity and Islam, contrary to religions of rites, such as Shintoism and Buddhism, relativise rituals in reference to beliefs. Rituals, as periodic reunions, have the important function of revivifying the members' common faith, engaging them in its common manifestation. By such manifestations, rituals strengthen common sentiments which, if left to themselves, would soon grow weak.[4] What has been happening to ritual in the Catholic Church?

1 RAMP is a European study on Religious And Moral Pluralism done in eleven Western and Central European countries (Dobbelaere and Riis, "Religious and Moral Pluralism").

2 Young, *Rational Choice Theory and Religion*.

3 Dobbelaere, *Secularization*.

4 Durkheim, *The Elementary Forms of the Religious Life*, 240-241.

The rituals

In Belgium, weekly church attendance has dropped yearly since the registration began. It accelerated in the period 1967-1973 with 1,8 percent points per year and has diminished since then so the last 10 years of registration (1988-1998) has a mean loss of 0,8 percentage points per year (graph 1). The same pattern is visible in the Brussels region (1,3 and 0,3 respectively), in Flanders (2,3 and 1,1 respectively) and in Wallonia (1,6 and 0,7 respectively). The percentage of Catholics going to mass weekly was still falling in 1998, and the fall in percentage points was highest in the region that had the highest weekly church attendance, Flanders. Thus, the differences between the regions diminished each year: in 1967 there was a 19,1 percentage points difference between Flanders and Wallonia, and 9,6 percentage points more than the Brussels region. In 1998, these differences in percentage points between Flanders and Wallonia were reduced to 3,4 and to 3 percentage points more than the Brussels region. Is what happened in Belgium an exception?

Graph 1: Frequency of weekly church attendance in percentages in Belgium, the Brussels region, Flanders, and Wallonia, related to the total number of inhabitants 5-69 years old

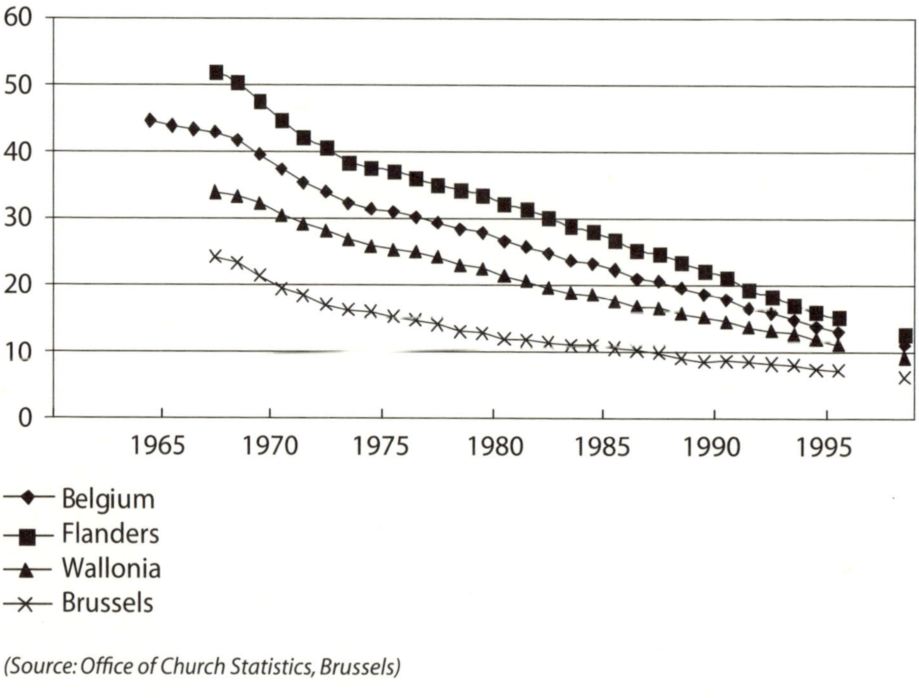

(Source: Office of Church Statistics, Brussels)

As can be seen from graph 2, the patterns of change in France and the Netherlands were both similar to Belgium. The decline in weekly church attendance accelerated in the latter part of the 1960s and the first part of the 1970s, and the drop in percentage points continued subsequently. These trends were confirmed for West Germany and Italy, except that in Italy church attendance in percentages rose again from the 1980s on.[5] Is the change simply a shift to going to church monthly instead of weekly, as is often suggested? Data to check this proposal are available only from France (see graph 3).

Graph 2: Frequency of weekly church attendance in percentages in Belgium
- calculated on the total number of inhabitants 5-69 years old, France
- calculated on the total population - and the Netherlands
- calculated on the Catholic population 7 years and older registered in the parishes

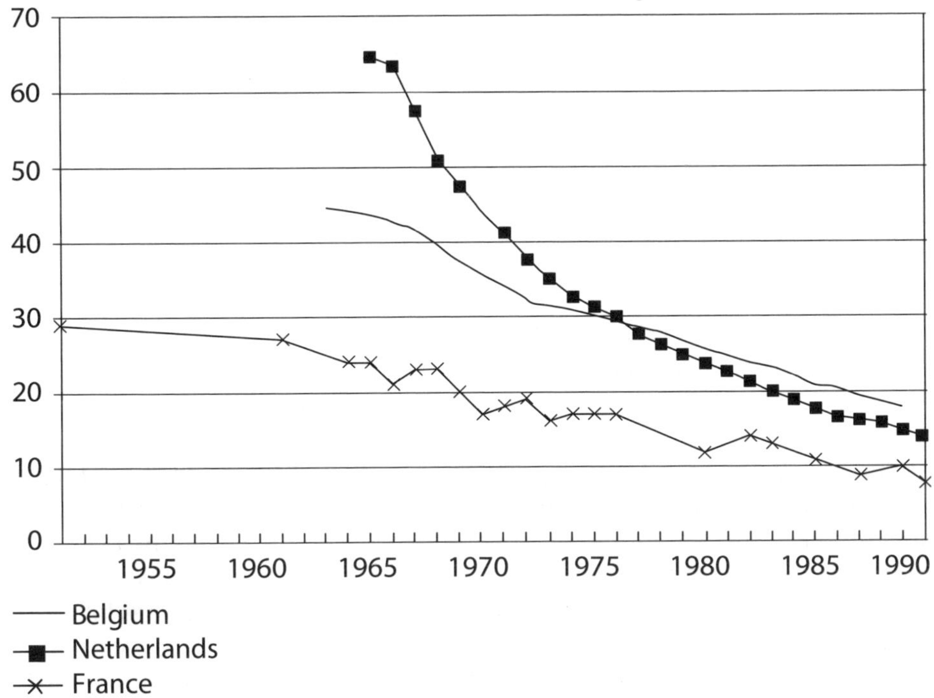

(Source: for Belgium: Office of Church Statistics, Brussels; for France: Dr. Y. Lambert, Centre National de Recherche Scientifique, Groupe de sociologie des religions et de la laïcité; for the Netherlands: Dobbelaere, "Secularization, Pillarization, and Religious Change in the Low Countries", 88-89, 121 and Informatie Bulletin *(KASKI).)*

5 Jagodzinski and Dobbelaere, "Secularization and Church Religiosity", 103.

Graph 3: Frequency of weekly church attendance compared with a monthly practice in percentages in France - calculated on the total population

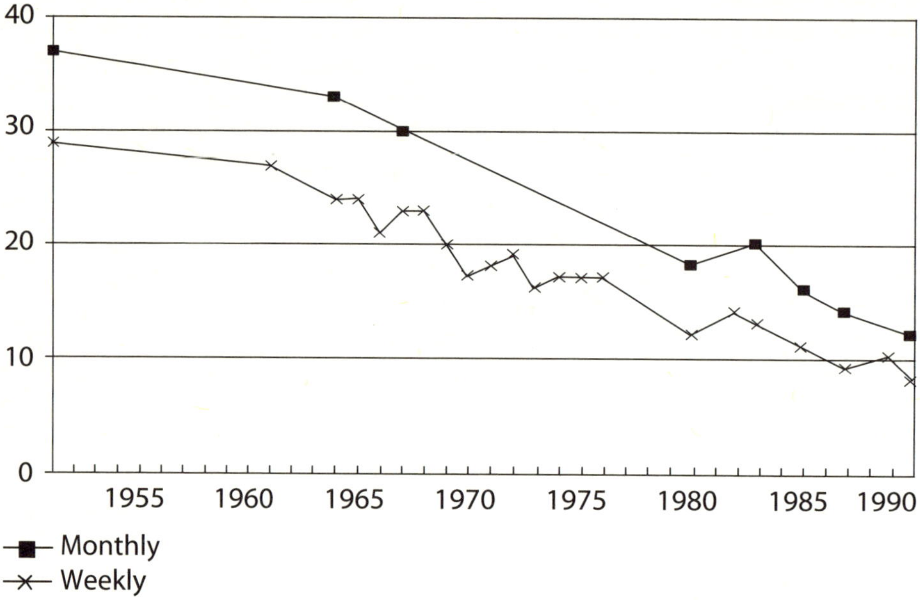

(Source: Dr. Y. Lambert, Centre National de Recherche Scientifique, Groupe de sociologie des religions et de la laïcité.)

If monthly church attendance instead of weekly is taken as the yardstick for defining core church members in the 1960s, then there is a growth of about eight percentage points. However, monthly church attendance has not augmented over the years as a result of the continuing decline of weekly church attendance. Even more, over the years, the growth had slowed to about four percentage points by 1990. These facts contradict the hypothesis of a simple shift from weekly to monthly church attendance. Had such been the case, monthly church attendance would have increased not decreased. We may conclude that in general weekly and monthly church attendance has fallen drastically in the latter part of the 20th century, especially in those countries where church practice was still high in the early 1960s. If we take Durkheim's analysis of the functions of rituals seriously, then this situation threatens the revivification of the common beliefs and sentiments within the Catholic community (cf infra).

Certain analysts have suggested that the Catholic Church was too demanding in imposing a weekly involvement compared to other organisations like voluntary associations and political organisations. They stressed the importance of participation in rites of passage as a criterion for church involvement.[6] Rites of passage take place on the occasions of baptism, of the profession of faith (also called solemn Communion) celebrated at the age of 12, of marriages and of funerals. In graph 4, the statistics allow us to evaluate the change in the percentage of people who celebrate such rituals in Belgium.

Graph 4: Frequency of baptisms (related to live births), Catholic marriages (related to total number of civil marriages), Catholic funerals (related to total number of deaths) and weekly church attendance (related to total number of inhabitants 5-69 years old)

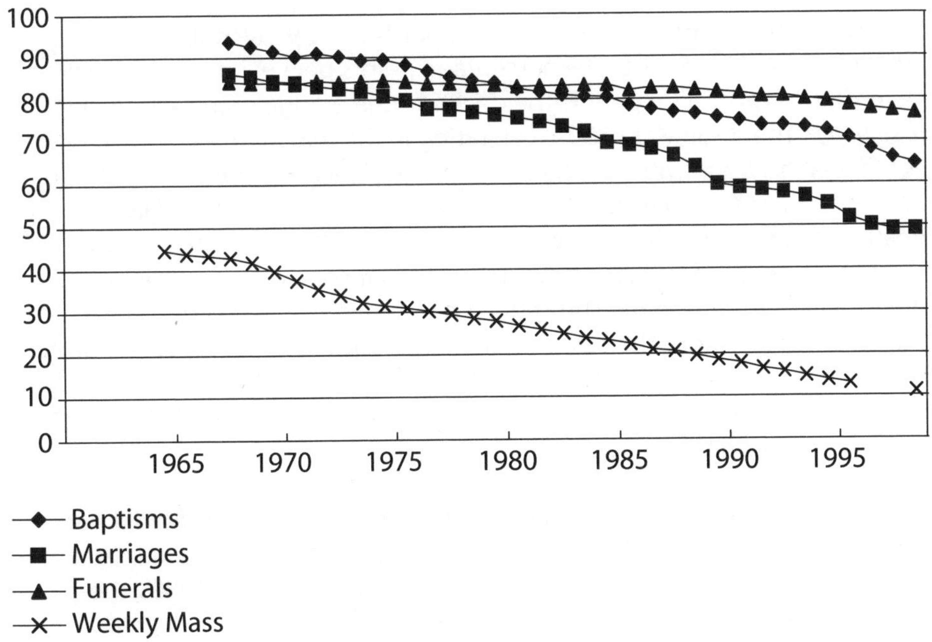

(Source: Office of Church Statistics, Brussels)

6 Bonnet, *A hue et à dia*; Pannet, *Le catholicisme populaire.*

Graph 4 shows a decline also in the participation of rites of passage, albeit less pronounced than the decline in weekly church attendance. Within 31 years, the percentage of people buried with a Catholic funeral diminished by 7,7 percentage points, so 0,2 percentage points per year. During the last eleven years of the registration period, the decline accelerated somewhat to 0,6 percentage points per year. However, there is a problem with these statistics. They are calculated on the basis of the total Belgian population of which a small percentage is a member of other faiths (about 5% according to the European Religious and Moral Pluralism study done in 1998). Since we have no figures for members of other faiths who died during the years, we cannot correct burial statistics. The problems are similar for statistics on marriages and baptisms. However, these observations do not explain the decline, far from it.

Baptisms in the Catholic Church have diminished: 29,9 percentage points over a period of 31 years or 0,9 percentage points per year. In the last eleven years of the registration period, the decline's percentage points per year rose to 1,2. The decline started accelerating in the middle of the 1970s. If one compares this trend with the much smaller decline in Catholic funerals, the figures suggest two things. The hope, expressed in religious funerals, that the death of the body is not the end is deeply anchored in the Christian world. The high number of religious funerals in comparison with baptisms and religious marriages during the communist regimes in Eastern Europe also made this clear. Furthermore, the celebration of Catholic rites of passage has diminished more in the younger generations, those who have children, than in the older generations, those who die. Statistics confirm this also for the celebration of Catholic marriages.

The Catholic celebration of marriages has diminished most of all: 36,9 percentage points over a period of 31 year or 1,2 percentage points per year. This accelerating decline started much earlier. Since the early 1980s, the decline has been 1,5 percentage points per year. This trend means that since 1997 fewer than half of the marriages in Belgium were celebrated in a Catholic church. This decline is partly a consequence of the rising number of divorcees who remarry, but because of the norms of the Catholic Church, are not allowed to celebrate their new marriage in the Church. Taking that into account, and relating the number of Catholic marriages to all marriages that were contracted by people who suffered no impediment to marriage in the Church, we arrive at the trend that is presented in graph 5.

Graph 5: The percentage of marriages not confirmed in the Catholic Church between partners where a divorce of one or both partners was not an impediment

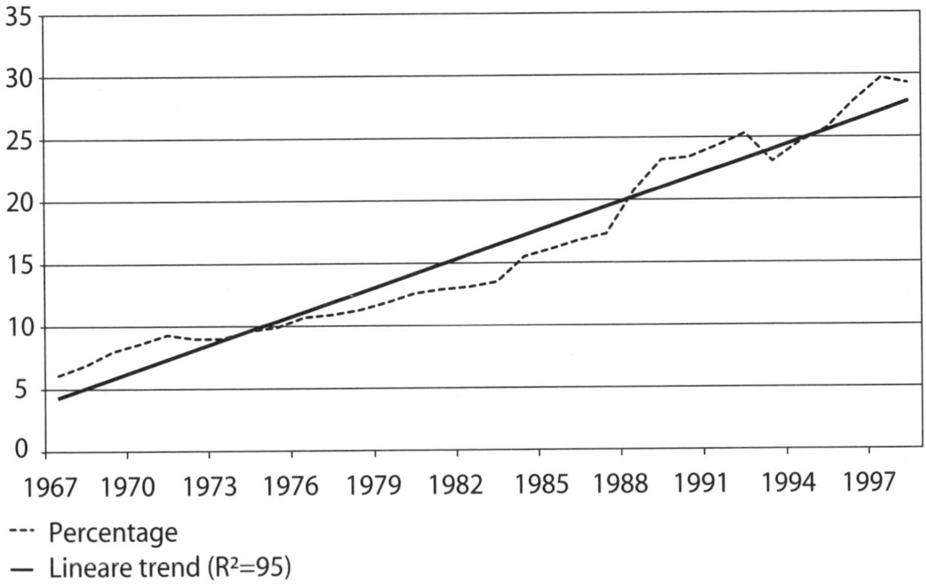

(Source: Office of Church Statistics, Brussels; calculations by Prof Koen Matthijs and Bart Noels, Dept of Sociology, Catholic University of Leuven)

The trend is clear: the number of marriages not celebrated in the Catholic Church, although there was no impediment, has risen for 30 years, but especially since the early 1980s. If we take into account that in this calculation the number of marriages celebrated in other religious communities could not, for lack of available data, be excluded from the total number of marriages contracted in a given year, then we can safely state that in Belgium, at the end of the last century, about 25% of the marriages between people who were entitled to marry in the Church were not so celebrated.

Is the change in ritual practice the result of changes only in the younger generations? A study of Flemish data by Billiet and Vanhoutvinck, comparing cohort trends over a 15-year period, indicates a decline in church practice within *all* cohorts, but more so in the younger than the older cohorts.[7] Comparing age categories over the same period, they found a lower percen-

7 Billiet and Vanhoutvinck, "Het stemgedrag van de Vlaamse bejaarden", 53.

tage of people going to church on Sunday and this was more pronounced in the younger than the older age categories. These trends suggest that we are witnessing *period effects* that have a differential impact on different cohorts. This result was confirmed by a cohort study by Jagodzinski and Dobbelaere of data from Belgium, France, Great Britain, Italy, the Netherlands, and West Germany, i.e. Catholic and religiously mixed countries.[8] The differential period effect in Belgian generations can be seen in the degree of involvement (from core members to unchurched) in the Catholic Church in Belgium in 1999 (table 1).[9]

Table 1: Church involvement in Belgium by generations in percentages

Church involvement	**born < 1940 + 59 years Pre-war**	**born 1940-1955 44-59 years Protest**	**born 1956-1970 29-43 years Lost**	**born > 1970 - 29 years Youngest**
Core members	17	8	6	2
Modal members	29	13	10	7
Marginal members	29	43	37	36
1st gen. unchurched	14	21	27	29
Several gen. unch.	11	15	20	26
(Total number)	100 (525)	100 (429)	100 (529)	100 (291)

(Source: Dobbelaere and Voyé, "Religie en kerkbetrokkenheid", 131)

In table 1, we distinguish four generations based on Becker's studies of generations.[10] Following him, we call those born before 1940 the "pre-war generation"; the "protest generation" was born in 1940-1955, they were socialised and matured in the protest period of 1968-1975 and were partly the life and soul of that protest; those born in 1956-1970 he calls the "lost generation",

8 Jagodzinski and Dobbelaere, "Secularization and Church Religiosity", 105-113.

9 Core members are practising at least once a month and are involved in church work or voluntary Christian associations. Marginal church members define themselves as Catholic but do not practise on weekends. Modal members situate themselves in between these two categories. The unchurched define themselves as not belonging to the Church and are divided into two subcategories: the first generation and those who have been unchurched for at least two generations.

10 Becker, "Dynamics of Life Histories and Generations Research"; Idem, "A Pattern of Generations".

their formative years were in a period of economic recession and the cool no-nonsense policy[11]; finally, we call those born after 1970 the "youngest generation", more distance is needed to typify them.[12]

In the pre-war generation, nearly one fifth were core member and only about 25% were unchurched. In the youngest generation, 55% declared themselves to be unchurched, of whom nearly half have been unchurched for at least two generations. In the three youngest generations, the number of core members was very low, and the number of those unchurched rose from 36 to 55%.
It should be noted, however, that declaring oneself unchurched does not mean that one is a-religious: only half of the first generation unchurched declared themselves not very or not at all religious. Even among those declaring themselves not very or not at all religious, 40% want a religious ritual on at least one of the rites of passage.[13]

This disposition helps to explain the mixed success of the educational course in Catholic religion. In non-denominational schools in Belgium, organised by the public authorities, there is a choice between classes on non-denominational ethics, Catholic or other religions, while in the Catholic schools a course on Catholic religion is one of the compulsory subjects (see tables 2 and 3).

11 Becker, *Generaties en hun kansen,* 13-14.
12 Ibidem, 107-119.
13 Dobbelaere and Voyé, "Religie en kerkbetrokkenheid", 129-130.

Table 2: Percentages of youngsters in Flemish primary and secondary education who follow religious classes, Catholic (1) or other (2) (Protestant, Anglican, Islamic, Jewish or Orthodox), non-denominational ethics (3) and who are exempt (4) (dispensed or provided with a special curriculum) according to the school year in primary and secondary education

School year	**Primary education**					**Secondary education**				
	(1)	**(2)**	**(3)**	**(4)**	**Total *N***	**(1)**	**(2)**	**(3)**	**(4)**	**Total *N***
1980-81	93,6	1,0	5,4	0	100 *506.614*	86,6	0,7	12,7	0	100 *479.512*
1985-86	91,4	2,6	5,8	0,2	100 *428.614*	84,9	1,0	14,1	0	100 *479.537*
1990-91	90,2	3,1	6,4	0,3	100 *430.578*	85,4	1,5	13,0	0,1	100 *435.094*
1995-96	88,8	3,3	7,1	0,8	100 *413.022*	84,0	2,1	13,3	0,6	100 *450.973*
2000-01	87,0	3,8	8,3	0,9	100 *35.535*	83,1	2,5	13,7	0,7	100 *429.106*

(Source: Statistisch Jaarboek van het Vlaams Onderwijs, *Departement Onderwijs, Brussels)*

If parents want their children to be eligible for their First or Private Communion (at the age of 7 or 8) and their confirmation (at the age of 12) in the Catholic Church, then their children should not choose non-denominational ethics. Indeed, for a child to study non-denominational ethics in primary education is a clear indication of the parental rejection of religion, an attitude which, in the last twenty years of the 20th century, has slowly risen by 2,9 percentage points.

The difference in percentage between those who have and have not studied Catholic religion in primary and secondary education shows the importance that parents, even a great number of nominal Catholics and the unchurched,

still attach to these rites for their children, especially confirmation, which is the transitive rite of passage from childhood to adolescence. Indeed, in 1980-1981, 93,6% studied Catholic religion in primary school, but five years later, when most of them were in secondary education, only 84,9% continued to take Catholic religion; at the same time, in the same group of students, the percentage of those taking non-denominational ethics had gone up from 5,4 to 14,1%, when they were in secondary education and had been confirmed. Such changes recur in the later school years as can be seen in table 2.
The difference in percentage points diminishes over the years with the rising percentage of those taking non-denominational ethics in primary school.
Can the same trend be detected in the French-speaking part of Belgium (see table 3)?

Table 3: Percentages of youngsters in ordinary primary and secondary education in the French Community of Belgium (the Walloon region and the French-speaking children of the Brussels' Region) who follow religious classes, Catholic (1) or other (2) (Protestant, Anglican, Islamic, Jewish or Orthodox), non-denominational ethics (3), and who are exempt (4) (dispensed or provided with a special curriculum) according to the school year

School year	**Primary education**					**Secondary education**				
	(1)	**(2)**	**(3)**	**(4)**	**Total (*N*)**	**(1)**	**(2)**	**(3)**	**(4)**	**Total (*N*)**
1990-91	77,8	6,6	15,6	--	100 *301.702*	71,7	4,3	24,0	--	100 336.389
1995-96	77,1	6,6	16,3	--	100 *311.031*	70,5	5,8	23,7	--	100 329.080
1999-00	74,2	7,1	18,7	--	100 *319.180*	69,1	5,9	23,2	1,8	100 330.846

(Source: Ministère de la Communauté française: Service général de l'informatique et des statistiques)

First of all, the percentage of primary school children taking non-denominational ethics is much higher in the French-speaking part of Belgium than in Flanders, by about 10 percentage points. This reflects the decline in church commitment that started much earlier in Wallonia and Brussels. Furthermore, the percentage of those studying other religions is twice as high in the French-speaking part of Belgium, due to the much larger number of immigrants, mostly Muslims. The difference in percentage points between studying Catholicism in primary school and five years later in secondary education is down 7 to 8 percentage points, indicating the same tendency as in Flanders. This suggests that some parents there, too, still see the Catholic rites of passage as important for their children, especially confirmation.

We may conclude that the Catholic rites of passage, especially those for children, baptism, first Communion and confirmation, and for the deceased, church burial, are still very much in demand. In a study on baptism, Van Meerbeeck illustrated the complex motivations of marginal Catholics and the unchurched in seeking Catholic baptism for their children; both the cultural tradition of the country and the familial tradition were important elements.[14] These persons were all socialised in the Catholic tradition, which they claimed to have appreciated. Consequently, they wanted to transmit this culture to their children. In their opinion, it would be up to their children, when they were old enough, to decide if they wanted to continue practicing or not. They thought that it was better to raise them as Catholics and to allow them to decide later on if they wanted to stay Catholic. Since they themselves had had the chance to choose after having received a Catholic education, their children should have the same opportunity. By undergoing the basic rituals, the children would be socialised in the basic values of their culture while preparing for their first Communion and confirmation. The parents considered this gave their children a "good start".

This study clearly points out that while some people still ask for religious rites of passage, the sense of the rites has changed: it expresses more cultural and familial traditions rather than religious ones. A recent study, directed by Hiernaux and Voyé, of Catholics in French-speaking Belgium who want a religious burial, makes that point very clearly. About one hundred in-depth interviews were conducted which were then supplemented by participant observation.[15] According to these observations and interviews, "the priest is no longer the grand commander of the rite faced with a passive congregation", he "is now very often relegated to the role of performer". "Either he just carries out the orders of the funeral director or when the families have a relatively high socio-cultural status, the priest performs in a scenario designed by the

14 Van Meerbeeck, "Dopen: waarom niet?", 204-214; Idem, *Het doopsel*, 125-266.

15 Voyé, "Death and Christmas Revisited", 288-296.

closest relatives of the deceased".[16] In the past, when Latin was used in ritual and hymns, the priest had the central role. He used standardised formulae, which he knew and understood, creating a distance between daily life and afterlife: the ritual was centred on the life to come and the mystery surrounding it. Now, through the introduction of the vernacular, the ritual is centred on the deceased: his/her life, his/her loves and friendships, his/her accomplishments. The texts read, the songs and the music played, are chosen by the family with reference to the deceased. If religious texts and hymns are used, they are chosen to express the qualities of the deceased and not because they refer to God. Quite often, "God is never brought up, except in the rare sacramental words pronounced by the priest".[17] The authors of these changes are not the professionals of the religious institution, but the funeral directors or the close family, who de-sacralise the ritual and bring about organisational secularisation. Religious rites seem to survive easily in as far as they are partly secularised, which cannot be done with the weekly mass: here, the religious professional is still the grand commander of the rite and participation is very low. If we take Durkheim's analysis of rituals seriously, this must have an impact on beliefs since they are neither revivified week by week, nor communally celebrated.

The beliefs

Together with rituals, beliefs are a constituent element of religion. To analyse some trends in the acceptance of dogmatic points, we looked at data on beliefs available from the European Values Study (EVS). However, these only go back to 1981.

Table 4 makes clear that the number Belgians believing in God has dropped significantly in the two last decades of the 20th century. Belief in a life after death is quite stable. The percentage of people giving a Christian interpretation of this belief - the belief in heaven and hell - has diminished significantly however. And "life after death" may be interpreted by some as "re-incarnation", a concept alien to Christian doctrine, but quite stable in Belgium, adherents ranging from 13 to 15%. The same may be said of the attitude towards sin, which dropped significantly, and even those professing sin to be possible may not understand it in the Christian sense.

16 Ibidem, 291.
17 Ibidem, 292-293.

Table 4: Percentage of Belgians who believe in different points of faith and according to their conception of God in the EVS

Believe in	**1981 N= 1.145**	**1990 N= 2.792**	**1999 N= 1.912**
God	77	63	65**
Life after death	37	37	37
Heaven	33	30	26**
Hell	18	15	13*
Sin	44	41	38*
Conception of God			
Personal God	39	29	26**
Spirit or life force	24	20	36**
Agnostic	15	29	20*
No God, spirit nor life force	8	14	16**
No answer	14	8	2**

*The decline over the years is significant: * p<.05; **p<.01*
(Source: Dobbelaere and Voyé, "Religie en kerkbetrokkenheid", 141)

Not only did the belief in God decline, the Christian conception of God as a person also fell significantly even though it was already low in 1981, when two out of five people believed in a "personal God". Evasive responses to the question "Which of the statements (about God) comes closest to your beliefs" have diminished significantly since 1981. This resulted in a statistically significant rise in those stating that they conceive of God as "a spirit or life force", which is not a Christian notion, but also in the number of people who deny the existence of God. Agnosticism has also slightly risen. Are these results limited to Belgium or more widespread?

Using the same data set, Lambert suggests that nine West European countries[18] share the same trends in stability or decline except for the belief in hell and the conception of a personal God that have both risen.[19] Looking more closely at the EVS-data, we observed that this so-called rise resulted primarily

18 Belgium, Denmark, France, Great Britain, Ireland, Italy, the Netherlands, Spain and Western Germany.

19 Lambert, "Religion", 134 and 150.

from the Italian data, where the belief in a personal God was abnormally low in 1981 (26%) rising in 1990 to 66%.[20] A rise of 40 percentage points in 9 years is an artefact produced by the wording of the 1981-questionnaire. That it was abnormally low in 1981 is confirmed by the stability of the percentage in 1999, 70% compared with the 66% of 1990. The same is true for the belief in hell. Consequently, we may conclude that the situation is not particular to Belgium, but quite widespread in Western Europe.

Looking for a Theoretical Perspective to Explain the Trends

To make sense of these trends, two theoretical perspectives, which are the most prominent theories in the sociology of religion today - Rational Choice Theory (RCT) and Secularisation Theory (ST) - will be examined in light of religious pluralism. It should be noted, however, that a full exposition of these theories can not be developed here: only the theoretical propositions that may explain the developments described above will be discussed.[21]

The test will be based on data from the European Religious and Moral Pluralism (RAMP) study.[22] A subsample from this data set was used: all Catholics and the first generation unchurched Catholics, 6100 individuals in total, living in seven different countries: Belgium (1224), Great Britain (185), Hungary (576), Italy (1828), the Netherlands (401), Poland (1091) and Portugal (795). Due to sufficient numbers of Catholics and former Catholics, the Nordic countries, Denmark, Finland, Norway and Sweden, part of the original study, were not included (so 33 individuals). The 6100 Catholics and former Catholics live in four so-called Catholic countries, Belgium, Italy, Poland and Portugal (4938), and three mixed countries, Great Britain, Hungary, and the Netherlands (1162). Another classification of these countries is that all are West European (4433), except the Central European countries of Hungary and Poland (1667).

20 The reliability of the 1981 percentage is questionable and probably due to the translation of this question in Italian.

21 See footnotes 2 and 3.

22 For information on this study see Dobbelaere and Riis, "Religious and Moral Pluralism".

Testing the effect of pluralism

RCT and ST predict religious pluralism's effect on church commitment differently. For RCT, three important propositions are relevant for our purpose. First of all, RCT postulates a latent religiosity on the demand side[23] which, in its second proposition, should become manifest by active competition between religious firms on the supply side.[24] However, this is only possible via its third proposition where, in a pluralistic religious situation, religious firms compete for customers but only to the extent that the supply-side is not limited by state regulations that suppress or subsidise some religions, in other words, to the degree that these states are secularised on the societal level.[25]

ST, however, predicts a decline in religiosity in a situation of religious pluralism. The sociological explanation of societal secularisation starts with the process of *functional differentiation*: religion becomes a subsystem alongside other subsystems (e.g. economy, polity, science, family and education). These subsystems affirm their autonomy and reject religiously prescribed rules, i.e. the *autonomisation* of the subsystems. One of the major effects of autonomisation is the relativisation of religions.

Autonomisation undermines the credibility of traditional religion, which has to open up the religious subsystem for competing religious, a-religious and non-religious meaning systems: a *pluralistic religious "market" develops*.[26] According to traditional ST, religious pluralism augments the relativity of the respective religious messages or in Berger's terms "it relativises their religious contents", their religious message is "de-objectivised", and more generally, "the pluralistic situation … *ipso facto* plunges religion into a crisis of credibility".[27] More recently, in reference to the American situation, Berger has reformulated his position by stating: "What pluralism does (and there I was right) is to undermine all taken-for-granted certainties, in religion as in all other spheres of life. But it is possible to hold beliefs and to live by them even if they no longer hold the status of taken-for-granted verities".[28] This revision has been refuted by Bruce[29] who confirms the traditional position in secularisation

23 Stark, "Bringing Theory Back In", 8.
24 Ibidem, 17.
25 Iannaccone, "Rational Choice", 40-41; Finke: "The Consequences of Religious Competition", 50-51.
26 Dobbelaere, "Towards an Integrated Perspective", 235-236.
27 Berger, *The Sacred Canopy*, 150-151.
28 Idem, "Postscript", 194.
29 Bruce, "The Curious Case of the Unnecessary Recantation", 98-100.

theory: pluralism undermines the plausibility of religion, which in turn promotes a decline of church commitment, a position we also have defended.[30]

The selection and construction of the variables[31]

To take not only the ritual and belief dimensions into account, but also the consequential dimension, an index was constructed. This construct called "church commitment" is based on the following variables. The ritual dimension is measured by three variables: public practice which is based on whether or not one belongs to a church or religious community and on the frequency of participation in public religious services; the frequency of private religious practices, i.e. praying; and the importance a person attaches to religious rites of passage at the occasion of birth, marriage and death. The belief dimension can also be called "Christian orthodoxy" and is measured by a set of statements on belief in God[32] and by the Christian conception of Jesus Christ.[33] The consequential dimension is measured by two variables: the saliency of one's religion measured by its influence on decisions in daily life[34]; and the degree to which one's religion is perceived as having moral consequences.[35]

To explain the level of church commitment, we have used several measures of religious pluralism, which should allow us to test the two propositions common to the RCT and ST, but which end with opposite predictions. First of all, the *Index of Religious Heterogeneity* is measured by a diversity index which takes the number and relative importance of a country's denominations into account. Other measures refer to the degree to which respondents have lived in lasting, stable and traditional settings: *geographical mobility* and *urbanisation* of the place where they live.

30 Dobbelaere, *Secularization,* 193-194.

31 More information on the measurement models is to be found in Billiet et al, "Church Commitment".

32 Based on the person's concept of God: personal God, spirit or life force, God inside each person, do not believe, and do not know what to believe.

33 A cumulative scale built on the beliefs in Jesus as God and man, as a prophet, as a religious leader, and the denial of the existence of Jesus.

34 Operationalised by two questions "My religious beliefs have a great deal of influence on my daily life" and "My religious beliefs have a great deal of influence on how I make important decisions", both with a seven point scale, going from "definitely not" to "definitely yes".

35 Refers to the answers on the question "If you need to decide what is right or wrong, good or bad, how strongly are you influenced by your religion?", going from "not at all" to "strongly influenced" on a seven point scale.

The results of the test with a multi-level regression model

In the first step of the analysis (see table 5 in annex), individual characteristics were introduced as explanatory variables (mobility and degree of urbanisation: two measures of religious pluralism; gender, level of education, generation: variables that, according to most studies, have an effect on church commitment, and science as a meaning system; see below model 1a); in a second step two contextual societal variables, the religious heterogeneity index and GNP per capita (see below), were introduced (model 1b); finally, we introduced childhood church commitment to control for socialisation effects of the family (model 2b).[36]

The RCT predicts a higher church commitment in a pluralistic situation. The results of the regression analysis point out (see table 5 model 1b) that the religious heterogeneity index is negatively associated with church commitment, although statistically not significant at the level $p<.05$, which is contrary to the predictions of RCT and is in the line with the ST. The two other explanatory variables pointing to pluralism, i.e. mobility and urbanisation, are also in line with the ST (see table 5 model 2b). It could be argued of course that the conditions expressed in the third proposition of RCT are not met in some European countries: in Italy, for example, church and state are not deregulated. However, two mixed countries and two so-called Catholic countries, where a separation of church and state legally exists, also manifest weekend practice that is the inverse of the RTC predictions. In the two mixed countries, the Netherlands and Hungary, the number of people going to church at least one

36 The standardised parameters in the multilevel regression models in tables 5 and 6 indicate the percentage of change (increase or decrease) in the dependent variables (church commitment, or compartmentalisation) per unit change in a metric predictor. The change is expressed in units standard deviation. For the categorical predictors, the parameters must be interpreted as unit change when an individual does not belong to the reference category but to the examined category. The t-values (parameter/standard error) indicate the statistical significance of the parameters. See for example the effect of gender in table 5, model 1a. Men compared to women, controlling for all other explanatory variables in the model, are less committed to the church (-0.095), and this effect remains statistically significant (t-value > 2.6) even after the introduction of contextual variables (model 1b) and religious commitment in childhood (model 2b). The degree of religious commitment decreases about 10% when men are compared with women (reference). An example of a positive effect is found in the variable 'religious commitment in childhood' (also table 5, model 2b). Religious commitment has a significant positive effect on actual church commitment that is stronger (in absolute value) than the effect of all other explanatory variables. Actual church commitment increases by about 40% when the metric predictor 'church commitment in childhood' increases with one standard unit. The country-specific effects are indicated by interaction (* sign). The parameter 'values' indicates whether there is a specific effect (increase or decrease) for a variable in a country, compared with the reference category (the Netherlands).

weekend a month is 26 and 18% respectively, which is lower than in the two Catholic countries Belgium and Poland, 28 and 78% respectively.[37] Furthermore, the religiously most pluralistic regions in Belgium (Brussels and Wallonia) have the lowest church attendance (see graph 1). The results of our analysis and the comparison between and within some European countries show that ST explains the European situation of Catholics better than RCT.

According to our analysis, the negative impact of religious pluralism may be curtailed by family socialisation. When we introduce church practice at the age of twelve into the model (see model 2b), it has a strong positive effect on actual church commitment, so the effect of religious heterogeneity is reduced (the t-value is reduced from -2.51 to -1.07). This indicates that Catholic families may create a plausibility structure that controls contextual effect. However, that is not the case in Great Britain. In applying Merton's reference groups theory, we could hypothesise that the family of origin will be the religious reference group for Catholics if it is homogenously, solidly, church committed and if the other primary groups to which a person belongs and will belong are overwhelmingly solidly church committed. The religious context will have its effect if the primary groups to which a person belongs, the family, the peer groups, friends and colleagues, are religiously heterogeneous.[38] This hypothesis is more plausible since society was religiously more homogeneous when the second oldest generation was in its formative years. That the hypothesis does not hold for Great Britain may be explained by the fact that most Catholics there are Irish immigrants who are motivated to integrate and be accepted in British society at large.

A further test of Secularisation Theory

Since the test of the effect of religious pluralism among Catholics in Europe does not point towards RCT, let us further test the ST. Another effect of the autonomisation of the subsystems is the development of *functional rationality* within the organisations established in the so-called secular subsystems. The economy loses its religious ethos.[39] Goals and means are evaluated on a cost-efficiency basis. This typical attitude implying observations, evaluations, calculation and planning - which is based on a belief that the world is calculable, predictable and controllable[40] - is not limited to the economic system.

37 Halman, *The European Values Study*, 78.
38 Merton, *Social Theory and Social Structure*, 332-335.
39 Weber, *Gesammelte Aufsätze zur Religionssoziologie*, 163-206.
40 Wilson, *Contemporary Transformations of Religion* and Idem, "Secularization".

The political system is also rationalised, leaving little room for traditional and charismatic authority, as modern states develop their rational administration. Since these economic and political organisations need more and more people trained in science and techniques, the educational curriculum has to change: a scientific approach to the world and the teaching of technical knowledge increasingly replace a religious-literary formation. The development of scientifically based techniques also has its impact on daily life: domestic tasks become increasingly mechanised and computerised, even the most intimate human behaviour, sexuality, becomes governed by it. The so-called natural method of birth control proposed by the Catholic Church, the Ogino-Knauss method for example, is based on the basal temperature of the woman registered when waking and plotted on a chart. On the basis of an evaluation of the temperature-curve, the fertile and infertile periods can be calculated. Sexual intercourse can then be planned to prevent pregnancy.

In most of the rational institutional spheres organisations develop (e.g. business organisations and agencies) in which individuals assume positions and perform roles. The organisation supervises and is concerned exclusively with efficient task-performances: the individual is "replaceable as a person in proportion to the increasing anonymity of specialized roles that are determined by the functionally rational institutions".[41] What Wilson calls a "rational empirical orientation to the world", the opposite of a magical-religious orientation, predominates.[42] Control is technical and bureaucratic, not moral or religious: "It has become impersonal and amoral, a matter for routine techniques and unknown officials".[43] The relationships that develop here and become more and more typical for the different functional spheres are "gesellschaftlich" (Tönnies) or "secondary" (Cooley). They are, indeed, positional, contractual, formal, utilitarian, confined to segments of the person, and transferable. The individual is no longer regarded as an end in oneself, as in the *Gemeinschaft,* where the dominant relationships are "primary" (Cooley), i.e. affective, total, and regulated by habits. "A community really involves face-to-face relationships of known persons. [...] Society, in contrast, involves the interaction of role-performances of unknown role-players".[44]

This bureaucratic type of relationship extends into the social world. City life, commerce, welfare, school, entertainment and even the neighbourhood are basically *gesellschaftlich*. As the community, the *Gemeinschaft*, ceases to be

41 Luckmann, *The Invisible Religion*, 96.

42 Wilson, *Contemporary Transformations of Religion*, 11.

43 Ibidem, 20.

44 Wilson, "Aspects of Secularization", 264.

the basic principle of social organisation and develops in a more and more *gesellschaftlich* manner (Weber called it "Vergesellschaftung" and Wilson "societalization"), religion loses momentum. As Wilson points out, religion offers "redemption" and this personal, total, "indivisible ultimate", unsusceptible to rational procedures or "cost-efficiency criteria", is offered in a "community".[45] He explains the diminishing impact of religion by the decline of community: "My thesis is that secularization is the decline of community: secularization is a concomitant of societalization".[46]

The selection and construction of the variables and the hypotheses[47]

As context variables, we have used *country*, *Religious Heterogeneity of the country* (cf supra) and *Gross National Product* (GNP) per head in 1998, which is used here as a proxy for functional rationality. According to ST, the higher the GNP per head the lower church commitment will be. Further predictions based on the ST suggest the following variables. *Generation*, the working hypothesis is that the younger generation will be less church committed since they have always lived in a secularised society, while the older generation has known a society where religion was more important (the generation born before 1940 is the reference category in our analysis). *Level of education* (higher, secondary, and lower as the reference category), the idea is that the higher the level of education, the more people have been exposed to science and technical knowledge. Another classical individual variable is *gender* (reference category is 'men'), the hypothesis being that men are more exposed to functional rationality than women. To that argument should be added that women, more than men, are concerned with the integration and the problems of the family. Most prayers read in churches and chapels are by women. These requests refer to illnesses in the family, inter-marital relations, problems with children, family-members' exams and the like. Women's concerns for family may draw them, rather than men, closer to religion.

Secularisation is not a latent consequence solely of functional differentiation, it is also the result of voluntary action to insulate sectors of society, such as culture, education and the family, from religious influences, i.e. the process of laicisation. The emergence and development of Enlightenment ideas, with their forceful opposition to religious and sacred myths and to religious authority, was instrumental in this process. Its guiding idea was that human-

45 Ibidem, 273.
46 Ibidem, 265-266.
47 More information on the measurement models is to be found in Billiet et al, "Church Commitment", 139-143.

kind should develop rational knowledge of the world and discard supernatural dependencies.[48] The development of science, technology and education were considered powerful instruments to liberate man from myths. In our research, this attitude towards science is measured by agreement with a single assertion "Science can, by itself, give life a meaning". This is a 7-point Likert scale and is called *science as a meaning system*.

Finally, we have introduced *previous religious involvement*, measured by questions about belonging to a church in the past and the participation in public religious services at age twelve, to measure the impact of the religious socialisation in the family of origin. The working hypothesis is that the family can build a religious plausibility structure to protect its children against environmental a- and antireligious influences.

The results of the test with a multi-level regression model

Contrary to our expectation, the negative association between GNP per capita, a proxy for functional rationality, and church commitment is not significantly negative as far as the Catholic population is concerned. All other individual explanatory variables confirm ST when the context variables and the socialisation variable are introduced (see model 2b).

Catholic men are significantly less church committed than women, which is even more true in Great Britain (apparently Irish men adapt more easily than women to the society where they have immigrated), Hungary, Italy, Poland and Portugal. Analysing this result in detail for Belgium, Voyé and Dobbelaere concluded that, as far as public practice was concerned, women working outside the home are more akin to men than to housewives. However, women engage in private practice (i.e. praying) more frequently than men, and there are significantly more women than men who define themselves as religious. Many factors may play a role here. Going to church on the weekend offers housewives external contacts. Otherwise, they less than the others come into contact with the secularised world that stands in opposition to the value rationality of the Catholic Church. They also live more in a *gemeinschaftliche Umwelt* that is more open to religion. It is probably concern for the family that draws women closer to religion than men, since family values are more akin to religious values than are the values of the other subsystems. The fact that women who are professionally engaged do not externalise their religiosity by going to church services on weekends may be the result of the work load

48 Dupront, *Qu'est-ce que les Lumières?*, 19 and 32.

at home which, for lack of time during the week, they have to take care of during the weekend.[49]

As predicted by ST, higher education has a negative impact (see table 5 model 1a and 1b) on the church commitment of Catholics, and in Great Britain this is so even for secondary education. When we control for religious socialisation in childhood, the effect of secondary education has also significant negative effects on church commitment (see table 5 model 2b) in all countries, but this effect is stronger in Great Britain than elsewhere. As predicted by ST, science as a meaning system also has a negative effect on the church commitment of Catholics, and this effect is stronger in Great Britain then in the other countries. Finally, Catholics born since the start of World War II are much less committed to their church than those born before that war. The pre-war generation was socialised and had lived in a society where religion had a much more important societal role than it has had since World War II. It is clear that these results confirm the general trend of our analysis described above. A more detailed analysis based on ST does explain the actual church commitment of Catholics in Europe to a large extent. We may conclude from our analysis that societal secularisation has had a negative effect on church commitment. In other words, many Catholics are also secularised. Does that help explain the sharp decline at the end of the 1960s and the early 1970s?

What Happened at the End of the 1960s

The standard model of generational change, which may help to explain the sharp decline in church practice, suggests that change is largely restricted to "formative" years. "Once beliefs, norms and values are internalised and behaviour becomes routinized, change is less likely to occur".[50] This model that predicts a gradual change can be combined with Inglehart's idea of formative affluence.[51] "Then we would not expect a gradual decline of church involvement but a watershed between the post war and older cohorts".[52] On the basis of a cohort analysis of core church members in Catholic (Belgium, France, and Italy) and mixed countries (Great Britain, the Netherlands and West Germany) Jagodzinski and Dobbelaere came to the conclu-

49 Dobbelaere and Voyé, "Religie en kerkbetrokkenheid", 149-150.
50 Jagodzinski and Dobbelaere, "Secularization and Church Religiosity", 105.
51 Inglehart, *Culture Shift in Advanced Industrial Society*.
52 Jagodzinski and Dobbelaere, "Secularization and Church Religiosity", 106.

sion that neither generational model of change fitted the data and they formulated the "contagion model" which suggests that the younger cohorts are more affected by a process which affects *all* cohorts.[53] This model was largely confirmed by a cohort analysis of church disengagement in the same countries, although in a few exceptional cases some modifications of the model were needed.[54]

We will now describe the process that affected all cohorts, but most of all the younger generations, at the end of the 1960s and the early 1970s. We do this in response to the need "to explain the so-called 'massive exodus' that occurred at that period".

In his book, the Belgian historian Van Isacker explains the "massive exodus" of the faithful and the simultaneous "desertion by the priest" in the Western world as a result of the Second Vatican Council.[55] The Council as emphasis upon "humanism", "democracy" and "ecumenism" resulted from the infiltration of Masonic, relativistic ideas about God, truth, and religion and created a climate of confusion.[56] The profanation became eminently clear in the liturgical changes: the Tridentine missal was banned, Latin language and sacred music were replaced by the vernacular, jazz, folk, and electronic music; and the priest now faced the people. "Now, one sits comradely, 'democratically', and '*sans gêne*' before the unnameable God. And, immediately, the mystery that should surround the attitudes of humans toward their God is gone".[57]

However, Greeley and his associates have refuted on empirical grounds the hypothesis that the exodus of the faithful might be accounted for by the Vatican Council. Instead, they explained the exodus as a violent reaction of a large number of Catholics to the 1968 birth-control encyclical, *Humanae vitae*.[58] However, a comparative analysis across countries demonstrates that the exodus from the Church is explained neither by the Second Vatican Council nor by *Humanae vitae*. In Belgium and the Netherlands, the sharp decline started before the publication of the encyclical[59] and in France the exodus began in the early 1960s, which was well before the impact of the Council

53 Jagodzinski and Dobbelaere, "Secularization and Church Religiosity", 107-111.
54 Ibidem, 111-113.
55 Van Isacker, *Ontwijding* (Profanation).
56 Ibidem, 58-60.
57 Ibidem, 67.
58 Greeley, *American Catholics*, 55-57; Greeley, McGready and McCourt, *Catholic Schools*, 116-152; Hout and Greeley, "The Center doesn't hold", 332-335.
59 Dobbelaere, "Secularization, Pillarization, and Religious Change", 88-95.

was felt. Indeed, regular church attendance in France dropped from 38 to 20% between 1961 and 1966 (3.5 percentage points a year). It fell even further to 10% by 1981.[60] In addition, the decline in church attendance was not limited to the Catholic Church: it also occurred in the Protestant denominations in the Netherlands.[61] In the German Federal Republic, church attendance figures for Protestants declined: from 15% in 1963 to 10% in 1967-1969 and further to 6% in 1982.[62] This decline in church attendance in the Protestant churches cannot be explained by Catholic institutional factors. Furthermore, *institutional* factors do not explain why in Belgium, as in Canada, the attendance drop-off was far from uniform across these countries.[63] An analysis of the available evidence points rather to the *contextual* factors of industrialisation and modernisation. The acceleration of these processes in Quebec and Flanders in the 1960s explains the belated and more dramatic declines that occurred there.

Our theoretical explanation is based on the centrality of the belief in a "personal God" for the preservation of traditional beliefs and church involvement and now this belief has been impacted by functional differentiation, rationalisation and societalisation, which produced societal secularisation (cf supra). As a consequence of functional differentiation and rationalisation, many people, especially the young, conceive of the physical, psychic, and social world as more and more controllable and calculable. Consequently, many can no longer believe in God because "*they* have the world in *their* hands". And if for some people, the notion of God still lingers on, God is more and more conceived of as a "higher power", "something vague and general", and not as a "personal" God. Durkheim[64], Swanson[65], and other anthropologists and sociologists have shown that people develop a concept of personified supernatural beings directly from the model which their society provides. How could God be thought of as a "personal God" in a society in which people experience fewer and fewer "personal relationships" in public life? In a society where impersonal, segmented role relations prevail, belief in a "personal God" and, consequently, the celebration of a person's relationship with God in religious services appears as an anachronism for many modern women and men. As Durkheim suggested, the more general and vague God becomes, the more

60 Gellard, Valadier and Donegani, *Regards sur le catholicisme français*, 56.
61 Van Hemert, *En zij verontschuldigden zich*, 10-11.
62 Köcher, "Religiös in einer säkularisierten Welt", 221.
63 Bibby, *Fragmented Gods*, 19-21; and supra graph 1.
64 Durkheim, *The Elementary Forms of the Religious Life.*
65 Swanson, *The Birth of the Gods.*

removed God is from the world and the more ineffective God is.[66] At the same time, such a belief is very shaky. It is a belief in an abstract notion without any real impact on people's lives, and one that can easily be disposed of.

As early as the 1960s, the impact of modernity strongly undermined the belief in a "personal God" as well as belief in other articles of faith, but overt, traditional behaviour simply continued under the weight of social traditions. A vast number of priests and religious persons together with the Catholic community regimented the faithful. However, Sunday mass had become for many a "duty", a "tradition" not supported by strong beliefs. In the second half of the 1960s, a discussion began about a number of issues raised in Bishop Robinson's book *Honest to God* (1963), *Humanae vitae* (1968), and the implementation of the conciliar resolutions. Add to that local issues such as the dividing up of the *Universitas Louvaniensis*, in Belgium; in the Netherlands the *Pastoral Council* and the *Dutch Catechism*, and in the USA the *Underground Church*. One could, for the first time, in public discourse and the mass media, acknowledge that the religious understanding of beliefs, church ethics, and church authority were very much undermined. In the secular world, too, institutions and authority came under heavy criticism. This discussion broke down the "dikes" the Church had established to protect the faithful; the existence of a Catholic "pillar" was being challenged.[67] In the same period, many in the clergy left the Church, an event that had repercussions upon the beliefs, attitudes, and behaviour of lay people. The sharp decline in weekly mass attendance at the end of the 1960s and the early 1970s may, consequently, be seen as the collapse of traditional behaviour that was no longer supported by the belief in a "personal God" and the traditional values that the Church proclaims. What occurred was the convergence of *public* behaviour and the *personal* general disbelief in the doctrines and values of the Church. Since that time social control has increasingly had a completely different impact: it started to keep people out of church rather than inducing them to attend. This can be seen in the behaviour and beliefs of the youngest generation.

Jagodzinski and Dobbelaere's "contagion model" does not deny differences between pre-war and post-war generation. However, these differences are not caused by post-war affluence; they are rather the consequence of public criticisms that turned inner doubts into overt behaviour.[68] And as we have seen (table 1), the two generations born between 1940 and 1971 were the

66 Durkheim, *The Division of Labor in Society*, 144 and 272-276.

67 Dobbelaere and Voyé, "Western European Catholicism", 213-214.

68 Jagodzinski and Dobbelaere, "Secularization and Church Religiosity", 111.

more affected. The oldest generation reacted less rapidly to new norms and ideas, although the pre-war generation was also affected by it according to the study of Billiet and Vanhoutvinck referred to above. It is, however, more difficult for older people to give up internalised beliefs and values and to change routinised behaviour. The youngest generation, born after 1970, was socialised in an a-religious culture and by parents expressing their religious scepticism, which reinforced the decline in church attendance.

Do we reduce our explanation to a monocausal model? Important historical changes as we described cannot be explained monocausally. Other factors, institutional as well as contextual also had an impact. In the 1970s and the 1980s, the reactionary policy of the Holy See, blocking the "aggiornamento" discouraged a number of Catholics who wanted to adapt the Church to the world in the light of the conciliar spirit.[69] Moreover, structural changes were also important. Functional differentiation produced the individuation of decisions[70], an event that stimulated "*religion à la carte*" or "religious bricolage" (see below, Liliane Voyé's paper). This had an exceptional appeal for the upper middle and upper classes and especially intellectuals. They no longer accepted the "given" answers. And because the Church lost credibility as a consequence of scientific discoveries, and since the process of secularisation divested the Church of its capacity to legitimise the status of the upper classes, members of these classes dissociated themselves from the Church.
That explains why, after the 1960s, change occurred in the well-established relationship between the upper classes and church involvement. Today all social classes practise very little.

Moreover, structural changes were also important: in the 1960s and 1970s, an increasing number of people obtained more leisure time, not only more vacation time but Saturdays were also freed from work and school, and a leisure culture developed. Consequently, in a period when, for a growing number of people Sunday mass became a "traditional" behaviour, a "sheer duty", it became more located in a period of extended leisure time. The feeling associated with leisure time, being primarily a time of "exemption from external pressures", heightened the awareness of "duty" associated with religious "obligations". Bit by bit, a culture emerged that conflicted directly with traditional religious values, which legitimated a "culture of duties and self-restraint" and was based on the notion of "community". In contrast, leisure culture stressed

69 Schillebeeckx, *Mensen als verhaal van God*, 5-6; Dobbelaere and Voyé, "Western European Catholicism", 215-224.
70 Luhmann, *Funktion der Religion*, 232-248.

freedom, individualism, "private niches", massification, emotionalism, pleasure and ecstasy. This culture is supported by consumerism and advertising, both of which stress novelty, new trends, new fashions, new products.[71] Religion, in contrast, is supported by collective rituals that "repeat" the same gestures and the same texts, stressing continuity and tradition.

Will Secularisation Continue?

Functional differentiation produced the secularisation of society which in turn, together with accompanying processes like individuation, produced the secularisation of individuals and the decline of church commitment. Does it also have an effect on "secularisation of the mind" or *compartmentalisation*? This concept tries to measure the extent to which people see a separation between the religious subsystem and the juridical, the educational, the economic, the family, the scientific, the medical, and the political subsystems. In other words, do they think that religion should *not* inform the other subsystems, that the subsystems are autonomous and that any interference of religion in these subsystems should be eradicated and disallowed?

The latent variable compartmentalisation is measured by six observed indicators. Three of these variables are part of a sub-dimension of secularisation: agreement (Yes/No) with prohibition of religious symbols in (public) schools, degree of financial support of religious schools that met the normal educational standards, and agreement with financial support of none, some, or all religions. The three other indicators deal with agreement with the practice in courts of swearing an oath with reference to God, the consultation with religious leaders by the state when making laws on moral questions, and the desirability of religious influence in politics.

Which social and religious variables influence a compartmentalised attitude? In order to explore the total effects of the demographic and the contextual variables on compartmentalisation, no individual religious variables were included in the first model (see table 6 model 4a).[72] In the second model two religious variables, actual church commitment and commitment at the age of 12, are introduced (see table 6 model 4b).

71 Balandier, *Le detour,* 184-195; Yonnet, *Jeux, modes et masses.*

72 See annexe table 6 for multilevel regression models for compartmentalisation.

In the first model, we do not register a significant effect of the societal context variables on compartmentalisation. However, when the individual religious variables are introduced (model 4b) we see that religious heterogeneity has a negative effect. It is clear that the more Catholics are committed to their Church, the less they are opposed to the impact of religion on the other subsystems [-0,669 (-39.27)], and this is more so in societies with a heterogeneous religious composition [-0,221 (-5.55)]. In a mono-religious Catholic society, the more church-committed Catholics are, the more they oppose the secularisation of society. They want financial support for their Church and Catholic schools and religious symbols in state schools. They think that religion should influence politics and that laws on moral questions, e.g. abortion, euthanasia and experiments on embryos, should be informed by religious leaders. In religiously pluralistic countries the effect on Catholics is stronger. They more strongly defend the Church's position, confronted as they are with the standpoints of other religions. They see the stakes because religions do not have a uniform view on moral issues and Protestant churches, for example, lay more stress on individual responsibility rather than seeking to impose their views on the whole society. Catholics in contrast stress the societal level and want the position of the Church institutionalised on the societal level so that the Catholic religion has an impact on the other subsystems.

Apart from this strong opposition to the secularisation of society according to church commitment and the effect of the country's level of religious heterogeneity we see that church involvement in childhood has no impact on attitudes towards secularisation. Some positional characteristics (having had secondary education and being part of the protest generation) still have a significant effect, but these are weaker and are positive towards the secularisation of society.

Conclusions

What is happening to church commitment in Europe can only be understood in a comparative perspective and is best explained by Secularisation Theory. Rational Choice Theory cannot explain the European situation, since most of the conditions for its functioning are not present in Europe: there is no real religious competition. The mono-religious situation prevails in most countries, and even if a country is religiously mixed, the religions are more or less regionally segregated, for example as in the Netherlands and Germany. Only sects and New Religious Movements are active on the supply side, but their freedom of action is limited by political interventions in many European countries. Belgium, Germany and France are paradigmatic in this respect.

Our study does not imply that RCT is falsified: the theory should be reformulated for Europe and our study suggests ways in which this could be done. First of all, it is not sufficient to measure religious pluralism on the supply side in the countries under study: the degree of *competition* between religions should be measured. Secondly, not only is religious pluralism important, but so is "pluralism of meaning systems", which would allow a measurement of the competition between religious meaning systems themselves and with a- and antireligious meaning systems. Moreover, research is needed on the so-called postulated latent religiosity on the demand side. Recent research in Belgium allowed us see that the number of individuals defining themselves as religious declined steadily according to the number of generations in the family of origin that are unchurched.[73]

The secularisation of European societies is a consequence of societal processes that were not manifestly intended to secularise society: functional differentiation, functional rationalisation, individualisation and societalisation. However, secularisation has also been promoted by political action, which is called the laicisation of society. Since church commitment is declining in all the societies under study, so not limited to Catholics, we may expect that the opposition to the secularisation of society will become weaker, and that popular support for parties opposing secularisation will increasingly fade away in the future if this point has priority on their political agenda. Indeed, "secularisation of the mind" or compartmentalisation is a consequence of the secularisation of society. A compartmentalised view is typical of members who are less church-committed, and that includes the great majority of Catholics as well as the unchurched, who are a growing category in European societies.

73 Dobbelaere and Voyé, "Religie en kerkbetrokkenheid", 129-130.

The beliefs of the great majority of Catholics are "general and vague": God is conceived more and more as a "spirit or life force" and belief in an afterlife exceptionally expresses itself in the typical Christian notions of heaven and hell. Consequently, weekly church practice is very low. However, the rites of passage still have a high participation rate. This expresses a vague religiosity that is also expressed in private prayers, which may have a magical character: a demand for help in difficult situations. The participation in rites of passage also symbolises a traditional Catholic identity, a participation in a particular culture without great knowledge of this culture's content. Participants are not part of a "*lignée croyante*"[74] but rather continue a "ritual memory". However, as we have noticed, studies have pointed out that lay people appropriate the "rites of passage", which for them express rather cultural and family traditions than religious ones. This is a form of organisational secularisation. For a vast majority, Catholicism, in Davie's terms, becomes a "vicarious religion"[75], offering nominal and lapsed Catholics the possibility of a sacred celebration at important "passages" in the life cycle by means of secularised rituals. To what extent this is the basis for a continued identification is a big question. The growing number of unchurched, who in the youngest generation are at least two generations unchurched, makes this problematic. Indeed, in Belgium, as Dobbelaere and Voyé noted, in this category fewer people than in the first generation unchurched define themselves as religious or maintain a private practice.[76]

74 Hervieu-Léger, *La religion pour mémoire*.

75 Davie, *Europe*, 19-20.

76 Dobbelaere and Voyé, "Religie en kerkbetrokkenheid", 129-130.

Table 5: Multilevel regression models for church commitment (Catholics and former Catholics, baseline the Netherlands); (1) Standardised parameter, (2) t-value

Explanatory variables	**Model 1a**		**Model 1b**		**Model 2b**	
	(1)	**(2)**	**(1)**	**(2)**	**(1)**	**(2)**
Fixed part						
Intercept	0.331	(2.70)	0.343	(3.84)	0.117	(0.91)
Gender: Men (Reference: Women)	-0.095***	(-4.86)	-0.095***	(-4.86)	-0.090***	(-4.74)
Level of education (Reference: Lower)						
Secondary	-0.023	(-1.78)	-0.022	(-1.73)	-0.028	(-2.26)
Higher	-0.029	(-2.48)	-0.029	(-2.44)	-0.037*	(-3.22)
Generation (Reference: born < 1940)						
1940 - 1955	-0.139***	(-10.81)	-0.140***	(-10.83)	-0.161***	(-8.91)
1956 - 1970	-0.223***	(-16.70)	-0.224***	(-16.73)	-0.185***	(-14.10)
1971 - 1982	-0.197***	(-14.92)	-0.197***	(-14.95)	-0.159***	(-12.19)
Geographical mobility	-0.027	(-2.47)	-0.026	(-2.42)	-0.027*	(-2.60)
Degree of urbanization	-0.085***	(-8.14)	-0.084***	(-8.08)	-0.066***	(-6.47)
Science as a meaning system	-0.076***	(-6.55)	-0.076***	(-6.58)	-0.073***	(-6.56)
*Gender * Great Britain*	-0.142	(-2.11)	-0.150	(-2.24)	-0.159	(-2.44)
*Gender * Hungary*	-0.146**	(-3.75)	-0.146**	(-3.75)	-0.117*	(-3.09)
*Gender * Italy*	-0.071*	(-2.65)	-0.071*	(-2.65)	-0.061	(-2.35)
*Gender * Poland*	-0.075	(-2.38)	-0.075	(-2.36)	-0.069	(-2.25)
*Gender * Portugal*	-0.091*	(-2.64)	-0.091*	(-2.65)	-0.070	(-2.11)
*Secondary * Great Britain*	-0.166	(-2.42)	-0.147	(-2.16)	-0.166	(-2.49)
*Science * Great Britain '(continued...)*	-0.184*	(-2.70)	-0.187*	(-2.74)	-0.180*	(-2.69)
Religious commitment in childhood					0.402***	(19.98)
*Rel. com. in childh. * Gen. 1940-1955*					0.058*	(3.00)
*Rel. com. in childh. * Great Britain*					-0.400*	(-3.13)
GNP_cap of country			-0.097	(-1.18)	-0.214	(-1.06)
Religious heterogeneity of country			-0.196	(-2.51)	-0.124	(-1.07)
Random part						
Level 1. Countries (var. of intercept)	0.104	(1.72)	0.035	(1.27)	0.072	(1.26)
Level 2. Individuals (res. variance)	0.611***		0.611***	(54.40)	0.572***	(54.34)
R^2 at individual level	13,4%		21,7%		22,0%	
R^2 at country level	11,8%		11,8%		17,4%	

** p <.01; ** p < .001; *** p < .0001*

Table 6: Multilevel regression models for compartmentalisation (Catholics and former Catholics); (1) Standardized parameter, (2) t-value

Explanatory variables	**Model 4a**		**Model 4b**	
	(1)	**(2)**	**(1)**	**(2)**
Fixed part				
Intercept	-0.008	(-0.11)	0.211	(4.64)
Gender: Men (Reference: Women)	0.123***	(6.29)	-0.009	(-0.53)
Level of education (Reference: Lower)				
Secondary	0.076***	(4.84)	0.058***	(4.35)
Higher	0.022	(1.48)	0.011	(0.88)
Generation (Reference: born < 1940)				
1940 - 1955	0.136***	(8.59)	0.045**	(3.29)
1956 - 1970	0.173***	(10.58)	0.030	(2.06)
1971 - 1982	0.126***	(7.76)	-0.002	(-0.14)
Geographical mobility	0.044**	(3.28)	0.027	(2.33)
Degree of urbanisation	0.080***	(6.27)	0.025	(2.23)
Science as a meaning system	0.029	(1.95)	-0.025	(-1.90)
Church commitment in childhood			0.001	(0.02)
Religious commitment			-0.669***	(-39.27)
*Gender * Belgium*[1]	-0.100*	(-2.96)	-0.034	(-1.15)
*Gender * The Netherlands*	-0.188**	(-3.60)	-0.088	(-1.98)
*Gender * Italy*	-0.080*	(-2.70)	-0.060	(-2.34)
*Higher * Portugal*	0.109	(2.50)	-0.057	(1.54)
*Urban * Great Britain*	-0.393	(-2.15)	-0.303	(-2.31)
*Science * Portugal*	-0.085	(-2.15)	-0.094*	(-2.80)
Religious commitment Belgium*			0.073	(2.39)
Rel. commitment The Netherlands*			0.113	(2.37)
GNP_cap of country	0.098	(1.49)	0.032	(0.80)
Religious heterogeneity of country	-0.078	(-1.21)	-0.221**	(-5.55)
Random part				
Level 1. Countries (var. of intercept)	0.021	(0.85)	0.007	(1.05)
Level 2. Individuals (res. variance)	0.922***	(54.40)	0.672***	(54.34)
R^2 at individual level	8,2%		33,9%	
R^2 at country level	5,2%		30,9%	

** p < .01; ** p < .001; *** p < .0001; 1 Reference group: Poland*

Contemporary Syncretism in Europe

Liliane Voyé

For a long time, syncretism was exclusively associated with continents other than Europe, and with Africa and Latin America in particular. It was perceived as evidence of these peoples' irrationality that, in this way, they blended gods, beliefs and practices that the colonisers defined as incompatible and mutually antagonistic. Anthropologists have demonstrated, however, that, far from lacking coherence, this syncretism was an attempt by people to preserve their identities. This held especially true when colonisation disrupted social structures (for example the systems of lineage) as well as daily life (notably with the spread of schooling and the development of urbanisation). Syncretism was, therefore, used by the natives in order to guarantee that certain spaces remained free and yet avoid confrontation with the colonisers.

Faced with these manifestations of syncretism, Europe has perceived itself as (relatively) homogenous and coherent, showing as much confidence in the radical superiority of its religion - Christianity - as in the supremacy of its economy, political system and culture. During the synod of European bishops held in Rome in 1991 the journal *La Croix* published the "Christian map of Europe" which was followed by numerous others and which clearly manifests this attitude.[1] Such a view involved ignoring the existence of discrepancies, the intermingling of traditions (with popular religion and superstitions, in particular) and dissident appropriations (religious practice as a sign of social status, for example) which have always relativised this representation and opinion.

Nevertheless, things have changed in the last fifty years or so. Europe continues voluntarily to identify itself as Christian[2], but this identification is often

1 Voyé, "Religion in Modern Europe".
2 Ibidem.

more nominal than substantial: practice has diminished drastically; beliefs are becoming indistinct; respect for moral norms is disintegrating. The different movements that exist within Christianity, ranging from fundamentalism to a "couldn't care less" attitude, are increasingly revealed for what they are. The present attitude towards the Church often resembles that of a client rather than of a worshipper. Syncretism, quite unaffected by any feeling of guilt, is developing more or less actively, by means of diverse and multiple borrowings.

It is this last aspect which I examine here, limiting my study to Catholicism in Europe. I rapidly outline the most common elements in syncretic compositions, before suggesting some interpretative hypotheses.

A Wandering Christian Europe: Various Modalities of Composition

I already mentioned that Catholics have always combined the Church's practices and beliefs with others taken from popular religions and even belonging to the register of superstitions and beliefs. Little has changed today, despite the fact that during the 1960s and 70s, swept up in the wave of projects for general rationalisation which made its mark on our societies at that time, the Catholic Church attempted to purify its practices and beliefs. Wishing to re-focus these practices and beliefs on God, it eliminated from its hagiography a whole series of saints, whose statues disappeared from churches as a result, strongly discouraged requests for the benediction of houses, cars and animals and transformed the 'solemn Communion' into a 'profession of faith', by which it indicated its desire to re-focus the rite on its original meaning and to strip it of garish profane trappings.

Popular religion and parallel beliefs

This project was never fully carried out by the ecclesial authorities. Certainly if, at the same time, some people abandoned the obligatory practices, and in particular Sunday worship, they nonetheless continued to have recourse to many popular religious practices: after a short period of relative regression, requests for benediction, pilgrimages, reinstating cults of various saints and so on, began to multiply again. However, these various practices came within the scope of client-type relationships (that is, initiated privately or by individuals), mostly autonomous of any sort of institutional framework. This is particularly the case with pilgrimages. It is interesting to note that these varied practices are mostly initiated by requests concerning personal health and that of family and friends, as well as by questions relating to daily life, especially concerning matters such as good family relations, successful exams or finding a job. Contrary to what could be understood by 'popular', these practices, which are not obligatory and are composed primarily of gestures and emotions, rather than words, are common to people of all social backgrounds and ages even if these social variables induce differences in locality, in types of request or even in the manner of expression.[3]

A survey concerning "Religious and Moral Pluralism" (RAMP) carried out in eleven European countries[4], between 1997 and 1999 (depending on the country) gives us some additional information.[5] In the four dominantly Catholic countries (Belgium, Italy, Poland and Portugal) and in the two mixed countries (Hungary and the Netherlands) where the survey was carried out - the number of Catholics in the sample being too low in the other countries surveyed to make analysis possible - the more people participated in religious practices, prayed and had orthodox beliefs, the more sacred objects such as crosses and medals they owned and the more they believed in their effectiveness.[6] The ratio is highest where is most prayer; perhaps this should be seen as an instance of religiousness expressed particularly through requests for protection, help and support in the resolution of daily problems - a religious characteristic more often of women than of men. Incidentally, the relationship between beliefs in exogenous power through objects (for example, the possessions of talismans and belief in them) and in the consultation of horoscopes, on one hand, and religious practice and the frequency of prayer, on the other, is very weak, and is negative in examples of orthodox faith: the higher the incidence of orthodoxy, the less frequently such beliefs

3 Voyé, "Religion populaire et pèlerinages en Europe"; Idem, "Le rite en question"; Idem, "Popular Religion and Pilgrimages in Western Europe".

4 The eleven countries studied in the RAMP survey were Belgium, Denmark, Finland, Great Britain, Hungary, Italy, the Netherlands, Norway, Poland, Portugal and Sweden. The surveys in Germany and France, which had participated in the preparatory studies, could not, unfortunately, be completed, as the researchers did not obtain the funding they had expected. Some results were already published, see Piedmont and Moberg, *Research in the Social Scientific Study of Religion*, Vol. 13, 159-243 and Vol. 14, 129-159.

5 Dobbelaere, Tomasi and Voyé, "Religious Syncretism".

6 We have searched for patterns of syncretism in the whole sample and in sub-samples - among other religious affiliations, countries, gender, and levels of education -, however, no pattern emerged. We therefore had to study the inter-relatedness of the respective syncretic elements on a binary basis (Dobbelaere, Tomasi and Voyé, "Religious Syncretism", 227).

are found.[7] It would therefore appear that those who attain relatively high scores for the three variables characteristic of adhesion to the Church come within the scope of a traditional mode of monolithic religious adherence, where everything is interrelated and constitutes an indivisible unit, sealed from intrusion by any element foreign to the practices and corpus of beliefs defined by the Church.[8]

The RAMP survey further shows that the most fervent Christians and those without religious beliefs are less likely to be attracted by parallel beliefs than more nominative Christians who, it shout be noted, represent the majority of the population.

The survey also notes that the socio-professional category, level of education and urban or rural place of residence do not appear to have any influence on the incidence of recourse to popular religion and parallel beliefs. This is not the case where gender and age are concerned. Women proved more frequently to own holy objects and to express confidence in their efficacy than men. More women also pray and more frequently. No doubt this seems to indicate, as in other areas, that despite the changes that have come about, women remain more preoccupied than men by basic daily problems such as their families' health, their children's success at school and healthy relationships with their partners. Indeed, it is these themes which receive priority under their signatures in the books available in various churches, chapels and places of pilgrimage; and one could hypothesise that these are the same concerns which occupy their prayers. Women also consult horoscopes more often; of course, horoscopes are commonly found in womens' magazines, but the above hypothesis is also probably an explanatory factor - horoscope-reading is not limited merely to the reader's zodiac sign, but is extended to include the signs of those close to the reader.

Another particularly important factor revealed by this survey is that the ownership of talismans is primarily a feature of young people and, independently of what has just been said regarding the influence of gender, it is also

7 The same is true of Protestants but, for them, there is a curvilinear relationship between practice and prayer, on the one hand, and the possession of talismans, on the other: it is those for whom the frequency of the two religious measures is intermediary who most often own talismans; however, a linear relation can be observed with the consultation of horoscopes.

8 We noted, for the sake of information, that for the Protestant populations of the four Scandinavian countries and, to a lesser degree, of Great Britain, a significant linear relationship exists between orthodoxy and practice on one hand and the ownership of holy objects on the other; however, it is with the frequency of prayer that the positive relationship is clearest (with the exception of Great Britain).

they who consult horoscopes most frequently. Although horoscopes may be more frequently in the media and the markets for which they are the main target, the most likely interpretation would seem to lie in the uncertainty and risks threatening every aspect of their lives, even more so than for their elders. I shall return to this subject.

It is important to note that this resort to parallel beliefs and magic cannot be interpreted as an abandonment of scientific rationality. In the case of young people in particular, it is not rare to see that even though they continue to hope science will improve everyone's conditions of life, science is nonetheless considered unfinished and therefore likely in the future to offer a rational understanding of phenomena which today are seen to escape its explanations.[9] The achievement of so many things that existed until recently solely in science fiction serves only to encourage this view. At the same time, as this rational knowledge has been little by little 'disenchanting' the world, it has created a vacuum for the marvellous and for fairy tales, which no doubt explains the crazes surrounding examples such as the Brazilian child of the shanty-town who becomes a great footballer, the ex-drug addicted single mother who marries a prince or the immigrant servant who becomes a famous singer. No doubt the same is also to be observed in popular literature, where science fiction novels now find themselves outstripped by works of "heroic fantasy"[10], populated by witches, angels and magicians, as the enormous current successes of *The Lord of the Rings* and, above all, *Harry Potter*, show, as well as in the increase of works on esotericism, ranging from alchemy to parapsychology.

Psychosomatic therapy and parallel medicine

The integration of parallel beliefs into European Christianity is not the only element which reveals the wanderings and the borrowings from other belief systems and other spheres. A similar combination occurs notably in psychosomatic therapy and natural or parallel medicine, both of which experience increasing popularity. In both cases, the person is reconciled with his own body and with nature, while attributing to the latter two a dimension and an importance which go beyond their material reality. Thus, for example, seminars and sessions are organised so that moments of physical exercise and of thought and reflection are intermingled; the rhythms of life are thereby harmonised with those of nature and a cosmic meaning is given to the ingre-

9 Boy and Michelat, "Les Français et les parasciences", 209.
10 Piras, "Nouveaux mysticismes", 91.

dients of the nourishment. Many such practices are associated with the New Age movement, which insists on a rediscovery of the divine essence in the human person and on the necessity of learning to fulfil oneself by partaking of various therapies which will assist self-transformation and thereby progressively change social structures.

Exotic religions and philosophical traditions

Combinations also occur with borrowings from several major exotic religious and philosophical traditions. Thus, Europe has witnessed the emergence of various groups claiming Buddhism as their inspiration and accepting members whose concerns are to respect the world and to develop the self in every way. In order to realise this objective, they carry out exercises that are both spiritual (for example meditation, recitation of mantras, the practice of positive thinking) and physical (for example relaxation and breathing exercises), thereby demonstrating their concern to acknowledge the positive character of both the emotional and bodily dimensions. If such groups have always been and remain in the minority, the ideas, practices and rituals which characterise them have spread far beyond and can now often be observed in more or less free combinations with traditional Christian beliefs and practices. For example, there now exist groups of people who practise what they call "Christian Yoga" and who intend to develop the practice of this physical and spiritual discipline, which is intended to free people of inhibitions and material preoccupations and to teach them self-mastery in order to assist their total development. A certain priest (who has since been condemned by his superiors but has nonetheless remained active) has successfully organised yoga, Zen and divination sessions for priests in his area and proposed to teach them how to 'believe in life'. Elsewhere, regularly practicing Christians meet periodically at a Carmelite monastery for 'positive thinking' sessions where, basing themselves on a medical model, they learn to breathe and to eat more naturally and to relax their bodies. (They did not understand the negative reaction of a priest who found an advertisement for these activities in his church). In another example, a parochial council member organises courses in anthroposophy and initiation into 'life-energy' and a certain group of Christians meets once a week in order to pray and conduct an in-depth psychological discovery of what they call "the seven layers of man". Examples abound. Together they give evidence for the ubiquity and what might be called the 'banality' of the current intermingling of Christian beliefs and practices with other beliefs freely inspired by oriental traditions and other influences, whose intention is to reconcile the material and the spiritual, the body and the spirit, the emotional and the rational, humanity and nature.

Incidentally, it is interesting to observe that the form and content of traditional religious practices and beliefs are also dissolving somewhat. This fact obviously testifies to the progress of religious deregulation and to the powerlessness of the ecclesial authorities to ensure conformity of belief and to contain that belief within doctrinal limits. A very clear example is the conception of life after death. Apart from the clear increase of doubt on this subject ("I don't know if there is anything") often accompanied by hope ("... but I hope that death is not the absolute end"), researchers were surprised to see, in the results of the European Values Study (EVS), that in 1999 about 24% of Europeans believed in reincarnation, clearly expressed by the terms: "I believe that we will be reborn into this world". Italy and Belgium, each with 18%, and Germany with 19% represent the lowest scores in Western Europe, the other percentages being 21% in the Netherlands, 23% in Ireland and in Greece, 24% in Luxemburg, and 29% in France and Portugal.

Apart from these figures, which are surprising in countries with a strong Christian tradition and include people declaring themselves to be Christian, it is particularly interesting to examine exactly what the term 'reincarnation' means to those who say it. It is this question that makes subsequent quantitative research possible. To believe in reincarnation does not mean that the term is understood in its exact, essentially Buddhist, original sense. Most of those asked were ignorant or had only vague ideas as to its meaning. Nevertheless, as Mary emphasises, this kind of appropriation depends on "the symbolic negotiation of two traditions of thought", through which "the substantial re-used or borrowed terms, have not, even in the very essence of the imaginary relationship, lost their differential value, their 'original integrity', even if this last is drawn from an approximate perception".[11] Thus, as these quotations demonstrate, belief in reincarnation clearly expresses two things which freely alter two 'originally integral' aspects of reincarnation and which distance them from the Christian belief in resurrection: by reincarnation, one is permitted with a more or less altered 'physical materiality' to remain on or to return to 'this earth'.

Belief in reincarnation does not solely depend on more or less approximate and vague borrowings from Buddhism. In just as imprecise a manner, it is also nourished by scientific and para-scientific sources, generally based in ecology

11 Mary, *Le défi du syncrétisme*, 483-484.

and its associated philosophy. From this perspective, reincarnation is considered to be a reintegration of the body through the 'general vital force' in which all living beings participate: "thus, I will be re-absorbed into nature; my body will participate again and again in the creation of new lives which will be manifested through different forms".[12] This type of statement is becoming relatively frequent and no doubt partially explains the increasing preference for cremation and the dispersal of the ashes. People who take this view often say that they would prefer cremation to burial, and dispersal of the ashes to their conservation in an urn because, according to them, this accelerates the process of reintegration back into the universal principal of life in a manner which is both more hygienic and more dignified than that of the slow and degrading rot of the buried corpse. Incidentally, God is often associated in such discourse with this principle of life which flows eternally through every living being.

The attraction of oriental religions and philosophies could also be linked to the fact that they seem closer to nature and appear to have more respect for the natural order and to lack any complicity with the Christian Western world's disenchanted materialism.

Scientific reference

A sort of reconciliation also seems to be appearing between beliefs and science. Verlinden has shown that various parallel beliefs have more chances of being followed and combined - 'in all good faith', one might say - with a definition of oneself as a religious or even Christian person, if these beliefs present a scientific image. Thus, she states, "clairvoyance, telepathy, astrology, divination, biorhythms [...] have a higher degree of authenticity than, for example, four-leaved clovers or black cats, because they can be said to use scientific methods [...]: their approaches are difficult, the ideas which underlie them are complex, making them work requires calculations and technical apparatus - just so many elements that contribute to producing an impression of things scientific".[13] Besides the fact that this image brings legitimacy and validity to such beliefs, it allows them to distance themselves both from other cultures, African in particular, and from the past - spaces and times considered to be less developed and therefore prone to superstitions.[14]

12 Voyé, "Religion in Modern Europe".
13 Verlinden, *Het ongewone alledaagse*, 154.
14 Ibidem, 166-167.

One additional point should be emphasised. If the various ways of combining elements of Christianity with practices and beliefs from many other sources are observed in this fashion, the flexible, nomadic character of these compositions becomes evident. Indeed, most people involved in such 'combinations' often multiply their experiences of them, move from one group to another, borrow successively or simultaneously from different sources. This mobility is facilitated by the multiplicity of seminars, fairs, festivals, websites and so on, which provide information and propose meeting-points where experiences can be exchanged, the available possibilities explored and - most importantly - validation for one's heterodoxy can be found in that of others who are also in search of themselves.

Reasons for this Wandering

Several elements seem to explain this phenomenon of wandering which radically opposes not only institutional expectations but also the cold rationality of the eighteenth century, which did indeed make its mark on many areas of collective life, including that of religion, during the first period of modernity.

Secularisation incontestably plays an important role here; I shall not dwell on this except to recall that, as Dobbelaere states[15], it is rooted in functional differentiation and causes the religious representative to lose his former tutelary power as much over other domains as over people. This emancipation was, no doubt, the condition necessary for the present liberation of practices and beliefs of which I have given some illustrations. It was essential that religion and, more specifically, Catholicism, lose its power to impose and inhibit, and that its complicity with other areas be reduced for this wandering of beliefs and practices to be made possible without guilt. It is, therefore, on this basis of secularisation that the latter must be interpreted.

The affirmation of the individual autonomy

One factor seems decisive: the affirmation of the individual as a centre of meaning and of planning and the consequent responsibility to reconstruct the self repeatedly. To paraphrase Luhmann, we have left behind us a normative mode, where life was governed by norms and institutions whose purpose was to reduce potentialities, in favour of a cognitive mode, which calls for

15 Dobbelaere, *Secularization*.

an eternally open apprenticeship and the practice of reflexiveness.[16] I take this later term in Giddens' sense: as a permanent revision of one's manners of being and of thinking in the light of information and fresh knowledge available through communication of all sorts.[17] Thus, the individual is no longer trapped within a definition of himself that is given once and for all, nor in predefined attributed roles: on the contrary, he can increasingly choose who he understands himself to be and define newly-negotiable roles. The importance of finding ways which permit a person to engage in endless self-construction - an endlessness that includes the possibility of multiple compositions and of varied wanderings - can be understood in this way.

Realisation of the self, including emotions and body

Although these ways can always be revised, they are all guided by the quest for the promotion and realisation of the self, as envisaged in all its different dimensions - that is, corporal, emotional and spiritual - which are considered to be closely interrelated. It should be noted that Christianity, and Catholicism in particular, as it has often been taught, is perceived as closed to recognising the importance of the corporal dimension: instead, it is the suffering body which is proposed as a reference. Furthermore, the efforts at rationalisation which the Church has undergone since the 1960s have often led it to disregard emotions in favour of a more intellectual and more consciously attended religion. As I have already mentioned, the transformation of the 'solemn Communion' into a 'profession of faith' is, in this sense, more than simply a change of name: it indicates the intention to strip this religious act of its various profane and festive attributes in order to emphasise the conscious, voluntary engagement that it is meant to express. Of course, such attempts at 'purification' have not fully succeeded - far from it. But they have, no doubt involuntarily, contributed to highlighting those expressions that leave room both for the emotions and for the body and that offer ways which seem able to give preference to expression and harmony. We should not, therefore, be surprised at the relative success in our countries of Buddhism and of everything associated with it, even in quite unorthodox ways. In the more or less undisciplined interpretations of this doctrine, what is constantly retained is the possibility of freeing oneself from all kinds of suffering, thanks to a combination of mental and physical techniques which are intended to lead to a full realisation of the self and of happiness. There is certainly, therefore, a type of

16 Luhmann, *Essays on Self-Reference*.
17 Giddens, *Modernity and Self-Identity*, 20.

elective affinity between these revised versions of Buddhism and the self-construction of human persons today.

This way of valuing the body and the emotions and their vital role in the realisation of the self also allows us to understand the attraction of the various therapies which draw on the psychosomatic realm and are often borrowed from parallel or exotic medicines, para-sciences or techniques such as group dynamics, and even scientific disciplines such as psychology. Where these new religious movements generally pay great attention to health and offer their followers techniques which are meant to assist the maintenance, re-establishment or improvement of their health, Christianity, oriented towards saving the soul in the afterlife, seems not to have such techniques. People's present relationship with themselves strives to satisfy all aspects of this relationship, for body and soul, spirit and emotions, and to allow their significance to emerge through the immediacy of daily life. The search to save the soul proves thus to be doubly unsatisfactory: it appears to ignore the other human dimensions and projects itself into an afterlife perceived as problematic; an inversion of signification can therefore be observed. "In the traditional Christian universe, the theme of healing is regularly associated with the problematic area of salvation [... In some new spheres of influence, particularly charismatic ones,] an inversion of perspective can often be observed: the theme of salvation no longer refers to the culturally devalued expectation of a complete life in another world. Salvation operates as a symbolic reference point which causes the demand for healing to be enlarged and include all aspects of self-realisation."[18]

A holistic view of the world

From this perspective, the health, equilibrium and well-being of the body often take on a larger dimension. Just as some natural catastrophes, everything from floods to contemporary illnesses such as cancer or AIDS, which are often called 'diseases of civilisation', are widely reinterpreted in apocalyptic terms as chastisements sent to punish people for their pretensions and negligence, whereas health and harmony within oneself seem, against this background, like the signs of a recovered equilibrium, not only for the individual, but also, by extension, for the world and for creation itself. To look after one's body, to live and eat healthily while respecting nature - of which the human person is both an intrinsic part and for which he is responsible - would seem to guarantee that a better world can be found. This type of cosmic vision is

18 Hervieu-Léger, "Renouveaux émotionnels contemporains", 242.

commonly found in small, neo-rural Christian groups, but is also present, even if in a less conscious or ideological way, among many individuals, whether Christians or not, who search for health in the holistic sense. Of course, not all the approaches undertaken with the intention of guaranteeing health share the same meaning, but the success of these approaches, amplified and 'vulgarised' by media pressure, is probably founded on the unease caused by a world increasingly perceived as disturbed and menacing. This feeling, in certain cases, turns fully towards a religious understanding, and then the recourse to various psychosomatic therapies can also take on a more or less explicit religious dimension.

Necessary guardianship of nature

In tandem with this concern for a fully developed self, another explanation for these combinations appears to be based on a similar preoccupation. Although confidence in science and in its technological advances seems to be persist, the negative effects, however, create an unease with science's pretension to answer all questions, to explain all mystery. This is becoming increasingly clear. Thus, although the first years of modernity ('the glorious thirties')[19] were devoted to developing humankind's promethean mastery over nature, since the end of the seventies, a new concern for nature can be observed, even if it is still tentative. Ecology's emphasis on humanity's prominent, complex place in nature and on its responsibility for it, and ecology's opinion that humanity should be nature's enlightened guardian, have often naturally led to religious-type questions, supported more or less freely by sacred texts (for example, the Flood, the Plagues of Egypt, the Apocalypse, as well as humanity's mission as the chosen guardian of the created universe). The multiplication of natural catastrophes and threats to the planet have also contributed to the simultaneous development of a feeling of powerlessness to deal with nature's rebellion and an awareness of a force superior to humans which they cannot neglect or scorn. This new vision combines religious, scientific and para-scientific elements, and considers them of equal importance. It is not surprising, therefore, that the individual adheres to beliefs and practices from various sources and combines them in a belief system indifferent to the limits of disciplines and of religions.

19 This expression commonly refers to the years 1945/50-1975/80 which in European countries were characterised by great economic development, a sizable rise in the standard of living and an increasing role of the welfare state.

A culture of risks

The growing unease with nature's increasing rebellion is also based on the modern world emphasis that risk and uncertainty characterise all existence, at every level. Examples are the effects of nature's outraged rebellion, as we have seen; risks from wars using nuclear, chemical and biological weapons, which have ongoing destructive forces; from a type of terrorism that fails to recognise borders, sex or age. Many uncertainties also affect daily life: family break-ups, drugs, unemployment, urban insecurity and disintegration of the familiar elements that once organised life and gave it a rhythm through important rites of passage. This life fit into a certain structure and was ruled by clearly defined norms which gave it a sense (that is to say, both meaning and direction); now, everything has become complicated, subject to debate and to questioning. Stating that the emancipation of the individual is one of its many causes does not to challenge this situation. But it is important to emphasise that if this autonomy brings liberty and responsibility which allow the individual to grow, it also renders him fragile because there is, as yet, no mechanism that can regulate one's relationships with others. The recourse to horoscopes, fortune-tellers and other magicians should also be understood in the context of these increasing causes for uncertainty. Religions which present events as easily resolved and without profound complexity are badly equipped to appease such uncertainty. This also explains the combinations we have mentioned: as former certainties set out by the Church fade away, the individual finds himself condemned to uncertainty and to a constant search for supports.

Incidentally, it is interesting to point out that these combinations are certainly not individual constructions but are very much based on the same logic as the modern 'lifestyle'. In this logic, the individual subscribes to models of living shared by a greater or lesser number of people who function through networks (that is, voluntarily, often at a distance from one another and even virtually) and who find approval for their beliefs and practices through these networks. It is, therefore, no longer the religious institution that gives legitimacy and coherence to these beliefs, but rather the simple observation that others share the same orientation. These 'lifestyles' are mobile and fluid as a rule: individuals can change their lifestyle as often as they like, according to the newly mobile character of an identity which remains constantly open to revision and redefinition.

A religious market

This fluidity has increased because 'the religious market' has been liberalised and is no longer under the control of institutions which formerly had the monopoly. As the affirmation of individuals allows them to make choices in a domain which was formerly closed to choice, two elements have rendered his access to this market much easier.

One of these elements is the importance of the media, in particular of television and the Internet, which broadcast programmes and offer numerous sites respectively, for general information about different spiritual and religious movements. These movements often enhance their credibility in two ways. First, sports or entertainment recount their experiences, or second 'ordinary people' in whom anyone can recognise himself speak. Approval for beliefs and practices is, therefore, no longer required from ecclesial authority, but is sought in the similarity of real experiences whose immanence seems to guarantee the capacity for conviction.

Globalisation

There is another characteristic of contemporary society which also contributes to the various mixtures, particularly those that borrow from other religious traditions: globalisation. Quite apart from its economic dimensions, it also has an important cultural aspect. Today, because of migration, travel and the media, cultures can meet and be directly present to each other. Concerning religious matters in particular, models of thought and of practice which before were unknown outside of their own lands or which could only be theoretically accessed through more or less difficult, scholarly literature, are always accessible. Of course, this often requires some form of alteration/simplification, but each person can nevertheless freely access various references from which he/she is free to create combinations. As much research shows, most people believe that "all religions are equal", that there are good and not so good elements in each religion, and that initially belonging to one religion or another depends solely on the place and time into which one is born.

Conclusion

What can we conclude from all this? Evidently we are observing in Europe various forms of syncretism which, although not radically absent before, were formerly and pejoratively associated with the 'savagery' of Africans or American Indians. The originality of this present type of syncretism is its basis in Christianity and that it operates openly and without any sense of guilt. Apart from this, Western syncretism shares many characteristics identical to those observed by Mary in African societies.

This similarity is one primarily of form, as this syncretism integrates only "decontextualised bits and pieces" from other cultures and sources or from scientific advances. Those involved find themselves in a "relationship of exteriority with a system of meanings, the logic of whose entirety they are thereby incapable of grasping".[20] However, Mary insists that "the cultural heterogeneousness of the sources does not exclude the possibility of [an] original creation" of a coherent system.[21]

This similarity is also one of meaning. Trapped between, on the one hand, the rejection of institutional norms and, on the other, the necessity to construct themselves amidst a confused and helpless modern world, individuals attempt to negotiate their identity and their relationship with themselves, with others and with the world. Thus, as well as reconciling what seems irreconcilable, they must carry out the symbolic task of overcoming contradictions in order to attain a synthesis which makes sense for them in the complex situations they experience. The autonomy imposed upon them forces them to confront this alone, uncertain and as a wanderer. As an anthropologist specialising in Africa said, "When new problems arise that cannot be solved by the old gods, these gods and their religions are abandoned in order to turn to other gods, in the hope that they will be more apt for the emerging questions."

20 Mary, *Le défi du syncrétisme*, 478.
21 Ibidem, 15.

The American Exception? Secularisation and Religion in the United States, 1945-2000

Jon Butler

Historians face a puzzle in assessing American religion after World War II, if not a paradox. In the nation often thought to epitomise the triumph of secularity, religion maintains a presence so extraordinary that it almost defies description as well as analysis. By any measure - statistics on membership, active participation, financial contributions and health, construction of new church buildings and (with the exception of rural America) maintenance of old buildings - religion is as healthy in the United States in 2003 as it has been in almost any other time, including the vaunted Puritan era of seventeenth-century New England. Churches, synagogues, and mosques are prospering. Private spirituality is flourishing. Religion counts in American politics, and it stands at the center of one of the nation's most volatile political issues - whether government should provide "voucher" or tuition subsidies to pay part, if not all, of the costs of a religiously tracked elementary and secondary education. Foreign visitors discover quickly that rumors about popular religiosity in America are true. Americans actually attend religious services regularly, and churches, synagogues, and mosques in every area of the nation (with the possible exception of the Pacific northwest) are jammed, not with foreign tourists but with observant Americans.

Historians and scholars have offered many explanations for the strength of religion in a society where one might have imagined the secular to triumph. But one fact seems particularly important. Pluralism - the presence in America of so many different religions and several versions of the seemingly same religion - has reinforced rather than retarded religious inclinations. Among the denominations, the presence of Protestants seems to have increased Roman Catholic church attendance and loyalty, while Protestants certainly used the Roman Catholic "menace" as a deft recruiting tool from the 1820s well into the 1950s. Indeed, much to the chagrin of many denominational leaders, New Age spirituality, often pursued individually through book purchases from the "New Age" sections of major chain bookstores in America, seldom harms participation in more traditional Christian or Jewish congregations and may even help sustain the traditional religious activity of some otherwise seemingly traditional worshipers.[1]

Nor has secularity - the growth of technology, market economies, urbanisation, suburbanisation, industrialisation, and computerisation - either retarded or suppressed widespread traditional religious commitment among Christians, Jews, or Muslims in the United States since 1945. Like the reputed challenge of "New Age" religion, the forces customarily associated with secularisation have, if anything motivated religious belief, commitment, and activism in America to provide meaning for the secular developments that seem so threatening. In America, religious groups and individuals not only have adapted, but they have adapted successfully to all the major forces of modernisation. Seldom have they been stymied by any or all of them.[2]

Thus the surprise of religion in America since 1945, and indeed, throughout the twentieth century, should be no surprise at all. Religion has inflected every aspect of American life throughout the century. It has helped shape every stage of the life cycle through rites of passage that stretch from birth through marriage and death and that customarily are channeled through religious rites and liturgies. Religion has affected almost every region, although not without regional variation. Southern California and Florida are and have been as "religious" as New York, Massachusetts, Ohio, and Minnesota. Even San Francisco and Seattle, the most secular of America's twentieth-century cities, evidence vigorous religious participation nonetheless, although not at levels found in other American cities. Indeed, the cities themselves, once viewed as American religion's charnel houses, have instead become the beacons of religious faith and practice. Organised religion has prospered, not died, in almost all American cities, and virtually all major denominations are headquartered in America's urban centers, either metropolitan or suburban, not for sheer convenience but because that is where their principal work lies, as well as their principal strength.[3]

1 Thomas, *Revivalism and Cultural Change*; Roof, *Spiritual Marketplace*.

2 Heinze, *Adapting to Abundance*; Idem, "The First Mass Market Rabbi".

3 Dixon, *Failure of Protestantism in New York*; Laidlaw, "Christ and the City"; Idem, "Third Sociological Canvass"; Schauffler, "The Present Condition of New York City"; Spalding, *The Religious Mission of the Irish People*; White, "A City Block in 1896".

But what do we mean by "religion" in the United states after 1945? This is not the place to explicate a new or even old conceptualisation of religion. But it is the place to discuss what so many Americans seem to have understood and experienced as religion since 1945. We can do this by focusing on three changes that occurred in American religion and religious practice between 1945 and 1980.

One change centered on religion and politics, at least politics in a broad sense. This transformation was most powerfully described by the Princeton sociologist Robert Wuthnow in his well known book, *The Restructuring of American Religion: Society and Faith Since World War II*. Wuthnow argued that after World War II, "religion" ceased to be associated primarily with specific denominations, particularly with denominational creeds, and came instead to be associated with broad ethical and political trends generally clustered along familiar "liberal" and "conservative" political lines.[4]

One of Wuthnow's most potent observations is central to understanding the transformation of American religion after World War II. Put simply, after 1945 and down to the present, in the United States it has become far less important to say that one is Roman Catholic or Presbyterian or Lutheran than it has been important to say that one is a "conservative Roman Catholic" or a "liberal Presbyterian" or a "moderate Lutheran". Of course, it could be said that something very similar was true in late sixteenth-century England, when the Puritan movement fissured as it faced such sophisticated and resolute opposition from Elizabeth, dividing in several different political and theological directions. Yet the Elizabethan incident remained relatively self-contained, its potential realised only a half-century later in the English Revolution of the 1640s, while the post-1945 U.S. transformation bespoke a fundamental shift in the way Americans thought about religion and used it in both culture and politics.[5]

This amalgamation of religion with a strongly general sense of politics in the United States after 1945 stemmed from at least two causes. It reflected the breakdown of already weak creedal and denominational foundations among traditional religious denominations. Laypeople in many denominations knew little about church doctrine or theology, largely because most denominations

4 Wuthnow, *The Restructuring of American Religion*; Silk, *Spiritual Politics*.

5 As a measure of the acceptance of Wuthnow's views on American religion after 1945, see the treatment of post World War II American religion in two recent general books on American religious history: Butler, Wacker and Balmer, *Religion in American Life*, and Gaustad and Schmidt, *The Religious History of America*.

did a poor job teaching either or both, despite what surely was the largest Sunday School establishment in the world, at least among Protestants. In a democratic society, Protestant denominations had never successfully democratised the teaching of theology on a mass scale. In addition, many if not all denominations became deeply invested in the American anti-Communist crusade after 1946. They set Christianity against Marxism and took the struggle between east and west as a contest between Christianity and an atheistic, materialistic Marxism, a language Marxists themselves accepted, albeit with reverse values and connotations.[6]

In addition, after 1945 America's Christian denominations imbibed "American civil religion" - a near worship of American culture itself - which the sociologist Will Herberg described in his famous 1955 book, *Protestant-Catholic-Jew: An Essay in American Religious Sociology*. In post World War II America, organised religion tied itself to rudimentary American values, not only including freedom and democracy but also success, problem-solving, and individual betterment, goals also associated with what American historians call "therapeutic religion". This was an old American theme that extended back into the 1890s and produced the "New Thought" movement, Christian Science, and a variety of smaller, less well known religious movements. Of course, this also links back to common Christian and Jewish themes - prayer and supplication in times of need, personal as well as national. Yet where traditional religion placed the fate of individuals and nations in the hands of God, postwar "therapeutic" religion all but guaranteed success if the individual acted properly, wisely, and persistently. The greatest exemplification of this trend, Norman Vincent Peale's 1952 book, *The Power of Positive Thinking*, placed as much emphasis on power as on the positive - and certainly placed little emphasis on thinking. The popular 1950s television program "Life is Worth Living" featuring Roman Catholic Bishop Fulton J. Sheen stressed "coping" far more than Roman Catholic doctrine, a fact that accounted for its popularity but also resentment from Sheen's fellow bishops. Parish and congregational activity among Catholics, Protestants, and Jews alike increasingly emphasised therapeutic elements and also therapy itself, including marriage and sex counseling.[7]

6 Regrettably, there is no substantial study of catechisation in American religion beyond that of studies of the American Sunday School. See Boylan, *Sunday School*; Lankard, *A History of the American Sunday School Curriculum*; Glock and Stark, *Christian Beliefs and Anti-Semitism*.

7 Herberg, *Protestant-Catholic-Jew*; Peale, *The Power of Positive Thinking*; Lynch, *Selling Catholicism*; Massa, *Catholics and American Culture*; Reeves, *America's Bishop*; Sheen, *Peace of Soul*.

Third, in post World War II America, religion persistently informed American politics. In the immediate aftermath of the Second World War, all the major varieties of religion in America identified strongly with stands on the threat of Communism. Roman Catholics, led by New York's Cardinal Francis Spellman, and conservative Protestants, epitomised by the young evangelist Billy Graham, castigated the Soviet Union as the epitome of evil and agent of the apocalypse because it suppressed Christianity and persecuted Christians. Liberal Protestants and Jews stressed the conditions that led to Communist takeovers in eastern Europe and especially China, particularly endemic poverty and maldistribution of land, and vigorously opposed the anti-Communist campaign of the conservative Wisconsin Republican - and Roman Catholic - Senator Joseph McCarthy.[8]

The crusade to achieve civil rights for African-Americans took its strongest roots within America's active post World War II religious communities from the 1950s into the 1970s. The work of the Southern Christian Leadership Conference (SCLC) scarcely could have played a more dramatic and central role. The SCLC mobilised African Americans fearful of violent retaliation for their civil rights activism in the south and combated the often reticent stance by leaders within the principal African-American denominations - African Methodist Episcopal Church, Zion, and the National Baptist Convention. And liberal Protestants, Roman Catholics, and Jews provided critical support that helped suppress the most vicious forms of physical violence used against African-Americans in the south and produced the important legislative victories in the United States Congress that dismantled the Jim Crow legislation passed throughout the south between the 1890s and the 1920s.[9]

The anti-war movement that protested American involvement in the Vietnam conflict proved to have its intellectual and organizational center as firmly within religious institutions as did the American civil rights movement. Certainly, critical support and direction came from obviously secular sources, especially organizations like Students for a Democratic Society (SDS), whose Marxist sympathies sat awkwardly next to religiously motivated anti-war activism. But antiwar protest depended heavily on a distinctly religious leadership, exemplified in the Josephite priest Philip Berrigan and his brother, the Jesuit Daniel Berrigan, in organisations like Clergy and Laymen Concerned, and in major figures ranging from Martin Luther King to the

8 Frady, *Billy Graham*; Miller, *Bishop G. Bromley Oxnam*.

9 Findlay, "Religion and Politics in the Sixties"; Idem, *Church People in the Struggle*; Garrow, *Bearing the Cross*; Fairclough, *To Redeem the Soul of America*.

prominent Jewish theologian Abraham Joshua Heschel. The nation's Roman Catholic bishops expressed deep concern about the enveloping war in 1966, and the United Presbyterian Church and other Protestant denominations followed in the next several years.[10]

The emergence of the "Moral Majority" and what historians term the "Christian Right" in the 1970s only deepened the links between religion and politics in America and moved them in directions substantially different from those created by the civil rights and anti-war movements. The Moral Majority, founded in 1979 by the evangelist Jerry Falwell, was succeeded in the early 1990s by the Christian Coalition, founded by the televangelist Pat Robertson. Historians often have credited the Moral Majority with a critical role in electing George Bush to the American presidency in 1988, just as historians have blamed Bush's failure to court his critical conservative evangelical voters while in office for his reelection loss to Bill Clinton in 1992. In these elections, the Christian Right consistently bemoaned America's moral decay - the elimination of prayers in the public schools through U.S. Supreme Court decisions in the 1950s and 1960, contests with the U.S. Internal Revenue Service over tax exemptions for "Christian" schools, and the general tenor of American social life witnessed in rising divorce, growing sexual freedom, increasing teenage pregnancy, the legitimation of homosexuality and lesbianism, rampant drug use, and the general sordidness of American movies and television programs.[11]

American debate over the abortion issue crystallised the growing polarisation of American religion itself along political lines. The 1973 U.S. Supreme Court decision in Roe v. Wade that legalised abortion unleashed a firestorm of protest and brought together groups previously regarded as doctrinal and creedal opposites. This did not occur immediately, however. The nation's Roman Catholic bishops were the only substantial religious officials to protest Roe v. Wade immediately. The conservative Southern Baptist Convention actually approved the decision because it honored the separation of church and state, meaning that it did not recognise the Roman Catholic position on abortion as U.S. law. But old denominational barriers fell in the next decade. Roman Catholics and politically conservative Protestants and Jews began working together to overturn Roe v. Wade. By the mid-1980s these conserva-

10 Rossinow, *The Politics of Authenticity*; Polner and O'Grady, *Disarmed and Dangerous*; Hall, *Because of Their Faith*; King et al, *Dr. Martin Luther King*.

11 Ammerman, *Bible Believers*; Bruce, *Pray TV*; Idem, *The Rise and Fall of the New Christian Right*; Lienesch, *Redeeming America*; McGirr, *Suburban Warriors*.

tive forces said far more about their agreement on opposition to abortion than they ever said about their doctrinal and creedal differences. The coalescence of these formerly highly antagonist religious groups within the post-1980s anti-abortion "pro-life" movement bore eloquent testimony to Robert Wuthnow's argument that the years after World War II had indeed transformed American religion and, with it, American society and even politics.[12]

Thus, in the very decades when scholars and intellectuals of the 1890s or the early 1900s might have predicted the last gasps of religious allegiance and the triumph of secularisation in the world's most modern society, the decades after World War II brought forth an almost astonishing persistence and even triumph of religion in the United States. After 1945, religion became more important in shaping American values, politics, and life, not less important. The measure is most dramatically conveyed in American presidential politics. From the famous statement by President-elect Dwight D. Eisenhower in December 1952 that "America needs religion, and I don't care what it is" to the "Catholic issue" that dogged the campaign of John F. Kennedy in 1960 to Jimmy Carter's open espousal of evangelically-based liberal politics to the romance between conservative Protestant evangelicals and Ronald Reagan, George Bush, and George W. Bush to Bill Clinton's extraordinary empathy with African-American Christians and religious style, religion has played major roles in the making of the American presidency for fifty years at the very end of the twentieth century.[13]

Suburbanisation accelerated both denominational growth and the increasingly fuzzy but appealing mix of therapeutic faith and religion's engagement with larger cultural patterns. As a result, organised religion won the suburbs, it did not lose them. Suburbs more often linked to church membership and activity than did either cities or rural areas in America. On the surface, this middle class attachment to organised religion might have reinforced the view that religion was epiphenomenal, a secondary byproduct of class itself. Yet not all suburbs were middle class, and organised religions prospered as fully in poor and wealthy suburbs as they did in middle class suburbs. Here, too, the emphasis on services proved as telling as elsewhere. Roman Catholic, Protestants, and Jewish congregations alike provided child care, nursery schools, youth organisations, sports leagues, marriage and sex counseling for

12 Dillon, "Religion and Culture in Tension"; Idem, *Catholic Identity*; Ginsburg, *Contested Lives*; Hankins, *Uneasy in Babylon*.

13 Henry, "'And I Don't Care What It Is'".

adolescents and adults, career seminars, and activities for the elderly, all in addition to tradition worship and religious training.[14]

The sum of all these parts created something simple and important: after 1945 religion increased its ability to shape national life in the United States. This occurred not on the basis of religion's historical legacy in America but as a dynamic part of the present. Of course, historians point to the words of the Puritan governor, John Winthrop, aboard the ship Arbella as the Puritans departed from England for Massachusetts in 1630 as the foundation of this achievement: "We must be knit together in this work as one man, we must entertain each other in brotherly affection. We must delight in each other, make others' conditions our own, rejoice together, mourn together, labor, and suffer together, always shaving before our eyes our commission and community in the work, our community as members of the same body". In fact, "delight" gave way to division, bitterness, even death by hanging in Massachusetts (during the infamous 1692 witch trials), and Puritan New England bears questionable credentials as the source for modern American sentiments about religion as the balm of community.[15]

Instead, religion's centrality to creating and maintaining community in twentieth century America had its own contemporary origins in denominational and lay engagement with the social process. Consider the transformation of religious affection and its growing relevance in America for immigrants from southern Italy arriving from the 1880s into the 1930s. Often, they carried deep antagonism toward the Church from home because of the papacy's opposition to Italian nationalism and Church links to an enforced peasantry in Italy's rural south. But in America - certainly not without struggle - Italian immigrants slowly transformed their relationship with Roman Catholicism.
In Italian Harlem they recreated *festas*, often in the face of recalcitrance from Irish priests and New York's archdiocesan hierarchy, that slowly made the ethnic Italian parish the center of Italian community life in vibrant ways that had not been true in Italy. For these and other immigrants - Poles, German, Irish underwent similar transformations if in different ways - the twentieth-century American experience transformed both their own Catholicism and, subtly, the Roman Catholic Church itself, and it owed nothing to the heritage

14 Diamond, *And I Will Dwell in Their Midst*; Ammerman and Farnsley, eds., *Congregation and Community*; Cohen, "The Orthodox Synagogue"; Conzen, "The Place of Religion"; Hudnut-Beumler, *Looking for God in the Suburbs*; Jackson, *Crabgrass Frontier*; Kelly, *Why Conservative Churches are Growing*; Miller, *Suburb*; Sussman, "The Suburbanization of American Judaism"; Winter, *Suburban Captivity of the Churches*.

15 Winthrop, "Model of Christian Charity".

of religion and community reputedly descending from the Puritans. It is scarcely surprising that long after the old immigration ceased, and well into the third, fourth, and fifth generations between 1945 and 2000, religion and community remained deeply entwined in American ethnic communities despite the reputed progress of secularism in so many other aspects of American life.[16]

The American exception to the expectation for rising secularism in the twentieth-century west proved to be more than merely an assertion of traditional religion in the face of modern challenges. It raises intriguing questions: Did developments in America represent new ways of configuring religion within a changing society, especially a "modernising" society? Is the post-1945 American reconfiguration of religion more elusive, more subtle, and perhaps even quietly subversive of both "religion" and secularity? Do we have in post-1945 America not merely the sacralisation of the secular (or the secularisation of the sacred) but some new kind of relationship between traditional forms of both the sacred and the secular? If so, how can we judge?

One possible difference can be found in the relationship to power. Even the most commanding members of twelfth century European society accepted the exceptional limitations, if not helplessness. But in post-1945 America, where so much religion survives and prospers, power has been everywhere present and religion has been intimately involved in its exercise on a scale that could be said to challenge that of medieval Europe.

In the United States, religions in all forms - Roman Catholicism, Protestantism, Protestant Fundamentalism, Judaism, Islam, Hinduism, and Buddhism, to say nothing of many sectarian groups including Scientology - have all but universally accepted and mastered the relevant forms of power in modern life. The coming and triumph of modern technology, urbanisation, industrialism, suburbanisation, and post-industrialisation all have not only been accepted by America's principal religious groups - not always happily in their earliest encounters - but have subsequently constituted the foundation of organisational entrees into America's modernizing culture. In short, America's organised religious groups have largely accepted a market model of society that assumes the conscious manipulation of political and social power and have adapted it to their own religious purposes, a model adopted among European Christians after 1945 with seemingly less enthusiasm and success.

16 Orsi, *The Madonna of 115th Street*; Vecoli, "Prelates and Peasants"; Di Giovanni, *Michael Augustine Corrigan*.

The result in America is an anomaly. On the surface, the persistence, survival, and success of religion in the United States makes America resemble the so-called "third world" of the Middle East, Africa, parts of Asia (but not much of Japan and China), and Latin America in their support for religion. By comparison, the United States least resembles the Europe from which it traditionally traces its cultural and religious origins.[17]

But what is this "religion" in America? Is it religion as traditionally meant in previous centuries? Certainly, much traditional religion still exists in twenty-first century America. It can be seen in Americans' widespread resort to prayer and worship, in the acceptance of human limitation even as Americans engage technology and world politics, in the persistence of doctrinal and creedal disputes among and within religious groups, and in the resort to divine explanations of inexplicable events, whether accidents or personal tragedy or calamitous national events, such as the attacks on the World Trade Center and the Pentagon of September 11, 2001. Certainly, traditional religion faces immense crises in the United States. Virtually every major Christian group, with the possible exception of conservative evangelical Protestants, faces major crises in furnishing clergy for congregations. Many congregations pay very poor clerical salaries despite all the seeming financial support given to religion, and divinity schools and seminaries report steadily shrinking enrollment. In many Roman Catholic parishes in the United States in 2003, for example, lay men as well as women do much of the work of visiting the sick and elderly that priests formerly performed and which was once understood to be an all but exclusively priestly function.[18]

Yet much of this traditional expression of religion in the United States since 1945 and certainly in 2003 also is indelibly linked with a remarkably comfortable and expected sense of power - the conviction that humans can reshape life and its elemental conditions. This expectation and achievement does not wait on supplication but on human enterprise. In the United States, religion's involvement with politics, conservative or liberal, has openly proved attractive because its subscribers saw it as the foundation for major social and political change. Liberals who sought to bring justice to race relations in the American south in the 1950s and 1960s saw their crusade as an expression of Christian brotherhood. Conservatives who have sought to return prayer to the public schools and place the text of the Ten Commandments in courthouses in the

17 Finke and Stark, *The Churching of America*.

18 On various aspects of the "clerical crisis" in the United States, see Messer, *Send Me?*; Hoge et al, eds., *Money Matters*; Hoge, *The Future of Catholic Leadership*; Schoenherr, Young and Cheng, *Full Pews and Empty Altars*; Schoenherr and Yamane, *Goodbye Father*.

1970s, 1980s, and 1990s sought to return America to its "Christian roots". Each employed fascinating but often mythical evocations of America's religious past to support their cause combination of resort to the seeming religious history of America's past, although they leaned most often on highly charged and very successfully constructed contemporary theological passion, coupled with vivid denunciations of contemporary moral squalor. Throughout, these activists eagerly turned to politics to implement their religious visions, sometimes in blatantly partisan fashion. As a result, America's late twentieth-century political parties have exemplified as much religious division as America's religious groups once evidenced political divisions a century ago in the 1890s. America's religious "liberals", coming from many denominations and extending beyond Roman Catholics and Protestants to Jews as well, cluster within the Democratic party while its religious "conservatives", exhibiting equal denominational breadth, cluster inside the Republican party.[19]

In emphasising broad "values" rather than specific creeds and doctrines, and in stressing religion's capacity to generate power and produce political and cultural change that would guarantee a triumph over life's adversities, as well as one's opponents, religion in post World War II America has fashioned a formidable and perhaps frightening model for the twenty-first century. Whether this American exception constitutes a model others would wisely emulate seems more than an idle question. For better or worse, the lure of the American model in establishing religion's "success" amidst the competition of the secular seems all too obvious. In our modern times, does not "success" speak for itself? Perhaps in the right hands, we might applaud. But when men and women pursue world transformation and eternal life through a fusion of "religion" with modern power in all its technological dexterity, as happened on September 11, 2001, we might wonder whether America's post-1945 religious "success" is a wise model after all.

19 On the use of history in conservative politics, see Reed, *Active Faith*; Thomas and Dobson, *Blinded by Might*.

II
Some Basic Issues in Postwar Church Life

Fundamental Changes in the Social Ethic of the Christian Churches

Johan Verstraeten

The social discourse of churches is not an unhistorical doctrine but "a continuing learning process"[1] which results in a series of texts developed in a permanent dialogue with the secular world, its movements and its theories.[2] An adequate understanding of the fundamental transformations in the social discourse of churches requires, consequently, an examination of the changing social, political and economic realities and their popular as well as scientific interpretations (*Sollicitudo rei socialis* 41). This does not mean that churches are passive actors reacting to historical circumstances and trends in thinking. As living social realities intertwined with the world, they actively participate in processes of change.

In this paper, I will point out how the social teaching of the Catholic Church and partially of the Protestant churches, mainly as represented by the World Council of Churches, have evolved during the last fifty years under the influence of historical circumstances and how these churches have in turn influenced society. The sequence of Catholic Church and Protestant churches does not imply any judgment about which of the two communities has preceded the other in developping ideas. My focus will not be Europe as such, but the broader context of the world churches. This is an unavoidable methodological option since the most important innovations concern problems at a global level such as the disco-very of the Third World and rapid changes in world capitalism.

1 O. von Nell Breuning, as quoted in McCormick, "Laborem Exercens and Social Morality", 228.

2 For an excellent reflection on the role of the social movements see: Mich, *Catholic Social Teaching and Movements*.

The changes in the social ethics of the churches will be described in three steps. The focus will be first on concrete changes in the world which have influenced the social agenda of the churches. In a second reflection these thematic changes will be linked with a reflection on the churches' methodology for the social ethics. Finally some conclusions will be drawn from the perspective of questions such as: "Do the churches respond adequately to the great transformations in the contemporary world, and does their methodology do justice to their potential role as innovators sufficiently?"

The Great Changes in Society which Have Directly Influenced the Social Agenda of the Christian Churches

Apart from secularisation and post-modernity, which are sufficiently analysed by others, several historical events or trends have had a direct impact on the social agenda of the churches: the cold war, the proclamation of the universal declaration of human rights in 1948, the discovery of the 'Third World' which put the themes of development and later of liberation on the political agenda, the neo-liberal reaction and its pro-capitalism debate, the environmental agenda, globalisation, migration and the culture clash between Christianity and Islam.

The cold war and peace politics

The post-war era, particularly in Europe, was dominated by the cold war until 1989. The West's anxiety about the Communist threat found an echo in many official and semi-official peace documents devoted to the arms race, deterrence, ABC weapons and non-violence.[3]

In its reaction to the cold war, the Catholic Church shifted from virulent anticommunism to becoming a proponent of détente and 'Ostpolitik' (although something of its anticommunism continued in the form of a struggle against the Marxist influence on liberation theology, see further). Simultaneously there was also a paradigm shift "from just war theory to praxeology of peace".[4]

3 Only the texts of the popes on the occasion of the yearly peace day from 1968-1986 add up to 246 pages (Pontifical Commission Iustitia et Pax, *Ways of Peace*).

4 Czempiel, "Die Christen und die Auswärtige Politik". See also Van Ouwerkerk, "De moraaltheologische discussie over de moderne oorlog", 121.

The turning point was *Pacem in Terris* (1963), which was as influential by what it said as by what it did not articulate.[5] As response of John XXIII to a new era of detente after the Cuba crisis, this encyclical not only refused to repeat the classical condemnation of "godless Communism", but it also proclaimed that "it no longer makes sense to maintain that war is a fit instrument with which to repair the violence of justice" (*Pacem in Terris* 127). Peace would be from then on a matter of "negotiation and agreement" (*Pacem in Terris* 126).

The Second Vatican Council continued on the same line, but not without a reaffirmation of the right to legitimate defence.

For *Gaudium et spes*, peace was "not merely the absense of war". It had to be defined in positive terms as "an enterprise of justice" which required that "personal well-being is safeguarded" and that "men freely and trustingly share with one another the riches of their inner spirits and their talents". It also required a determination "to respect other men and peoples and their dignity, as well as the studied practice of brotherhood" (*Gaudium et spes* 78).

Gaudium et spes also praised "those who renounce the use of violence in the vindication of their rights [...]", provided that it "can be done without injury to the rights and duties of others or of the community itself" (*Gaudium et spes* 78). Despite this nuance, the statement can be considered as a genuine, official recognition of non-violence as method to resolve conflicts.[6]

The council also condemned, but not unambiguously, counter population warfare with the historical words that: "any act of war aimed (*tendit in*) indiscriminately (*indiscriminatim*) at the destruction of entire cities or extensive areas along with their population is a crime against God and man himself" (*Gaudium et spes* 80). This apparently clear condemnation could have been much stronger, if the original words referring to a real bombing of citizens (*secumfert* or *pertinet ad*) had not been replaced by the more cautious *intendit*. By doing this, the council fathers, under the influence of an American pressure group (The Catholic Association of International Peace[7]), wanted

5 Cf. Nagel and Oberhem, *Dem Frieden Verpflichtet*, 37-40.
6 Coste, *L'Eglise et la paix*, 74-75.
7 Cf. O'Brien, *Morality, Nuclear War and the Schema on the Church in the Modern World*, 6-8 and Dwyer, *An Analysis of Nuclear Warfare in Light of the Traditional Just War Theory*, 162.

to avoid an unambiguous condemnation of the obliteration bombardments during World War II or of the nuclear bombing of Hiroshima and Nagasaki.[8]

All the popes after the Second Vatican Council have in one or other way confirmed the new and positive way of thinking about peace. Paul VI proclaimed development as the new name for peace and Pope John Paul II became one of the strongest opponents of the Gulf War of 1990-1991 against Saddam Hussein.[9]

Not only the popes but also bishops' conferences paid much attention to peace problems, particularly during the early eighties. European bishops' conferences in Germany (first East, then West), France, Hungary, Holland and Belgium wrote peace letters on the occasion of the debate about the new Pershing II and cruise missiles as response to the SS 20 missiles of the Soviets. The Western European letters were, despite their differences, influenced by the drafts of the peace letter of the NCCB, the National Conference of Catholic Bishops in the US (*The Challenge of Peace, God's Promise and Our Response*, final text 1983). This peace letter determined the parameters of the debate, particularly as an attempt to balance or combine the gospel values of non-violence with just war thinking. This diplomatic attitude paved the way towards a cautious, conditional (leading to mutual and progressive disarmament) and temporal acceptance of the nuclear defence system of NATO, or, in the case of the French bishops, with fewer nuances, the French "force de frappe".[10]

The most fundamental development, however, did not emerge from the bishops' peace ethics, but from new forms of peace praxis initiated by new movements. The most striking example is the innovative second track diplomacy of the Sant' Egidio movement which succeeded in ending the almost hopeless civil war in Mozambique.[11]

8 Cf. Glatzel, "Neueste Kirchliche Lehrverkündigung zur Sicherheits und Rüstungsdebatte". According to him there is no doubt that the council fathers made use of a subtile act with double effect reasoning. According to Dubarle and Herr, however, this is not the case (cf. Herr, *Sauver la paix*, 33-65).

9 See Langan, "The Just War Theory after the Gulf War" and also Pope, "You Can't Keep a Good Theory Down".

10 *Gerechtigkeit schafft Frieden* (West Germany) was published on April 27th, 1983, followed by *Vrede en Gerechtigheid* (the Netherlands, May 5th, 1983), *The Challenge of Peace* (USA, May 1983 after previous drafts had been published in June 1982, October 1982 and March 1983), *Ontwapenen voor de vrede* (Belgium, July 19th, 1983), *Gagner la Paix* (France, November 8th, 1983).

11 See Reychler, "Religion and Conflict" and Appleby, *The Ambivalence of the Sacred.*

In the Protestant churches and the World Council of Churches the theme of peace has been almost permanently on the agenda, but it has at times also caused great division among church members and churches.

The first Assembly of the World Council of Churches (Amsterdam 1948) criticised modern warfare as such without considering nuclear and conventional weapons as separate problems.[12] The second WCC general assembly at Evanston adopted a text "urging the prohibition of all weapons of mass destruction under the provision of international inspection and control along with the reduction of all other types of armaments". Simultaneously the text stated that a constructive step towards the restoration of confidence could be "a renunciation of or the use of nuclear weapons or the threat of that use". It also called for safeguards in the further testing of the hydrogen bomb.[13] The third general assembly condemned counter population warfare and indiscriminate use of weapons, and an appeal was made to stop the arms race. New, and preceding the Catholic Church in this regard, was the linking of disarmament and development.[14] Since then the WCC has not ceased to criticise the new nuclear policies (for example the first use option included in the 'flexibility in response' strategy of NATO during the fourth general assembly in 1968 at Uppsala).

During the 1983 debates the Protestant churches in Europe and especially in Germany were quite divided between a balanced and prudential way of thinking (similar to that of the Catholic bishops) and a more radical pacifism. Characteristic of this was the 'Moderamen' of the German Reformed League, which called for a return to a confessing church ('Bekennende Kirche') and the proclamation of the so-called 'status confessionis'. This proclamation means that in exceptional circumstances such as the Barmer Thesen at the time when the Nazi's introduced their laws against the Jews, a decision about political matters coincides with faith. According to the authors of the text, "Peace is a matter of faith. Through it, the status confessionis enters for us because the confession and the denial of the gospel truth are involved in the position on questions of mass-destruction" and "for Christians on the basis of confessing God as creator, reconciler and redeemer, there applies an unconditional no, a no without any yes".[15] For the German Reformed League, faith in Christ

12 Solms, "The World Council of Churches on Disarmament and Peace", 1.

13 Ibidem, 2.

14 Ibidem, 5.

15 Moderamen des reformierten Bundes, *Das Bekenntnis zu Jesus Christus und die Friedensverantwortung der Kirche*, 6.

implied necessarily and immediately a rejection of the new Pershing II and cruise missiles, and Christians who dare to say yes to these innovations put themselves in a 'status separationis', which means that, by accepting nuclear weapons they ipso facto excluded themselves from the church community. Far from being the dominant voice in the Protestant churches, the question of the 'status confessionis' shows how the radicalisation of peace ethics had become a real cause of division among Christians.

The proclamation of the Universal Declaration of Human Rights

The second historical event that influenced the social teachings of the churches was the proclamation of the Universal Declaration of Human Rights in 1948. Since that moment the human rights discourse, combined with a personalistic ethic focussing on human dignity, has gradually become an alternative, or more adequately, a parallel approach to the natural law ethics.

Despite the condemnation of many freedom rights in the nineteenth century, the Catholic Church has gradually adopted the human rights vision of the United Nations. Pius XII sporadically used a human rights terminology in his messages, but, according to Czempiel, he was quite reluctant to acknowledge the universal moral authority of a secular institution such as the United Nations. This distrust disappeared totally during the pontificate of John XXIII whose encyclical *Pacem in Terris* (1963) can be considered as a breakthrough in this regard, although Catholics had to wait for an unambiguous acceptance of the right to religious freedom until the *Constitution on Human Dignity* of the Second Vatican Council which was promulgated soon after.

The hesitation of the Catholic Church with regards to Universal Declaration of Human Rights is quite paradoxical, since the declaration itself is clearly influenced by Catholic thinking, as the use of words such as human family and human dignity indicate. According to Mary Ann Glendon, it was the European Catholic philosopher Jacques Maritain who contributed in a substantial way to the UNESCO draft of the text and who had, moreover, an indirect but constitutive influence on the definitive text of the declaration via the many Latin American diplomats who were familiar with his philosophy.[16] Angelo Roncalli, later Pope John XXIII, discussed human rights related issues as nuntius based in Paris with Réné Cassin, one of the writers of the text of the declaration.[17]

16 Glendon, "The Sources of 'Right Talk'" and Idem, "The Forgotten Crucible".
17 Cf. Ukken, *The contributions of Jacques Maritain to the Universal Declaration of Human Rights*.

Since the sixties the human rights discourse has become fully integrated into Catholic social thinking and moreover theologically radicalised and deepened by John Paul II. In many documents of the European bishops' conferences human rights are the cornerstone of their moral argument on problems such as migration, asylum, refugees, and racism.

Much more than in the Catholic Church, in the Protestant world and especially in the World Council of Churches, the concern for human rights has culminated in the struggle against apartheid and racism. This world wide struggle, partially steered by Holland, has not only mobilised many Christians, but it has also been very efficient. It influenced many secular international institutions such as the United Nations, as well as the corporate world, where the acceptance of the Sullivan principles and the decision of shareholders to threaten the apartheid regime with a total withdrawal of investments from multinationals in South Africa, has ultimately produced sufficient pressure for terminating apartheid and for the release of Nelson Mandela.[18] The struggle against apartheid is one of the most striking examples of the churches' real mobilising force in the economic and political world.

The discovery of the 'Third World'

The third political fact which had a direct influence on the social teachings of the churches was the process of decolonisation, followed by the appearance of the so-called 'Third World' on the international political scene. It resulted in a fundamental shift from churches as guardians of the established order (or the established disorder as Mounier contended), to churches becoming critics of this order and so perceived as a danger to the market economy.

In the beginning of the 1960s, the concern for the poor in the Third World was prudentially framed in terms of 'development'. John XXIII had a quite naive concept of it, since he interpreted development mainly as a sort of export of the Western welfare society (based on Keynesian economic thinking) to poor countries. He neglected the fact that the rise of the Western welfare state was partially based on neo-cololonial trade relations.[19]

The real breakthrough of the church's commitment to the Third World started with the Second Vatican Council. Despite the predominantly liberal and intra-

18 Cf. Sethi and Williams, *Economic Imperatives and Ethical Values in Global Business*.
19 This judgment follows Dorr, *Option for the Poor*.

ecclesial agenda, determined by European and American cardinals and bishops, some Third World bishops, such as Helder Camara from Brazil, gradually gained sufficient influence to put the poor of the Third World on the agenda.[20] It resulted in surprisingly radical standpoints, especially in the chapter of *Gaudium et spes* on economic and social life. This chapter can be considered as the paradigmatic ratification of the shift in Catholic social thinking from an almost 'liberal' private property ethic (cf the use of liberal concepts 'natural' 'sacred' en 'inviolable' with regard to property in *Rerum novarum*) to a relativisation of private property in light of the primacy of the universal destination of goods.[21] This shift was already present in abstract terms in the social ethics of Pius XII, but *Gaudium et spes* gave it real meaning by articulating its concrete implications and by proclaiming in No 67 the right of the poor in extreme necessity to procure what they need out of the riches of others. When more than thirty years later, bishop Muskens from the Netherlands used this text in an interview, saying that in extreme necessity a poor person has the right to steal bread, this was perceived by the Dutch society, minister president Kok included, as an unacceptable negation of the Western work and property ethos. The same sort of radical thinking is expressed in No 71 of *Gaudium et spes* according to which large and extensive rural estates "should be distributed to those who can make these land fruitful". It was applied in Portugal after the Pink Revolution where it was considered and later abolished as too dangerous for the ethic of property. In using a radicalised property ethic, the Church moved from being mainly a defender of the rich, to making an option for the poor.

Very soon after *Gaudium et spes* the language of development became challenged and replaced by a more radical discourse. In *Populorum progressio* of 1967, Paul VI still tried to maintain a prudential and top-down ethics of development in which revolution was excluded on moral grounds (except in extreme cases and even then with a severe caveat, No 31).

But one year later the attitude of the Church changed drastically, particularly in Latin America. During the meetings of Latin American bishops in Medellin in 1968 a new vocabulary was adopted which became the object of a twenty year long controversy in the Catholic Church. From then on the key words were: structural injustice and structural sin, liberation and option for the poor. In Europe this discourse had a real impact on theologians, on all sorts of jour-

20 For a fundamental analysis of this point see Palathinkal, *Goods of the Earth Destined for All*, 245-306.

21 This is clearly demonstrated in Palathinkal, *Goods of the Earth Destined for All*, 245-306.

nals on missiology and mission and even in letters from bishops' conferences, especially the French. But Europe contributed more than a passive reaction: many outstanding liberation theologians had studied in Europe where they became influenced by social sciences and the political theology of Metz and Moltmann.

The language game of liberation was adopted at the level of the universal Church for the first time in 1971 during the general synod of bishops on justice. In the prophetic document *Justice in the World* the bishops wrote that "action on behalf of justice and participation in the transformation of the world" must be considered as a "*constitutive* dimension of the preaching of the gospel" and "of the Church's mission for the redemption of the world, the human race and its *liberation* from every oppressive situation". This text caused serious interpretation problems since the word 'constitutive' was inadequately translated as 'essential' in Dutch and German. *Justice in the world* also created discord between the large majority of bishops who had accepted the document and a small minority of bishops who rejected it as dangerously challenging to both classic theology and the established order.

As a consequence of the controversies, *Justice in the World* became the last final text of a general bishops' synod written and approved by the participating bishops. After the next synod on evangelisation in 1964, Paul VI decided that henceforward the pope (and his ghostwriters), and not the conference of bishops would be responsible for the final text. Hence a more nuanced and less radical 'apostolic exhortation' on evangelisation in 1975 (*Evangelii nuntiandi*) included a clear but conditional acceptance of the liberation discourse.

Later on, when John Paul II became pope, the controversy about liberation and the theologies related to it, continued and provoked sharp conflicts in the Church community, even in Europe, not least because the German cardinal Ratzinger played a key role in this discussion. One of the neuralgic points in this controversy on liberation was the question whether the Marxist 'class struggle' concept could be used as a tool for analysis without having to accept the entire Marxist ideology. The answer from Rome was clearly no, the answer of the community of theologians varied from a clear yes from Christians for socialism, to a nuanced hesitation or rejection by others. The culmination point of the controversy was the publication in 1984 by Cardinal Ratzinger of an official document in which he both acknowledged the longing for liberation and radically condemned all sorts of liberation theology which were according to him flirting with Marxism (*Libertatis nuntius*). This document was followed two years later by a more positive document on the relationship between Christian freedom and liberation (*Libertatis conscientia*, 1986). Last but non least the Catholic Church contributed to the development discussion on the occasion of the Jubilee Year 2000: everywhere reflection and action concerned debt relief.[22]

In the WCC there was a similar development, with a shift from a more conservative European to a more radical Third World perspective. In the beginning, during and since the first general assembly in Amsterdam, the key concept of the WCC social ethics was *responsible society*, a concept that stands "as a symbol of the social arrangement maintaining in dynamic equilibrium freedom and order, liberty and justice".[23] This equilibrium based idea of a responsible society did not refer to an alternative political or social system but, according to the WCC general assembly in Evanston (1954), it was conceived as a criterion to judge "all existing social orders".

During the World Council's meeting in Evanston the first signs of radicalisation appeared in a new descriptive term: *rapid social change*. It refers to countries and situations in which a process of rapid social change takes place. Later on it became a more radical and normative concept under the direct influence of the theology of revolution of that time. The expression 'rapid social change' became the Protestant alternative for the Catholic term liberation. During a special "Church and World" meeting in Geneva (1966), the concept of rapid social change became explicitly connected with a theology of revolution which is "a legitimate claim if one remembers that for centuries theologians have taught nothing but a theology of order and had a vision of an entirely static human universe". And in the same text we can read that "as Christians we are committed to working for the transformation of society. In the past we have usually done this through quiet efforts at social renewal, working in and through established institutions, according to their rules. Today, a significant number of those who are dedicated to the service of Christ and their neighbour assume a more radical or revolutionary position [...] they are searching for a new strategy which brings about changes in society without too much delay. It is possible that the tension between these two positions will have an important place in the life of the Christian commu-

22 Cf. Verstraeten, "Debt Forgiveness, Social Justice and Solidarity". On the occasion of the Jubilee Year the Belgian bishops published *Het jubeljaar 2000*.

23 Duff, *Social Thought of the Worldcouncil of Churches*, 191.

nity for some time to come".[24] This tension has indeed become reality in both the Catholic and the Protestant churches.

Reaction: the pro-capitalism debate

The fourth social fact which influenced the social discourse of the churches was an immediate consequence of the previous discussion. The controversy about liberation generated a crusade against the influence of Marxist thinking, combined with an effort to produce a more free market friendly ideology.

The resistance to liberation theology and its 'Marxist' influences started as a violent political fact. According to John Desroches, a Rockefeller report from 1969 (one year after Medellin) warned president Nixon and the business community about the growing influence of Marxism in Latin American and, if we may believe Desroches, even the bishops' conference of Medellin as well as liberation theology were under suspicion. It is not a mere coincidence that in the following years the "theory of national security" became a language of justification for installing military regimes in several Latin-American countries. Anyone suspected of having communist, Marxist, or socialist ideas was persecuted. Christian basic communities and theologians of liberation were among the suspects. In the decade after 1968 over 850 religious, priests and bishops were jailed, kidnapped, tortured, expelled or even killed. Msgr. Romero and the Jesuits of El Salvador are the examples par excellence. Their martyrdom had an enormous resonance in Europe, as for instance the *doctorate honoris causa* of Archbishop Romero in Leuven, two weeks before his death testifies.

But the violent crusade was only the tip of the iceberg.[25] A more subtle response to the perceived threat by left wing movements and their support by the Church was worked out: scholars hired and paid by the business community started producing texts in favour of a "corporate world friendly" theology. It is amazing how much interest the business community showed in Catholic social thinking. The movement started in America, but had a great influence in Europe. Think tanks and lobbies such as the American Enterprise Institute, the Washington Centre for Public Policy Research and later on the Acton Institute, invested money in the production of a pro-capitalist Catholic theology and social ethics. Symptomatic of this turn was Michael Novak's famous address of to American business leaders in which he urged them to be not only competitive in business, but also in the market of ideas. His book

24 Quoted in Fey, *The Ecumenical Advance*, II, 254-255.
25 Desrochers, *The Social Teaching of the Church*, 315-322.

The Catholic ethic and the spirit of capitalism[26], in which he provided a Catholic alternative for the Weberian interpretation of the Protestant ethic as a moral basis for capitalism, is symptomatic of this endeavour. He contributed so successfully to this new competition, that he even directly influenced *Centesimus annus*, one of Pope John Paul II's most important encyclicals. This was the first official document of the magisterium in which the benefits of the free market and profit were praised. It is however not chapter four which has become most controversial since its approval of the market and of profit remains very conditional. The crucial chapter is the fifth in which the pope radically criticises the European social assistance state. The text has, quite surprisingly, more affinities with and resemblances to the pro-capitalist "lay letter" which was written against the American bishops' letter on justice for all (definite version published in 1986). While the bishops' letter was an exemplar of a clear, partially classical and biblically founded actualisation of Catholic social thinking with a strong communitarian angle[27], the lay letter represented a very American version of Catholic thinking which was congruent with the business community's interests. While the bishops had written their document in dialogue with the most influential Catholic scholars and universities, the lay letter, in which Novak played a crucial role, represented a radically opposite 'new' Catholic version of neo-liberal and more individualistic thinking.[28] After almost hundred years of Church concern for justice, Novak succeeded in inserting his concern for liberal 'freedom' in official Catholic social thinking at the cost of social justice.

In *Centesimus annus* Novak's influence is more than a hypothesis derived from similarities between the encyclical and the lay letter. It is a historical fact that Novak's direct influence on *Centesimus annus* came through Rocco Buttiglione (connected with Comunione e Liberazione), one of the authors who influenced the second, and less Third-World friendly, draft of the encyclical.[29]

A later example of the free-market lobbies' direct influence of is the fact that the Pontifical Council for Justice and Peace published a semi official 'agenda' of the church's social doctrine where one of the co-editors, Robert A. Siricco,

26 Novak, *The Catholic Ethic and the Spirit of Capitalism*.
27 For a fundamental discussion of the history and the content of *Economic Justice for All* (1986) see Verstraeten, ed, *Economie en rechtvaardigheid*.
28 *Toward the Future*. The Lay Commission was led by William Simon and Michael Novak.
29 See Verstraeten and Van Liedekerke, *Naar een samenleving met een menselijk gelaat*.

president of the Acton Institute for the Study of Religion and Liberty, is explicitly mentioned.[30]

The question is whether or to what extent Pope John Paul II really agreed with the turn to capitalism. On the one hand it is clear that he put several caveats about the market in the paragraphs of *Centesimus annus*. On the other hand one cannot deny that the discourse on justice is sometimes overshadowed by a discourse on solidarity. Whether there is a real shift from social justice to social love in his social ethics needs further inquiry[31], particularly from the perspective of the complexity of John Paul II's understanding of solidarity and of his turn to a radical ethic of witness.[32] In Cardinal Ratzinger's second letter on liberation theology (*Libertatis conscientia,* 1986) this shift is manifest.

A most interesting question in this context concerns the role of the new movements or *movimenti*. Are they the carriers of the more market-friendly social ethics, and is this, as Comblin states, a consequence of their sociological positioning in the middle class? Or, do they move in the direction of new alternatives which cannot be simply framed in terms of the old oppositions? The response to this question is not simple and again requires further research. Even without clear results one can already ascertain that some new initiatives do make a difference, such as, for example, "the economy of solidarity" of the Focolare movement which tries to reconnect with the tradition of

30 To characterise the opinions of Father Robert Sirico, we can refer to a text on recent developments in Latin America in *Religion and Liberty*, 13 (2003) 4, 15. The title is: "Latin America Imprisoned in Liberation Theology" (the year 2003!). It starts as follows "Old-style leftist politics is making a huge comeback in Latin America. In Brazil, an avowed socialist and anti-capitalist has taken power in a landslide vote. Luiz Lula da Silva's first day as a president ended with a dinner with Cuba's Fidel Castro (...)". And after also referring to Hugo Chavez, president of Venezuela he writes: "These political leaders' platforms are also fueled by a religious component: a reversion to liberation theology which twists the gospel call to assist the poor in their plight into a redistributionalist political agenda that threatens violence and uses anti-American sentiment to secure political power (...). All of this recalls the heady days of the 1980s when liberation theology was at its height in Latin American Policies. Lead by theologian intellectuals, the liberation theology religious movement allied itself with Soviet-backed political interests to call for revolution against the capitalist classes, etc... This time, redistribution, not revolution, is the watchword..." His solution of the problem is "free trade and openness".

31 Cf. the research project of Jude Njoku, *Examining the Foundations of Solidarity in the Social Encyclicals of John Paul II*. Promoter was the author of this article.

32 For a more detailled account of the solidarity concept of Pope John Paul II see: Verstraeten, "Solidarity and Subsidiarity".

Genovesi, a tradition marginalised by neoclassical economics based on the thought of Adam Smith.[33]

The pro-capitalist turn is not a monopoly only in the Catholic world. The same sort of evolution is clearly present in the Protestant world where some new evangelical movements have become the allies of neoliberal and pro-capitalist thinking. While classical denominations continue to defend either liberation theology or a form of social market economy[34] and have developed a sort of bureaucratic institutionalisation of their concern for justice[35], radical right-wing fundamentalist Protestant groups have become an influential factor in politics, not only in North America, but also in Latin America where the number of Catholics has decreased, and these new groups, also exporting a 'spirit of capitalism', have gained not only members but also influence.

The environmental agenda and globalisation

Since the warnings of the first Club of Rome in the early 1970s and the many publications on issues such as the greenhouse effect and the destruction of the rain forests, the environment has been put continuously on the agenda of the churches, and it has given a new impetus to ecumenical collaboration. The combination of ecumenism and action for the environment was clearly present in the "conciliar process" which was triggered off in 1986 by Carl Friedrich von Weizsäcker during a Kirchentag in Düsseldorf with his famous talk, "Die Zeit drängt" (1986). After the successful European ecumenical meeting in Basel (1989), which received the full support of the Catholic Church, the WCC organised a world convocation on "Justice, Peace and Inte-grity of Creation" (1990). Also during the 1992 world summit on the environment in Rio, both the Catholic and Protestant churches were very active.

From the side of the Catholic Church there are so many texts on the environment that it is hardly possible to summarise them here. Two excellent publications by the Pontifical Council for Justice and Peace can be most helpful here: a theological reflection written by Sr Marjorie Keenan, *Care for Creation. Human Activity and the Environment* (2000) and *From Stockholm to Johannesburg. An Historical Overview of the Concern of the Holy See for the Environment, 1972-2002* (2002).[36]

33 Bruni, "Economy of Communion".
34 Cf. the ecumenical document *Für eine Zukunft in Solidarität und Gerechtigkeit*.
35 Bellah, *The Good Society*, 179-219.
36 Keenan, *Care for Creation* and Idem, *From Stockholm to Johannesburg*.

Later, the ecological agenda became connected to globalisation which has now become a main concern, as is testified by John Paul II in his call for a 'globalisation of solidarity'.[37] The theme of globalisation has become the object of a document of a COMECE commission, the conference of Catholic bishops from EU countries.[38]

The migration agenda

Last but not least the problems of migration, asylum, refugees and multiculturalism have found their way to official church documents. The Pontifical Council for Justice and Peace as well as local bishops' conferences have written documents on this problematic field.[39]

Methodology Shift and its Consequences

Behind changes in the attitude toward particular social problems we can discern a more fundamental change in the methodology of the social teaching. Both in the Catholic and Protestant churches there is a 'conflict of interpretations' between on the one hand an open and realistic approach starting from an analysis based on social sciences and, on the other hand, a more doctrinal theological approach leading to a new self-understanding of the church as a contrast or witness community.

A new method

Catholic social teaching after the war was characterised by a most fundamental shift from a deductive (and Eurocentric) *third way* model towards a more analytic and prudential approach. That this methodological shift became unavoidable demonstrated Marie-Dominique Chenu in his magisterial book, *The Catholic Social Doctrine as Ideology* (1971). Chenu pointed out that the old idea of a particular Catholic socio-political alternative had become impossible. When one starts from the *duplex ordo* of natural law and revelation in order to deduce from it an 'unchanged and unchangeable' Catholic socio-economic harmony model, which pretends to be the third way between

37 Pontifical Council for Justice and Peace, *From Stockholm to Johannesburg*.

38 *Global Governance*.

39 The Pontifical Council for Justice and Peace has published documents on racism (1988) and on the problem of homeless people (1986). A significant document from the bishops is: Comité épiscopal des Migration (France), *Un peuple en devenir*.

Marxism and liberalism, one ends up with an ideology, a false representation of reality. The solidaristic socio-political model, defended as a deduction from God's eternal order, has contributed to a time-bound, highly problematic socio-political model which has served as an ideological instrument for the legitimation of undemocratic or autocratic regimes under such leaders as Mussolini, Franco, Salazar and Dollfuss. We cannot forget that it was Pius XI himself who declared in the period before the Anschluss in Austria that the autocratic regime of Dollfuss was the realisation of the *Quadragesimo Anno* state. After the war, Oswald von Nell Breuning, the ghostwriter of *Quadragesimo Anno*, explicitly distanced himself from the few passages which Pius XI had added to the text, where his attitude vis-à-vis the fascist system in Italy was highly ambiguous.

It is consequently not surprising that after the war and especially after Chenu's intervention, the method of deducing a specific Catholic model of society from the *duplex ordo* has been totally abandoned by the magisterium. Even John Paul II declared in unambiguous terms that the time of the third way was over (*Sollicitudo rei socialis* 41). The deductive method became replaced in *Mater et magistra* (1961) by the 'see judge act' method of the Young Christian Workers Movement, and it was theologically refined by the Second Vatican Council with the expression: "scrutinizing the signs of the times and interpreting them in light of the gospel".

The valorisation of social sciences

One of the immediate consequences of this shift to a more analytic approach was a dialogue with the social sciences and the introduction of some of their concepts, such as that of socialisation in *Mater et magistra*. But as soon as Marxist thinking became an important ingredient of the social sciences (since the sixties), the magisterium of the Catholic Church became very cautious, and particularly distrustful of the class struggle model as an analytic tool. While this distrust was still moderate in *Octogesima adveniens* (1971) with its nuanced approach to socialism and Marxism, it became quite sharp in the teaching of John Paul II. His response to the problem was: less social science, more theology. A fragment of *Centesimus annus* is characteristic: "The human sciences and philosophy are helpful for interpreting man's central place within society and for enabling him to understand himself better as a 'social being'. However, man's true identity is *only* fully revealed to him through *faith*, and it is precisely from faith that the church's social teaching begins (54) [...]

The church's social doctrine [...] belongs to the field of theology and particularly of moral theology (55)".

Before elaborating further on this second shift from social science and analysis to theology, it is necessary to explain one of the reasons why the magisterium became so concerned: the shift had serious consequences for its own authority, although it was Pope Paul VI himself who acknowledged that this was inevitable. In *Octogesima adveniens* No 4 he declared that it is impossible as pope to give a unified message with a solution which - as the text literally says - would be "congruous with all local situations" (*qua solutio, omnibus locus congruens, proponatur*). His response to this problem is clear: It is "up to the Christian communities [a clear reference to the integral ecclesiology of *Lumen Gentium* chapter 2] to scrutinise (*perscrutentur*) with objectivity the situation which is proper to their own country, to shed on it the light of the gospel's unalterable words and to draw principles of reflection (*principia cogitandi*), norms of judgment (*iudicandi normas*) and directives for action (*regulas operandi*) from the social teaching of the Church [...]. It is up to these Christian communities [in other words it is not only the task of the magisterium or of bishops' conferences!], with the help of the Holy Spirit, in communion with the bishops, who hold responsibility and in dialogue with other Christian brethren and all men of good will [ecumenical perspective and open attitude towards secular movements!], to discern (*discernere*) the options and commitments which are called for in order to bring about the social, political and economic changes seen in many cases to be urgently needed".

With this text he gave full-fledged legitimacy to a "top-down bottom-up" approach in which the sapient grassroots experience of people is valorised. But this raised the question: who represents or expresses this thinking? Is it the task of local commissions for justice and peace? In that case one has to resolve the problem of the many tensions between these local commissions and the bishops. (For example: the Flemish document on human rights in the Church, which was translated and spread throughout Europe, was far from being warmly welcomed by the Belgian bishops). The turn to local communities and their analysis engendered a serious "conflict of interpretations".

Together with other sources of discord and division among Catholics, such as the controversy about liberation theology, this caused a real conflict in the Catholic community. It remained unresolved, despite John Paul II's attempt through centralisation and insistence on the unity of the 'doctrine'.

Again a New Approach: Social Ethics as Theology

The preceding remark should not lead to simplistic conclusions, since particularly in the social teaching of Pope John Paul II something new and hopeful appeared: a more narrative and biblical approach, leading to a new self-understanding of the Church as a witnessing community.

When John Paul II talked about 'doctrine' he had not in mind merely a theory, but the articulation of a radical commitment of the Church. "Today", he wrote in *Centesimus annus*, "more than ever the Church is aware that her social message will gain credibility more immediately from the witness of actions than as a result of its internal logic and consistency". And in *Veritatis splendor* he pleaded for a radical ethics of martyrdom. According to him, Christians must be ready, if necessary, to sacrifice their life for the dignity of the life of others. He called it an attitude to which all the members of the Church community are called. Thus, when Pope John Paul II talked about social ethics and solidarity, these were not merely theoretical concepts, but he articulated a commitment to a radical ethics of witness.

This sort of theologisation of the social ethic was not simply a reaction against the contribution of social sciences. It was more an expression of a shift from theory to praxis. In this regard John Paul II was not an anti-modern, but a post-modern thinker whose theology had unintended affinities with the contrast church model or the witness ethics of Protestant thinkers such as Stanley Hauerwas or the Anglican proponents of a new orthodoxy such as Milbank and others.

For Pope John Paul II Catholic social doctrine was more than an interpretation or analysis of facts, more than a critical judgment on society and even more than a prophetic task to condemn social injustices. For him it was also and first and foremost the "proclamation of a new life" expressed in an alternative and radically Christian community life. Something of this new approach was also visible in some texts of the French bishops, which were very much grounded in the gospels.

Concluding Remarks

There is no such thing as a monolithic social teaching of the churches, since this teaching is influenced by post-modern fragmentation and its conflicts of interpretation.

In some regards the social discourse of the churches expresses progressive concerns in line with the basic inspiration of liberation theology. In other regards there are clear attempts to use the churches as hired legitimators of the established order or the market. It would be, however, a mistake to reduce the changes in the social teaching of the churches to merely an opposition between progressive thinkers and conservatives or between left-wing and right-wing movements and theories.

Later developments in the thinking of John Paul II and of many theologians and bishops do not fit into this scheme. The theologisation of Catholic social teaching and the option for the poor leads to a gospel-based, radical witnessing church model, which is not simply a reaction to historical developments in society. The social thinking of other churches is also innovative. They are not only scrutinising the signs of the times, but they do this in light of the gospel, and this leads to "a proclamation of new life". The implications of this turn have been engagingly discussed by the French theologian Henri Jérôme Gagey. According to him the question will be: can the church make a difference and become a dynamic actor which, by being different, contributes to a process of change and humanisation in a complex society?[40] If the church succeeds in becoming an 'avant garde', she will be capable of transcending the old oppositions mentioned in our survey.

40 Unpublished communication during a meeting of the International Association for Catholic Social Thought, Leuven, September 2002.

The Affirmation of Women's Religious Leadership A "Modern" Issue?

Anne-Marie Korte

In the summer of 2001, I attended an international celebration of the Eucharist led by three female priests. These ministers included a Lutheran priest from Sweden, an Anglican priest from England, and an Old-Catholic priest from Germany. All women were in their thirties, feminist theologians and officially ordained. They had created a celebration that was, on the one hand, in line with their respective church orders and with interconfessional agreements, and, on the other hand, expressed the style and content of feminist liturgies. This second aspect meant that, for instance, mutual contact, bodily experience and references to daily life were prominent in the celebration. I was moved by this celebration, not only because of this unique performance of three young female priests, but especially by the efforts they had made to hold on to their different and partly opposing loyalties: the loyalty to their respective bishops and church communities, to women's movements in and outside of the churches, and to the circles of feminist theologians with their often sharp criticism of current church practices. They had confronted an almost impossible mission. The fact that so many churches, the Roman Catholic Church in particular, still oppose the ordination of women, underlined the exceptional status and symbolic meaning of this celebration.

The event I recall here mirrors one of the major changes that have taken place in twentieth century's church history, namely the rise of the religious leadership of women in the traditional Western Christian churches.[1] As it is well known, this phenomenon forms a highly controversial issue within and between many Christian churches. Particularly, in the last quarter of the

1 See a.o. Behr-Sigel and Ware, *The Ordination of Women in the Orthodox Church*; Wessinger, ed, *Religious Institutions and Women's Leadership*; Dowell and Williams, *Bread, Wine and Women*; Field-Bibb, *Women Towards Priesthood*.

twentieth century in Western countries, conflicts in the churches over women's religious leadership have increased and have become more prominent. In the same period, the churches in Western countries have been confronted with a radical decline of adherents, and a substantial loss of public status, political influence and cultural meaning. The relation between these two processes is complex and has been interpreted in different ways. Should we consider the new and contested female leadership in the Christian churches as the result of and even the ultimate sign of modernity, as some have suggested? Does modern culture enter and take over the traditional Christian churches particularly by women's influence and leadership, as others fear? Or is it the other way round, and are women in their new leading roles the ones who will save and renew the Christian heritage as others expect?

In this contribution, I will discuss several ways of perceiving and evaluating the rise of the religious leadership of women in the traditional Western Christian churches in the past two centuries in its relation to processes of emancipation and secularisation.[2] After a general exploration of this subject matter, I will turn to the challenging insights of American sociologist of religion, Marc Chaves, regarding conflicts over ordination and women's emancipation, and I will discuss the well-documented case of the changing position of women in the Dutch Catholic Church to comment on these insights.

Women's Emancipation and Secularisation

In recent years, interest has grown in relating the fate of church and religion in modern times to the changing position of women. The question of if and how women's emancipation contributes to the waning of the institutional Christian churches and to the rise of new forms and styles of religiosity has become a fairly common topic in all kinds of research. The relationship between emancipation and secularisation seems to attract the most interest. An interesting example that I came across forms one of the attempts to explain the large differences within the Western world with respect to the

2 A Dutch version of this paper has been published as Korte, "Erkenning van religieus leiderschap van vrouwen". This paper has its origins in two articles I have written in cooperation with sociologist dr José Sanders, former researcher at the KASKI in the Netherlands. These articles aim to evaluate the changing position of women in the Catholic Church in the Netherlands, in particular women in leading functions and offices, in the context of emancipation processes and gender policy. Cf. Korte and Sanders, "Vrouwen en kerkelijk leiderschap"; Idem, "Mannenbolwerk of vrouwenorganisatie?".

degree of secularisation by using the database of the European Values Survey. The researchers, social scientists from the University of Tilburg in the Netherlands, state that they were surprised by the finding that the 'masculine' or 'feminine' character of a culture seems to be one of the best indications of the degree of secularisation in the various countries of Europe.[3] In a more masculine culture, they argue, structures and concepts of difference and hierarchy, especially between men and women, are emphasised, while in a more feminine culture, for example the Netherlands and the Scandinavian countries, men and women both prefer open, non-hierarchical relationships and put emphasis on equality. Welfare and gender patterns prove to be the most important single variables that point to the degree of secularisation: in a more emancipated culture and highly advanced welfare state, there are less religiously oriented and orthodox people.[4]

An underlying concept in this type of research is the idea, already formulated by Max Weber in the beginning of the twentieth century, that there is a direct relation between women's emancipation, the general loss of traditional Christian faith and the processes of secularisation.[5] As feminist researchers have shown, Weber himself seemed to have been ambivalent towards this

3 In this research project Johan Verweij and Peter Ester have compared religious market variables with indices of modernisation and culture to explain differences in religious mentality and religious activity between sixteen European countries. They have used data from the 1990 European Values Survey. They show that, in general, culture and modernisation are more important than the religious market structure. Although church membership, as they point out, is explained by the religious market structure, the effects are opposed to the expectations. Of the modernisation and cultural indices, development of welfare state and masculinity/femininity appear to be the most relevant characteristics. Of the market variables, level of state regulation is more important than religious pluralism. See Verweij and Ester, "Secularization as an Economic and Cultural Phenomenon".

4 Verweij and Ester explain the functioning of gender patterns as follows: "In "masculine" societies, gender roles are clearly distinct, i.e., men are supposed to be assertive, tough, focused on material success, while women are supposed to be modest, tender, concerned with the quality of life. In "feminine" countries, gender roles overlap. (...) The Judeo-Christian heritage, the basis of the predominant religious tradition in most Western countries, seems best to flourish in a masculine culture. (...) Catholic countries may also be different from Protestant ones in that their religious practice and imagery is more culturally masculine. The Catholic religious domain is clearly marked by boundaries dividing men and women. (...) Countries with a feminine culture may be more secularized than countries with a masculine culture because they are more open for contradictory value systems (including nonbelief) and accept pluryformity as a state of life. In feminine cultures, men and women both prefer open, nonhierarchical relationships and put emphasis on equality. Such a preference is not really compatible with concepts of difference and hierarchy as expressed in some modes of the Christian tradition." Verweij and Ester, "Secularization", 312 and 317. Verwey and Ester do not comment on the exceptional status of the Netherlands that has a comparatively high (62,80) percentage of Catholics and a very low cultural level of 'masculinity'.

5 Weber, *Gesammelte Aufsätze zur Religionssoziologie.*

phenomenon. He supported women's right to achieve emancipation and assumed that women therefore have to abandon the non-rational realm of the private sphere, which cannot guarantee equality or freedom. On the other hand, Weber feared the dehumanising consequences of this development because he considered the private sphere as the space where community ties and values were guarded under the guidance of traditional religion, and such ties and values would no longer be esteemed in modern, rationalised society.[6] A consequence of this ambivalence in Weber's analysis is that advocates, pro as well contra secularisation, have resorted to his approach to interpret the women's position, and that this way of connecting women's emancipation to secularisation has become quite dominant and well known.

It is important to note that Weber's analysis as such depends on a rather dualistic perception of the social position of women and their religious orientation. Only two types of female behaviour are recognised: on the one hand, there is 'woman under religion', the passive keeper of traditional values, and on the other hand, we find the emancipated woman who is actively involved in modern rational society and for whom religion has lost its relevance, namely, the 'free woman beyond religion'.[7] The idea that women's emancipation can also take place in and through mainstream religion (and not only in the contexts of sects and marginal cults, as Weber supposed) or that modern emancipated women might be seriously interested in mainstream and institutionalised religion obviously does not fit into this model. Actual phenomena like the rise of women's religious leadership in the traditional churches and the influx of highly educated and emancipated women in evangelical and charismatic movements, in New Age circles and as new converts to the Catholic Church, cannot be understood by assuming a direct relation between women's emancipation and secularisation.

In this contribution, I will concentrate on the rise of women's religious leadership in the traditional churches and on the questions *if* and *how* this can be related to processes of emancipation and secularisation. An interesting case to start discussing these questions is the view presented by Marc Chaves, who has studied the developments and debates around women's ordination in more than hundred denominations in nineteenth and twentieth century America.[8] First, I will discuss his view, which is rather generalising, and then

6 Bologh, *Love or Greatness*, 196-197.

7 McPhillips, "Modernity, Rationality and the Problem of Women's Religious Agency"; Erickson, *Where Silence Speaks*.

8 Chaves, *Ordaining Women*.

I will turn to a case study, namely of women's actual position in the Catholic Church in the Netherlands, to confront Chaves's findings with a refined analysis of rising female religious leadership in a context of emancipation and secularisation.

Conflicts over Women's Ordination: Modern Culture and Religious Identity

In his book, *Ordaining Women: Culture and Conflict in Religious Organizations*, sociologist of religion, Marc Chaves, states that he was intrigued by the gap existing in many churches between official rules regarding women's ordination and everyday practices. Examples of this divergence can easily be found. The Roman Catholic Church is one of those churches showing great discrepancy between its formal teachings and its actual practices concerning women's religious leadership. During the past three decades, official Roman Catholic teachings on the exclusion of women from the priesthood have been stressed and sharpened while, as several researchers have observed, during this same period women have come to fulfil all kinds of 'priestly' tasks in Catholic parishes in the United States of America, Canada, Australia and Europe.[9] Especially in rural and remote areas, the clergy shortage can be so acute that for pragmatic reasons women are allowed to administer complete Roman Catholic parishes. As sociologist Ruth Wallace has found out, most of the three hundred American parishes without priests are 'pastored' by women. Here women function as priests in almost every sense, including presiding at worship and distributing Communion. They are often called 'pastor' by their parishioners, by male priests, and even by their bishops, despite the fact that this title is formally prohibited to them.[10]

There are also examples showing the reverse side of the gap between rules regarding women's ordination and everyday practices. During the past two centuries, a number of Christian denominations have opened their ministerial functions to women, but this does not mean that women within these denominations have started to occupy these positions or even want to do so. There is also no direct relation between the number of women enrolled in seminaries and theological faculties, and the formal rules of the diverse denominations concerning the ordaining of women. To have a substantial

9 Weaver, *New Catholic Women*; Brotherton, ed, *The Voice of the Turtledove*; Raab, *When Women Become Priests*.

10 Wallace, *They Call Her Pastor*.

percentage of women studying theology does not correspond directly to the possibility of fulfilling a ministerial function, as, again, the situation in the Roman Catholic Church demonstrates. And admitting women to be ordained does not mean that a particular church actually has female students in theology who are preparing themselves for the ministry.[11]

Paradoxical findings like these brought Chaves to write a comprehensive study on the external as well the internal factors that influence the churches' stances towards women's ordination (here defined as the granting of full clergy rights to women). Using quantitative as well as qualitative material, Chaves charted the developments and debates regarding women's ordination in the one hundred largest Christian denominations in the United States. The results of this investigation confirm the observation that formal rules concerning women's ordination are only very loosely connected to the actual position and activities of women in the churches. External pressure, public opinion, and the churches' alliances with other churches have more impact on their policies toward women's ordination than the need to regulate or respond to what women are actually doing inside their own churches.

That does not mean that women did not and cannot influence the churches' stances regarding women's ordination. Chaves' records show that women, organised and individually, have influenced the debates and policies on women's ordination in several ways. Firstly, the broad, secular women's movements of the nineteenth and twentieth centuries have formed a prominent and persistent source of external pressure on denominations in favour of women's ordination. By claiming equal rights for women in all sectors of society, the women's movement has set the agenda that forms the cultural context of the debate over women's ordination. Moreover, many denominations have been direct targets of this movement during its two waves of high mobilisation and activity. The women's movement has also influenced denominations more indirectly by diffusing gender equality as a value among opinion leaders and policy makers in the churches. Furthermore, in the context of this movement, women also have individually operated to seek ordination for themselves and have sometimes been successful in achieving formal access to the ministry. The most recent wave of the women's movement has generated a number of action groups and national, as well as international, organisations advocating women's ordination, who exert constant and inescapable pressure on the churches. And finally, feminist theologians

11 Chaves, *Ordaining Women*, 18-19, 36-37.

have influenced the debate by offering new analyses and arguments on the basis of theological research and gender studies.[12]

However, the official stances of the various churches towards female clergy do not primarily depend on the ambitions or militancy of the women in their own midst. Far more important are other factors like external cultural pressure, interdenominational alliances and the need for the churches to profile their identity towards their cultural environment. Therefore, according to Chaves, formal rules about female clergy are best understood as identity markers. They are a symbolic display that is part of a broader process by which denominations construct their public identities. Attitudes toward women's ordination signal to the world the denominations' location vis-à-vis modern culture, a culture that stresses individual rights and free moral choices and that cherishes a modern ethos for which gender equality is a key symbol. To support gender equality means to support the larger project of modernity; to reject gender equality means to resist that project.[13] For the Catholic Church, to resist gender equality forms the next step in a series of anti-modernist stances that would respectively oppose church-state separation, higher biblical criticism, evolution theory and Marxist social theory.[14] Chaves emphasises that the women's movement itself has played a crucial role in the construction of women's ordination as a symbol for liberal modernity. Before the rise of the nineteenth century women's movement, the ordaining of women was not spoken about in terms of gender equality. In the nineteenth century, the phenomenon of women seeking ordination occurred in the context of religious and social movements like revivalism, temperance and abolition. Women justified their request to be ordained by appealing to a personal and extraordinary call by God. When the women's movement started arguing over women's ordination in terms of gender equality, it offered a completely new interpretation to the practice of women's ordination, linking it to the secular principle of gender equality. In this way, Chaves argues, the women's movement has directly contributed to the rise of the symbolic significance of women's ordination and to its abstraction from whatever practical consequences it may bring to women and men.[15] The thesis that contemporary debates and conflicts over women's ordination primarily mirror identity policies towards modern culture and that they address the women's position only in a very abstract and symbolic way, both is interesting

12 Chaves and Cavendish, "Recent Changes in Women's Ordination Conflicts".
13 Chaves, *Ordaining Women*, 6, 129, 192.
14 Ibidem, 120-127.
15 Ibidem, 182-192.

and attractive. It has explanatory and, at the same time, reassuring power. This interpretation helps one to understand the often contradictory policies and practices regarding the ordination of women in and between the churches. It explains why the resistance towards women's ordination in some churches continues to increase, while at the same gender equality as a norm has received almost general acceptance. It is then understandable why all the hard theological work being done to bring about new scholarly insights to the ordination debate does not seem to make any difference. It is also a thesis capable of reducing tensions surrounding women's ordination, for its central message is that conflicts over women's ordination in the Christian churches are not primarily about women, and do not consist of conflicts between the sexes. So women do not have to take personally their churches' stances toward female clergy and church leaders need not be blamed for trying to save their church's identity vis-à-vis modern, secular culture.

But is not this thesis too convenient? Can and should the highly controversial issue of women's ordination be so easily tamed? Is it true that the fights over female clergy address the women's position only in a very abstract and symbolic way, namely as modern individuals claiming equal rights? To answer these questions I will discuss the recent rise of female religious leadership in the Christian churches in more detail by focussing on a comprehensive, documented case, namely the involvement and growing professional activity of women in the Catholic Church in the Netherlands.

The Professional Influx of Women in the Roman Catholic Church: the Dutch Case

As has already been mentioned, in the Roman Catholic Church, formal rules about female clergy and everyday practices do not correspond. We have seen that since 1976, about the time that the second-wave women's movement became very manifest and militant, the official Roman Catholic teachings on the exclusion of women from the priesthood have been stressed and sharpened, and traditional hierarchical gender divisions have been underlined.[16] Notwithstanding this hard-line policy, during the past three decades there has been a substantial influx of well-educated and often theologically trained women at almost every level of the Catholic

16 See the Vatican declaration *Inter Insigniores* (1976), the encyclical *Mulieris Dignitatem* (1988), the papal letter *Ordinatio Sacerdotalis* (1994) and the apostolic letter *Ad Tuendam Fidem* (1998). See for a critical analysis a.o. Raab, *When Women Become Priests*, 21-55.

Church in Western countries, in functions that are now open to lay persons and that in most cases were formerly fulfilled by ordained men.[17]

The actual situation in the Netherlands forms a telling case in point.[18] In the Netherlands, as in most European countries, women traditionally form the greater part of those who are actively involved in the Roman Catholic Church. They constitute the majority of the regular church attendants and of the volunteers. Since about 1970, women have begun to perform other tasks and functions apart from their more traditional forms of church participation. Around this time, the function of the lay pastoral worker was established and the theological education required for church functions became accessible for lay people, including women. In the Netherlands today, approximately 40% of all officially appointed pastoral workers are women, and in some dioceses there are already more than 50% female pastoral workers.

In the theological faculties and other centres of theological training, more than half of the students are female. By studying theology, often as a supplement to or as a continuation of previous education, many women qualify for church positions that are open to lay persons. Their occupational entrance into the Church is nearly always via a pastoral function, for most women who opt for church functions define their motivation in terms of care and concern for the people they want to serve.[19] But during the past twenty years women have also started to work at executive levels in the national, diocesan and deanery bureaus of the Catholic Church. We now find women also working as canon lawyers, juridical advisors, pastoral advisors, policy officials, diocesan representatives, members of diocesan councils et cetera.

The effect of women's emancipation is the main force behind this professional influx. This becomes clear when we notice that the occupational influx of women, since about 1970, has been an analogous process in many other Christian churches in Western countries, regardless of whether these churches ordain women or not, and regardless of whether these churches have a clergy shortage or not.[20]

17 Brotherton, ed, *The Voice of the Turtledove;* Wallace, *They Call Her Pastor.*

18 See Sanders, *Vrouw en beleid*; Kits, *De pastor is een vrouw*; Oomen-van der Vegt, *Vrouwen in het pastoraal werk.*

19 Wallace, *They Call Her Pastor*, 199; Janssen, *Naar een kerk op twee benen*, 47-73; Oomen-van der Vegt, *Vrouwen in het pastoraal werk*, 75-101; Pieper et al, *Charisma, ambt, professionaliteit*, 11-32; Kits, *De pastor is een vrouw*, 131-149.

20 Brotherton, ed, *The Voice of the Turtledove*; Wallace, *They Call Her Pastor.*

Implications for the Affirmation of Women's Religious Leadership

What are the consequences of this professional influx for the establishing and acknowledging of women's religious leadership? Here I will point to the most interesting results of the investigations in the Dutch case.

The fact that women have entered the pastoral function and now make up 40% of the officially appointed pastoral workers is a very substantial change. This percentage is high enough to cause significant changes within church organisation, for as gender research shows, it takes the presence of at least 30% women to influence the structure and culture of male-dominated organisations.[21] On the other hand, when the influx rises above 30%, another mechanism starts working, as sociologist Paula Nesbitt has shown.
She studied the so-called feminisation of the clergy in American denominations that have come to ordain women. According to Nesbitt, when a great number of women enter the clergy in a relatively short time, a gendered reordering of tasks and functions takes place in order to restore the status and image of the church offices. Functions of higher status and income again become separated and reserved for males. The fact that religious authority in Christian discourse and imagination from early on is shaped after male models has great influence on this process.[22]

We can also find both aspects, change and re-ordering in relation to the rise of women's leadership, in the Dutch case. The great influx of women in pastoral functions has enabled acceptance of women in leading functions by the religious community, by male colleagues, and by women themselves.
Their collective entrance as professionals has made it possible for female pastoral workers to start seeing themselves as religious leaders and to act according to this self-perception, by moving on, for instance, to other leading functions and positions. The occupation of pastoral functions works in this way and is indicated by research showing that almost all women in leading and higher functions in the Catholic Church in the Netherlands are former pastoral workers.[23]

21 See Granovetter, "Threshold Models of Collective Behavior"; Reskin and Roos, *Job Queues, Gender Queues*.

22 Nesbitt, *Feminization of the Clergy in America*; Idem, "Clergy feminization".

23 Kits, *De pastor is een vrouw*, 175.

Interestingly, during the past two decades the Catholic Church in the Netherlands has supported this professional influx of women in its own organisation by several forms of emancipation policies. Committees and executives for women's and gender issues have been installed, and general intentions have been proclaimed to further emancipation aspects and to combat injustice towards women in church and society. In some dioceses, even new functions have been created to make it possible to appoint women in higher church positions.

All of this seems to contradict the official regulations regarding women's position in the church, but we need to recognise that the Roman Catholic Church does not oppose gender equality in general. Since the Second Vatican Council, the Catholic Church has supported the movement for individual rights and gender equality in the secular world, but declared the Church, its own sacred sphere, immune from that movement, at least with respect to the priesthood. Official Catholic opposition to gender equality is "one of limiting its scope rather than resisting it altogether" as Chaves puts it.[24] It will be clear that this dual stance creates constant border conflicts, but it also produces border crossings, as can be seen in this case.

As the more general effects of the professional influx of women show, the Dutch case also displays the second mechanism of the re-ordering of tasks, positions and policy in reaction to the growing presence and activity of women. First of all, the upward mobility of women to higher and policy-making church functions turns out to be very limited and remains substantially behind the percentages of women in leading functions in comparable organisations in the Netherlands. We also see new gender divisions taking shape, in this case between lay men and lay women in leading, policymaking and management functions. For in the higher church positions that do not require ordination, women are hardly represented.[25] Moreover, nearly all of the emancipatory investments of the past two decades have been recently withdrawn, officially for financial reasons, but also probably because the professional influx of women has worn out the argument that women's subordinate position has to be set right. Now that the physical and professional presence of women in the church organisation has become quite normal, emancipation and equal right policies have lost their function as well as their moral appeal.[26] So, now that the further implementation of women's

24 Chaves, *Ordaining Women*, 178-179.

25 See Sanders, *Vrouw en beleid.*

26 See Korte en Sanders, "Mannenbolwerk of vrouwenorganisatie?".

equal participation and the public affirmation of women's religious authority has to start, the process obviously stops.

Concluding Remarks

In summation, studying the professional influx of women in the Catholic Church in the Netherlands has led me to two observations. The first is an affirmation of what we have already seen before in Chaves's analysis: without having formal access to the ministry, women have actually come to fulfil leading and higher functions in the internal organisation of the Catholic Church in the Netherlands. The second observation is even more surprising: the public affirmation of female religious authority keeps on being resisted even though it is official Church policy to promote gender equality within its own organisation.

This brings me to the insight that conflicts over the ordination of women, whatever they may symbolise for the different parties involved, are directly related to real existing conflicts over the public affirmation of women's religious authority. The symbolic meaning of women's ordination is not confined to modern issues of equality and individual rights, but addresses the fundamental problem of how to imagine Divine presence or performance and its authority. The affirmation of women's religious authority supposes equality, but it is essentially much more than that, for it requires, at the same time, the positive recognition of difference. For as the phenomenon of female priests in other episcopal and sacramental churches has already shown, Christian discourse and ritual alter if women, with their own history and corporeality, come to represent Christ.[27]

In conclusion, I do not think that conflicts over women's ordination are best approached by considering them as expressions of the churches' self-positioning towards modern culture. This thesis conveys the impression that the issue of women's ordination should no longer be considered as intrinsically related to gender issues. In my opinion, this forms a delusive point of view, for women's ordination is not only about formal gender equality, that is to say, the affirmation of individual rights. It also concerns the affirmation of female religious authority, a deep and already longstanding problem in

27 See a.o. Methuen, "Women Priests Have Real Presence"; Raab, *When Women Become Priest*; Hopkins, "The 'Other Priest' and the Body of Christ"; Eakins, *Priestess*; Sered, *Priestess, Mother, Sacred Sister*.

Christian history and theology that cannot be reduced to gender equality or to modern preoccupations as such. The question of whether women (can) possess religious authority and what kind of authority they may lay claim to has occurred over and again in Christian history, whether it was is related to female apostles, missionaries, deacons, abbesses, saints, miracle performers, mystics, or to theologians, pastoral workers and ministers. It formed part of a strongly gendered rhetoric of authority that has shaped Christian religious role models from early on.

Therefore, instead of seeing the women's ordination debate primarily as a new version of the modernity debate, it seems to me more interesting and productive to address it as a new version of the much older debate over women's religious leadership and authority.

God has no Favourites
Ecumenism and Interreligious Dialogue: the Unity of God's Creation

Anton Houtepen

Ecumenism at the Crossroads: its Successes and its Recent Crisis

When we speak about tranformations of the churches in the second half of the twentieth century, ecumenism and interreligious encounter seem to be two of the most striking examples.

Ecumenism, "the great new fact of our era" (Visser 't Hooft), has changed church life and societal relations considerably. The increase of mixed marriages, the exchange of liturgical forms and organisational patterns of the churches (e.g. forms of synodality in the Roman Catholic Church, forms of episcopacy in various Reformation churches), a multiplicity of theological dialogues, the osmosis of ideas and scholarly cooperation beyond confessional boundaries: all these have reshaped the idea of confessional identity. Through the ecumenical movement no church tradition has remained the same. Christians have become aware of a 'legitimate diversity' both within and among churches.[1]

We are witnesses to the phenomenon of 'partial identification' or even 'multiple loyalty' of church members: many people are affiliated to diverse confessions during their lifetime, most church members do not fully identify themselves with all aspects of their own tradition ... Christians may adhere to various spiritual movements and modalities within one and the same church or belong to common layers of spirituality across denominational boundaries.

1 Evans, *The Church and the Churches*. The expression 'legitimate diversity' was first used by Pope John Paul II in his encyclical *Ut unum sint* § 50 (1995) and, in contrast to 'illegitimate diversity', the rich variety of traditions and historical contexts was seen as 'integral to communion' by the World Council of Churches' VIIth Assembly in Canberra 1991: Kinnamon, ed, *Signs of the Spirit*, 173.

Important theological agreements on core questions of Christian confession were reached. Despite our divisions we share 'the faith of the church through the ages' as a "Treasure in Earthen Vessels".[2] The convergence text on "Baptism, Eucharist, and Ministry" (Lima 1982) documented major agreement on the Christian sacraments and the structures of the church. The common explication of the Nicene Creed, presented to the churches in *Confessing the One Faith* (Budapest 1989), has laid the basis for ecumenical catechesis on the fundamentals of the faith. The ecumenical movement has rediscovered the servant position of the Church in Vatican II's constitution *Gaudium et Spes* and in the Faith and Order Study *Church and World*, received in 1993 in Santiago de Compostela, followed by the studies on "Ecclesiology and Ethics" (1994-1997)[3], received by the Harare Assembly 1998. The World Council of Churches has given a strong lead to common witness against racism, oppression, militarism, economic injustice and ecological exploitation. Over the past thirty years a network of bilateral dialogues of the Christian World Communions has produced more than 1500 pages of international theological agreements between different church traditions, especially on soteriology, ecclesiology, sacraments and ministry.[4] Far reaching agreements on episcopacy between Lutherans and Anglicans in Germany, the Scandinavian Countries, the USA and France (the Meissen, Reuilly, Porvoo and ELCA Agreements on Episcopè 1993-1999)[5] have accessed an important ecumenical 'inner market' in Europe and the USA. The very important "Joint Declaration on the Doctrine of Justification" (1999) between the Lutheran churches worldwide and the Roman Catholic Church marks a decisive step towards reconciliation. If such a document could have been prepared before the Tridentine Council, it would probably have prevented the split of Christianity in the West at the beginning of the 16th century. Local and regional Councils of churches have fostered pastoral cooperation in matters of catechesis, diaconal service and prophetic witness to society. So we may say that we Christians share a real, yet still imperfect but growing *communion* or *koinonia*.

These encouraging results of the Ecumenical Movement, however, were overshadowed and absorbed by two factors of regression: first by the hesitations of church leaders to really receive the agreements reached between theologians and to draw the consequences thereof for church life by a mutual recognition of churches, their members and ministers, second by the general

2 Thus the title of a Faith and Order Report on issues of hermeneutics.
3 Best and Robra, eds, *Ecclesiology and Ethics*, 2-91 (Reports from the Study Process).
4 Meyer and Vischer, eds, *Growth in Agreement*; Gros, Meyer and Rusch, eds, *Growth in Agreement II*.
5 *The Meissen Common Statement*; *The Porvoo Common Statement*; *Called to Common Mission*.

societal climate of globalisation, pluralism, secularisation and post-modern thinking on differences and syncretism (*bricolage*). A general criticism of the 'hegemony of tradition' has come to the fore, especially in contextual theologies from the Third World and in feminist theology.[6] This trend, though an understandable reaction against prevailing patriarchal and colonial domination, is inclined to deconstruct the very idea of a common Christian tradition, implying a shared faith, 'confessed in all times and at all places and by everyone' (*quod semper et ubique et ab omnibus creditum est*, Vincent of Lérins). Why, then, try to reach consensus of traditions, when everything in tradition is a matter of ever-changing cultural construction? When we no longer have any criteria to judge the insights and expression-forms of the sovereign other precisely as other? Moreover, why should we foster formal dialogues between churches and confessional traditions, when formal church adherence seems to decrease in favour of *informal religion* and 'religious shopping', new religious movements and all kinds of independent or 'newly emergent' churches?[7] According to the recent edition of David Barrett's *World Christian Encyclopedia*, nearly half of affiliated Christians belong to such informal religious groups like charismatic, pentecostal or evangelical communities, scarcely committed to any ecumenical endeavour or even opposing it. The crisis within the World Council of Churches, brought into the open by the criticisms of the Orthodox member churches on the apparent loss of tradition in Western Christianity[8], is only one sign of this ecumenical *aporia*.

Karl Rahner[9] once labelled this global cultural situation one of 'epistemological tolerance': none of us is able anymore to cope with the whole historical richness of tradition. Konrad Raiser, at the WCC's Assembly in Harare 1998 and in his recent book *For a Culture of Life*, speaks positively of an ecumenical space for the churches to transform a culture of globalisation and violence into a culture of life. Because cultures differ so much, intercultural communication between them becomes the special task of the ecumenical movement. Robert Schreiter would even call this culture of local diversity within the worldwide web of global communication and a global exchange of material and cultural goods *A New Catholicity*. Would, thus, the conclusion be: Let us be happy with our diversity and let us hail together ecumenism as 'reconciled diversity', good relations and peaceful communication?

6 Pranger, *Redeeming Tradition*.
7 Cf. Houtepen, "Hermeneutics, Mission and Ecumenism".
8 Cf. Idem, "Evangelisation and Ecumenism".
9 Rahner and Fries, *Einheit der Kirche*.

Interreligious Dialogue: its Failures and its Hopes

One factor seems to be easily overlooked in these positive evaluations of the increased flow of ideas and products on the global market: that is the lasting divisions among the world's living faiths, responsible, as Huntington has contended, for much of "the clash of civilizations"[10] which he foresaw in 1991 for the beginning of the 21th century. His vision, we may say after the tragic events of 11 September 2001, was highly prophetic. Is it true that Christianity and its 'ecumenical space' or 'catholicity' would have the potential to tranform the violent aspects of our globalising culture and multi-cultural cohabitation into a 'culture of life'. I would argue that such a role and responsibility would imply a much more intensive interreligious dialogue and a realistic program to implement the beautiful ideas of the Second Vatican Council expressed in the declaration on the Non-Christian religions *Nostra Aetate*, the dogmatic constitution on the Church *Lumen Gentium* and the decree on the Missionary activity of the church *Ad Gentes*. To quote just one passage from these texts: "The Catholic Church does not reject anything of what is true and holy in other religions. With sincere respect she considers certain rules of conduct and commandments, prescripts and doctrines which, however different in many regards from what she herself teaches and follows, not seldom mirror a ray of that '*truth which enlightens all people*'. She herself, however, proclaims and must do so incessantly the Christ, who is 'the way, the truth and life' (John 14,6), in whom people may find the fullness of religious life and in whom God has reconciled everything to Himself (*Nostra Aetate* § 2)."

How can the Catholic respect for the truth enlightening all people, and the Christian message of God's reconciliation with all of creation in Christ be brought together in concrete forms of conversation, cooperation and common celebration of the unity of creation and the dignity of human life?

Parallel to inner-Christian confessional dialogue, interreligious dialogue did bear fruits after World War II especially: first in the dialogue between Judaism and Christianity after the tragedy of the Holocaust, then, from the Second Vatican Council onwards, in the dialogue with Islam and the Asian religions, and after the Nairobi Assembly of the WCC 1975 also with aboriginal or traditional religions in Africa, Australia, Latin America and Canada. Three special synods of bishops held for Africa, Asia and the two Americas under the Pontificate of John Paul II have promoted these dialogues, as did John Paul II

10 Huntington, *The Clash of Civilizations*.

himself during his frequent visits to Christian churches in all continents.[11] The Roman Catholic Secretariat for the Dialogue with Non-Christians and for the Dialogue with Non-believers, together with the Secretariat (now Pontifical Council) for Promoting Christian Unity, has given a firm and open lead to this dialogue. This interreligious dialogue was both an exchange on the level of ideas and a conversation on the level of daily life about practical issues of tolerance, freedom of religion, human rights, economic solidarity and peace. The increased migration from Asian and African countries to Europe has changed the religious habitat of people, most of all in the urban centres. In many cities of Europe Turks, Moroccans and Algerians form large minorities, whose children dominate schools, sportsclubs and other areas of city life. The prognosis of the Social Cultural Planning Office in the Netherlands for the year 2020 is that there will be a 7% Muslim population in the country, equal to the number of Protestants and scarcely less than Roman Catholics (10%).[12] Though Christians and Muslims together will form only a minority of believers - about one quarter of the population -, tensions between them will increase. These will be caused by cultural differences, opposing views on human rights and on the rights of women, economic rivalry, general prejudice and international political suspicion, caused by terrorism and fundamentalist threats.

A multicultural society, hailed by some politicians and firmly rejected by others, has become a matter of fact in daily life, where most of people configure their own lifestyle by borrowing elements from foreign cultures: combining Japanese fish with Belgian beer and Italian pasta, playing Gregorian chant while chatting with an African or Indian friend. The actual coexistence of different religious communities in most cities of the world must be the starting point, therefore, of interreligious dialogue and conversation at the local level.

11 For a survey of these texts, see: Houtepen, "From Freedom of Religion Towards Really Free Religion".

12 Sociaal en Cultureel Planbureau, *Sociaal en Cultureel Rapport 2000.*

Positive Theological Markers of the 'Unitive Pluralism' of Religions

Starting point for such a dialogue must be, of course, the respect for the diverse and long-standing religious traditions and cultures of the other living faiths. Exclusivism and proselytism preclude every real dialogue and violate the human right of freedom of religion. Since the Second Vatican Council the old Christian adage *extra ecclesiam nulla salus* was left behind or was at least seriously reinterpreted.[13] A '*theologia religionum*' developed which was based on such general theological markers as 'anonymous Christianity' (K. Rahner)[14], 'the cosmic Christ' (R. Panikkar)[15] and 'Christ-centered syncretism' (M.M. Thomas)[16], the unity of God's creation (W. Pannenberg)[17], a 'universal *Welt-ethos*' (H. Küng)[18] or 'Konvivenz' (Th. Sundermeier)[19].

Not unlike interconfessional dialogue, however, this field of interreligious dialogue is also threatened by absorption by a general plea for epistemological pluralism, the critique of institutionalised religion, and the shift of attention in both cultural anthropology and the general study of religions to religion as a cultural construction of reality.[20] We therefore need a much more specific theology of religions than we have articulated thus far in abstract terms of exclusivism, inclusivism, parallelism or pluralism.[21] We need a basic debate on anthropological and hermeneutical starting points, on historical prejudices and on enemy-imaging, as was needed at the beginning of the ecumenical movement. The declaration *Dominus Jesus* of September 2000, condemning both exclusivism and pluralism, did not really deal with such specific aspects of real-life conversation with people of other faiths, and especially not with the problems of the 'Abrahamitic Ecumenism' between Jews, Christians and Muslims.[22] In her survey of interreligious dialogue thus far,

13 See Sullivan, *Salvation Outsude the Church?*

14 Rahner, "Christianity and the Non-Christian"; Idem, "Anonymous Christianity and the Missionary Task of the Church; Idem, "Observations on the Problem of the 'Anonymous Christian'".

15 Panikkar, *The Unknown Christ of Hinduism*; Idem, *The Cosmotheandric Experience*.

16 Thomas, *The Acknowledged Christ of the Indian renaissance*; Idem, "Jesus Christ Frees and Unites", 306; Idem, "Christ-Centered Syncretism"; Idem, "Modern Man and the New Humanity in Christ".

17 Pannenberg, "Die Wirklichkeit Gottes und der Götter in der Erfahrung der Religionen".

18 Küng, *Projekt Weltethos*.

19 Sundermeier, *Den Fremden wahrnehmen*; Idem, *Den Fremden verstehen*.

20 Cf. Geertz, *The Interpretation of Cultures*; Pranger, *Redeeming Tradition*.

21 Cf. Knitter, *No Other Name?*

22 Kuschel, *Streit um Abraham*.

Jutta Sperber concludes that such a dialogue on the real neuralgic points that divide us has not yet taken place.[23]

Abrahamitic Ecumenism: its 'Skandala' and Perspectives

Within 'Abrahamitic Ecumenism' - to which I would like to limit my reflections in this article, because it is the most common context of the European Churches -conversation should be foremost on the mutual neuralgic points or 'skandala' of history, of which I mention three: (1) the refusal to pray together and to adore the same God - YHWH-Abba - Allah; (2) the prejudices and misunderstandings with regard to Christologies and the inner-Christian quarrels about it, especially with regard to the theologies of incarnation, the salvific meaning of Jesus' crucifixion and the docetic interpretations of it, both in early Christian and in general Muslim thinking; and (3), perhaps the most important of all, the use and misuse of power and violence in all three religions where they became dominant and foster their beliefs and lifestyles with the sanctions of public law (*societas christiana, sharia*, the state of Israel).

The challenge of common prayer: the unity of creation and the praise of the Creator and Father of all people

Both the Jewish and Christian Scriptures as well as the Koran, though in several instances favourable to exclusivist ideas like election, predestination, forced conversion and holy war, testify to the final mercy of God, who does not sanction human greed or prejudice, chosenness or exclusion. Because all are created in the image and likeness of God, God has no favourites (Acts 10,34; Rom 2,11; Gal 2,16; Kol 3,25; 1 Petr 1,17; Koran 2, 136). God wants to be adored by all: God has 'put his eye in the hearts of men' (Sirach 17,8). He has enthroned Adam as his prophet and messenger: *rasul* and *khalif*. God wants 'a house of prayer for all peoples and nations' (Is 56,7; Mk 11,15-18). The credibility of Abrahamitic monotheism depends, indeed, on the will of all believers to submit (= *islam*) to the one God, Creator and Father of all and to respect the prophets and apostles who were his messengers in history sucessively. Until the end of times Moses, Jesus and Mohammed will be in a salvific and peaceful competition, even if in this terrestrial situation Jews will opt for the unique position of Moses as giving us the Torah, Christians for the unique gift of

23 Sperber, *Christians and Muslims*, 95.

Jesus, who gave himself for the life of all on the cross and Muslims for God's messenger Mohammed, who completed the revelations to and the covenant with all true believers since Abraham or even since the prophet Adam.[24]
At the same time, however, religious pluralism and interaction in an agnostic culture like ours should be aware of its common but precarious responsibility for the adoration of the one Creator and Father of all life. We cannot afford to pray against one another. We should stop banishing the other followers of Abraham from our churches, mosques and synagogues or forcing them into our own religious community. There should be no hindrance to love and intermariage. We should not be afraid from sharing our economic and civil resources when others seek refuge from persecution or from poverty. Synagogues, churches and mosques have shared the skyline of beautiful European cities like Granada, Serajevo, Mostar, Istanbul for centuries. Why, then, complain about a similar phenomenon which begins to mark the urban atmosphere of Antwerp, Brussels, Rotterdam and Amsterdam? In many of these cities we now find active Councils of Religions beside Councils of Churches, Councils of Mosques (fostering inner-islam ecumenism between e.g. Turks, Moroccans, Shi'ites and Sunnites) and Councils of Jews. In many cases it is the Christian churches that took initiative in this, but it stimulated a climate of trust among the diverse religious communities, which demands further forms of spiritual sharing. Common prayer would underline the unity (*tawhid*) of God and the obedience (*islam*) of his creatures. Was it not Jesus himself who wanted the temple in Jerusalem to be "a house of prayer for all peoples"?[25] And does not the Koran itself criticise our quarrels about common prayer, saying: "Do you quarrel with us about God, though he is our Lord and your Lord? (Koran 2, 140 cf 29,46) ... Wherever you are, Allah will bring you together (Koran 2, 149) … It is no virtue, whether you direct your faces to the East or to the West. True virtue is in him who believes in Allah, in the Last Day, in the angels, the Book and the prophets and who shares out of love for God his possessions with his family, with orphans, with the poor, the travellers, the beggars and for the redemption of slaves. He who is faithful in praying and in paying the taxes for the religious community (Koran 2, 178). Your God is One, there is no God except God, the Merciful, the One full of Grace."

24 Cf. Steenbrink, *Adam redivivus*.

25 The story of Jesus' cleansing of the temple has a central place in both the synoptic gospels and in John, who has put it at the very beginning of Jesus' public life (John 2,13-16), referring to his 'zeal for the house of God' (Ps 69,10) as the main cause of his passion and rejection, like that of the psalmist. The synoptics allude to Is 56,1-7, where it is said that pagan eunuchs and foreigners will be admitted to the temple for prayer and sacrifice. Mark especially stresses Is 56,7: "... for my house will be called a house of prayer for all the peoples".

This common Abrahamitic monotheism is under attack in a society which hails 'the return of the gods'. It uses the idea of God as a mere metaphor for human passion or instrumentalises it in a magical way for the economy of our fears and desires. The one God, worthy to be adored by Jews, Christians and Muslims alike, is the Creator and Carrier of an economy of salvation, which transcends all human will to control, to calculate and to plan. Our Scriptures refer to this Creator with many images and metaphors: the Word of YHWH, the kingdom of heaven, the will of Allah. We may call this economy the promised land, the new earth or paradise, but none of these can ever be identified with the final purpose of God, who is 'beyond any category', 'hors categorie', and therefore unique, *monos,* the only One, without any rivals, being nobody's property. God does not know of any *prosopolèmpsia*: God has no favourites. His covenant is a universal covenant, without exceptions and without any privileges.[26] This Abrahamitic monotheism also excludes any form of metaphysical dualism: God has no powerful enemies with whom He must compete. He is not one pole in a field of polarities, like that of good and evil, light and darkness, the sacred and the profane, the public and the private, the spirit and the body or we and the other. God is the one Creator of everything that we experience as either good or bad, the familiar and the alien, the particular and the universal. The final judgment thereof is only His.[27] This unity of God creates peace and equality in humanity, it provides for equal chances in the economy of salvation and for shared responsibilities. Any competition or strife about God is alien to monotheism.

26 Pannenberg, *Systematische Theologie*, 133-206 (esp. 143-150). Pannenberg stresses the fact that monotheism looses its credibility when it starts to proclaim, that the one God of other monotheisms is not the one true God of our own community. The claim that 'our God' is the one and universal God implies that it cannot be a tribal or particular God of one group exclusively. Christianity started precisely by the claim that the God of Israel, YHWH, is also the God of the Gentiles. With regard to Islam it cannot be otherwise. Even if Jewish, Christian or Muslim believers could not fully agree on their ideas, concepts and images of God, they still share the covenantal promises and the blessings of Abraham, expressing God's own love for all who confess God as the Creator of the Universe, the Guide, the Shepherd and the merciful Judge of all believers.

27 Both within Judaism and in Christianity and Islam dualistic ideas have crept in from Persian sources and have been retained in religious imagery over the centuries: satan (*sjetan, iblis*) and all kinds of demons, angels and spirits (*djinn*) populate the symbolical universe of monotheistic believers. Finally they have to submit to the one God, who creates both the good and the evil things (Is 45,7), but meanwhile these ideas suggest a kind of permanent competition between God and the forces of evil. Is 45 is a hymn of praise to the one God, unrivalled: 'there is no other God besides me', which is very similar to the Islamic confession of the oneness of Allah in Surah 2.

A second skandalon: our Christological quarrels

Throughout the centuries Christians have reproached both Jews and Muslims for not recognising and honouring the figure of Jesus as God's final envoy[28], denying him such messianic dignity as expressed by the titles of Son of God, Son of Man, Servant of the Lord etc. Both Jews and Muslims argue, however, that we Christians ourselves are hopelessly divided on the sign of Isa (Koran 19,36-37; 21,93; 23,53; 43,64-65): about his origin, about the policy of God which he proclaimed, about the meaning of his death and resurrection and about his final coming and judgment at the end of time. This division in our Christological and soteriological interpretation of the event of Jesus implies a deep confusion among us about God's own being-with-us. The early church dogma of the mystery of God's threefold presence with us in creation, in the history of his Word and his Spirit and in the life and death of his servant and messenger Jesus of Nazareth, was for Muhammad and most Jews the big *skandalon* throughout the centuries. But did we take our own *aporias* in this field seriously enough? Do we realise how many schisms we have caused or at least tolerated in defending one or the other of the human articulations of this mystery of God's presence with us? Why can we not take seriously the protests and questions of Judaism and Islam against trinitarian and Christological models which seem to violate the absolute unity and sovereignty of God? Would not the internal ecumenical Christian debate e.g. on the economic Trinity or on the biblical parallelism of Jesus' incarnation and resurrection clarify historical Jewish and Muslim misunderstandings, as if Christians would think about God, Jesus and the Holy Spirit in terms of a divine family? And of God generating a Son from the Virgin Mary in some miraculous but still anthropomorphically procreative way? Jews and Muslims could learn from such dialogue that Christians do not simply identify Jesus and God, and Christians would understand why the Koran stresses so much that Jesus himself, as well as his mother Mary, glorify God in an unambiguous way, never claiming divine honour for themselves (Koran 5,17; 5,72; 5,116; 9,30).

Apparently we Christians, in formulating our Christologies and soteriologies, have not succeeded in safeguarding the unity and uniqueness of God, which was the core of Jesus' own faith, and in making this faith clear to Jews and Muslims. From recent exegetical and historical studies about the 'Christologies' of the New Testament and the Early Church[29], we have learned, that the

28 Cf. De Jonge, *God's Final Envoy*.

29 E.g. Hahn, *The Titles of Jesus in Christology*; Moule, *The Origin of Christology*; Schillebeeckx, *Jesus: An Experiment in Christology*; Dunn, *Christology in the Making*; Vermès, *Jesus and the World of Judaism*; Sanders, *The Historical Figure of Jesus*; Schnackenburg, *Jesus in the Gospels.*

early Christian communities could only formulate their vision of the Christ-Event within the framework of Jewish thinking. They could only believe in Jesus as God's final servant, prophet and envoy, who announced the coming of the kingdom of God, who wanted to do the will of God and who identified himself throughout his life and death with a mission given to him by God, whom he called Father. In his divine mission, he was replenished by the Spirit or *ruach* of God and he faithfully served the cause of God. He related to God as the heir and the Son, preaching the Word of God and doing the works of God in signs and miracles. Early Christology glorified, in a highly *theocentric* way, the one God and Father of all creation and derived the mission of Christ outside the borders of Israel from his unity with the one Creator of all humankind. The gospel of John, especially, proclaims the divine *logos*-character of the person and work of Jesus, *sent* by God into the things of God and sending his disciples into the world of the nations in the name of God, Father and Spirit as well as in his own name, the Son of God, representing the one God of all peoples from the beginning of creation. He represents the invisible God and is the perfect *icon* of God, but nowhere he is replacing God or just identical with God: he praises and glorifies God, he prays towards God and surrenders his life and spirit to God: he is in intimate relationship with God, but he is no 'second God' or a 'substitute' for God. All of this might be clarified in Christian-Jewish-Muslim trialogue, comparing the authentic Christological sayings of the Koran and of the Gospels. It would then become clear that the Koran teaches a rather 'high' Christology of Jesus as God's envoy (*rasul*) who is overshadowed by the Word and the Spirit of God. We should learn again to spell out the many images of divine-human encounter, like the adoption of the sons of God, God's Spirit overshadowing Mary, the disciples at Pentecost, and even Jesus, which accompany the idea of God's Word and Wisdom sent to us in the person of Jesus, born from woman (Gal 4,4) and raised by God from the dead. Much of this imagery is present in both the Koran and the New Testament and borrowed from the Jewish Scriptures. The Koran, thus, does not minimise the significance of Jesus in the creative and revelatory work of God, nor do the Gospels forget about the ever greater reality of God, the one and all encompassing merciful Father.[30]

The later Christian quarrels about Christology and soteriology refer mainly to the divine origin and the doctrine of the incarnation of God in Jesus

30 De Jonge, *God's Final Envoy,* 123: "Jesus the Son, the exemplary envoy, in complete obedience to the will of his Sender, in loving unity with the Father, speaks and acts as the Father. Hence 'the Father and I are one' (Jn 10,30), and 'whoever has seen me has seen the Father' (Jn 14,9; cf. 12,45). Yet it is self-evident that 'the Father is greater than I' - the Father to whom the Son returns at the completion of his mission (Jn 14,31)".

Christ, interpreted in terms of Greek ontology, which was alien both to the New Testament[31] and to the Koran. A common rereading of the Scriptures of both communities with regard to the role and the figure of Jesus would be a primary task of dialogue. Forty years of exegetical and historical reflection on the Christian interpretation of the Christ-Event, which has tried to reconcile the New Testament Christologies with the strict monotheism of the Yahwistic tradition of Israel must still be communicated with both Jews and Muslims. Similarly, newer readings of the Koran and its vision on the mission of Jesus needs reception in Christian theological and catechetical teaching.[32]

On the Muslim side it is the denial of the crucifixion of Jesus that marks a *skandalon* for Christians. For Christians the crucifixion of Jesus is one of the most certain facts of history and crucial for their view on the prophetic mission of Jesus, whereas Muslims see the crucifixion of a divine prophet as a final failure of his mission. Christians have interpreted the poor fate of Jesus - his modest birth, the protests against his teaching and his shameful execution on the cross - in a paradoxical way, transforming his painful fate into victorious signs of God's eschatological kingdom: a Christ, in the end triumphant over injustice and death. In the nativity gospels of Matthew and Luke, Jesus' cradle became the proleptic focus of adoration by both the Jewish underclasses - the shepherds - and the oriental wisemen, and even a source of fear for Roman governors like Herod. Jesus' cross and his grave became the place of God's victory over death and decay, over human injustice and violence, a theophany in view of which the Roman guardians trembled. The Koran accepts Jesus' miraculous birth and wonderful deeds, but rejects his crucifixion and what happened at his grave: "They [the Jews] did not manage to kill him, they did not crucify him. They merely saw the appearence of it. No, God himself has raised him up to himself and God is mighty and wise" (Koran 4, 157-159). A true prophet like Jesus, who is himself able to raise the dead, cannot fall prone to decay. So Islam is inclined to glorify Jesus as a miraculous man and a divine prophet, raised up by God to his throne, but cannot see him as the suffering servant of God, who offered himself to death for the sins of the world. It glorifies the results of the works of the prophets and preaches the triumph of Muhammed as well as that of other prophets, among them foremost Isa-Jesus. We must confess that on the Christian side as well, the triumphant Christ - *Dominus Jesus* - frequently has been borrowed from a more kenotic vision of Jesus - *Ebed YHWH*. This is, perhaps, our common

31 See the findings of James Dunn in his *Christology in the Making*, quoted in note 34.

32 Much preparatory academic work has been done in this field in the last decades. See: Goddard, *Muslim Perceptions of Christianity*; Leirvik, *Images of Jesus Christ in Islam*.

skandalon. Neither Judaism, nor Islam thus far, have really accepted the idea of a suffering Messiah. Christianity itself, though essentially based on the gospel of the crucified Jesus, has often succumbed to an aggressive theology of the cross: *in hoc signo vinces.* The essence of religion is at stake here: is it to foster our own desires for power, prosperity and success, or is religion first of all a cry from the depths of human misery, a protest against violence and a support of solidarity with the weak and powerless in the name of God and to the glory of God?

The third skandalon: a history of violence

The third skandalon, related to the first and the second indeed, is our violent common past of mutual excommunications, persecutions, crusades, unholy alliances, colonial exploitation, genocide. Terrorism and wars on terrorism: unholy violence, blasphemously defended in the name of God.[33]

In the ecumenical movement and in Christian theology, and even in post-modern philosophy such appeal to God for the support of our own power claims and acts of vengeance has been consistently rejected. We might speak of a general *metamorphosis of the idea of God* in the second half of the twentieth century. God's energy and will are no longer expressed in terms of power, force and domination, but in terms of participation, relatedness and compassion. The mystery of God's merciful gratuitousness and donation is expressed in a new kind of negative theology. The God of Abraham is not just better and more powerful than all other gods, powers and forces in the universe, but his *dynamis* and *energeia* are of a different order, the order of what people like Marguerite Yourcenar and Gianni Vattimo have called 'the weak forces'. God is neither an almighty king nor a deistic watcher of the universe. God is no longer the natural ally of political or ecclesiastical rulers, claiming to act as his direct viceregents. God is not the solution for our physical or metaphysical puzzles about life and death. God is not a patriarch, granting men the right to behave like gods towards women. God cannot be claimed for one religion alone.

Such metamorphosis is the result of the critique on religion since the Enlightenment, of a critical rereading of the Scriptures and of the ecumenical movement

33 See the historical analysis of Watt, *Islamic Political*. For more recent developments, see: Donohue and Esposito, eds, *Islam in Transition*; Mortimer, *Faith and Power*. For traditional Islamic points of view on war and violence, see the reprint of Khadduri, *War and Peace in the Law of Islam*.

itself.[34] There we have heard the cry of the victims of power: the poor, the black, the oppressed, and the voices of women. There we have pleaded for justice, peace and the integrity of creation, the abbreviation *JPIC* nearly becoming a new *tetragrammaton* for the God of Abraham, God of mercy and grace, in whom there is no violence.

Conclusion

Ecumenism and interreligious dialogue have transformed the cultural position of the churches and the religious attitudes of their members considerably in the second half of the twentieth century. An 'ecumenical space' of tolerance, mutual respect and intercultural exchange has been created, fostering 'a culture for life' (Raiser) indeed.

Within this space, however, conversation among Christians and within and between the adherents of the three Abrahamitic religions especially, should concentrate on the unity of God's creation as a theological basis for human dignity and human rights and on the scandals of our violent past: the refusal to adore our God YHWH, Elohim, Abba, Ruach, Allah as the one God of Abraham; the refusal to accept a suffering and crucified prophet as the final envoy and messiah of God and the unholy alliance of faith and power, religion and violence in defense of particular and private interests, attitudes of conquest and imperialistic ideologies.

God is a living God, a God of life, mercy and grace, praised be He. This is the core kerygma of Islam, which resembles the core message of the Jewish Scriptures and of the Gospel of Jesus: that there is one Holy God, from Whom and to Whom everything exists and without Whom nothing can exist, Who has no rivals against Him nor equals aside. This God demands justice among all humans, who are created in equal dignity by God. All humans should live in grateful obedience to this one God, who will judge all people in the end of times and in life hereafter without any *prosopolèmpsia:* then God has no favourites.[35]

34 See my *God, An Open Question*.

35 Platti, *Wat gelooft een goede moslim?*, 71.

Ecumenism and Interreligious Dialogue

Hans Ucko

French Reformed theologian, F. Lovsky, has in his book, *La Déchirure de l'absence: Essai sur les rapports de l'Église du Christ et du peuple d'Israël*, a chapter entitled "Le peuple d'Israël, pivot œcuménique du peuple de Dieu".[1] Here, he puts in relation the "Mystère de l'*É*glise" and the "Mystère d'Israël" and says that this relationship obliges us to realise that the unity of the Church cannot be conceived without the people Israel, which is the root of the Church. The other is thus intrinsically part of the self-understanding and unity of the Church. Elaborating, he sees the theory of rejection and exclusion of the other to have been the guiding principle in the history and theology of the Church, much to its own detriment. The Jew first, followed by so many others excluded.

The way to proper Christian self-understanding would then be in and through a sincere encounter with the other. Interreligious dialogue is certainly about meeting the other. However, dialogue is equally, and maybe even more, about meeting oneself. There is an unexpected discovery about oneself waiting in an encounter with the other. Fernand Braudel once wrote to a French student, who was about to leave Paris for one year's studies in London: "Living in London for one year does not automatically imply that you will know England very well. But in comparison, in the light of the many surprises that you will have, you will suddenly have understood some of the deepest and most original features of France, those you did not know before and could not learn in any other way".[2]

1 Lovsky, *La Déchirure de l'absence*, 231-265.
2 Braudel, *Écrits sur l'histoire*, 59.

The Catholic Church and many Protestant churches have realised that, post-Holocaust in the words of a report from the First Assembly of the World Council of Churches (Amsterdam 1948), "To the Jews our God has bound us in a special solidarity linking our destinies together in His design".[3] Judaism truly challenges Christian claims, and the real dialogue between Jews and Christians on these vital theological issues has barely just begun. Although Judaism remains a particular *Doppelgänger* for Christian theology, the other, whether Jewish, Muslim, Hindu or Buddhist, each in their own and particular way, is a significant other not only for Christian theology but also for ecumenism itself. There is no particular confessional (Lutheran, Baptist, etc) stance on religious plurality. While there may be interesting confessional emphases, which should be taken seriously, the various Christian confessions and churches are largely and equally challenged by the reality of religious plurality. The challenges of religious plurality therefore serve as an intensifier of the Christian fellowship and *koinonia*. The otherness of the other could and should strengthen ecumenism among Christians towards a Christian assessment of what religious plurality really signifies.

The Greek word, *oikoumene*, from which we derive the English word 'ecumenical', occurs fifteen times in the New Testament, whose writers used it to describe "the whole inhabited earth", or, more specifically, the Greco-Roman world. The ecumenical councils of the early Church were designated as such since representatives attended from churches throughout the known world. By the year 381 CE, its meaning had been more sharply defined by the Council of Constantinople to refer to that which is accepted as authoritative for the whole Church, and by the sixteenth century, it had ceased to have any meaning other than a narrow ecclesiastical one, referring to councils, creeds, and the Patriarchate of Constantinople.

With the rise of the modern missionary movement, the concept 'ecumenical' began to be used to denote the whole worldwide Church, although such usage was sporadic up until the First World War and the development of the Faith and Order and Life and Work movements, the precursors to the World Council of Churches (WCC).[4]

What we now know as the *ecumenical movement* is widely regarded to have begun with the convening of the World Missionary Conference in Edinburgh

3 Report of Committee IV, *Concerns of the Churches*, chapter 3: "The Christian Approach to the Jews".

4 Visser 't Hooft, "The Word Ecumenical", 735.

in 1910, and with the dawning realisation that Christian unity, rather than being an end in itself, was necessary for the sake of mission. The attempts towards an organised ecumenical movement of the early twentieth century has, in this respect, not changed, but has been focusing on what it has understood to be Christian concerns and *oikoumene* or 'ecumenical' is limited to that which concerns Christian faith. *Oikoumene* does not, in traditional Christian thinking, reckon with the whole inhabited world as the religiously plural world it is, nor are people of other faiths, by virtue of living in the world, considered to be part of the *oikoumene*. The word and concept 'ecumenism' is so closely linked to the search for Christian unity that one would have difficulty thinking in other categories.

The ecumenical movement has, as a Christian movement, enabled Christians of different confessions to discover each other. Jürgen Moltmann wrote at the time of the fiftieth anniversary of the Faith and Order movement (1977): "After fifty years of concerted theological effort we now have to say quite openly to Christians and church authorities that there are no longer any doctrinal differences which justify the division of our churches."[5] His comment seemed to be borne out when, five years later, in Lima, the Faith and Order Commission received the final text of the document, *Baptism, Eucharist and Ministry*, which exhibited a remarkable convergence of thought. One commentator noted, "that theologians of such widely different traditions should be able to speak so harmoniously about baptism, Eucharist and ministry is unprecedented in the modern ecumenical movement".[6]

The remarkable convergence notwithstanding, there is still quite a long way to go. We find ourselves today in a time of "ecumenical eclipse" and there are signs contradicting the positive notes. Baptism is not the undeniable sign of Christian unity. The Eucharist does not bring us into communion with each other. The question of common worship was a controversial feature of the Harare Assembly and has again re-emerged as a major issue in the life of the WCC in the first years of this millennium. There is a clash in the basic self-understanding of Orthodox and Protestant churches and the way in which they relate to the One Church of Jesus Christ. This contrast has influenced an often heated debate about the nature of the fellowship that is experienced in the WCC. There have been chronic protests about the ways in which ecumenical institutions such as the WCC have gone about the task of inter-Christian encounter and activity. Questions are consistently raised as to how churches

5 *Lausanne 77*, 39.
6 *Baptism, Eucharist and Ministry*, ix.

are represented, how decisions are taken and how these are spelled out in the priorities, programmes and "ethos" of the WCC. The WCC Assembly in Harare (1998) created a special commission to address these concerns. The final report included sections on worship and prayer, which make common worship between Orthodox and Protestants quite difficult. Distinctions are made between "confessional" worship and "interconfessional" experiences to avoid the difficulties of praying together.[7]

Following the collapse of State socialism, the question of religious freedom has become an issue in Eastern Europe and it is divisive. When Western Protestant groups go to Russia to proclaim the Gospel in Russia, are they then infringing upon Orthodox territory? If the WCC were a fellowship of Christian churches, would this not be the forum for a genuine and thorough Christian exchange between those who claim the freedom to evangelise and those who wonder how they are to understand the Protestant interpretation of *koinonia*?

Many member churches of the WCC report on the mushrooming of new evangelical, charismatic or indigenous churches, the majority of them not being particularly interested in ecumenism or membership of the WCC. The Roman Catholic Church relates similar experiences. In countries where Roman Catholics, Orthodox or Protestants were in undisputed majority, new churches are emerging. In Roman Catholic Latin America, Pentecostal churches challenge the present status quo. In Africa, traditional churches with their roots in colonialism stagnate, while so-called African instituted churches flourish. Similar stirrings can be seen in hitherto secularised societies, even if new churches may not be the only appearance. Instead there is an upsurge in new religious movements of various kinds.

The divide between so-called evangelicals and ecumenicals has become a significant feature of Christianity today. The new churches, charismatic, evangelical, indigenous, seem to prefer other ways of fellowship than the approach of the ecumenical movement. The quest for spirituality goes rather in the opposite direction of the ecumenical movement. The ecumenical movement is perceived to be too rationalistic and too secular itself to be considered any longer. In society at large, the voice of the ecumenical movement is not heard or it is not possible to distinguish from all other voices.

7 *Final Report of the Special Commission on Orthodox participation in the WCC.*

Mainline churches in the Western world, faced with aging membership and dwindling resources, are turning inward. Churches have become increasingly preoccupied with questions concerning their own survival. The vision of a church united and uniting, in order that it may bare witness to the purpose of God for wholeness seems to have been lost. The vision has shrivelled up, shrunk and one has to accept it.[8]

There are those who refer to the present times as a time of "ecumenical winter". The policy document of the WCC, *Towards a Common Understanding and Vision of the World Council of Churches*, explains the context of the WCC in the following words: "The WCC and the ecumenical movement are passing through a period of uncertainty. There are signs of a weakening of ecumenical commitment, of a growing distance between the WCC and its member churches, and of a widespread perception among the young generation that the ecumenical movement has lost its vitality and does not provide relevant answers to the pressing problems of today. Internal factors are preventing many churches from maintaining their level of financial support, thus obliging the WCC to reduce its activities; and some member churches are experiencing internal conflicts and even the threat of schism because of their participation in the ecumenical fellowship."[9]

And yet, in spite of these ominous signs and events, the ecumenical movement has supported and encouraged movements within itself that will and could be a factor to reckon with in the transformation of what it means to be Church. Among them are the concerns for a changed view of our relation to creation, the role and place of women in church and society and the dialogue and relations with people of other faiths. The latter is now my focus.

Interreligious dialogue today has acquired an important role in the life of the ecumenical movement and is considered a core activity within the WCC. What used to be in the margin of the WCC, the ecumenical movement and reserved for a few academic specialists has become a prism for dealing with some of the thematic programs in the WCC: youth and interreligious relations, women and interreligious relations, education and interreligious relations, indigenous peoples and interreligious relations, to mention but a few. More than ever, we

8 During a consultation of the WCC in Wittenberg 1997, "Die Sendung der Kirchen in den säkularisierten Gesellschaften Europas", the discussion centred on shrinking membership in the churches. A German pastor said with some weariness, "Well, we'll just have to bake fewer bread rolls for the church coffee". Same procedure as last year, only fewer rolls this year.

9 *Towards a Common Understanding and Vision of the World Council of Churches*.

sense a growing need not just for dialogue with people of other faiths but for genuine relationships with them. In spite of our religious diversity, we find ourselves able to address issues of common concern.

The theological interpretation of what we are doing in interreligious dialogue remains, however, controversial in the ecumenical movement. What does it mean for us as Christians to relate to people of other faiths?[10] The establishment in 1971 of the Sub-unit for Dialogue with People of Living Faiths and Ideologies (DFI) was, in the WCC Central Committee of those days, emphasised as "a common adventure" of the churches. Meant to indicate dialogue as a positive challenge for the church, dialogue instead became increasingly perceived as an adventure riskier than usual and the question was raised whether those engaged in dialogue were entirely theologically responsible. The WCC Assembly in Nairobi 1975 almost jeopardised the whole ecumenical engagement in interfaith dialogue and obliged the then Director, Stanley Samartha, to travel to Nordic countries and explain his theology of dialogue.

In spite of positive wordings about other faiths in statements by the churches, there is an ambiguity in relation to religious plurality. Christian statements abound, which, on the one hand, maintain the primacy of Christ and, on the other hand, remind the Church to recognise that God is creatively and redemptively at work in the religious life of all humankind. The question then arises that, if God is truly redemptively at work in our religious plurality, why is there a primacy of Christ? Or what does the primacy of Christ mean?

The discovery of the other as a significant other through interreligious dialogue has for some in the ecumenical movement been of utmost importance. This is particularly apparent as one result of the Jewish-Christian dialogue. Through the Jewish-Christian dialogue a considerable literature by Christians on Christian anti-Judaism emerged in the 1970s. There is no "previous experience of this kind in religious history", says John Cobb. We have in the last century experienced how one religion has realised how its theology and teaching has led to the denigration of another religion. From the "teaching of contempt" (Jules Isaac), Jewish-Christian relations have become a success story.[11] Obviously, such a conversion has had repercussions on Christianity itself and Christian

10 I will in the following use 'faith' and 'religion' as well as 'interfaith' and 'interreligious' interchangeably, although I personally prefer 'religion' and 'interreligious'. Not every religion considers itself to be a faith. But interfaith has gained such coinage, which today cannot be ignored.

11 Rabbi James Rudin calls the Jewish-Christian dialogue the success story of the twentieth century.

self-understanding. It has dented a self-sufficient theology. John Cobb continues, "... few want to continue teachings or practices once they recognize their anti-Jewish nature. [...] [There is a beginning realisation] that commitment to Jesus Christ [has] a dark side in their implications for Jews."[12] This learning constitutes an important dimension. The other enables me to question myself and challenges me to refocus. "For the church to learn and grow in interaction with the Greeks, Romans, and Germans, and now with Muslims, Hindus, and Buddhists, is to continue the process we discern in the canon, of the Hebrews learning through interaction with Canaanites, Egyptians, Babylonians, Persians and Greeks."[13]

Similar experiences have been had by Christians engaged in other interreligious encounters. Ernst Lange said that the Christian conscience has to learn to adjust itself to the larger household to which it was from the very beginning "called out" and toward which it was directed, namely, to the household of the whole inhabited earth.[14] It is this understanding that has led us back to the beginning, to an understanding of *oikoumene* as referring to "the whole inhabited earth".

While not departing from the commitment to seek the unity of the Body of Christ, many Christians will today set as a priority the participation in the healing of creation, making common cause with all people of good will, whether they be people of faith or not, towards a world that is just, participatory and sustainable.

Could the discovery of the other as other and as a God-given other in such undertakings help the churches rediscover themselves? Could the spirituality of the other help inform Christian self-understanding? Urgent moral issues forge the way faith has to be lived out and reflected upon. In facing them, the Church will often need to work with other communities of good will, sharing in their expertise and commitment. Christians would be frequently motivated and challenged by the dedication and urgency that others bring to this task.

Internalising the reality of religious plurality brings challenges to the ecumenical movement. The world has always been a plural world. With increased communication and mobility, this plurality has, in a new and sometimes challenging way, entered every place in the whole world. Today, it is obvious that

12 Cobb, *Reclaiming the Church*, 15-16.
13 Ibidem, 58.
14 *The Ecumenical Review*, 23 (1978) 1, 8.

no religion is an island. We witness a multireligious reality from which there is definitely no return. We are not any longer living in geographically defined areas: Buddhists, Christians, Jews, Hindus and Muslims. We live next door to each other in the whole world.

Taking seriously religious plurality is a challenge to the nature and scope of the ecumenical movement. Multireligious plurality is in many situations and contexts a complex reality which has prompted the ecumenical movement to begin reflecting in new ways how best to respond and live a relevant ministry. Religious plurality is one facet in the ongoing transformation of the churches today, either as a problem to overcome or a possibility with which to reckon. In 1980, Wilfred Cantwell Smith complained that the word "ecumenical, that should in reality mean the search for the unity of all humankind, had unfortunately been appropriated lately to designate a rather internal development within the on-going church".[15] The use of "New Ecumenism", "Mega Ecumenism", "Wider Ecumenism", etc point to the need for the religious traditions to grow closer together but has not received much welcome. There is a fear that this concept would in the end undermine the Christian search for unity. But this is not the case. Christians still need to find ways to speak, act and engage together to fulfil their common calling to be a church in the world. Yet, the ecumenical movement can no longer be satisfied with the unity of the church to the exclusion of the search for a wider unity. The relationship between the two movements needs to be understood and related. In fact there had been attempts in the past to deal with this question in the Faith and Order studies on "The Unity of the Church and Unity of Humankind". The contemporary religious awareness has gone far beyond the parameters of that study, and a new attempt to understand the issues has become urgent.

There is resistance to reconsidering the use of 'ecumenical' towards an understanding that sees humankind, the whole inhabited world, as the focus. The WCC policy document *Towards a Common Understanding and Vision of the World Council of Churches* says: "More recently, a growing number of voices from the churches, especially in Asia but also in Latin America, have spoken of the need for a 'wider ecumenism' or 'macro-ecumenism' - an understanding that would open the ecumenical movement to other religious and cultural traditions beyond the Christian community. These ambiguities surrounding the understanding of 'ecumenical' create the real danger of introducing competitive divisions into the ecumenical movement. What is the meaning and purpose of this movement? Who are its subjects? What are its goals

15 Smith, "The Christian in a Religiously Plural World", 87.

and methods or forms of action? What is the source of the dynamic, which warrants speaking of the 'ecumenical movement' beyond its institutional manifestations in the WCC and elsewhere? [...] The ecumenical movement, while it shares in other efforts at international, inter-cultural, and interreligious cooperation and dialogue, is rooted in the life of the Christian churches. Yet, it is not limited to the concern for inter-church relationships and is wider than the various organizations in which it has found expression. The ecumenical movement seeks to foster cooperation and sharing, common witness and common action by the churches and their members. More specifically, however, it is a renewal movement in and through the churches, which has found expression in diverse initiatives and networks among lay people, especially women and youth. It is committed to the search for visible unity, not as an end in itself but in order to give credible witness 'so that the world may believe' and to serve the healing of the human community and the wholeness of God's entire creation. While the ecumenical movement has a worldwide scope - in line with the original use of the word *oikoumene* for 'the whole inhabited earth' - it points more specifically to the catholicity of the church, that is, globally. In each place and in all places, the ecumenical movement is concerned with the true being and life of the church as an inclusive community."[16]

While these arguments are certainly valid and persuasive, they reflect the uneasiness regarding a correlation between ecumenism and interreligious relations. There are apprehensions affirming that interfaith relations and inter-Christian ecumenism are woven together and, even more so, discovering the need to make some theological sense out of our involvement in interreligious dialogue. While one welcomes the so-called dialogue of life, one is less interested in dealing with theological conclusions coming out of interreligious relations. There is nervousness seeing that the logic that once spurred the ecumenical movement and the demand for Christian unity is the same that generates a passionate commitment to interreligious dialogue among Christians throughout the world today. The enthusiasm that sparked the ecumenical movement is perhaps found again today among those who have discovered the affinity between people of different religions and have been enriched through interfaith dialogue. Many are those, who through interfaith dialogue have found new inspiration. What we hear expressed is something of a confession. People say, "I find it easier and more enriching to talk with people of other faiths, across the confessional boundaries than with members of my own church". The dividing line is no longer exclusively between reli-

16 *Towards a Common Understanding and Vision of the World Council of Churches.*

gions but is more and more expressed as a theological split within religion. Ernst Simon expressed the same experience in the following way: "The people I can pray with, I can't talk to and the people I can talk to, I can't pray with".

The present longing for a refocusing of ecumenism towards a "wider ecumenism" comprising people of different religions is not the outcome of indifferentism or fatigue with traditional Christian ecumenical concerns. People have made experiences in and through interreligious dialogue and have become convinced that there is a need to clear the ground towards the open horizon. Historical theological differences meant a great deal but today the issues which concern people are elsewhere. There is also an increasing recognition that the world's problems are not "Christian problems requiring Christian answers", but human problems that must be addressed together by all human beings. Whether it is the issue of justice, peace, human rights or the destruction of the environment, we realise today that we need to work across the boundaries of religions, nations and cultures. There is a growing interest today in multifaith approaches to issues of common concern: peace and religions as peacemakers, supporting the work of the United Nations from an interreligious perspective, multifaith initiatives articulating and formulating declarations of global ethics, human responsibilities, guidelines for interreligious interaction and commitments, highlighting the importance of values and hence, of ethics. Other interreligious initiatives are expressed in conjunction with societal and global issues, injustice, physical poverty, violence and environmental destruction. Religions are requested not to shirk their responsibility towards the planet on whose life our lives depend. Alliances are called for between the religions and economic, societal or issue-oriented institutions or organisations on the subject of poverty, development or environment. Exchanges between religious leaders and political and economic leaders are sought to improve the state of the world, creating global partnerships with business, political, intellectual, religious and other leaders of society to define and discuss key issues on the global agenda and to bring in the moral authority of religion to help solve the problems dividing communities and nations.[17]

True and sincere interreligious dialogue and engagement will prompt a theological reflection. "[The] issue of "how ecumenical 'ecumenical' should be" is no longer a question of semantics or inclusion; it is a theological question. It has to do with a reassessment of our understanding of God, the scope of God's saving work, and of the agents of God's mission. Such reflections, of

17 Ucko, "Reflections on international and global multifaith initiatives".

necessity, affect our present understandings of the mystery of the Incarnation and the being and meaning of the church as the Body of Christ."[18]

The new awareness of religious plurality raises questions for the basis on which discussions on mission and dialogue are carried out within the ecumenical movement. There needs to be a new framework for our theological discussion on the reality of other religious traditions and our relationship with them.

Although the ecumenical movement is well placed to facilitate a rethinking of Christian theology with attentiveness to the fact that others also have a contribution to make to the subjects of our theological explorations, the road ahead will be difficult and strenuous. At the General Assembly of the World Council of Churches in Vancouver in 1983, the theological significance of other religious traditions still remained a controversial issue. When a report recognising the work of God in the lives of people of other faiths was presented on the Assembly floor, it was hotly contested. A dozen substitute formulations were offered. The Assembly finally settled for a recognition of "God's creative work in the seeking for religious truth among people of other faiths". During the confusion of the plenary debate, delegates were unsure about the "finding".[19] The question of whether people would find God in seeking God in and through their own religious tradition was, according to how WCC Assemblies have ruled, not addressed.

This is not to say that there is silence. Constructive and productive missiological thinking on religious plurality came out of the Mission Conference in San Antonio in 1989. It pointed out the dilemma of the church in mission: "In reaffirming the "evangelistic mandate" of the ecumenical movement, we would like to emphasize that we may never claim to have a full understanding of God's truth. [...] We cannot point to any other way of salvation than Jesus Christ; at the same time, we cannot set limits to the saving power of God. [...] Dialogue has its own place and integrity and is neither opposed to nor incompatible with witness or proclamation. [...] [There is] the possibility that the God we know in Jesus Christ may encounter us also in the lives of our neighbours of other faiths. [...] We are well aware that these convictions and the ministry of witness stand in tension with what we have affirmed about God being present in and at work in people of other faiths; we appreciate this

18 Ariarajah, "Wider Ecumenism".
19 Eck, "On Seeking and Finding in the World's Religions".

tension, and do not attempt to resolve it."[20] The question is, of course, where this tension will take you, if it enables you to probe deeper or it leaves you in a theological limbo. Where do we go with challenges such as the following? Are we to speak of God's work in the lives of all men and women only in tentative terms of hope in order that they may experience something of him, or, more positively, in terms of God's self-disclosure to people of living faiths? What is the relationship between God's universal action in creation and his redemptive action in Jesus Christ?

At a broad ecumenical gathering in Baar, Switzerland in 1990, the Dialogue sub-unit of the WCC attempted to build on the question from Vancouver and the statement from San Antonio as a challenge to the Assembly in Canberra in 1991. The deliberations were dense and expressed the conviction that, "God has been present in their seeking and finding, that where there is truth and wisdom in their teachings, and love and holiness in their living, this, like any wisdom, insight, knowledge, understanding, love and holiness that is found among us, is the gift of the Holy Spirit."[21]

It was hoped that the statement would help animate and facilitate the discussion at the Seventh Assembly in Canberra in February 1991. But the document was not picked up anywhere and Methodist theologian Kenneth Cracknell reflects on the role of the WCC and interfaith dialogue that it both in its theology and its policy operates with "two diverse sets of values, the one quite negative and exclusive, the other open to dialogue and co-operation".[22] He continues with reference to the Declaration from Baar: "It is deeply regrettable that no attention was paid to the Baar Declaration by the four thousand or so Christians gathered in Canberra. Furthermore I find no reference to the Baar Declaration in the Minutes of the Central Committee Meetings since 1991. It is almost as though it had never been."[23]

While there certainly is a lot of fear squarely addressing the significance of religious plurality for Christian self-understanding, there is also a significant shift in our assessment of religion in today's world. Religion is present both as a blessing and a curse and we may not have quite fathomed the presence of religion in today's world as an intensifier of conflict and as a lethal weapon for a political agenda. The word fundamentalism has developed legs of its own

20 "The San Antonio Conference", Reports of the sections: IV "Witness among people of other living faiths", 351-352.

21 *Baar Statement on Theological Perspectives on Plurality.*

22 Cracknell, *In Good and Generous Faith*, 178.

23 Ibidem, 202.

and walks outside its original context in the Protestant world. It implicates today all religions. Many now rightly try to stem the tide and focus on dialogue as way of achieving a necessary modus vivendi in a plural world. This is already a Sisyphean challenge. A parallel challenge is however also the theological task ad intra. The intra-Christian theological exploration of the significance of religious plurality and Christian self-understanding cannot be set aside. The Mission Conferences following the San Antonio conference did so far not strongly enough focus on the issue of a Christian theological reflection in relation to interreligious relations and dialogue.

Attempts by the dialogue office of the WCC in collaboration with the desks for mission and evangelism and Faith & Order engaged in a process of several years to articulate a way beyond San Antonio. The document "Religious Plurality and Christian Self-Understanding", mandated by the governing bodies of the World Council of Churches was however never received or adopted by the same bodies; it found eventually its place as a background-document for the Porto Alegre Assembly in 2006.[24] It was however preceded by a caveat, which confirmed some of the reflections of Kenneth Cracknell referred to above about the "one step forward and two step back-mentality of the WCC". The preface to the background document says: "The present document is the result of a study process in response to suggestions made in 2002 at the WCC central committee to the three staff teams on Faith and Order, Inter-religious Relations, and Mission and Evangelism, and their respective commissions or advisory bodies. [...] It must be emphasized that the paper does not represent the view of the WCC. Discussions in commissions showed how important but also how controversial the matter is. Much careful theological work is needed. This document is shared as a background document for discussion and debate. Further comments, critiques and suggestions from assembly participants or churches and other partners are welcome and will be fed into the continuing reflection on the key issue of Christian self-understanding and witness in a religiously plural world."[25] There is, however, so far not very much of a follow-up as a programmatic thrust.

The potential role of religion in conflict and the growing place of religion in public life maybe received more attention in the WCC than the issue of theological explorations of dialogue. The role of religion in conflict requires a

24 <http://wcc-coe.org/wcc/what/interreligious/cd45-02.html>.

25 <http://www.oikoumene.org/en/resources/documents/assembly/porto-alegre-2006/3-preparatory-and-background-documents/religious-plurality-and-christian-self-understanding.html>.

simultaneous work towards greater understanding and cooperation among people of diverse faiths. This thrust is strongly emphasised in the revision of the 1979 WCC *Guidelines for Dialogue*, entitled in their final form: "Ecumenical considerations for dialogue and relations with people of other religions - Taking stock of 30 years of dialogue and revisiting the 1979 Guidelines."[26] How can we find common ground to address issues when we, irrespective of our religious traditions, see common challenges and understand our common responsibility? People experience each other across the religious barriers as potential partners through many of the issues that affect human life. Therefore, the ecumenical movement needs to pioneer the Christian willingness to explore all issues that confront humankind, not in isolation, but in partnership with others. The so-called Lund Principle of Faith & Order in relation to inter-church relations, which states, "that which we can do together we should not do separately", should be broadened to include our relationships and life with people from other religious traditions.

Today, the focus of the work of the WCC in interreligious relations and dialogue is on cooperation between faith communities. The name of the office has also been changed. It is no longer an office but a program and the name is Inter-religious Dialogue and Cooperation. Its various activities entitled "Inter-religious trust and respect", "Christian self-understanding", "Churches in situations of conflict" does reckon with the theological issue ad intra. It remains to be seen how one intends to pursue the theological agenda.

A particular feature of the dialogue work of the WCC merits attention. It concerns the work of the interreligious group initiated by the WCC called Thinking Together. It is a small group of people of different faiths with substantial experience in interreligious dialogue and therefore possesses the openness to focus together on some of the basic issues of belief. The group wants to go a little deeper than just stating the ideals of our respective faiths or making grand scale declarations, as is sometimes the case in many interreligious gatherings. One stirring question emerged as a consequence of the exposure to the interreligious exchange of ideas and realities: How can we, in the midst of our religious diversity, express common convictions and explore the core issues present in all our religious traditions? As people committed to different faiths, we are aware that we live in a world which deeply challenges our faiths in different ways. Religious plurality is one such challenge. How do our commitments as people of faith translate in our encounters with each

26 Document for WCC Central Committee 26.8-3.9.2002 and <http://www.oikoumene.org/index.php?id=3445>.

other? Does the other in his or her otherness challenge my faith or religion? Does my religious tradition provide space for the integrity of the other in his or her otherness? Can we, in each other's presence, wrestle together with some of the problems our faiths have to confront today?[27]

The new religious awareness today places on us challenges for such a radical departure. This is the way ahead. Some in the ecumenical movement will see any embarking upon this way as taking too many steps in a dangerous direction. It is, however, my opinion that here lies the key to the renewal of the ecumenical movement.

27 For a presentation of the group and its work on the issue of religion and violence, see *Current Dialogue,* 39 (2001) <http://www.wcc-coe.org/wcc/what/interreligious/cd39-01.html>.

Christian Churches as Social Capital
An Empirical Study of the Relationship between Church Commitment, Religious Pluralism and Tolerance, and the Attitude towards Immigrants in Eleven European Countries

Jaak Billiet, Karel Dobbelaere & Bart Cambré

Does church commitment affect social attitudes that are favourable to social integration? From a social capital viewpoint, social integration is understood as the maintenance of orientations and attitudes that are favourable to the justification and functioning of a pluralistic, democratic, political system. Social capital itself has been functionally defined as aspects of social relationships or structures that facilitate the purposeful co-operation of individuals within these relationships. These aspects are mutual obligations and expectations, the availability of information, purposeful social organisations, norms of reciprocity, civic commitment, and social confidence.[1]

An empirical study in Belgium has shown that the involvement in religious-ideological associations had a significant effect on several indicators of social integration.[2] It analysed whether religious involvement and active participation in voluntary associations had a moderating effect on several indicators of social disintegration, and if so, how much. These indicators were: distrust in others and in the future, feelings of being threatened by immigrants, racist views concerning newcomers in society, utilitarian individualism, political alienation, and the lack of political interest and participation. All these

1 Coleman, "Social Capital in the Creation of Human Capital"; Idem, *Foundations of Social Theory*, 306-313; Putnam, *Making Democracy Work*, 167.

2 Billiet, "Social Capital, Religious-philosophical Involvement and Social Integration in Belgium".

indicators were measured on the individual level of social attitudes.[3] As was expected, church involvement and active participation in voluntary associations were negatively correlated with these indicators of social disintegration. Those deeply involved in the Catholic Church and who participate actively in voluntary organisations were less likely to score high on the indicators of social disintegration than marginal Catholics and people with no philosophy of life. However, this was also the case for a-religious humanists ("free thinkers"). Finally, the effect of religious-philosophical involvement was not very strong.[4]

Why did we expect such a relationship between social capital and religious/philosophical involvement? Two aspects of religious-philosophical involvement were explored - the degree of church (or religious-philosophical) involvement in the strict sense (measured by adherence to belief systems and actual religious practice), and active involvement in associations with a religious-philosophical flavour. In both cases, people are embedded in interactive networks of social ties characterized by their value-orientation. It was believed that co-operative ties of this kind, based on values, are eminently suited to fulfilling the functions of social capital, not least because they can provide individuals with a buffer against the atomisation and social disintegration of society as a whole. This theme actually dates back to the nineteenth-century pioneers of sociology, such as Durkheim and Tönnies. According to Putnam, drawing on data from the 1991 *World Values Study*, members of associations have greater trust in others and participate more in political life.[5] The latter has been demonstrated in numerous studies.[6]

In this study, we investigate how far these findings are transferable to other European democracies. Is religious involvement a social capital in the sense that it prevents social disintegration? What aspects of religious involvement favour social integration and what aspects do not? For practical reasons, our focus is on one indicator of social (dis)integration, namely the attitude towards newcomers in society (immigrants). We choose this since we have no cross-national datasets in which extensive measurements of the other

3 For the meaningfulness of individual measurements see: Brehm and Rahn, *Individual Level Evidence for the Causes and Consequences of Social Capital.*

4 Billiet, "Social Capital", 243.

5 Putnam, "Bowling alone: America's declining Social Capital", 67-69, 73.

6 One of the leading studies is: Verba, Scholzman and Brady, *Voice and Equality: Civic Voluntarism in American Politics.*

indicators of social (dis)integration and religious involvement are available.[7] The *Religious and Moral Pluralism* (RAMP) cross-national dataset is most useful since it contains measures of the attitude towards immigrants and extensive measures of religious participation, and other relevant attitudes, such as religious pluralism and religious tolerance.[8] Thus we focus on the attitude towards immigrants as a proxy for the mentioned indicators of social integration with which it strongly correlates.[9] Both the measurement qualities and the cross-cultural equivalence of the attitude towards immigrants in RAMP have been extensively investigated.[10] This is an additional advantage of using RAMP for this study.

The Controversial Relation between Church Involvement and Ethnocentrism

Past research on the relationship between religious orientations and ethnocentrism has shown that this relationship has tremendous variation within all societies, religions, and kinds of immigrants.

In order to explain the variation in the relationship between religious orientations and ethnocentrism, one should reduce extra variation by selecting more or less comparable societies, for example Western European nations that are characterised by Christian traditions. Such a reduction is necessary for several reasons. First of all, in cross-cultural empirical research, it is necessary to obtain equivalent measurements for the theoretical concepts, and therefore the societies that are compared should belong to the same cultural and structural variety. Second, it is apparent that not all religious groups contribute to social capital. We need only think of Bosnia in the 1990s, or the conflicts in the Middle East or in Northern Ireland. However these conflicts are not manifestations of religious tensions alone since they are mixed with sharp ethnic, social, and economic cleavages. In such situations characterised by heavy conflicts within one society, it becomes clear that indicators for social

7 This is written in 2003 at the moment of the analysis. Now in 2008, other datasets of the *European Social Survey* are available with more indicators of social (dis)integration; however, the measurement of religious commitment is much restricted compared with the data of RAMP.

8 Dobbelaere and Riis, "Religious and Moral Pluralism".

9 RAMP also contained a measure of interest in politics, but this attitude is measured by one single question. For that reason, it is impossible to state the validity and reliability of this measurement.

10 See: Cambré, Welkenhuysen-Gybels and Billiet, "Is it Content or Style?"; Cambré, *De relatie tussen religiositeit en etnocentrisme*, 112-149.

integration from the viewpoint of one group are indicators for disintegration from the perspective of another. This makes it impossible to answer empirical questions about the effect of religious orientations on social integration. It is also clear that strong social relationships within some small religious groups such as sects, can demolish the opportunities of integration in a larger social environment. We can imagine that not all aspects of religious commitment contribute equally to social capital. For all these reasons, both a selection of comparable cases and accurate definitions of the concepts that are measured by the empirical indicators are necessary.

Even when we restrict ourselves to the elements of the out group aspect of ethnocentrism as a proxy for social (dis)integration, to involvement in a church, and both of these within the Christian world, one can still observe variability in the relations. Sometimes, the stronger the involvement in a church, the more likely the negative prejudices towards immigrants. In other contexts that relationship is just the opposite so Christians who are closely associated with their church are less likely to adhere to negative prejudices. In other occasions a curvilinear relationship was found in the sense that non-church members and strongly involved church members were less prejudiced than the weakly involved church-member (e.g. marginal Catholics). And in still other situations, there is no relationship at all between religious orientations and ethnocentrism.[11]

Cambré systematically investigated the (net) relationship between church involvement and ethnocentrism in thirteen Western European countries, controlling for a set of relevant, known, individual level co-variantes like gender, generation, education, and occupation.[12] He used both the RAMP dataset and the 1995 dataset of the *International Social Survey Program* (ISSP) that focused on national identity. In general, the non-church members were less likely than members to harbour negative attitudes towards immigrants; however, among church members the relationship between the degree of involvement and ethnocentrism varied greatly depending on countries and denominations. When a significant relationship was observed, the marginal church members were mostly (but not always) more likely to have stronger negative feelings towards immigrants. Attempts to explain the differences by variation in characteristics of the religious system failed. Cambré concluded

11 Eisinga, Felling and Peters, "Religious Belief, Church Involvement and Ethnocentrism in the Netherlands", 54-56; Billiet, "Church Involvement, Individualism, and Ethnic Prejudice among Flemish Roman Catholics", 225-226.

12 Cambré, *De relatie tussen religiositeit en etnocentrisme.*

that characteristics of the social system (nation) might be more important for explaining the variation. Because of the variation, one must check all interactions of these two variables, church involvement and ethnocentrism, with the country variable in any study that aims to study the effects of religious orientations on ethnocentrism in cross-national datasets.

Scheepers et al used the RAMP dataset in order to perform cross-national tests of the relationship between aspects of religiosity and ethnic prejudice.[13] They investigated several aspects of religiosity: religious denomination, church attendance, Christian doctrinal beliefs, saliency of religion, and religious particularism. Surprisingly, concerning church attendance, these researchers came to findings that contradict four large-scale surveys in Belgium and their own previous research in the Netherlands.[14] According to the recent study of Scheepers et al, the more frequently people attend church, the more prejudiced they are, and this relationship holds for all eleven countries in RAMP. The fact that this finding is so incompatible with the findings of Cambré who used the same data calls for a careful investigation of the measures that were used.

The most striking difference can be found in the operationalisation of ethnocentrism. Cambré systematically tested the measurement equivalence of all six indicators that were used in RAMP in order to measure ethnocentrism. He found that there were serious problems in wording and translation from the source questionnaire concerning the three positively worded ethnocentric items.[15] In a number of countries (languages) this wording must have led to confusion because of the double negations ("Immigrants are no less ... than ..." in the English source questionnaire, and in the Netherlands and Portugal) and deficiencies in translation ("Immigrants are as ... as." in Finland, Sweden, and Norway; "Immigrants are at least as ... as ..." in Italy; "Immigrants are just as ... as ..." in Great Britain). After the inclusion of a method factor in most nations, the six items did not measure two different concepts (ethnic prejudice and ethnic threat) but one more general concept.[16] But even after the inclusion of a method factor (acquiescence), the balanced scale with the six items was not a factorial invariant for any of the eleven nations.[17] Scheepers et al used a subset of the balanced six-item scale (called "ethnic prejudice"),

13 Scheepers, Gijsberts and Hello, "Religiosity and Prejudice against Ethnic Minorities in Europe".

14 Billiet, Eisinga and Scheepers, "Ethnocentrism in the Low Countries"; Billiet, "Church Involvement"; Cambré, *De relatie tussen religiositeit en etnocentrisme,* 79-91.

15 Cambré, *De relatie tussen religiositeit en etnocentrisme*, 66.

16 Cambré, Welkenhuysen-Gybels and Billiet, "Is it Content or Style?", 17: 408-409.

17 Ibidem, 64-71.

but they used the precise that part that was particularly poor concerning measurement quality and that was seriously biased.[18] For that reason, we do not support the conclusion of Scheepers et al that they have disentangled the controversial relationship between religion and prejudice within the European social context.[19] We will therefore re-analyse the RAMP dataset with a more valid and reliable measurement of ethnocentrism and look carefully for differences between countries by checking the interactions with nations.

Data and measurements

The data of RAMP were collected in 1997-1999 by means of face-to-face interviews in representative samples in eleven countries: Belgium (N = 1,630), Denmark (N = 606), Finland (N = 785), Great Britain (N = 1,466), Hungary (N = 1,000), Italy (N = 2149), the Netherlands (N = 1,004), Norway (N = 503), Poland (N = 1,134), Portugal (N = 982) and Sweden (N = 1,032).[20] In these countries, the principal investigators who are sociologists (of religion) controlled the data collection. They met several times during the preparation of the questionnaire. Since we are working in a cross-cultural context, we must assume that all the variables that are used in the analysis are equivalent. How plausible is this presumption? In case of the single indicator variables, one can only trust the question-designers who, in the preparatory meetings, have discussed the indicators and the single question wordings. Country specific variations are explained in the codebook prepared by the Central Archive for Empirical Research ZA No. 3170 (Cologne). In the case of multiple indicators that are combined into constructs, the situation is different. There we can rely on the concept of construct equivalence.[21] Following Rensvold and Cheung, construct equivalence is operationalised here as 'factorial equivalence', which means that the factor loadings of the indicators of each latent variable (construct) are invariant (or equal) in all countries.[22] The tests on factorial invariance are done by multiple group comparisons of measurement models with structural equation modelling using LISREL 8©.[23] Each test starts with a measurement model in which all the factor loadings

18 Cambré, Welkenhuysen-Gybels and Billiet, "Is it Content or Style?", 66. The reliability of the scale (measured by Cronbach's) is very weak (<= 0.60) in four countries, see: Hello, Scheepers and Gijsberts, "Education and Ethnic Prejudice in Europe", 11.

19 Scheepers, Gijsberts and Hello, "Religiosity and Prejudice against Ethnic Minorities in Europe", 258.

20 See Dobbelaere and Riis, "Religious and Moral Pluralism".

21 Poortinga, "Equivalence of Cross-Cultural Data".

22 Rensvold and Chung, "Testing Measurement Models for Factorial Invariance".

23 Bollen, *Structural Equations with Latent Variables*, 198; Jöreskog and Sörbom, *LISREL 8*.

and residual (co)variances are assumed to be equal (identical). The variances and covariances of the latent variables (factors) are not constrained and can thus vary between countries. When the model does not fit with the observed data, some of the equality constraints are relaxed. This means that for one or more countries, differences in the relations of some indicators to the latent variable are accepted (and reported). Minor differences are not a problem, but when substantial differences in the relationships between observed indicators and the variables occur in a particular country, one should be careful in interpreting that analysis since, in that case, the concept might have a somewhat different meaning. In other words, the measurement quality of the indicators in the different countries is evaluated by controlling structural relations between observed indicators and latent variables.

The dependent variable in this study is an aspect of ethnocentrism that is best defined as 'perceived ethnic threat'. This variable can be used as a proxy variable for several indicators of social (dis)integration since it is strongly correlated with the following: anomy, distrust of politics, utilitarian individualism.[24] *Perceived ethnic threat* is measured by three items: the feeling that the presence of immigrants in the country threatens 'our' way of life (v64), the feeling that immigrants are getting jobs at the expense of citizens (v66), and the feeling that the country has suffered from the arrival of immigrants (v68). Contrary to the complete balanced sets of items in RAMP, the measurement model for *perceived ethnic threat* is completely factorial invariant for all eleven countries.[25] Moreover the measurement quality is much better than the three positively worded (and confusing) indicators of *ethnic prejudice* that are used by Scheepers et al.[26]

The respondent's *actual denomination* is measured by the question about the subjective feeling of belonging to a church or religious group (v98 and v99). The following major categories are used in this study: Catholics, Protestants, other Christians, other religion, and un-churched (this is the reference category in the regression analysis).

24 See Billiet, "Social Capital"; Idem, "Church Involvement".

25 Fit indices of the completely factorial invariant model in a multi-group comparison: Chi-square = 224.94; RSMEA = 0.05; p-value of close fit = 1.0; NFI = 0.981. Accepting a residual covariant for the second and third item in Great Britain improves the model even significantly (Chi-square = 185.197; RMSEA = 0.047) but all other parameters remain unchanged. It is not necessary to accept this minor deviation of complete factorial invariance.

26 The general reliability (Cronbach's) is 0.77. It ranges from 0.72 to 0.79 over all nations.

The *participation in public religious services* is measured by its frequency (apart from social and familial duties). The scale ranges from never (score 0) to daily (score 7). Careful inspection of this construct shows that we can use it safely in a linear regression with ethnic threat as the dependent variable.[27]

In RAMP, religious orientation is measured by several variables. The belief dimension *Christian orthodoxy* is measured by a set of beliefs in God (v73) and by the Christian conception of Jesus Christ (v92, v93, v94 and v95).[28] As was found in previous research, this variable had no effect at all on perceived ethnic threat.[29] Two other religious orientations that are measured in RAMP are *religious saliency,* and the *importance of religious rites of passage*. The *saliency of one's religion* is measured by the self-assessment of one's religiosity (v83), the degree religion influences one's daily life (v84), and the perceived influence of one's religiosity on important decisions (v85). The *importance of religious rites of passage* at the occasion of birth (v89), marriage (v90) and death (v91) may express a sense of belonging to a cultural group and the importance attached to traditional cultural norms and practices. Therefore, a relation with perceived ethnic threat is expected.[30]

Religious tolerance is probably related to ethnocentrism. Six indicators measure two dimensions of religious tolerance. Two of the indicators are intended to measure the *attitude towards religious movements that are controversial* in the media. These indicators deal with the acceptance of publically practicing Jehovah's Witnesses (v123) and Scientologists (v124) and are both measured by 7-point response scales ranging from completely disagree (1) to completely agree (7). The other dimension deals with the *attitude towards some particularities* of religious groups: the 'chador' among young females as part of a religious tradition (v116); the use of soft drugs in the context of religious rituals (v117); the prevention of blood transfusion for children by their parents

27 The brut relationship between participation in public religious services and ethnic threat is not curvilinear, and it can be used in our linear regression. In order to be sure, the analysis was also done with a set of categorical dummy variables (second generation un-churched, first generation un-churched, irregular church practice, regular practice, and marginal members as reference category). The final conclusions were nearly the same as in models with a (quasi-) metric variable. The regular churchgoers feel significantly less threatened by immigrants.

28 A cumulative scale built on the beliefs in Jesus as God and Man (v92), as a prophet (v93), as a religious leader (v94), and the denial of the existence of Jesus (v95).

29 See Billiet, Eisinga and Scheepers, "Ethnocentrism in the Low Countries", 408-409.

30 We have not tested the equivalence of a measurement model for the different religious orientations since most are constructs made by combinations of the items scores. A second order factor model was tested, and this was, with some deviations in Italy, a nearly complete factorial invariant.

(v118); committing suicide for religious reasons (v119). These attitudes are also measured by 7-point scales (completely disagree 1 - completely agree 7). These two dimensions, which we call *tolerance towards controversial religion* and *tolerance towards religious particularities*, are confirmed in our multigroup test of the measurement model. However, the first indicator of the attitude towards religious particularities (the 'chador') is not included in the final model because it causes a number of residual covariances in various countries (correlated error).[31] Moreover, this item is somewhat contaminated by the dependent variable *perceived ethnic threat* because it refers to Muslims.

The variable *pluralism* is an additive scale based on two statements.[32] The first item (v120) states, "The increasing variety of religious groups in our society is a source of cultural enrichment". The second item is measured by the statement "Even if people belong to a particular religion, they should still feel free to draw on teachings from other religious traditions" (v122). We call it the *attitude towards religious pluralism in the country*.

Apart from these attitudinal variables at the individual level, a number of relevant background variables are measured. These are *gender* (reference category is 'men'), level of *education* (secondary, higher, and lower as the reference categories), and *generation*[33] (the generation born in 1940-1955, the generation of 1956-1970, the youngest generation born after 1970, and the generation born before 1940 as the reference categories). These are classical variables that appear in all studies. In addition, a dummy variable "whether (score 1) or not (score 0) *engaged in voluntary work* in non-religious organisations" (v54) is included since previous research has shown that active participation in organisations boosters social integration in general, and moderates negative attitudes towards immigrants in particular.[34]

31 According to the test criteria, this model is acceptable (RMSEA < .05 and NFI is close to 1). The factor loadings and the residual variances are invariant over the eleven cultural groups (countries). Moreover, all error covariances (correlated error) are fixed to zero, except for the residual covariance between the first and fifth indicator in Great Britain. The correlation between the two dimensions ranges from .11 in Italy to .45 in Great Britain. In most other countries, the correlation is higher than .25.

32 The attempt to construct a latent variable based on the five indicators (agree-disagree 7-point scales) for pluralism in the questionnaire failed, because these indicators clearly did not measure the same concept. Only two indicators with strongest correlation are used.

33 Based on Becker's generational studies. See: Becker, ed., *Dynamics of Cohort and Generations Research*.

34 Billiet, "Social Capital"; Elchardus, Huyse en Hooghe, eds., *Het maatschappelijk middenveld in Vlaanderen*.

We have included two variables that deal with the degree to which respondents have lived in lasting stable and traditional relations. This aspect is measured by the degree of geographical mobility (v55) and by the degree of urbanisation (v162) of the places they live. The first variable, *geographical mobility*, consists of three categories, those who have lived in different countries or societies (very mobile), those who have lived in a number of places within the same country or region (moderate mobile), and those who have always lived in the same neighbourhood (not mobile, this is the reference category in the analysis). The other variable, *level of urbanisation* (v162), is rather a context variable; however, it cannot be used that way since there is no identification of the villages or cities in the dataset. Therefore, that variable is used at the individual level.

However, we can use *country* as a context variable. This is a typical grouping variable, which is included in the random part (intercept) of the regression equation.[35] In order to investigate the differences between the groups (countries), the interactions with the other variables are explored in the fixed part of the equation. Two characteristics of the grouping variable are analysed in a further step of the analysis. These were *Gross National Product per head*, and *Index of Religious Heterogeneity* of the country. Religious heterogeneity is measured by the diversity index, which takes the number of denominations in a country into account.[36] However, as we will see, these two variables do not have a significant effect.

35 We will test a multi-level regression model by means of the MIXED MODEL procedure of SAS®. Sweden is the reference group in this analysis. In a simulation study (2007) on the applicability of multi-level analysis in the context of structural equation modelling (SEM) Meuleman and Billiet have found that reliable analysis are only possible with much more country samples than the number that is available in RAMP. However, we are not applying the analysis directly with latent and observed variables in SEM, but with constructs based on measurement models in a previous step. Our interest is mainly in cross-level interactions which specify differences in relations between dependent and independent variables according to groups. These parameters are presumably more reliable since these do not differ so much from classic regression analysis with dummies for countries.

36 In formula: $(1\text{-sum }(X_n^{\ 2}))/(1\text{-}1/k)$, where the X's are the different proportions of denominations and k is the number of denominations (source: RAMP data). Recently, this measure has been criticised when it is used a predictor for religiosity because the same indicators (memberships and participation) are measured for both variables. However we do not use this indicator as a predictor for religiosity but as a predictor for ethnic threat. See: Voas, Olsen and Crockett, *Religious Pluralism and Participation.*

Results

The relationship between church commitment, measured by *participation in public religious services* and *perceived ethnic threat* is tested in three steps. The effect parameters in the regression models indicate the amount of change (increase or decrease) in perceived ethnic threat per unit change in a metric predictor.[37] For (quasi) metric variables one can compare the amount of change since the variables are standardized before inclusion in the analysis. For the categorical predictors, the parameters must be interpreted as unit change when an individual does not belong to the reference category but to the examined category. The t-values (parameter/standard error) indicate the statistical significance of the parameters (See Table 1 p. 248-249).

In the first step (Model 1), only the effects of the social-background variables at the individual level, of the group variable (countries), of the country-level variable GNP, and of the interaction of background variables in nations with perceived ethnic prejudice are investigated. Only 16,4% of the variance level in the dependent variable at the individual is explained, and 7,1% at the country level. As expected, compared with the lower educated reference, ethnic prejudice decreases when the respondents obtained a degree in secondary or higher education. The younger generations are somewhat less prejudiced than those born before 1940. Geographical mobility, and living in urban regions, also tends to decrease ethnic prejudice. One may assume that people in these situations are more familiar with multi-cultural contexts and therefore feel less threatened. In general, gender has no significant effect on ethnic prejudice. As the significant interaction terms indicate, there are some country-specific variations in the relationships of some background variables and perceived ethnic threat (in Hungary, Italy, Great Britain, the Netherlands, and Portugal). We do not discuss these deviations from the main line, since we are primarily interested in the effect of the religious variables. The strongest moderating effect is at the country level since ethnic prejudice tends to be much lower in countries with a larger GNP per capita.

The second step (Model 2) is more interesting from the perspective of our research question since several religious variables are now included in the model. The explained variance at the individual level increases to 20,4%. Which religious variables are most responsible for this increase? Considering oneself as a Catholic, a Protestant, or in another denomination does not have

37 The change is expressed in units standard deviation. The regression models met the assumptions concerning linearity, normality, homeoskedasticity, and noncollinearity.

any impact on perceived ethnic threat. However, those belonging to another religion are somewhat less prejudiced (-0,064). This finding is not in line with previous research since in general, the un-churched tended to feel less threatened than those who belong to a religious denomination.[38] There is strong evidence that this must be explained by the presence of other religious variables (covariates) in the model, particularly the *importance of rites of passage*, since this is the major difference with the previous analysis of RAMP.[39] The importance attached to rites of passage increases ethnic threat significantly (+0,11), and this is more the case in Italy (additionally +0,198) than in the other countries. However, and in line with our expectation, participation in public religious services diminishes perceived ethnic threat significantly, but this effect is not very strong (-0,089), except in Italy where this effect is twice (another –0,098). This observation, that aspects of church commitment have different effects on perceived ethnic threat, will be discussed in the subsequent section.

In the third step (Model 3) some relevant subjective variables are included, and the explained variance at the individual level increases now to 26,1%. The explained variance at the country level (15,7%) is now also substantially higher than in Model 1. The newly included variables are related to the religious variables and that can explain why the *importance of rites of passage* and *participation in public services* are related to perceived ethnic threat. These variables are religious pluralism and tolerance towards 'controversial' religious groups or to religious particularities that are somewhat deviant from the viewpoint of the dominant culture. Persons that are more open to religious pluralism, and more tolerant, feel less threatened by ethnic minorities. The moderating effect of pluralism (-0,23) has the strongest effect in most countries. However, this is not the case in Hungary, Italy and Portugal, because of a country-specific effect in the opposite direction. The combination of the main effect and the specific country effects results in zero-relationships in these countries. The moderating effects of the two aspects of tolerance are about the same (-0,101 and -0,081), but they tend to disappear in Italy (+0,91 and +0,065). Tolerance towards controversial religions also has no impact in Finland.

38 See: Cambré, *De relatie tussen religiositeit en etnocentrisme*; Billiet, Eisinga and Scheepers, "Ethnocentrism in the Low Countries".

39 Cambré, *De relatie tussen religiositeit en etnocentrisme*.

Table 1: Multilevel regression models for perceived ethnic threat; Effect parameter [1]= (1), (t-value)= (2) (with v87b: church attendance or participation in public religious services) (N > 11,660)

* p <= 0.01; ** p <= 0.001; *** p <= 0.0001; [1] parameters are actually strictly unstandardised in the regression analysis, but they are computed on variables that are standardized before analysis.

Explanatory variables		**Model 1**		**Model 2**		**Model 3**	
Fixed part		**(1)**	**(2)**	**(1)**	**(2)**	**(1)**	**(2)**
Gender (Ref. Women):	Men	.005	0.50)	0.005	(0.52)	0.010	(1.06)
Level of education (Ref. Lower):	Secondary	-0.131***	(-12.38)	-0.112***	(-11.50)	-0.102***	(-9.91)
	Higher	-0.184***	(-18.75)	-0.169***	(-17.43)	-0.134***	(-13.95)
Generation (Ref. born<1940):	1940 - 1955	-0.032*	(-3.05)	-0.028*	(-2.63)	-0.012	(-1.19)
	1956 - 1970	-0.052***	(-4.95)	-0.050***	(-4.39)	-0.028	(-2.50)
	1971 - 1982	-0.059***	(-5.43)	-0.066***	(-5.06)	-0.022	(-2.06)
Geographical mobility		-0.075***	(-8.06)	-0.066***	(-7.20)	-0.050***	(-5.50)
Degree of urbanisation		-0.040***	(-4.50)	-0.040***	(-4.44)	-0.030**	(-3.44)
Engaged in voluntary work		-0.050	(-5.78)	-0.044***	(-5.16)	-0.030**	(-3.66)
*Gender*Hungary*		-0.096*	(-3.11)	-0.091*	(-3.00)	-0.069	(-2.27)
*Gender*Italy*		-0.070*	(-3.18)	-0.059*	(-2.67)	-0.061*	(-2.87)
*Higher*Great Britain*		-0.079*	(-2.89)	-0.072*	(-2.70)	-0.029	(-1.13)
*Generation 1956-1970*Netherlands*		-0.074	(-2.52)	-0.075*	(-2.60)	-0.047	(-1.70)
*Generation 1971-1982*Portugal*		-0.099**	(-3.63)	-0.102***	(-3.81)	-0102***	(-3.91)
*Geographical mobility*Netherlands (continued)*		-0.094*	(-3.80)	-0103**	(-3.43)	-0.056	(-1.91)

Actual denomination (Ref. un-churched): Roman Catholic			-0.029	(-2.13)	-0.024	(-1.78)
Protestant			-0.007	(-0.43)	-0.014	(-0.89)
Other Christian			-0.012	(-1.16)	-0.007	(-0.71)
Other religion			-0.064***	(-6.29)	-0.058***	(-5.79)
Participation in public religious services			-0.089***	(-6.79)	-0.089***	(-6.92)
Importance of rites of passage			0.110***	(9.34)	0.079***	(6.75)
Religious saliency			0024	(2.07)	0.044***	(3.83)
*Participation in public religious services*Italy*			-0.098***	(-3.82)	-0.112***	(-4.44)
*Importance of rites of passage*Italy*			0.198***	(8.24)	0.234***	(9.93)
Religious pluralism					-0.230***	(-18.25)
Tolerant towards controversial religions					-0.101***	(-9.52)
Tolerant towards religious particularities					-0.081***	(-7.94)
*Religious pluralism*Hungary*					0.215***	(7.17)
*Religious pluralism*Italy*					0.205***	(9.31)
*Religious pluralism*Poland*					0.148***	(4.77)
*Religious pluralism*Portugal*					0.275***	(8.67)
*Tolerant controversial religions*Italy*					0.091*	(3.24)
*Tolerant controversial religions*Finland*					0.095*	(2.77)
*Tolerant religious particularities*Italy*					0.065*	(3.08)
GNP_cap of country	-0.228***	(-4.09)	-0.221***	(-4.94)	-0.207***	(-5.50)
Religious heterogeneity of country			0.133*	(2.75)	0.143**	(3.52)
Random part						
Level 1. Countries (variance of intercept)	0.042	(2.08)	0.025	(1.90)	0.017	(1.86)
Level 2. Individuals (residual variance)	0.824***	(77.12)	0.799***	(77.05)	0.748***	(76.17)
R^2 at individual level	16,4%		20,4%		26,1%	
R^2 at country level	7,15%		8,36%		15,7%	

The new subjective variables are negatively related to our religious predictors, but since the latter have opposite effects on ethnic prejudice, we can expect a different impact from their inclusion into the model. If one of the religious variables (e.g. rites) decreases or even completely loses effect, it indicates that that variable's effect on ethnic threat is somewhat (or even completely) spurious, and that one of the new subjective variables (pluralism, tolerance) gives the real explanation. On the other hand, when one of the religious variables' effects becomes substantially stronger, it means that its effect is (partially) hidden because of its relation with one of the newly included subjective variables. What are the additional findings of Model 3? The effect of participation in public religious services remains unchanged and seems real. The effect of the importance attached to rites of passages diminishes slightly (from +0,11 to 0,079), and this is partially due to the interrelation with pluralism and tolerance. The effect of religious saliency now appears. This means that after controlling for religious pluralism and tolerance, people for whom religion is more salient feel somewhat more threatened by ethnic minorities.

Discussion

Our analysis of the RAMP data from in eleven European countries was done from the perspective of social capital. Does the people's involvement in church have a favourable effect on social attitudes that advance social integration in a pluralistic, democratic society? The conclusion from previous research in Belgium was affirmative for six indicators of social integration. We wondered whether that conclusion also holds for other European societies. The fact that only one of these six indicators, *perceived ethnic threat*, was adequately measured in RAMP was a serious limitation in this study, however it still showed a substantial relationship with the other indicators. Therefore, perceived ethnic threat was conceived as a valid proxy variable for the other social attitudes that are advantageous for social integration.

In line with previous research we found a small but significant moderating effect of *participation in public religious services* on perceived ethnic threat. More participation in public religious services, an indicator for church commitment, leads to a lower degree of perceived ethnic threat. Conversely, *attaching great importance to rites of passage* and *religious saliency* were positively related to perceived ethnic threat. Those who are strongly attached to rites of passage and those who regard their religion as important in their daily life feel somewhat more threatened by immigrants. Other religious variables like Christian orthodoxy and private religious practice had no effect. Contrary to some previous studies, we also found no difference in perceived ethnic threat between the members of the Christian churches and the un-churched. Only the members of the non-Christian religions feel somewhat less threatened by immigrants. This is understandable since it is likely that in the societies we have studied, many of those belonging to non-Christian religions are immigrants themselves, or belong to ethnic minorities.

How can we explain the opposite effects of the participation in public services and the two other indicators of religious involvement? The participation in public religious services (church attendance) is the reporting not of an attitude but of behaviour. More important it indicates participation in a community. This variable is thus clearly linked to sources of social capital other than the importance of rites of passage and the saliency of one's religion. Those who regularly participate in religious services often take part in other social activities within their local community. The studies on social capital have shown that embeddedness in communities and in voluntary organisations promotes social trust. One may also hypothesise that regular churchgoers more frequently hear sermons and other messages from pastors who often stress openness and charity towards foreigners.

The importance attached to rites of passage does not have the same affinity with social capital. Rites of passage, especially in the churches that are characterised by substantial amounts of marginal church members, are not an indication of strong religious feeling but of cultural conformism. For a large number of marginal churchgoers, religious services for birth, marriage, and for the deceased, fit into cultural and familial traditions and may be indications of the importance attached to traditional cultural norms and practices (customs).[40] Since the famous study of G.W. Allport, it is known that cultural conservatism is strongly related to ethnocentrism.[41] The idea that our "own way of life" is threatened by immigrants, is included in our scale.[42] The feeble relationship between religious saliency and perceived ethnic threat has, as far as we know, no theoretically meaningful explanation.

The variables that are introduced in Model 3, religious pluralism and tolerance, are also clearly linked to the (lack of) concern with one's cultural tradi-

40 This was of the conclusions of a PhD dissertation on baptism in Belgium. See: Van Meerbeeck, *Het doopsel*, 125-266.

41 Allport, *The Nature of Prejudice*, 72, 431.

42 See item v64: "The arrival of immigrants in [country] poses a threat to our own way of life".

tion. The more people hold for pluralism and tolerance, the less they feel threatened by immigrants in most of the countries under study. However, this is not the case for pluralism and tolerance in Italy. Moreover, religious pluralism does not play a role in Hungary, Poland, and Portugal, while tolerance towards religious particularities does not affect ethnic prejudice in Finland. The few context variables that are in our database are not able to explain these deviations from the general line.

In view of our explanation of the effect of 'importance of rites of passage' ('cultural traditionalism'), we expected that this effect would shrink considerably after the introduction of pluralism and tolerance, however this is only partly the case.

The effect of the context variable "religious heterogeneity of the country" is in line with existing theories about religious competition.[43] Citizens in religiously heterogeneous countries feel somewhat more threatened by immigrants because of the religious competition in multi-religious societies. Denominations tend to stress their particularity, and this leads to stronger in-group feelings. Since there were significant interactions of ethnic threat with some countries and other variables, there were other country-specific effects that are not controlled by the two variables in the Model (*GNP/cap of country*, and *religious heterogeneity*). With the information we have in this study, we cannot identify these characteristics. Further research is particular needed in order to identify them. Italy was an exception in many cases. Is this substantial or a measurement error? Food for thought.

In eleven European countries, we have found a moderating effect of church involvement, measured by participation in public religious services, on perceived ethnic threat, which is one of the indicators of social integration. The effect was not strong, but significant. This is in line with our social capital approach. We were not able to investigate the other indicators of social integration studied in Belgium, but we hope to do so in further research.

43 Scheepers, Gijsberts and Hello, "Religiosity and Prejudice against Ethnic Minorities in Europe"; Finke and Stark, "Religious Economies and Sacred Canopies"; Cambré, *De relatie tussen religiositeit en etnocentrisme*, 39.

III
Impact and Reception of Vatican II

La réception du Concile Vatican II dans la Curie romaine

Philippe Chenaux

À la veille de l'ouverture des travaux du Concile Vatican II, en octobre 1962, l'image de la Curie romaine dans l'Église catholique reste très négative.[1] De nombreux évêques, dans leurs *vota* envoyés à Rome en réponse à la consultation lancée par la commission antépréparatoire en juin 1959, avaient réclamé "des changements dans l'administration" centrale de l'Église.[2] La réforme de la Congrégation du Saint-Office n'était-elle pas devenue, au cours de la période de préparation, l'un des plus sûrs marqueurs d'"un esprit réformiste"?[3] Passé le premier moment de stupeur et d'incrédulité, la réaction des principaux responsables de la Curie à l'initiative du pape Jean de convoquer un Concile œcuménique avait été empreinte d'une grande réserve. Face à l'avalanche de propositions parvenues à Rome, de signe souvent contradictoire et partant difficiles à interpréter dans un sens univoque comme l'ont bien montré les différentes analyses réalisées sur cet important matériau, le réflexe naturel des chefs de dicastère romain, devenus présidents des dix commissions conciliaires mises sur pied par décret pontifical en juin 1960, avait été pour ainsi dire de canaliser autant que possible ces velléités de réformes en préservant l'acquis qui, pour l'essentiel, se confondait dans leur esprit avec l'héritage du pontificat de Pie XII.[4] Le poids des hommes liés de près ou de loin à l'ancien pontife (les "pacelliens" comme on les appelle) dans l'appareil curial au début du pontificat roncallien demeure un sujet d'interrogation pour l'historien. Tout en insistant, dès l'origine, sur la nécessaire séparation entre le gouvernement ordinaire de l'Église (Curie) et la préparation de cet

1 "Cela fait mille ans que la Curie romaine crée des problèmes à l'Église" (témoignage du cardinal Siri au procès de béatification du cardinal Schuster, cité dans Sani, *Da De Gasperi a Fanfani*, 194, note 44).

2 Voir par exemple, pour la France, l'étude de Hilaire, "Les vœux de évêques français", 107.

3 Selon l'expression de Fouilloux, "La phase antépréparatoire", 136.

4 Riccardi, "I 'vota' romani", 163-168.

événement extraordinaire qu'était le Concile Vatican II, Jean XXIII s'était bien gardé de promouvoir des hommes neufs aux principaux postes de responsabilité en vue de l'organisation du futur Concile.[5] N'avait-il pas confié la présidence de la commission antépréparatoire à l'un des plus proches collaborateurs du pape Pacelli, le cardinal secrétaire d'État Domenico Tardini? N'est-ce pas son confesseur, le cardinal jésuite allemand Augustin Bea, qu'il nomma à la tête du nouveau Secrétariat pour l'unité des chrétiens institué en juin 1960 dans le but de nouer des contacts avec les autres confessions chrétiennes? Le choix de la continuité devait s'avérer, dans le cas de Bea, "créateur" lorsqu'on sait le rôle capital que devait jouer ce dernier comme leader de la majorité conciliaire.[6] Il convient donc de ne pas projeter une image trop monolithique de la Curie à la veille du Concile: l'antagonisme Bea-Ottaviani durant la phase préparatoire ou, si l'on préfère, la tension entre les positions relativement ouvertes du Secrétariat pour l'unité et celles, résolument conservatrices, du Saint-Office préfigure en quelque sorte les débats de l'assemblée conciliaire. Entre les deux, existait pourtant toute une gamme d'attitudes différenciées qu'il serait sans doute utile d'analyser dans le détail, notamment par rapport à cet enjeu central autour duquel allait se cristalliser la future majorité conciliaire: la réforme de la Curie.

La Curie romaine devait connaître, dans les années suivant le Concile, "une forte accélération de son processus de réforme".[7] Jusqu'à Vatican II en effet, seul deux papes (Sixte V, Pie X) avaient osé s'attaquer à une réforme d'ensemble du gouvernement de l'Église: tandis que la bulle *Immensa aeterni Dei* (22 janvier 1587) jetait les fondements de la Curie moderne au lendemain du Concile de Trente, la constitution *Sapienti consilio* (29 juin 1908) réorgani-sait la plupart de ses dicastères dans le contexte nouveau créé par la fin du pouvoir temporel. Depuis la fin du Concile Vatican II, le fonctionnement de la Curie a été l'objet d'une attention particulière de la part des pontifes romains: Paul VI entreprit la mise à jour de ses structures au lendemain du Concile (constitution apostolique *Regimini Ecclesiae universae*, 15 août 1967)[8]; Jean-Paul II adapta son organisation aux nouvelles dispositions du Code de droit canonique (constitution apostolique *Pastor bonus*, 29 juin 1988).[9] Cette double réforme successive n'épuise certes pas le processus de "réception" des

5 Riccardi, "Preparare il Concilio".
6 Cf. la biographie bien documentée de Schmidt, *Augustin Bea*.
7 Astorri, "La segreteria di stato nelle riforme", 502.
8 Voir les contributions d'Uginet, "La constitution 'Regimini ecclesiae universae'", et de d'Onorio, "Paul VI et le gouvernement central de l'Église", ainsi que celle de Manzanares, "La reforma de la curia romana por Pablo VI".
9 Bonnet et Gullo, éds., *La Curia romana nella costituzione apostolica "Pastor bonus"*.

enseignements conciliaires au niveau du gouvernement central de l'Église, mais elle est révélatrice d'une indiscutable volonté réformatrice au sommet de l'appareil ecclésial dans la fidélité à la lettre et à l'esprit du Concile. La "nouvelle Curie" de Paul VI et de Jean-Paul II (moins italienne, plus internationale) a-t-elle joué le jeu de l'*aggiornamento*? S'était-elle voulu un instrument au service de la communion ecclésiale ou bien au contraire les réformes introduites ont-elles abouti à ce que le père Congar appelait "une nouvelle centralisation"?[10] Y a-t-il de ce point de vue continuité d'inspiration entre les deux réformes, voire entre les deux pontificats? Par-delà les réformes de structures et les changements d'hommes, l'historien se doit d'être attentif à ce qu'on pourrait appeler l'esprit de l'institution. Le bilan que dressait Mgr Giovanni Benelli, l'homme choisi par Paul VI pour mettre en œuvre la réforme de la Curie en sa qualité de substitut à la secrétairerie d'État, dans une conférence prononcée à Augsbourg en juillet 1973, est à cet égard éclairant: "J'estime sincèrement (...), déclarait-il, qu'ont été mises en place des structures de soi suffisantes et efficaces pour assurer des rapports féconds entre le centre de l'Église universelle et les Églises locales. Malheureusement, de nouvelles structures et de bonnes intentions ne suffisent pas pour que chacun mette en pratique le nouveau style et les nouvelles méthodes. D'autres "réformes personnelles continuelles", d'autres changements d'esprit sont encore nécessaires pour répondre aux légitimes attentes de l'Église".[11]

Est-ce à dire que la réforme de la Curie fut un échec (Giuseppe Alberigo)?[12] Avant d'examiner les réformes successives de Paul VI et de Jean-Paul II dans l'après-Concile, nous nous intéresserons à la façon dont cette idée de réforme de la Curie a été débattue durant le Concile.

La Curie et le Concile

Faute sans doute d'un accès direct aux sources (en particulier les archives du Concile), le rôle de la Curie durant les assises conciliaires n'a pas été beaucoup étudié. Dans son étude sur les "*vota* romains", Andrea Riccardi observait pourtant qu'il s'agissait là d'un chapitre "très important dans l'histoire de l'Église contemporaine".[13] Dans une optique beaucoup plus

10 Congar, "Remarques générales", 852.

11 Benelli, "Les rapports entre le siège de Pierre et les Églises locales", 1075.

12 L'historien parle d'une succession frénétique de réformes "de portée marginale, bien loin d'introduire un *aggiornamento* effectif aux nouvelles conditions de la foi et de la communion ecclésiale" (Alberigo, "Transizione epocale?", 617).

13 Riccardi, "I 'vota' romani", 148.

critique, Giuseppe Alberigo note, dans le chapitre conclusif du dernier tome de la *Storia del concilio Vaticano II*, que la Curie a représenté "un pôle de toute la vie de Vatican II"."La présence au sein même de la Curie de positions diverses, loyales envers le Concile, n'a pas modifié la donnée structurelle d'un pôle ecclésiastique influent et puissant, qui a poursuivi des buts divergents par rapport à ceux de la majorité conciliaire".[14] Dans l'attente de futurs travaux sur cet aspect important de l'histoire de Vatican II et plus généralement d'une histoire de la Curie romaine qui manque encore aujourd'hui, il nous paraît utile à ce stade d'esquisser un bilan des connaissances acquises à partir d'une historiographie malgré tout assez riche et de quelques documents inédits.[15] Lorsqu'on traite des rapports entre la Curie et le Concile, il convient, me semble-t-il, d'envisager les choses d'un double point de vue: la Curie en tant qu'acteur conciliaire, la Curie en tant qu'objet de débat.[16]

Sur le premier point, il n'apparaît pas douteux que les principaux responsables de la Curie ont soutenu des positions qui étaient proches celles de la minorité: la défense du primat et de ses prérogatives, le sauvetage du latin et du thomisme, la méfiance à l'égard de l'œcuménisme, la lutte contre la liberté religieuse et la déclaration sur les juifs. Peut-on parler pour autant d'un lobby, voire d'un parti curial qui aurait tenté de s'opposer systématiquement aux réformes pour conserver son propre pouvoir? Le cas du cardinal Arcadio Larraona (1887-1973), dont les archives sont conservées à Rome auprès de la Curie généralice des missionnaires clarétins, est de ce point de vue intéressant.[17] Ce religieux d'origine espagnol, longtemps professeur de droit romain à l'Athénée pontificale du Latran, fit son entrée à la Curie romaine en 1943 comme sous-secrétaire de la Congrégation des religieux. Réputé proche de l'Opus Dei, il joua un rôle déterminant dans l'élaboration de la constitution apostolique *Provida Mater Ecclesia* (2 février 1947) sur les instituts séculiers. En 1950, Pie XII le nomma secrétaire de la même Congrégation des religieux avant que Jean XXIII, qui l'avait fait cardinal en novembre 1959, ne le propulse à la tête de la Congrégation des rites et, partant, à la présidence de la commission préparatoire sur la liturgie (12 février 1962). Son attitude, comme président de la commission conciliaire liturgique, sera, on le sait, pour le moins

14 Alberigo, "Transizione epocale?", 604.

15 Sur l'histoire de la Curie au XIXe siècle, on dispose désormais de la somme doctorale de Jankowiak, *La Curie romaine de Pie IX à Pi X*.

16 Sur l'un et l'autre aspect, on verra l'étude de Routhier, "Il Vaticano II: avvio di riforma della curia romana".

17 Alvarez Alonso, "Claretiani al Concilio: Arcadio M. Larraona, Arturo Tabera e Anastasio Gutierrez".

"contestée" aussi bien à l'intérieur qu'à l'extérieur de cette dernière.[18] Les documents consultés donnent pourtant l'impression d'un Larraona assez activiste, voir réformiste sur des sujets (les réformes institutionnelles) qui, comme canoniste, lui tenaient sans doute plus à cœur que la réforme liturgique. Loin donc de s'opposer aux réformes, le cardinal espagnol cherche au contraire à persuader le pape d'anticiper le mouvement afin de garder le contrôle d'une situation devenue mouvante. La première période du Concile ne s'était-elle pas avérée "catastrophique" (Gilles Routhier) pour la Curie? Sollicité par Jean XXIII lors d'une audience en décembre 1962, il n'hésite pas à proposer une réforme radicale du Sacré-Collège qui, "dans le climat actuel d'union plus intime avec les Orientaux et de vive tendance à donner plus d'importance à l'épiscopat", ferait du "sénat du Romain pontife" un organisme vraiment représentatif, "une sorte de continuation du Concile œcuménique".[19] Sentant souffler le vent de la collégialité et sûr de l'attention bienveillante du pape Jean, l'homme de Curie se fait l'avocat d'une stratégie de mouvement de la part de la papauté destinée à prévenir toute remise en cause de l'institution. Il n'est pas étonnant de retrouver le même Larraona, un an et demi plus tard, à l'origine d'une autre initiative, collective celle-là, dont l'issue sera en apparence plus heureuse puisqu'elle débouchera sur la décision de Paul VI d'ajouter une "*nota explicativa praevia*" au chapitre trois sur la collégialité de la future constitution conciliaire sur l'Église (*De Ecclesia*).[20] La "note personnellement adressée au Saint-Père" en date du 13 septembre 1964 et signée de 25 cardinaux (dont 16 de Curie), devait pourtant susciter, sur le moment, l'irritation de Paul VI.[21] Dans sa réponse adressée un mois plus tard, le 18 octobre 1964, au cardinal espagnol, il tendait à relativiser la portée d'une initiative qui, à ses yeux, lui était personnelle et qui n'avait pas reçu l'aval des plus hautes autorités du Saint-Office (Ottaviani, Parente). Le ton de la missive était inhabituellement ferme: à travers son destinataire, c'est à l'ensemble de la Curie que le pape s'adressait pour lui demander "d'accueillir avec prompte et sagace faveur les conclusions du Concile".[22] Paul VI a-t-il reconnu dans le cardinal Larraona le chef de file d'une espèce de fronde curiale dirigée contre le Concile et ses décisions? Le moins que l'on puisse dire est que le courant ne passait pas vraiment entre les deux hommes. En janvier 1964, le pape lui avait l'affront de nommer un évêque résidentiel, le cardinal Lercaro de Bologne, à la tête de l'organisme chargé de mettre en application la réforme liturgique, le

18 Paiano, "Les travaux de la Commission liturgique conciliaire", 6-8.

19 Lettre du card. Larraona à Jean XXIII, 31 janvier 1963 (Archives Larraona, GL 14-2).

20 Les pièces de ce dossier ont été publiées par Caprile, "Contributo alla storia della 'Nota explicativa praevia'".

21 Caprile, "Contributo", 596-603, 619-623.

22 Lettre du 18 octobre 1964, reproduite in Caprile, "Contributo", 633-635.

Consilium ad exsequendam constitutionem de sacra liturgia, la première commission post-conciliaire dont le contrôle échappait ainsi à la Curie romaine.

Autant que Paul VI, le cardinal Larraona souhaitait une réforme en profondeur des congrégations vaticanes. Il avait, on l'a vu, commencé d'y réfléchir à la demande de Jean XXIII et de mettre par écrit un "projet de réforme" "audacieux" (selon ses propres termes) qu'il transmit à Paul VI sans suite apparente.[23] Le projet en question, non daté et conservé dans ses propres archives, permet de se faire une idée dont certains milieux de la Curie (le cardinal Larraona apparaît de ce point de vue assez représentatif) concevaient, à Concile ouvert, la réforme de l'administration centrale de l'Église. Plus que d'une adhésion véritable au principe de *l'aggiornamento*, il s'agissait surtout de sauvegarder une institution gravement menacée: "Les crises très graves que le Concile a révélées, peut-être même aggravées, et qui concernent de bien des manières l'unité vraie, solide, hiérarchique de l'Église, l'exercice libre et efficace de la primauté, le retour dangereux des nationalismes, l'intolérance et la hargne contre la Curie, nous obligent à considérer les questions touchant la réforme de la Curie d'une manière bien plus radicale et plus sérieuse que ce n'était le cas au temps de Pie X".[24]

Dans son projet, le cardinal pointait du doigt deux graves causes de "dysfonctionnement" de la Curie romaine: la première, à laquelle selon lui la constitution *Sapiente Consilio* (29 juin 1908) avait cherché en vain de porter remède, était le chevauchement des compétences, cette "plaie dans l'évolution de la Curie", qui bien souvent se résolvait au bénéfice du Saint-Office; la seconde était le manque de coordination entre ses différents dicastères. "Il faut créer quelque chose qui ressemble à un Conseil des Ministres" proposait le cardinal pour qui la réforme devait "être et apparaître sérieuse et de fond, même dans les plus petits détails". Pour le reste, ses propositions n'avaient rien de révolutionnaire: le cardinal reprenait à son compte, de manière mesurée, l'idée d'une meilleure représentativité internationale de la Curie (de l'ordre de 30 à 35% de non Italiens) et se prononçait pour une sélection plus rigoureuse des candidats à travers notamment le rétablissement des procédures de concours. S'agissant des congrégations romaines et de leur ordonnancement, la seule proposition

23 Lettre du 28 octobre 1964, in Caprile, "Contributo", 650.

24 "Le crisi assai gravi che il Concilio ha manifestato, forse anche acuito, e che in tanti modi riguardano l'*unita* vera, solida, gerarchica della Chiesa, l'*esercizio* libero e efficace del *Primato*, il risorgere pauroso di nazionalismi, l'insofferenza ed astio contro la Curia, ci forzano a condirerare le questioni riguardanti la *Riforma della Curia* in modo ben più serio e più radicale che non al tempo di S. Pio X" (Archives Larraona, GL 14-2).

25 Cf. l'analyse de Famerée, "Vescovi e diocesi".

vraiment innovante concernait la Congrégation du Saint-Office qu'il suggérait de rebaptiser "Sacrée Congrégation théologique" en diminuant au passage ses compétences (notamment dans le domaine disciplinaire). On peut d'ailleurs se demander si l'un des buts de sa réforme n'était pas aussi d'affaiblir la toute puissante congrégation du cardinal Ottaviani que le cardinal Frings avait violemment prise à partie lors du débat conciliaire sur le schéma *De episcopis* en novembre 1963.[25] Le projet du cardinal Larraona apparaissait bien en deçà des attentes du Concile exprimées dans les paragraphes 9 et 10 du décret sur la charge pastorale des évêques *Christus Dominus* (28 octobre 1965). Rien n'était dit par exemple sur l'insertion d'évêques diocésains dans les congrégations romaines. Le cardinal Larraona ne sera pas appelé à faire partie de la commission mise en place par Paul VI pour réfléchir à la réorganisation de la Curie, mais certaines de ses idées trouveront malgré tout leur place dans la constitution *Regimini Ecclesiae universae* promulgué le 15 août 1967.

Les réformes de Paul VI

Paul VI, le "prince réformateur" (Andrea Riccardi), attacha d'emblée une grande importance à la réforme de la Curie. En tant qu'ancien substitut à la secrétairerie d'État sous les pontificats de Pie XI et surtout de Pie XII (de 1937 jusqu'à son transfert à Milan en 1954), il en connaissait bien tous les rouages mais aussi les défauts et les insuffisances. Comme l'écrit Mgr Moreira Neves, "aucun autre n'était plus préparé que lui" pour mener à bien cette réforme.[26] Dans son premier discours à la Curie du 21 septembre 1963, il invitait cette dernière à "accueillir" positivement les critiques dont elle était l'objet: comme "un stimulant à la vigilance, un rappel à l'observance, une invitation à la réforme, un ferment de perfection". C'est de Rome en effet que devait venir l'exemple de *l'aggiornamento* voulu par son prédécesseur: "la résolution de moderniser les structures juridiques et d'approfondir la conscience spirituelle, non seulement ne trouve pas de résistance au centre de l'Église, à la Curie romaine, mais trouve cette même Curie à l'avant-garde de cette réforme continuelle dont l'Église a constamment besoin en tant qu'institution humaine et terrestre".[27] Bien décidé à aller de l'avant sur cet important dossier, Paul VI ne voyait pas encore très clair sur la manière de procéder et sur l'ampleur des changements de structures à apporter. Dès cette période, il chargea une commission cardinalice d'étudier l'ensemble de la question. Les données

26 Moreira Neves, "Paul VI et la réforme de la Curie", 57.
27 *Documents pontificaux de Paul VI*, I (1963), 248.

encore fragmentaires dont dispose l'historien ne permettent pas de se faire une idée précise du déroulement de ses travaux. Si l'on en juge par les explications de son secrétaire, Mgr Giovanni Pinna, lors de la présentation de la constitution *Regimini Ecclesiae universae* à la presse en août 1967, il semble que son fonctionnement ait été assez chaotique.[28] Deux de ses membres (les cardinaux Jullien, ancien doyen de la Rote, et Albareda, bénédictin, ancien préfet de la Bibliothèque vaticane) durent être rapidement remplacés pour cause de décès (le premier par le cardinal William Heard, le second par le cardinal Efrem Forni). Après une première phase d'étude et de consultation (congrégations, épiscopat, collèges romains), divers projets (trois au total, plus un avant-projet) furent élaborés et soumis au pape. À l'idée de départ d'un document unique, se substitua celle d'une réforme "graduelle" congrégation par congrégation dont Paul VI se fit l'écho dans ses interventions au cours de l'année 1965: la réforme annoncée se ferait de manière "progressive", en ménageant les étapes et sans "dramatiser", car, comme il le déclarait à un journaliste du *Corriere della Sera* en octobre à la veille de son voyage aux Nations Unies, "il n'y avait pas de problèmes graves" à résoudre.[29] Plutôt que de réformes ou de "changements de structures", il préférait d'ailleurs parler de "retouches", de "simplifications", de "perfectionnements" dans son grand discours au Concile du 18 novembre 1965: "La transformation attendue semblera lente et partielle, et il doit en être ainsi si l'on veut rendre aux personnes et aux traditions le respect qu'elles méritent, mais elle viendra".[30] Cette stratégie des petits pas aboutit à la publication, le dernier jour du Concile, du motu proprio *Integrae servandae* (7 décembre 1965) concernant la Congrégation du Saint-Office. En prenant le nom de simple "Congrégation pour la doctrine de la foi", cette dernière perdait à la fois sa prééminence et son caractère inquisitorial ("poursuivre les hérésies, et, par conséquent, réprimer les délits contre la foi" selon la constitution *Licet ab initio* de Paul III du 21 juillet 1542) au profit d'une mission doctrinale et pastorale positive: "promouvoir la saine doctrine et l'accomplissement par l'Église de ses plus importances tâches d'apostolat" en "corrigeant les erreurs et en ramenant dans la bonne voie ceux qui s'en sont écartés".[31] Quant à l'*Index librorum prohibitorum*, il devait être purement et simplement supprimé par une notification de ladite congrégation du 14 juin 1966.[32] Parallèlement à cette première réforme hautement symbolique réclamée par la grande majorité des Pères conciliaires, Paul VI s'attacha à créer de

28 "La genèse de la Constitution 'Regimini Ecclesiae universae'".
29 *Documents pontificaux de Paul VI*, III (1965), 515-516.
30 Ibidem, 611.
31 *La Documentation Catholique*, 48 (1966) 1462, 83.
32 Ibidem, 48 (1966) 1474, 1175-1176.

nouveaux organismes destinés à mettre en œuvre l'esprit du Concile: le Secrétariat pour le dialogue avec les non chrétiens (bref *Progrediente Concilio*, 19 mai 1964), le Secrétariat pour le dialogue avec les non-croyants (9 avril 1965), le Conseil pontifical pour les laïcs et la Commission "Justice et Paix" (motu proprio *Catholicam Christi Ecclesiam*, 6 janvier 1967). D'autres organismes seront créés dans les années suivantes (la Commission théologique internationale, la Commission pontificale pour la pastorale des migrations et du tourisme, le Conseil pontifical "Cor unum", le Comité pour la famille). Ainsi prenait forme, dans l'immédiat après-Concile, ce qu'on a pu appeler la "nouvelle Curie" de Paul VI, qui n'était rien d'autre que la traduction institutionnelle d'une Église en dialogue "avec les autres religions et avec la société civile".[33] Saurait-elle pour autant "fusionner" avec l'ancienne? Comment se ferait l'articulation entre tous ces organismes? Après avoir beaucoup tergiversé, la commission chargée de la réforme de la Curie opta pour un "document unique" proposant "une vision d'ensemble" sur le modèle des deux précédentes constitutions citées. Paul VI, assisté de deux de ses plus proches collaborateurs (Dell'Acqua, Martin) suivit personnellement, semble-t-il, l'élaboration de ce qui allait devenir la constitution *Regimini Ecclesiae universae* du 15 août 1967.[34]

Au terme de réforme, Paul VI préférait celui de "rénovation" dans le long préambule qui ouvrait la constitution REU: "il a semblé que la Curie romaine digne de tous les éloges en raison de sa piété, de son activité, de sa vaillance, de sa probité, devait être rénovée de telle sorte qu'elle soit comme un instrument pleinement adapté et efficace pour celui à qui ont été confiées les fonctions suprêmes de magistère et de gouvernement". Tout en maintenant le cadre institutionnel de l'ancienne Curie (la distinction entre les congrégations, les tribunaux, les offices auxquels venaient s'ajouter les secrétariats), la constitution introduisait des dispositions nouvelles en réponse aux attente exprimées par le Concile: la limitation des mandats des cardinaux membres, secrétaires et consulteurs à cinq ans, la cessation de droit de leurs fonctions à la mort du souverain pontife, le recrutement international de son personnel, le refus d'un droit automatique à l'avancement, l'introduction des langues vivantes dans son administration. En s'ouvrant davantage sur l'extérieur à la suite de la décision, annoncée quelques jours plus tôt (*Pro comperto sane*, 6 août 1967), d'admettre des évêques diocésains en qualité de membres au sein des congrégations romaines, la Curie se voyait dotée de nouveaux instru-

33 Acerbi, "L'ecclésiologie à la base des institutions ecclésiales post-conciliaires", 240.
34 *La Documentation Catholique*, 49 (1967) 1500, 1441-1473.

ments de coordination pour les affaires dites de compétence mixte entre ses divers dicastères (13-18). La Secrétairerie d'État (ou "Secrétariat du Pape") était investi d'un rôle de coordination tout à fait central (analogue à celui d'un premier ministre ou d'un chef de gouvernement) qui en faisait la clé de voûte de tout l'organisme curial et la mettait au-dessus de toutes les autres congrégations (19-25). Quant à la congrégation dite des "Affaires ecclésiastiques extraordinaires", jusque-là considérée comme la première section de la Secrétairerie d'État, elle s'émancipait de cette dernière pour devenir le Conseil pour les affaires publiques de l'Église, sorte de ministère des affaires étrangères du Saint-Siège chargé "de traiter tout ce qui concerne les rapports avec les gouvernements civils" (26-28).

Avec la réforme de 1967, les prescriptions du Concile concernant la réorganisation de la Curie (décentralisation, internationalisation, participation des évêques diocésains) trouvaient une première forme d'actualisation au niveau juridique tout au moins. Restait à les mettre en application, autrement dit de passer d'une "réception formelle" des décisions du Concile à une "réception pratique" effective. Il n'entre pas dans notre propos ici d'évaluer la portée réelle d'une telle réforme sur le gouvernement central de l'Église dans les années du pontificat de Paul VI.[35] Une telle évaluation nécessiterait des recherches dépassant le cadre d'une telle communication et, de toute manière pour l'instant, très difficiles à entreprendre étant donné la fermeture des archives. Certains historiens n'ont pas manqué de souligner les inconvénients d'une telle réforme: tandis que le renforcement du rôle de la secrétairerie d'État aurait diminué l'autonomie des congrégations et partant le rôle de "contrepoids institutionnel" traditionnellement dévolu à la Curie (A. Acerbi)[36], l'internationalisation de son personnel, effective dès la fin des années 1960 comme le montrait une étude du p. Cavalli dans la *Civiltà Cattolica*[37], aurait réduit son homogénéité pour en faire une sorte de bureaucratie sans âme sur le modèle des grandes organisations internationales (A. Riccardi).[38] Par-delà les critiques, justifiées ou non, que peut faire l'historien, mais jamais exemptes de présupposés idéologiques ou de préjugés personnels, au sujet de son fonctionnement, il convient de faire crédit à Paul VI de sa loyauté dans la mise en œuvre, non seulement des décisions du Concile, mais également de son esprit. La réforme des structures était une chose, la réforme des esprits en était une autre: "il est une autre réforme, au sens ascétique du mot, à laquelle Nous tenons

35 Je préfère renvoyer le lecteur sur ce point à la contribution déjà cité de d'Onorio, "Paul VI et le gouvernement central de l'Église".

36 Acerbi, "L'ecclésiologie", 239.

37 Cavalli, "Sviluppo dell'internazionalizzazione nella Curia romana".

38 Riccardi, *Le politiche della Chiesa*, 149-150.

beaucoup, qui n'est pas toujours l'affaire de normes juridiques, mais qui est l'affaire de chacun d'entre nous, de notre façon de penser, d'agir et de servir avec esprit de foi et de sacrifice" (discours au Sacré-Collège, 22 décembre 1967).[39]

La constitution "Pastor bonus" (28 juin 1988)

Publiée vingt ans après l'entrée en vigueur de la constitution *Regimini Ecclesiae universae*, la constitution *Pastor bonus* (28 juin 1988) se voulait comme elle "un fruit du Concile Vatican II".[40] Dans un long préambule sur lequel nous aurons à revenir, Jean-Paul II expliquait qu'il avait, "dès le début de son pontificat", ouvert "une large consultation" (auprès des cardinaux, des dicastères, des Églises locales), en vue d'une nouvelle organisation de la Curie romaine à laquelle Paul VI lui-même avait commencé de réfléchir à partir de 1972.[41] La réforme s'inscrivait dans un double contexte ecclésial marqué à la fois par l'adoption du nouveau Code de droit canonique (1983) et d'autre part par la tenue du Synode extraordinaire des évêques (1985). On sait que la révision du Code de droit canonique avait été soustraite à la compétence du Concile et qu'une commission cardinalice *ad hoc* avait été constituée dès avant la fin de ses travaux (1963). Ce n'est très exactement que vingt-quatre ans après l'annonce qu'en avait faite Jean XXIII dans son discours de convocation du Concile (25 janvier 1959) qu'était promulgué par Jean-Paul II le nouveau *Codex iuris canonici* (25 janvier 1983). Le lien avec les enseignements de Vatican II était très clairement indiqué dans la constitution de promulgation: le code se voulait une traduction, en langage canonique (*in sermonem canonisticum*) du Concile, et revendiquait un caractère de complémentarité par rapport à son magistère doctrinal, spécialement les constitutions *Lumen gentium* et *Gaudium et Spes*. L'ecclésiologie de communion, "comme structure portante, juridiquement déterminante, du rapport entre Église universelle et églises particulières" (R. Astorri), inspirait l'ensemble de la constitution.[42] C'est cette même ecclésiologie de communion qui allait être au centre des travaux du synode extraordinaire réuni en 1985 à l'occasion du 20ème anniversaire de la fin du Concile. Précédé par la publication d'un livre d'entretiens à grand succès du cardinal Ratzinger (*Entretiens sur la foi*,

39 *Documents pontificaux de Paul VI*, VI (1967), 811.
40 Texte français dans *La nouvelle organisation de la Curie Romaine*, 13.
41 Cf. Rossi, "Le tappe della preparazione della costituzione apostolica *Pastor bonus*".
42 Astorri, "Codex iuris canonici", 364-369.

1985) appelant à "redécouvrir le vrai Concile", le synode devait constituer un "tournant" dans la réception de Vatican II ou, si l'on préfère, une tentative de reconstruction ("restauration" diront certains) de la part du magistère romain, à partir d'une lecture non sélective des documents conciliaires centrée sur les notions de "mystère" et de "communion".[43]

Le long préambule de la constitution *Pastor bonus* s'efforce ainsi de repenser la nature et les tâches de la Curie sur la base de cette ecclésiologie de communion. Après avoir défini le ministère de Pierre et de ses successeurs comme un ministère (*diakonia*) de communion et d'unité, il en vient à expliciter les deux caractéristiques de la Curie romaine contenues dans le décret conciliaire *Christus Dominus:* son caractère "ministériel" (ou de service), son caractère "vicaire" (au nom et sous l'autorité du pape), pour ensuite aboutir à cette définition de la Curie: "La Curie romaine, lit-on ainsi dans l'article 1 de la constitution, est l'ensemble des dicastères qui aident le Pontife romain dans l'exercice de sa mission pastorale suprême pour le bien et le service de l'Église universelle et des Églises particulières, exercice par lequel se renforcent l'unité de foi et la communion du peuple de Dieu et est promue la mission propre de l'Église dans le monde".[44]

Pour le reste, la réforme, de "profil modeste" (G. Alberigo), n'apportait pas de grands changements structurels si l'on excepte la réorganisation de la secrétairerie d'État en deux sections (les affaires générales, les relations avec les États), la réduction au rang de conseils des secrétariats institués par Jean XXIII et Paul VI au moment du Concile pour promouvoir l'union des chrétiens, le dialogue avec les religions non chrétiennes et le dialogue avec les non croyants.[45] La Curie de Jean-Paul II, du moins telle qu'elle se dessine au début des années 1990 (terme assignée à notre étude), n'est donc pas si différente, dans son organisation et ses structures, de celle de Paul VI. A-t-elle pour autant pleinement assimilé le rôle de serviteur de la communion ecclésiale (entre l'évêque de Rome et les autres évêques) que lui assignait cet authentique "fils du Concile" qu'est Jean-Paul II? La question mérite d'être posée au terme de cette étude.

43 Theobald, "Le devenir de la théologie catholique depuis le concile Vatican II", 174-175.

44 *La nouvelle organisation de la Curie romaine*, 22.

45 Alberigo, "Le concezioni della Chiesa e i mutamenti istituzionali", 117.

Collégialité et primauté dans l'application de Vatican II

Jan Grootaers

Dans ce texte je veux esquisser brièvement une évolution qui couvre quarante années. Je me limite donc à quelques points saillants concernant l'application ou la non-application de la collégialité épiscopale, qui fut à Vatican II un des thèmes les plus significatifs du renouveau que la majorité des Pères conciliaires voulait mettre en œuvre.

La notion de "collège des évêques" était une réalité très ancienne, mais presque oubliée après Trente et après Vatican I. Elle est apparue à l'ordre du jour du Concile de 1962 comme une découverte, et, de fait, c'en était une pour de très nombreux participants de Vatican II.[1] Malheureusement, au Concile, "primauté" et "collégialité" furent ressenties par certains comme des réalités concurrentes, ce qu'elles n'étaient pas dans les projets de texte à l'origine des débats. Au cours des discussions finales de la constitution sur l'Église et du décret sur la fonction pastorale de l'épiscopat, on ne peut fermer les yeux devant les précautions imposées à l'exercice de la collégialité et destinées à sauvegarder la liberté de la primauté afin d'exercer celle-ci sans aucune limite.

À la clôture de Vatican II, l'*aggiornamento* de l'ecclésiologie dont on avait rêvé est en fait inachevé. En commission, les évêques de la majorité avaient introduit des pierres d'attente dans la version finale de *Lumen gentium*: à leurs yeux, elles allaient pouvoir servir à des élaborations postconciliaires. Cependant, des représentants de la minorité font de même en sens opposé. C'est une première hypothèque qui va peser sur la réception.

Après la clôture du Concile, il y aura bientôt parmi les protagonistes de l'héritage conciliaire deux visions très différentes. D'une part, une perspective

1 Rousseau, "Vatican II", 447.

dynamique chez ceux pour qui Vatican II est un point de départ vers l'avenir, et, d'autre part, la perspective de ceux pour qui c'est un point d'arrivée, à rattacher aux normes du passé à cause de la crainte des "dérives" de l'après-Concile. On ne peut nier que Paul VI, pendant la première moitié de son règne, a dans une large mesure appartenu à la première perspective. Il en sera autrement de Jean-Paul II. C'est une seconde hypothèque qui a influencé la réception.

Avant son élection au siège de Rome, l'archevêque de Cracovie avait eu une lecture de Vatican II qui n'était ni celle des "libéraux" de Vatican II, ni celle de l'opposition conservatrice du Concile. Très tôt après la clôture du Concile, le cardinal Wojtyla ne peut que désapprouver la "dérive" de ceux qui veulent considérer Vatican II comme un tremplin (reproche destiné notamment aux évêques d'Europe occidentale). À ses yeux, il convenait donc de relire Vatican II à la lumière de Vatican I et de Trente afin de rattacher le dernier Concile à la grande Tradition et ainsi en tempérer les textes trop tranchants. De fait, Mgr Wojtyla, proche de J. Ratzinger, ami de H. de Lubac et admirateur de H.U. von Balthasar, s'était rallié à une lecture à nos yeux réductrice, proche des "rénovateurs déçus".[2]

Lorsque le cardinal Wojtyla est élu pape à l'automne 1978, il symbolise pour la majorité de ses électeurs l'énergie et l'esprit de décision qui semblaient avoir fait défaut à son prédécesseur et il rassure ceux que certaines "dérives" de la réception du Concile n'avaient cessé d'inquiéter.[3]

Au cours de son long pontificat, Jean-Paul II a, plus d'une fois, fait allusion à cette perspective. Il nous semble qu'il l'a fait de manière particulièrement

2 Dès 1972, K. Wojtyla publie un commentaire de l'ensemble des textes conciliaires, dans lequel l'auteur ne semble pas prendre position et donne une lecture aseptisée d'un concile harmonieux et sans tensions internes. Il lit les textes comme s'ils n'avaient pas eu de genèse ni en commission ni en assemblée générale! Il s'agit de l'ouvrage *Sources of Renewal* (traduction anglaise), ou *L'arricchimento della fede* (traduction italienne). Celle-ci est préfacée par Halina Bortnowska, proche collaboratrice de Wojtyla. Elle écrit: "L'auteur se cache derrière de nombreuses citations du texte conciliaire. Souvent il ne révèle pas quelle est sa propre pensée (...). Tout se situe dans le contexte des seules citations et toute référence aux discussions post-conciliaires ou même directement conciliaires en est absente."

3 Ce Conclave de 1978 n'était nullement bipolaire. Entre les "majoritaires" de Vatican II qui soutiennent Benelli, et les "minoritaires" du Concile qui soutiennent e.a. Siri, il y a la préoccupation de ceux qui estiment que le pontificat qui vient de s'achever a manqué d'énergie et que, pour en compenser les lacunes, il faudrait un leadership à poigne et "réorienter" l'interprétation de Vatican II. Parmi eux, il y a les "pionniers déçus". Avec l'appui de l'Opus Dei, ils vont réussir à sortir le collège électoral de l'impasse en élisant un candidat imprévu mais au profil bien marqué, qui bientôt rallie une majorité enthousiaste.

explicite dans le discours qu'il prononça le 27 février 2000 à l'issue du "Congrès international sur la mise en œuvre de Vatican II". Parlant de la présence dynamique de l'enseignement conciliaire dans la vie de l'Église, le pape souligna la nécessité de ne pas perdre de vue l'intention authentique des Pères conciliaires: "Celle-ci doit plutôt être retrouvée *en dépassant des interprétations partiales et partielles* qui ont empêché d'exprimer au mieux la nouveauté du magistère conciliaire".[4] Il poursuit aussitôt: "Lire le Concile en supposant qu'il comporte une rupture avec le passé, alors qu'en réalité il se situe dans la ligne de la foi de toujours, c'est se tromper complètement".[5] Ces "interprétations partiales et partielles" peuvent être comprises comme une allusion aux "dérives" de la réception du Concile attribuées à la première phase du pontificat de Paul VI.

Nous allons donc nous intéresser à l'évolution de la collégialité vécue dans deux domaines significatifs: les synodes et les conférences épiscopales. Nous dirons quelques mots des deux synodes extraordinaires, celui de 1969 et celui de 1985. Quant aux conférences épiscopales, nous voudrions indiquer très brièvement leur flux (au cours du premier postconcile) et leur reflux (pendant les vingt-cinq dernières années).

Si cette esquisse rapide va nous amener à décrire la dévalorisation progressive de la collégialité sous Jean-Paul II, il convient de souligner clairement que ce n'est là qu'un des aspects d'un pontificat riche en développements positifs dans d'autres domaines. De même, si le choix du thème traité nous oblige à nous limiter à un seul aspect, cela ne signifie nullement que nous oubliions d'autres aspects importants du même pontificat.

En effet, la durée exceptionnelle du règne de Jean Paul II, la grande diversité des objectifs poursuivis par un pape pastoral et voyageur et enfin l'éventail de prises de position doctrinales et "théologiques" qui n'était pas toujours homogène, font qu'il est très difficile d'avoir en ce moment une vue d'ensemble. Cependant, il nous paraît certain que le pontificat wojtylien a pris un certain "virage" autour de 1990-1991 et de la chute des régimes communistes dans l'Europe de l'Est. Sans effacer le premier volet du règne, il nous semble que le second volet révèle un assouplissement des objectifs mis à l'avant-plan tels que deux encycliques œcuméniques, la préparation du Grand Jubilé, le thème du pardon à demander et l'urgence du dialogue interreligieux.

4 Les mots en italique le sont dans *La Documentation Catholique*, 82 (2000) 6, 252.
5 Ibidem, 252.

Dans la suite de cet article, ce second volet n'est pas pris en compte même s'il existe, pour nous, de manière indéniable.

Synodalité et collégialité

Au départ de Vatican II, une majorité des Pères conciliaires souhaitait organiser un "sénat" ou conseil délibératif composé de délégués des épiscopats, qui aurait pu entourer le pape en permanence et donner des directives à une Curie romaine en tant qu'organe uniquement exécutif. C'était un peu l'utopie.

Cependant, le motu proprio de Paul VI de septembre 1965, qui court-circuite les travaux de la commission conciliaire sur la fonction des évêques, instaure un synode des évêques uniquement au service de la primauté et donc sans compétence délibérative; il ignore dans son texte la collégialité.[6] Les trois objectifs majeurs que Paul VI attribue alors au synode des évêques sont: promouvoir la coopération entre le pape et les évêques, veiller à ce qu'une information directe soit disponible au sujet des problèmes auxquels l'Église est confrontée, et faciliter la "concorde" tout au moins à l'égard des points essentiels de la doctrine dans l'Église.

Malgré ce motu proprio restrictif, il n'y a aucun doute que la synodalité vécue par les évêques à Rome toutes les deux ou trois années a fait progresser leur prise de conscience collégiale. Dans de nombreux cas, la phase préparatoire du synode des évêques a valorisé les initiatives des conférences épiscopales et parfois même elle a donné lieu à d'importantes restructurations collégiales à la dimension d'un continent.[7] L'échange d'information concernant les Églises locales qui se réalise pendant la première phase de chaque synode a abouti à renforcer la solidarité et la vitalité des conférences épiscopales. Et plus d'une fois la convocation d'une assemblée synodale a donné lieu à une évaluation critique des "promesses non tenues" de Vatican II.

6 Lors de la présentation de ce motu proprio au Concile, le cardinal Marella déclare: "Le synode peut être défini comme un symbole, un signe de la collégialité, mais il n'est point l'explication de la collégialité en acte ou dans le sens doctrinal, comme c'est le cas, par exemple, pour un concile œcuménique."

7 Il est clair par exemple que la préparation du Synode de 1974, consacré au thème de l'évangélisation, a donné naissance à la Federation of Asian Bishop's Conferences, dont le rôle par la suite est devenu de plus en plus significatif, notamment à la suite de ses commissions spécialisées qui se réunissaient régulièrement entre les assemblées générales.

Ce sont là des aspects positifs qu'il faut reconnaître. Cependant, il y a aussi les aspects négatifs: chaque synode a été soumis à la "loi de l'entonnoir" qui a pour résultat que la seconde phase des travaux - celle de la rédaction des résolutions - ne fournit plus qu'un pâle reflet de l'apport des épiscopats. Cette procédure débouche sur des textes censurés par des instances supérieures et invisibles, textes dans lesquels souvent les évêques ne se reconnaissent plus.

En bref, on peut résumer le chapitre des synodes en constatant un fonctionnement généralement défectueux mais des résultats cependant significatifs au niveau du vécu.

En ce qui concerne le programme du Synode extraordinaire de 1969, il constitue en quelque sorte un complément au Concile, car on y discute de la collégialité après la "Nota Praevia", "Nota" que Vatican II avait dû voter sans avoir eu l'occasion d'en discuter. Cet ordre du jour de 1969 comprend principalement deux thèmes: les limites de la primauté et la réciprocité entre les conférences épiscopales et le Saint-Siège. Quant au Synode extraordinaire de 1985, il a pour thème principal le souci de faire une évaluation de Vatican II.

Il est difficile d'imaginer deux événements d'Église plus contrastés que ces deux synodes. Le contexte historique et l'atmosphère générale différaient; l'environnement théologique avait changé.[8] La procédure synodale de 1969 permettait encore une grande liberté de parole et d'action qui en 1985 est devenue plutôt "symbolique"; en outre, l'assemblée synodale de 1969 était encore habilitée à rédiger un véritable document de conclusion, une compétence qui n'existait plus en 1985.

8 Est tout à fait remarquable le fait que la plupart des Pères synodaux de 1985 ignoraient tout des conclusions de 1969 alors que les ordres du jour des deux assemblées étaient souvent parallèles et que les dirigeants du synode de 1985 n'avaient cure de rappeler les précédents de 1969 qui étaient très instructifs.

Le Synode extraordinaire de 1969 et l'exercice de la primauté

La question des limites de la primauté

Le cardinal Seper (à l'époque préfet de la Doctrine de la foi) souligne dans son rapport au Synode de 1969 que l'exercice de la primauté n'est pas illimité. Cet exercice est soumis à des normes objectives, telles que: la Parole révélée, la constitution de l'Église et la tradition de l'Église. Le secrétaire du Synode de 1969, le pr. A. Anton, poursuit cette énumération, car, à ses yeux, la primauté est aussi limitée par: le bien de l'Église (*bonum Ecclesiae*), les conciles œcuméniques du passé et le ministère des évêques. En conclusion de ce chapitre, le Synode exprime le vœu que la "collégialité" fasse l'objet d'une étude théologique approfondie.

Une collégialité horizontale et le Saint-Siège

Le deuxième point à l'ordre du jour de 1969 concernait la réciprocité des relations entre les conférences épiscopales et le Saint-Siège. Pour les évêques, il s'agissait de valoriser les réformes permettant aux Églises locales de "coopérer" à la rédaction de documents romains.[9] L'enjeu n'est plus la doctrine, mais concerne les structures. Alors que, selon le cardinal Marty, les principes de la collégialité sont clairement indiqués dans les textes de Vatican II[10], on regrette que les modalités d'application sont souvent incertaines. Les évêques souhaitent que de plus larges compétences soient attribuées aux conférences épiscopales. À la source de cette préoccupation il y a la crise de *Humanae Vitae* (1968) au cours de laquelle dans certains milieux épiscopaux on avait regretté que Paul VI n'avait pas tenu compte du rapport final de sa propre commission où avaient siégé des délégués de nombreux épiscopats.

Plaidant la cause d'une collégialité horizontale, une large majorité des Pères synodaux proposait d'associer davantage les épiscopats aux décisions de Rome et d'établir des communications plus directes avec le pape sans l'intermédiaire d'instances curiales. Cependant, au cours de la phase finale de la procédure, les "vota" exprimés se sont trouvés graduellement rétrécis. La proposition très applaudie du cardinal Poma, archevêque de Bologne, qui aurait

9 À l'arrière-plan de cette préoccupation se trouve évidemment la promulgation d'*Humanae vitae* au cours de l'année précédente, selon une procédure qui avait été ressentie par de nombreux évêques comme "anticollégiale".

10 Le rapport de Marty fait référence à deux sources: *Lumen gentium*, nos 22 et 23; *Christus Dominus*, n° 8.

fait du secrétariat du synode un organe représentatif afin d'assister le pape à Rome de manière permanente et afin de préparer le synode à venir selon les indications des épiscopats, ce plan Poma a été biffé par les instances romaines. Dans la version finale des "vœux", le rôle du secrétariat du synode est devenu insignifiant. L'accord quasi unanime des Pères pour obtenir une structure permanente comme support d'une collégialité vécue devient ainsi sans objet.

L'évaluation de Vatican II au Synode extraordinaire de 1985

Convoqué à courte échéance pour effectuer une évaluation de vingt ans de "réception" de Vatican II, le Synode de 1985 avait l'ambition de traiter une matière très vaste dans un climat de fortes tensions et de polémiques, notamment suscitées par le livre-interview du cardinal Ratzinger qui avait entrepris une critique parfois radicale de la collégialité et de l'épiscopat.[11]

Le rapport principal qui introduit la thématique du Synode de 1985 et qui remplace le document préparatoire est présenté par le cardinal Danneels. Celui-ci réussit à dédramatiser l'atmosphère. De manière nuancée, l'archevêque de Malines-Bruxelles refuse de suivre l'interprétation pessimiste et polémique que Ratzinger avait donnée de l'après-concile: Danneels s'y oppose implicitement mais clairement en soulignant l'accueil et les résultats positifs de Vatican II, malgré certains phénomènes négatifs qui ne sont pas passés sous silence mais traités avec modération et replacés dans le contexte des circonstances. D'emblée, le ton fut donné et ce ton conciliatoire contrastait avec l'atmosphère du moment.

Comme aux synodes précédents, ce fut le débat en séance plénière pendant les huit premiers jours qui constitua la partie la plus dynamique de la procédure de 1985. Ce débat a permis à la grande majorité des Pères synodaux

11 Déjà en 1969 le professeur Ratzinger avait publié un livre manifeste pour le grand public, qui allait à contre-courant et avait fait date. Il s'agit de *Einführung in das Christentum*, considéré à l'époque comme la plate-forme d'une mise à jour de l'antimodernisme catholique. Zizola (*La restaurazione di papa Wojtyla*, 94-97) reconnaît dans le jeune professeur "un théologien pour la restauration". En 1985, Ratzinger, devenu cardinal de Curie, se laisse interviewer par le journaliste Messori pour dénoncer les dangers et les responsables de la crise qui menace la foi. Ce *Rapporto sulla fede*, destiné lui aussi au public, non seulement déplut à une partie de la Curie romaine, qui estimait que la charge de préfet de la Doctrine de la Foi était incompatible avec des publications à caractère polémique - voir e.a. les prises de position de *La Civiltà Cattolica*, revue officieuse -, mais provoqua d'autre part un vif mécontentement parmi de nombreux évêques d'Églises locales.

d'exprimer leur attachement aux grandes avancées de Vatican II et leur désir d'en mieux valoriser les applications concrètes.

Trois courants d'opinion

Alors que la collégialité vécue et appliquée fut l'objet principal des interventions des représentants des Églises occidentales (premier courant d'opinion), aux yeux des porte-parole des jeunes Églises, l'inculturation constituait le problème le plus urgent, avec ses applications à la liturgie, à la catéchèse et aussi à la réflexion théologique (deuxième courant d'opinion). On pouvait d'ailleurs constater une interaction entre ces deux courants: la viabilité d'une inculturation se trouve essentiellement déterminée par l'espace dont peuvent disposer l'Église locale et la Conférence épiscopale. Ce "détour" caractéristique a eu pour conséquence que les interventions des orateurs des jeunes Églises étaient conçues de manière plus constructive, alors que certains porte-parole du monde nord-atlantique révélaient parfois un style plus critique à l'égard des instances romaines.

Un troisième courant d'opinion, que l'on pourrait appeler "minoritaire", s'avérait très critique à l'égard de la collégialité et de ses applications. Ces Pères ne reconnaissaient l'exercice d'un véritable magistère épiscopal que dans deux cas: celui d'un concile général et celui de l'évêque individuel dans son diocèse.[12] Cette interprétation restrictive de *Lumen gentium* débouchait sur la mise en cause d'un statut théologique des Conférences épiscopales. Ce courant en faveur de la centralisation dans l'Église est plus articulé qu'en 1969 et, en outre, il jouit en 1985 de l'appui d'instances curiales importantes. Ce courant est "minoritaire" du point de vue numérique, mais en fin de parcours, lorsqu'il

12 Dans le *Rapporto sulla fede*, le cardinal Ratzinger avait insisté sur la fonction particulière de l'évêque individuel, qui risque d'être écrasé sous le poids des conférences épiscopales avec leurs structures bureaucratiques souvent lourdes et qui, en outre, n'ont pas de base théologique. Cf. Ratzinger et Messori, *Entretien sur la foi*, 67-69. Il n'est pas sans intérêt de rappeler ici les prises de position de Mgr Marcel Lefebvre au cours du Concile et notamment dans une interview à Rome le 15 octobre 1963 avec le père R. Wiltgen de l'ordre missionnaire de Steyl: "L'évêque individuel court un grave danger. On peut facilement s'imaginer que quatre ou cinq évêques exercent dans la conférence épiscopale nationale une influence plus grande que les autres et que ces quelques évêques prennent en main la direction" (cf. Service de presse des Missionnaires de Steyl, 18 juin 1963). Par ailleurs, c'est au cours du Synode de 1985 que le préfet de la Doctrine de la Foi annonça que le dialogue avec l'archevêque dissident M. Lefebvre avait fait assez de progrès pour que le pape désigne le cardinal E. Gagnon comme visiteur apostolique de la Fraternité sacerdotale Saint-Pie X. Cette communication créa un certain malaise, plus spécifiquement parmi les évêques français particulièrement impliqués dans cette "affaire" et qui cependant n'avaient pas été consultés.

s'agira de rédiger les vœux du rapport final, ce courant aura le dessus, grâce à l'entourage le plus proche de Jean-Paul II.

Le rapport final

Dans le rapport final, qui malheureusement ne reflète plus l'ensemble des échanges synodaux[13], il faut distinguer les paragraphes explicatifs (27 au total) et les "suggestions" (6 au total). Le vote des pères ne portera que sur les "suggestions".

Dans le chapitre consacré à l'Église en tant que "communion", où se trouve traitée la collégialité, nous y remarquons quelques paragraphes explicatifs qui sont d'un grand intérêt pour aboutir ensuite à des "suggestions" proprement insignifiantes. Le passage consacré à la collégialité (II C 4) reconnaît: "L'ecclésiologie de communion offre le fondement sacramentel de la collégialité. De ce fait, la théologie de la collégialité est beaucoup plus étendue que son simple aspect juridique." Par la suite cependant, on introduit une distinction radicale entre d'une part la collégialité au sens strict, dont l'expression la plus évidente est dans le concile œcuménique, et d'autre part diverses réalisations partielles, ou indirectes et de droit ecclésiastique. Parmi celles-ci: le synode des évêques. Ensuite, le rapport reconnaît que l'esprit collégial trouve une application concrète dans les conférences épiscopales (II C 5). Ces paragraphes se terminent cependant tous les deux par une réserve explicite: les conférences épiscopales sont au service: du collège avec le pape; des évêques individuels dont la responsabilité personnelle est inaliénable. Cette double réserve limite explicitement par le haut et par le bas l'espace de liberté et de compétence dont peuvent disposer les conférences épiscopales.

Quant aux trois "suggestions" en conclusion, toute la pointe du débat synodal y est passée sous silence. On se contente de trois vœux: le désir que la codification orientale soit achevée le plus vite possible; le souhait que le "status" théologique et l'autorité doctrinale des conférences épiscopales soient étudiés, compte tenu de *Christus Dominus* n° 38 et du Code, can. 447 et 753 (cette dernière précision a été ajoutée au texte du rapporteur par une main non identifiée); la recommandation d'une étude pour examiner si le principe de subsidiarité peut être appliqué à la vie de l'Église.

Dans le rapport intermédiaire que le cardinal Danneels avait présenté à la veille des "circuli minores", on trouvait encore des traces des tensions qui

13 Cf. Komonchak, "Le débat théologique", 70.

s'étaient manifestées au cours du débat en séance plénière et que le Synode était appelé à clarifier: on y parlait de "la collégialité que de nombreux Pères souhaitent voir mieux approfondie et mise en pratique de façon plus efficace". Mais dans les "suggestions finales", cette mise en pratique souhaitée par la majorité des Pères synodaux a disparu, tandis que la mise en question de l'autorité doctrinale des conférences y a été introduite.[14]

Déjà au lendemain de Vatican II, le professeur G. Philips avait dénoncé le risque de tomber dans un monophysisme ecclésiologique: "D'autres, cédant à la tentation d'absorber tous les aspects humains de l'Église dans la majesté de son origine surnaturelle, arrivent par des voies différentes à un résultat identique: l'évacuation du mystère par destruction de sa réalité terrestre".[15]

Les thèmes importants que les épiscopats avaient cherché à mettre à l'avant-plan devant l'assemblée sont de fait absents du rapport conclusif: une évolution jugée regrettable. Mais la lacune la plus grave dans cette lecture sélective du patrimoine de Vatican II, est probablement la quasi-disparition de l'Église en tant que Peuple de Dieu.

On peut mesurer ainsi le recul que la lecture de Vatican II a subie au plan théologique au cours de cet après-concile. Alors qu'en 1969 la majorité cherchait principalement, si pas exclusivement, à obtenir des modalités pratiques de la collégialité vécue, sans y parvenir d'ailleurs, au Synode de 1985 la majorité des Pères est sur la défensive et cherche plutôt à préserver qu'à conquérir. Les instances dirigeantes en 1985 se méfient de la dynamique postconciliaire des Églises locales et, pour se justifier, prennent prétexte des phénomènes de crise.[16]

Si les synodes extraordinaires de 1969 et 1985 avaient donc eu comme unique fonction de résoudre la mise en pratique de la collégialité selon les textes de Vatican II, notre bilan serait uniquement négatif. Cependant ces

14 C'est le troisième courant d'opinion qui prend le dessus sur les deux autres courants.

15 Philips, *L'Église et son mystère*, I, 117-118. Le rapport conclusif cherche à relativiser l'importance des débats sur la structure dans l'Église d'une autre manière encore en faisant appel à l'esprit collégial et à son fondement sacramentel, "alors qu'on pourrait tout aussi justement soutenir que les questions naissent précisément de ce que les fondements sacramentaux et collégiaux requièrent des structures et des rapports mieux appropriés"; telle est l'opinion de Komonchak, "Le débat théologique", 75.

16 Ainsi, c'est en invoquant la dénomination abusive d'une "Église populaire" dans le contexte politique de l'un ou l'autre pays d'Amérique centrale que des dirigeants mènent avec succès leur offensive contre l'expression de l'Église Peuple de Dieu: pourtant un des fondements de *Lumen gentium*.

deux assemblées épiscopales ont aussi constitué des événements significatifs par la fonction d'évaluation critique et de concertation collégiale qu'elles ont réalisée dans les faits. Le Synode de 1969 a permis de réaliser une première prise de conscience de la valeur de Vatican II, le Concile ayant alors déjà été mis à l'épreuve des réalités des Églises locales. Le Synode de 1985, en tant qu'évaluation éloquente des résultats bénéfiques du Concile et en tant qu'expression très claire de la volonté d'en poursuivre la réception, constitue malgré son rapport final une étape importante de l'Église postconciliaire.

Même si la demande de reconnaître au synode des évêques une compétence délibérative - demande faite en 1969 et répétée en 1985 - n'a pas été entendue, l'assemblée synodale n'en reste pas moins une expérience réelle de collégialité vécue. Sous cet aspect, l'institution synodale garde une valeur importante pour l'avenir, même si les textes qui en résultent ne sont pas au niveau des délibérations plénières et ont généralement constitué un motif de déception.

Revalorisation et dévaluation des conférences épiscopales

Le statut des conférences épiscopales constitue un autre aspect significatif de la collégialité. Il est passé par deux phases au cours de la réception de Vatican II. La première phase est caractérisée par une revalorisation des conférences épiscopales au plan local mais aussi à Rome où Paul VI veille notamment à introduire sept évêques diocésains dans l'assemblée de chacun des dicastères de la Curie. Le temps nous manque pour en dire davantage. Par contre, la seconde phase - au cours des vingt-cinq dernières années - est marquée par une nette dévaluation des conférences épiscopales.

La dévaluation des conférences épiscopales sous le pontificat de Jean-Paul II semble faire partie d'un plan cohérent du milieu romain. Le professeur Legrand, observateur pourtant modéré de ces développements de la thématique ecclésiologique, n'hésite pas à parler d'une véritable "stratégie".
Aux yeux du père Legrand, cette "stratégie" des instances romaines commence par agir sur les théologiens, qui doivent se subordonner au magistère, ensuite sur les ordres religieux, qui sont rappelés à l'ordre, et enfin sur les évêques locaux, qui doivent reprendre conscience du fait que leur collège a un chef.[17]

17 Cf. Legrand, "Églises locales, Églises régionales et Église entière", 282-283.

Ainsi que nous l'avons indiqué, le Synode extraordinaire des évêques de 1985 avait conclu par la demande que le statut des conférences épiscopales fasse l'objet d'une étude théologique: leur statut mais aussi leur magistère. Alors qu'au Synode de 1969, on prévoyait encore que l'étude souhaitée sur la doctrine de la collégialité serait remise à la Commission Théologique Internationale - avec l'espoir de conserver un droit de regard sur ce travail -, le Synode de 1985, en souhaitant cette fois une étude sur les conférences épiscopales, ne spécifie ni l'instance chargée de cette étude, ni la possibilité d'en contrôler le déroulement. Au Synode de 1985, on avait craint que le rapport final soit en retrait par rapport à la fécondité des débats de l'assemblée, mais la réalité fut plus décevante encore: tout le relief des courants d'opinion et même la "pointe" des projets de résolution avaient disparu.

De fait, cette étude théologique est confiée par le pape à la Congrégation pour les évêques: tâche entreprise conjointement par la Doctrine de la Foi, l'Évangélisation des peuples et le Secrétariat du synode des évêques. En novembre 1987, on apprend que la Commission d'étude a terminé la rédaction d'un "document de travail", projet qui sera soumis pour avis aux présidents des conférences épiscopales.[18] En janvier 1988, le préfet de la Congrégation pour les évêques adressait aux épiscopats ce projet de texte avec un questionnaire à l'appui, leur demandant de proposer des amendements éventuels avant la date du 31 décembre 1988.

Pendant le temps de préparation de ce texte, le milieu des théologiens ne resta pas inactif. À l'époque, on a particulièrement remarqué le colloque qui s'est tenu à Salamanque - avant que le projet romain ne soit connu - pour étudier le fondement théologique des conférences épiscopales et leur autorité doctrinale.[19]

Ce texte romain part d'un chapitre introductif où le concept de "communio" est détourné du sens qu'il avait à Vatican II pour signifier de manière unilatérale la fidélité absolue que les Églises locales doivent à Rome. Reprenant en outre des arguments de Mgr Marcel Lefebvre à Vatican II, le document souligne les risques qui menacent le fonctionnement des conférences épiscopales à cause de leurs structures bureaucratiques et leurs commissions qui font

18 Voir "Statut théologique et juridique des Conférences épiscopales. Rapport du cardinal B. Gantin".

19 Voir Legrand, Manzanares et Garcia y Garcia, éds., *Les Conférences épiscopales*, 530; Müller et Pottmeyer, *Die Bischofskonferenz*, 304. La série des colloques ecclésiologiques de Salamanque s'est poursuivie en 1991 et 1996.

obstacle à la liberté des évêques individuels. Mais il est plus important de constater que la majorité des épiscopats émettent un avis négatif quant au projet romain, qui est destiné à amoindrir l'autorité des conférences épiscopales.[20]

Quoi qu'il en soit, la promulgation en mai 1998 d'un motu proprio *Apostolos suos*, signé par Jean-Paul II lui-même, a mis fin à toutes les incertitudes. Après avoir développé d'abord une théologie conciliaire du collège des évêques, dans la suite du texte les conférences épiscopales se voient réduites dans leur compétence et dans leur autorité par en haut et par en bas. Il semble au père Bernard Sesboüé que la "méfiance curiale ait conditionné les prises de position principales de ce motu proprio".[21]

Il y a réduction par le haut en déclarant qu'il n'y a d'exercice juridique de la collégialité que dans un concile œcuménique. La déclaration d'une conférence épiscopale ne constitue un véritable magistère qu'après une approbation à l'unanimité des évêques (une approbation par les 2/3 nécessite la "recognitio" de Rome). Ceci correspond dans les faits au retrait du magistère aux conférences épiscopales. Il y a réduction par le bas lorsque *Apostolos suos* prend la défense de l'évêque individuel, cherchant à protéger ses prérogatives contre toute "mainmise" par la conférence épiscopale. Les affirmations reprennent les termes et les expressions de Vatican II, "mais précisément, elle les reprennent dans la rigueur des énoncés, en inversant la dynamique de l'énonciation".[22] La dynamique inversée des textes de Vatican II signifie ici que ce qui était ouverture au Concile est déclaré maintenant sans portée juridique et sans valeur. C'est là un procédé qui a été fréquemment appliqué dans les relectures restrictives de Vatican II faites à l'époque par la Congrégation de la Doctrine de la Foi.

Ce que nous avons tenté d'esquisser ici à partir d'une documentation des quarante dernières années est revenu brusquement à l'avant-plan de l'actualité à partir du Consistoire extraordinaire convoqué par Jean-Paul II en 2001.

20 Cf. "FABC urged to reject Vatican draft on Bishop's conferences", 1 et 5; Bole, "U.S. Bishops blast critique of episcopal conference", 23; "Response to Vatican Working Paper on Bishop's Conferences"; "U.S. Bischöfe: Kritik an römischen Vorstellungen über Bischofskonferenzen", 12-13. À l'époque, les avis négatifs de deux conférences épiscopales importantes sont mis en circulation de manière privée: "Stellungnahme der Deutschen Bischofs-konferenz zum *Instrumentum laboris*" (5 pages dactylographiées); "Response of the Episcopal Conference of the United States to the *Instrumentum laboris*" (8 pages dactylographiées).

21 Cf. Sesboüé, *Le magistère à l'épreuve*, 237-242.

22 Cf. Ibidem, 239.

À partir de cette assemblée destinée au "rodage" des nouveaux cardinaux, les langues se sont déliées. Un grand nombre d'intervenants ont critiqué la dévalorisation des synodes et ont plaidé en faveur d'un renouveau de la collégialité. De nombreux commentaires - dont celui du cardinal Danneels - ont déclaré à cette occasion que la thématique concernant la collégialité des évêques allait se trouver en tête de l'ordre du jour du prochain conclave.[23]

23 Cet exposé présenté en septembre 2002 s'arrêta à un moment où un large courant d'opinion parmi l'épiscopat catholique exprimait ses attentes quant à une réforme du synode qui donnerait à celui-ci une compétence délibérative, une possibilité prévue déjà lors de son instauration en 1964. Cependant les événements de 2005 ont démenti ces perspectives trop optimistes. (Post-scriptum de mai 2008.)

Réception et conséquences de Vatican II
Un point de vue protestant

André Birmelé

Le processus de la réception est une donnée complexe. Dans la foulée du Concile Vatican II le théologien catholique Yves Congar en a proposé une définition qui est aujourd'hui largement admise en vie ecclésiale et en théologie. Nous la reprenons à notre compte: "Par *réception* nous entendons ici le processus par lequel un corps ecclésial fait sienne en vérité une détermination qu'il ne s'est pas donnée à lui-même, en reconnaissant, dans la mesure promulguée, une règle qui convient à la sienne. Il y a dans la réception, bien autre chose que ce que les Scolastiques entendent par obéissance. Pour ces derniers, elle est l'acte par lequel un subordonné règle sa volonté et sa conduite par le précepte légitime d'un supérieur, par respect pour l'autorité de ce dernier. La réception n'est pas la pure et simple réalisation du rapport *secundum sub et supra*; elle comporte un apport propre de consentement, éventuellement de jugement, où s'exprime la vie d'un corps qui exerce des ressources spirituelles originales".[1]

La réception de Vatican II est en cours. Elle dépasse la simple approbation de quelques décisions et consiste en une appropriation par l'ensemble de l'Église catholique des options proposées par ce Concile. Elle est polymorphe et exige du temps.[2] Elle est loin d'être achevée, une période de 40 années étant même trop brève pour permettre une véritable évaluation de ce processus.

Quelle a été la réception du Concile en protestantisme? Si l'on s'en tient à la définition de Congar, on ne peut pas parler d'une réception directe vu que les familles ecclésiales issues de la Réforme n'avait pas à s'approprier des vérités

1 Congar, "La 'réception' comme réalité ecclésiologique", 370.
2 Cf. à ce propos: Routhier, *La réception d'un concile*.

promulgués par un Concile qui n'était pas le leur. Néanmoins Vatican II a été, aussi pour ces Églises, un moment majeur de la seconde partie du XXe siècle. Elles l'ont reçu d'une manière plus "indirecte". On pourrait mentionner la manière dont l'Église catholique a, par ce Concile, essayé de relever les défis contemporains en vue de parvenir à un meilleur témoignage dans une société en voie de sécularisation. Le souci de l'*aggiornamento,* la plus grande ouverture au monde et aux religions, a été suivi avec la plus grande attention, vu que ces mêmes questions se posent à toutes les familles ecclésiales. Mais ce n'est pas là l'essentiel de cette "réception plus indirecte". L'impact majeur réside dans le fait que les grandes décisions conciliaires, les options théologiques et les réformes mises en œuvre ont transformé le catholicisme, qui par ce même Concile s'ouvrait au dialogue avec les autres familles chrétiennes. Une telle évolution a inévitablement des conséquences pour l'ensemble des familles chrétiennes. Même si la communion demeure imparfaite, tout événement touchant un partenaire devient une cause partagée.

Nous nous intéresserons à la situation actuelle, 40 années après Vatican II. Nous ne nous concentrerons pas sur la manière dont ce Concile a été perçu par les partenaires protestants au moment de sa tenue. Ce point a fait l'objet de diverses études.[3] Nous évoquerons d'abord les données qui sont aujourd'hui, d'un point de vue protestant, comprises comme les percées majeures de Vatican II. Nous mentionnerons dans un second moment les défis que ce Concile pose aussi au protestantisme et que ce dernier s'efforce de relever. Enfin nous aborderons dans un troisième temps une question plus délicate mais non moins importante, celle de l'impact sur le protestantisme de la réception du Concile en catholicisme.

3 Je me permets de renvoyer aux indications bibliographiques mentionnées dans mon étude: Birmelé, "Le Concile Vatican II".

Les percées majeures

Avec le recul de 40 années qui est aujourd'hui le nôtre, deux moments de réception nous semblent avoir été, d'un point de vue protestant, les plus marquants. Ils ont profondément modifié la relations des familles issues de la Réforme à l'Église romaine.

Il est indéniable que la première percée retenue en protestantisme est l'entrée de l'Église catholique romaine en œcuménisme. Certains développements la laissait peut-être présager, mais les refus catégoriques maintes fois répétés ne laissaient guère entrevoir l'avancée que proposera le décret sur l'œcuménisme, *Unitatis redintegratio,* promulgué le 21 novembre 1964.
On gardait le souvenir de l'encyclique romaine *Mortalium animos*, qui répondait en 1928 à la première assemblée œcuménique de *Foi et Constitution* (Lausanne 1927) en interdisant toute participation catholique à une démarche de ce type.

Pour les traditions protestantes *Unitatis redintegratio* fut la première traduction concrète de la nouvelle compréhension ecclésiologique catholique romaine définie par le même Concile dans la Constitution dogmatique sur l'Église (*Lumen gentium*). Trois orientations nouvelles apparaissaient et ont été largement confirmées par 40 années de dialogues qui ont été engagés dès la fin du Concile et qui se poursuivent avec toutes les familles chrétiennes et le Conseil Œcuménique des Églises, dont l'Église catholique n'est toujours pas membre, tout en ayant intégré le mouvement Foi et Constitution.

- L'identification traditionnelle de l'Église de Jésus Christ et de l'Église romaine est remplacée par l'affirmation que l'Église du Christ "subsiste dans" l'Église catholique (*Lumen gentium* 8). Le changement peut paraître infime, il est fondamental car il signifie que l'Église du Christ peut aussi exister ailleurs, hors des limites de l'Église romaine même si cette dernière se considère encore comme seule expression pleine de la véritable Église (*Unitatis redintegratio* 3 et 4). Le décret sur l'œcuménisme peut donc parler d'autres "Églises chrétiennes" ce qui n'était pas imaginable dans l'Église romaine préconciliaire.
Le décret demeure prudent, seules les Églises orthodoxes sont appelées Églises, les Églises issues de la Réforme du XVIe siècle sont quant à elles des "communautés chrétiennes". Un pas décisif a cependant été fait. Les "hérétiques" sont devenus des "frères séparés" avec lesquels il faut chercher une communion nouvelle même si l'Église romaine reste, aujourd'hui encore, très prudente quant à la qualité ecclésiale des autres familles.

- Une seconde évolution décisive de ce décret a été l'introduction de la notion de "hiérarchie des vérités" (*Unitatis redintegratio* 11). Toutes les vérités bibliques ne sont pas à mettre sur un même plan. Il n'est donc pas nécessaire qu'il y ait accord sur tous les points de doctrine. Certains sont plus importants que d'autres et exigent l'unanimité, d'autres par contre peuvent exprimer une légitime diversité. "Pour rétablir ou garder la communion ou l'unité, il ne faut rien imposer qui ne soit nécessaire" (*Unitatis redintegratio* 18). Une des grandes tâches du mouvement œcuménique sera de définir ce qui est essentiel et d'harmoniser les "hiérarchies" souvent fort différentes d'une tradition à l'autre. Ce travail n'est pas achevé, mais le décret sur l'œcuménisme a ouvert une porte importante: l'unité n'exige pas l'uniformité, elle comprend et appelle une légitime diversité.

- La troisième perspective nouvelle est l'affirmation de la nécessité de "réformer" l'Église. "L'Église est à la fois sainte et toujours à purifier" (*Lumen gentium* 8). Il n'est plus question d'une Église catholique sans faute comme l'affirmait encore le pape Pie XII dans l'encyclique *Mystici corporis* de 1943. Le décret ne parle pas d'erreur de l'Église elle-même, mais cette dernière "demeure en ses membres exposée au péché" (*Unitatis redintegratio* 3). La cause de la division n'est donc pas à chercher exclusivement chez les autres. Toutes les Églises sont à rénover, tous doivent se convertir, se rapprocher des autres, prier ensemble pour que, dans une Église renouvelée, tous réapprennent à vivre l'unité que Dieu seul donne (*Unitatis redintegratio* 5 à 12).

Pour rendre compte de la réception de cette entrée de l'Église catholique en œcuménisme, il nous faudrait raconter toute l'histoire œcuménique de ces 40 dernières années. Nous ne saurions le faire ici. Il est cependant indéniable que cette percée a fondamentalement modifié l'histoire de toutes les familles chrétiennes et entraîné une période de dialogues sans précédent dans l'histoire de l'Église. Même si de nombreuses interrogations et questions ouvertes subsistent, ces dialogues ont profondément modifié l'ensemble des identités ecclésiales. C'est là la première dimension de la réception du Concile en protestantisme.

La seconde percée majeure n'aura connu son aboutissement qu'en octobre 1999 à Augsbourg par la signature par les Églises catholique et luthériennes de la "Déclaration commune à propos de la doctrine de la justification".[4]

4 Texte français dans: *La Documentation Catholique*, 79 (1997) 2168, 875-885. Pour une analyse détaillée de cette déclaration et de son histoire je me permets de renvoyer à mon ouvrage: Birmelé, *La communion ecclésiale*.

Cette déclaration entérine, plus de 30 ans après que ce consensus ait été constaté par les théologiens[5], le fait qu'il y a accord entre catholiques et luthériens à propos de la compréhension du salut. Pareil progrès n'aurait pas été envisageable sans le Concile Vatican II, son fort accent christologique, son insistance sur la mort et la résurrection du Christ pour le salut de l'humanité, la vie nouvelle offerte gratuitement au croyant, la donnée qui est, pour les traditions de la Réforme, l'*articulus stantis et cadentis ecclesiae*. Même si cette signature n'engage du côté protestant pour l'heure que les Églises luthériennes, cet événement est décisif pour l'ensemble des familles issues de la Réforme. Sans entrer ici dans le détail de cet accord, relevons seulement le fait que les deux traditions déclarent officiellement que l'autre communauté proclame le même salut dans le même Christ Jésus. Ce fruit des dialogues est des plus importants et peut sans conteste être compris comme un moment majeur de réception du Concile. L'événement dépasse la seule compréhension commune du salut et concrétise des ouvertures méthodologiques rendues possibles par Vatican II.

- L'approbation de la déclaration commune inaugure une autre qualité de relation entre ces deux familles qui malgré certains rapprochements récents, demeurent séparées. D'une relation d'exclusion mutuelle on est passé à un rapport d'Églises qui se déclarent portées par une même conviction commune, même si bien des étapes demeurent sur le chemin de la pleine communion. La percée opérée par la déclaration vient de la sanction ecclésiale de ce consensus. Pour la première fois dans l'histoire des relations entre les traditions protestantes et catholique, une conclusion de dialogue proposée par des théologiens a été officiellement ratifiée par les Églises. On ne saurait sous-estimer ce fait.

- La déclaration commune à propos de la doctrine de la justification n'affirme à aucun moment que les options des uns et des autres seraient identiques. Luthériens et catholiques ne proposent pas une seule compréhension du salut. Le consensus n'est pas synonyme d'uniformité. Il ne tolère pas seulement mais il inclut la différence. Après une affirmation commune et le rappel du témoignage biblique, la déclaration reprend, les uns après les autres, les sept points qui ont été le lieu des condamnations réciproques dans l'histoire. Pour chacun de ces domaines elle souligne le souci commun puis présente

5 Ainsi le rapport dit de Malte dans: Commission internationale catholique-luthérienne, *Face à l'unité*, 28-34. Il s'agit d'un texte de 1972 reprenant les conclusions acquises dès 1967. Le comité mixte catholique-protestant (luthériens et réformés) français l'a affirmé sans ambiguïté en 1986 (cf. *Consensus œcuménique et différence fondamentale*).

les options des deux traditions qui demeurent différentes. Une compréhension fondamentalement commune[6] est traduite dans les deux familles par des options particulières différentes mais ces "développements qui demeurent différents ne sont plus capables de provoquer des condamnations doctrinales".[7] Certaines différences sont donc légitimes et font partie du consensus.

- Il faut ici rappeler le discours par lequel le pape Jean XXIII ouvrait le Concile Vatican II. Il proposait de distinguer entre la "vérité révélée", intangible et immuable et les diverses "formulations" qu'elle est appelée à recevoir au cours des siècles: "En effet autre est le dépôt lui-même de la foi, c. à d. les vérités contenues dans notre vénérable doctrine, et autre est la forme sous laquelle ces vérités sont énoncées, en leur conservant toutefois le même sens et la même portée".[8] En affirmant que la continuité historique de l'Église réside dans la substance de l'énoncé et non dans les formulations historiques, le pape inaugurait une nouvelle époque. Les formulations historiques de la vérité sont ouvertes au dialogue, plus encore une même vérité pourrait être rendue par d'autres formulations. Cette option herméneutique proposée par Jean XXIII trouvera une traduction concrète dans la déclaration commune à propos de la doctrine de la justification. Il s'agit là d'une évolution dont toutes les conséquences n'ont pas encore été tirées. Cette démarche qui n'a rien à voir avec un faux compromis ou une politesse œcuménique, est nouvelle dans le dialogue entre protestantisme et catholicisme. Elle devra ultérieurement faire ses preuves dans d'autres domaines. Il n'en demeure pas moins que Rome peut concevoir qu'une même vérité de foi peut être rendue en d'autres termes que les siens. L'unité de l'Église n'exige pas le dépassement des différences mais la transformation de leur nature. Elles doivent perdre leur caractère séparateur pour participer au consensus qui met un terme aux condamnations passées. La déclaration est la traduction concrète de cette conviction œcuménique.

La déclaration n'implique pas encore la célébration commune de l'eucharistie et la pleine reconnaissance mutuelle dans une légitime diversité mais elle est un premier pas décisif dans cette direction. Cette déclaration est une conséquence directe de l'entrée en dialogue et des nouvelles orientations proposées par le Concile. Elle est un moment de réception du Concile et plus particulièrement de son décret sur l'œcuménisme, *Unitatis redintegratio*.

6 "Déclaration commune", 14 à 17.

7 Ibidem, 5 cf. 40.

8 Dans: *La Documentation Catholique*, 44 (1962) 1387, 1383.

Le Concile de la clarification ecclésiologique

Dans un second moment nous évoquerons les défis que Vatican II a posé et pose aux traditions protestantes. La réception peut, là-aussi, être qualifiée d'indirecte. Elle n'en est pas moins réelle. Ces défis se situent avant tout dans le domaine de l'ecclésiologie.

Que Vatican II ait présenté une redéfinition de l'ecclésiologie catholique avec une nouvelle insistance sur la communion, l'Église comprise comme peuple de Dieu, l'Église définie comme sacrement, une insistance sur l'eucharistie, un recentrage ministériel sur l'episcopè, une redéploiement liturgique sont des données connues. Au sein du catholicisme les études ecclésiologiques post-conciliaires sont nombreuses. Les possibilités ouvertes par le Concile sont loin d'être toutes explorées.

Cette insistance sur les données ecclésiologiques n'est pas restée sans conséquences pour les Églises issues de la Réforme. L'ecclésiologie y a été remise à l'ordre du jour et il n'y a probablement jamais eu dans l'histoire et au sein même de ces Églises une période aussi intense en réflexions ecclésiologiques que ces 40 dernières années. L'impact de Vatican II n'en est peut-être pas la seule raison, mais il fut certainement déterminant.

1. Cet intérêt pour l'ecclésiologie des Églises issues de la Réforme vient tout d'abord des dialogues œcuméniques. Dialoguant immédiatement après le Concile avec des théologiens romains, les représentants protestants furent rapidement interpellés quant à leur approche ecclésiologique. En effet le but du dialogue étant de parvenir à un rétablissement de l'unité, il s'avéra que les questions vraiment séparatrices relevaient toutes du domaine ecclésiologique. La question de la référence à l'Ecriture sainte et du rôle de la tradition ou la compréhension du salut qui avaient longtemps été considérées comme raisons majeures de la rupture, cédèrent rapidement la place à des entretiens à propos des sacrements en particulier l'eucharistie, les ministères et plus généralement la compréhension du mystère de l'Église. Même si ces thèmes demeurent toujours séparateurs d'Églises, le dialogue a permis de dépasser de nombreux préjugés et l'on peut à présent identifier clairement les lieux de consensus et les lieux d'opposition. La pensée ecclésiologique de Vatican II et en particulier le dépassement d'une approche traditionnelle marquée par Bellarmin, a largement contribué à cette clarification.

- Il nous faut d'abord mentionner le consensus aujourd'hui acquis. Toutes les traditions confessent l'Église une, sainte, catholique (universelle) et apostolique (Credo de l'Église ancienne). Elle est l'œuvre de l'Esprit Saint et, à ce titre, une donnée centrale de la foi. L'Église n'est pas simplement un rassemblement humain ou une société de convertis. Elle est le corps du Christ et n'a ni son origine ni sa finalité en elle-même. Elle est fondée et maintenue par Christ, incarnation de la Parole de Dieu, dont elle ne dispose pas et qui demeurera toujours son vis à vis créateur et critique.

L'Église est la communion des croyants. Même si le Nouveau Testament n'applique pas directement le terme *koinonia* (communion) à l'Église, cette notion, centrale pour Vatican II et qui a toujours été à la base de l'ecclésiologie protestante, a une dimension ecclésiologique fondamentale: elle caractérise la relation nouvelle unissant Dieu et le croyant et par voie de conséquence les croyants entre eux. En participant à la mort et à la résurrection du Christ par le baptême (Rm 6), en célébrant l'eucharistie qui unit les membres du seul corps du Christ à leur Seigneur (1 Co 10 et 11), en étant saisis par la Parole qui suscite la foi (Rm 10,14s.), les croyants sont incorporés au Christ et à l'Église. La nouvelle relation à Dieu est synonyme de participation vivante à la communauté ecclésiale et engendre une nouvelle qualité de relation entre les croyants.

L'Église n'est pas pour autant une réalité spirituelle abstraite insaisissable. À cette compréhension de l'Église comme donnée de la foi, correspond une réalité vécue, une Église qui dans la pluralité de ses formes historiques, sociales et géographiques est perçue empiriquement. À la confession de foi s'ajoute des conceptions théologiques, des contenus doctrinaux, des pratiques, des piétés et des spiritualités diverses qui témoignent de la vocation de l'Église à s'inscrire dans le tissu social environnant. L'Église est ce mystère qui a à la fois une dimension divine et humaine. Elle est en ce sens *sacramentum* pour reprendre un option majeure de Vatican II, une option à laquelle de nombreuses traditions protestantes peuvent adhérer. Pareille compréhension de l'Église est aujourd'hui le lieu d'un large consensus entre toutes les familles chrétiennes.

- Le dialogue post Vatican II aura aussi permis de clarifier la question majeure qui demeure en suspens entre l'Église romaine et les Églises protestantes, celle de la compréhension de la nature de l'instrumentalité de l'Église dans l'œuvre salvatrice de Dieu. L'enjeu n'est ni la compréhension de la parole, ni celle du sacrement, ni celle du salut mais la place précise qui revient à l'Église dans l'ensemble du mystère divin. "La divergence ... ne concerne pas le fait de l'instrumentalité de l'Église dans la transmission du salut, mais la nature de cette instrumentalité: l'Église est-elle sanctifiée de manière à devenir elle-même sujet sanctifiant?".[9] Les protestants deviennent plus réservés quant à la compréhension de l'Église comme sacrement dès que cette sacramentalité tendrait à confondre la médiation ecclésiale et la seule médiation du Christ. L'Église est certes signe et instrument de Dieu et de son règne, elle proclame la Parole et célèbre les sacrements mais c'est Dieu lui-même et Dieu seul qui suscite la foi et donne la grâce. L'Église ne peut à aucun moment devenir source ou auteur du salut des humains. Toute compréhension de l'Église comme prolongement du Christ, toute notion de médiation sacramentelle de l'Église dont dépendrait la présence du Christ ou toute compréhension sacrificielle du sacrement eucharistique, des approches présentes dans Vatican II, sont comprises comme atteintes à la seule souveraineté de Dieu. L'Église écoute, prêche, confesse, célèbre, témoigne, chante et fête. Elle est intendante des mystères de Dieu (1 Co 4,1). Mais ce faisant c'est Dieu et lui seul qui agit en et à travers elle le salut. L'action propre de l'Église est fondamentalement réceptive, caractérisée par la passivité créatrice de la foi. Sa vie et son action sont toujours transparentes pour la seule œuvre de Dieu. De ce fait les traditions protestantes interpelleront Vatican II. Elles demanderont une meilleure clarification de l'analogie entre Christ et l'Église affirmée par *Lumen gentium* 8. Le même constat vaut pour le ministère que les Églises issues de la Réforme considèrent une donnée essentielle de l'Église. Elles y verront cependant toujours comme une donnée seconde soumise et radicalement dépendante de la parole et des sacrements. Lorsque Vatican II affirmera qu'il existe entre le sacerdoce ministériel et celui de tous les baptisés "une différence d'essence et non seulement de degré", que le ministère particulier est pourvu "d'un pouvoir sacré" particulier qui est transmis par l'ordination lui permettant de former et de conduire le peuple de Dieu et en particulier de célébrer le sacrifice eucharistique (*Lumen gentium* 10), les protestants feront entendre leur différence.

On pourrait multiplier les exemples et passer en revue l'ensemble des thèmes majeurs ecclésiologiques. Le constat sera toujours le même: Vatican II aura permis et provoqué le dialogue. Ce Concile aura mis les questions ecclésiologiques au cœur du dialogue œcuménique naissant. Il y a tout lieu de comprendre ce fait comme une réception de Vatican II.

9 *Consensus œcuménique et différence fondamentale*, §11.

2. On peut même faire un pas supplémentaire et affirmer que Vatican II aura provoqué une réflexion ecclésiologique au sein même des Églises protestantes. Il y a certes eu de nombreuses autres raisons qui ont conduit ces Églises à repréciser leur identité. La perte des identités sociales habituelles ou des repères institutionnels traditionnels, la sécularisation et bien d'autres données y auront contribué. Mais il n'est pas moins évident que l'engagement dans le dialogue œcuménique a été une raison majeure qui a conduit ces familles à réfléchir à leur finalité et à se réassurer de leur identité. Ainsi les luthériens et les réformés européens ont pour la première fois depuis le XVIe siècle été amenés à présenter un texte ecclésiologique fondamental qui montre précisément que la compréhension de l'Église est pour eux centrale, même si elle n'est pas celle de Vatican II.[10] Ce texte insiste sur la célébration authentique de la parole et des sacrements comme marques de la vraie Église. Il rappelle la priorité que les Églises issues de la Réforme accordent à l'œuvre salvatrice de Dieu. Le salut en Christ est la clé de lecture qui permet de comprendre l'Ecriture sainte et la norme de toute vie ecclésiale. Toute vie d'Église doit constamment être lue, interprétée et réformée à la lumière de ce seul message. Le ministère épiscopal est évoqué et jugé nécessaire mais, à la différence de l'approche de Vatican II, ce ministère sera considéré comme second. Il ne saurait être le pilier de l'ecclésiologie.

Un autre exemple de cette réception que l'on pourrait appelé "en creux" de Vatican II est donné par le modèle d'unité mis en œuvre par les Églises issues de la Réforme dans les 30 dernières années. L'enjeu de la recherche de l'unité est la reconnaissance mutuelle dans la diversité et la communion ecclésiale qui en résultent. Les Églises luthériennes, réformées, anglicanes ou méthodistes se comprennent comme une expression, mais non l'expression unique, de l'Église de Jésus-Christ. Cette dernière a d'autres visages incarnés par d'autres familles ecclésiales. Le dialogue avec une autre tradition doit conduire à l'affirmation que la célébration de la parole et des sacrements indique que cette famille est, elle aussi, une forme authentique de l'unique Église du Christ. Cette condition est nécessaire et suffisante. Lorsqu'elle est remplie, les partenaires du dialogue se reconnaissent mutuellement comme Église du Christ et se déclarent en pleine communion ecclésiale quant à la célébration de la parole et des sacrements, cette communion comprenant aussi la reconnais-

10 Cette vision ecclésiologique commune a été approuvée par l'assemblée générale des Églises luthériennes et réformées européennes réunie à Vienne (1994): "L'Église de Jésus-Christ". On peut en outre renvoyer à des ecclésiologies récentes comme le dossier "Église" dans Gisel, éd, *Encyclopédie du protestantisme*.

sance mutuelle des ministères qui président à ces célébrations.[11] Cette approche n'est pas opposée à la compréhension de Vatican II, elle s'en distingue cependant par le fait que ces Églises n'éprouvent aucune difficulté à admettre une certaine relativité de leurs identités ecclésiales empiriques qu'elles comprennent comme une expression parmi d'autres possibles de l'incarnation de l'unique Église du Christ en ce monde. Un consensus différencié en ecclésiologie relève de l'évidence. Ce n'est pas là l'approche du Concile.

Les questions ecclésiologiques demeurent en partie ouvertes et interdisent la plein communion entre les familles chrétiennes. Elles représentent des défis à relever. Vatican II aura indéniablement été à l'origine de cette réflexion même si le protestantisme fait entendre sa différence et reçoit le Concile en précisant sa position autre.

L'impact en protestantisme de la réception du Concile en catholicisme

Dans une troisième et dernière partie nous aborderons la question de l'impact sur le protestantisme de la réception et des conséquences de Vatican II en catholicisme. Les Églises et les théologiens protestants sont très intéressés de voir quelle interprétation des développements et des textes conciliaires finira par s'imposer au sein même de l'Église catholique. On pourrait parler de "la réception de la réception de Vatican II".

C'est de la réponse à cette question que dépendent et dépendront les relations interecclésiales futures. Le théologien protestant sait que la réception de Vatican II n'est pas uniforme, qu'elle est loin d'être achevée et que le constat qu'il fait aujourd'hui, peut être démenti demain. Il n'en demeure pas moins qu'une certaine inquiétude se fait jour et que les interrogations quant à une réception "conservatrice" de Vatican II en catholicisme se multiplient en protestantisme.

11 Cette approche et cette vision de l'unité ont permis dans les dernières années des progrès considérables entre les familles luthériennes, réformées et anglicanes. Au niveau européen la concorde de Leuenberg lie depuis 1973 luthériens et réformés, l'accord de Meissen (1987) l'Église d'Angleterre et les Églises luthériennes et réformées allemandes, celui de Porvoo (1993) les Églises anglicanes britanniques et les Églises luthériennes scandinaves et baltes, celui de Reuilly (2001) les Églises anglicanes britanniques et les Églises luthériennes et réformées françaises, celui de Vienne (1997) les traditions méthodistes, luthériennes et réformées en Europe.

L'exemple aujourd'hui le plus souvent cité est la déclaration *Dominus Iesus* sur l'unicité et l'universalité salvifique de Jésus-Christ et de l'Église que le cardinal Ratzinger a publié au nom de la Congrégation pour la Doctrine de la Foi en été 2000.[12] Ce texte a provoqué les réactions que l'on connaît au sein de l'Église catholique et au-delà. Il est vrai que les paragraphes 16 et 17 de cette déclaration décrètent qu'il n'y a qu'une seule véritable Église, celle conduite par l'évêque de Rome, le successeur de Pierre et les évêques en communion avec lui. Il n'y a qu'un chemin vers l'unité: le retour de tous les chrétiens au bercail romain, seul lieu du salut véritable. Une affirmation de ce type ne pouvait que provoquer une large désapprobation même si elle ne fait que répéter des positions connues.

Le théologien protestant interrogera l'herméneutique des textes de Vatican II mise en œuvre dans cette affirmation. Il lui semble que les constitutions et décrets y sont lus avec une clé d'interprétation restrictive.

- Une percée majeure du Concile Vatican II - nous l'avons déjà signalée - consistait à remplacer un "est" par un "subsistit in". Alors que depuis des siècles la doctrine catholique considérait que l'Église de Jésus-Christ "est" l'Église romaine, les Pères conciliaires modifiaient ce "est" présent dans la première rédaction de *Lumen gentium* en un "subsistit in": ainsi que l'Église du Christ "subsiste dans" l'Église catholique.[13] Cette modification que nous avons évoquées, était majeure et ouvrait la porte du dialogue œcuménique. Il était à présent envisageable que l'Église du Christ subsiste aussi ailleurs, donc dans d'autres familles chrétiennes. Le Concile ne le disait pas *expressis verbis*, mais la simple lecture des actes indique que ce fut bien là l'enjeu. Lors des débats le cardinal Liénart de Lille demandait "expressément que l'on supprime l'article 7 qui équipare de façon absolue l'Église catholique et le Corps mystique".[14] De même le futur cardinal Grillmeier précisait dans le commentaire du Concile du *LThK*: "La commission théologique a décidé de se satisfaire du simple *subsistit* pour laisser consciemment ouverte la question du rapport de l'Église une aux Églises. Elle a ainsi rendu possible un développement d'une portée considérable". À l'opposé de ses deux collègues acteurs des débats conciliaires, le cardinal Ratzinger propose dans *Dominus Iesus* sa lecture particulière: "Par l'expression *subsistit in*, le Concile Vatican II a voulu proclamer … que

12 Texte français dans: *La Documentation Catholique*, 82 (2000) 2233, 812-822.

13 *Lumen gentium* 8.

14 Le professeur H. Legrand que l'on ne saurait soupçonner d'opposition systématique au cardinal Ratzinger rappelle fort opportunément cette intervention du cardinal Liénart dans une interview à *Témoignage chrétien* en octobre 2000 suite à la publication de *Dominus Iesus*.

malgré la division entre chrétiens, l'Église du Christ continue à exister en plénitude dans la seule Église catholique" (*Dominus Iesus* 16). Sa démarche consiste à lier la question du *subsistit in* à celle de la plénitude. En effet le Concile ne doutait a aucun moment du fait que l'Église catholique soit Église en plénitude. Mais ce n'était pas là l'objet du débat conciliaire sur le *subsistit in* comme le laisse entendre le cardinal. Pour établir ce lien Ratzinger introduit un "seulement" qui, après avoir qualifié la plénitude (*Dominus Iesus* 16), finit par qualifier d'une manière tout à fait générale l'unicité ecclésiale de l'Église catholique romaine.

- Un second développement confirme cette interprétation. Après avoir mentionné les Églises orthodoxes le paragraphe 17 dit à propos des communautés ecclésiales issues de la Réforme qu'elles "ne sont pas des Églises au sens propre" (*Dominus Iesus* 17). Une fois de plus les citations de Vatican II abondent. Il faut cependant noter que ce jugement de valeur à propos de l'ecclésialité des Églises issues de la Réforme est un rajout de Ratzinger qui ne peut pas se réclamer du Concile. Le décret conciliaire sur l'œcuménisme notait certes diverses lacunes dans l'ecclésialité des autres familles, en particulier dans leur conception du ministère.[15] Ces points devront, selon le Concile, faire l'objet de dialogues. Mais le même décret constatait à propos des Églises issues de la Réforme qu'"il est très difficile de les définir et nous n'en avons pas ici l'intention".[16] Conséquent avec l'interprétation théologique qu'il propose, le cardinal Ratzinger se prononce quant à la qualité ecclésiale de ces familles. Il ne parle plus avec le Concile et l'encyclique de Jean Paul II (*Ut unum sint*, 1995) d'"Églises et communautés ecclésiales" issues de la Réforme mais seulement de "communautés ecclésiales".[17]

- Un troisième développement est quelque peu différent mais relève aussi de l'herméneutique des déclarations magistérielles antérieures. Après avoir rappelé l'unicité et la plénitude de la révélation de Dieu en Jésus-Christ, le cardinal Ratzinger rappelle dans la section consacrée aux autres religions les propos de Vatican II: "En effet puisque le Christ est mort pour tous et que la vocation dernière de l'homme est réellement unique, à savoir divine, nous devons tenir que l'Esprit Saint offre à tous, d'une façon que Dieu connaît, la

15 Décret sur l'œcuménisme, *Unitatis redintegratio* 3, 22.

16 *Unitatis redintegratio* 19.

17 L'encyclique de Jean-Paul II, *Ut unum sint* (*Qu'ils soient un*) est une bonne illustration de l'option romaine de ces 30 dernières années. Elle ne se prononce pas quant à l'ecclésialité des ces familles et parle des "autres Églises et communautés ecclésiales d'Occident" (para. 64ss.). La question de l'ecclésialité des Églises issues de la Réforme est consciemment laissée ouverte. Ratzinger souhaite la clore.

possibilité d'être associé au mystère pascal".[18] Il complète ce texte par un extrait d'une encyclique de Jean-Paul II: "La présence et l'activité de l'Esprit ne concernent pas seulement les individus, mais la société et l'histoire, les peuples, les cultures, les religions ... Le Christ ressuscité agit désormais dans le cœur des hommes par la puissance de son Esprit ... C'est encore l'Esprit qui répand les 'semences du verbe' présentes dans les rites et les cultures, et les prépare à maturation en Christ".[19] Mais ces citations explicites n'empêchent pas le cardinal de réduire les expériences religieuses des autres religions à un "ensemble d'expériences et de réflexions, trésors humains de sagesse et de religiosité, que l'homme dans sa recherche de la vérité a pensé et vécu, pour ses relations avec le Divin et l'Absolu". Et pour bien souligner la "grave indigence" des autres religions, Ratzinger fait appel au pape Pie XI et à son encyclique *Mystici corporis* de 1943.[20]

On me pardonnera cette analyse trop détaillée et de ce fait trop longue. Elle voulait exprimer la crainte actuelle du partenaire protestant qui est surpris par cette manière de lire les références officielles. Avec une partie de l'Église catholique romaine - mais de loin pas tous ses croyants, ses théologiens et ses évêques - le cardinal Ratzinger souhaite imposer une interprétation restrictive. Pour y parvenir il n'hésite pas à "compléter" les textes conciliaires, à recourir à des documents préconciliaires et à citer, comme interprétations autorisées, des textes postérieurs de la Congrégation pour la Doctrine de la Foi, des textes dont il est généralement lui-même l'auteur. Il sait évidemment que la réception des textes conciliaires est loin d'être achevée. Dans l'histoire de l'Église la vérité qui finit par être reçue dans la compréhension des fidèles (*sensus fidelium*) n'est pas toujours la vérité objective d'une affirmation conciliaire mais l'interprétation qui se sera lentement imposée au fil des ans. Le cardinal Ratzinger souhaite de toute évidence favoriser une certaine réception du Concile. Et cette réception de Vatican II ne manque pas de provoquer un certain scepticisme protestant.

Nous conclurons cette présentation en insistant, une fois encore, sur la portée historique de ce Concile qui aura marqué l'histoire de toutes les Églises au XXe siècle. Le théologien protestant que je suis pourra même avouer une petite jalousie. Il s'interrogera sur la capacité conciliaires des Églises issues de la Réforme qui ont pourtant une grande tradition synodale. Seraient-elles capables de convoquer une assemblée de ce type qui serait en mesure de redire

18 *Gaudium et Spes*, 22.

19 *Dominus Iesus* 12 qui cite l'encyclique *Redemptoris Missio*.

20 *Dominus Iesus* 7 puis 22 qui cite Pie XII (encyclique *Mystici corporis*, DH 3821).

aujourd'hui d'une manière autorisé la quintessence du message qui a été celui de la Réforme? La réponse est loin d'être évidente. Il n'est pas exclu que les Églises de cette tradition soient encore pour un bon moment contraintes de se référer à leurs textes qui datent du XVIe siècle, là où leurs partenaires catholiques disposent d'une référence contemporaine.

Reception and Implementation of the Second Vatican Council Religious Institutes

Joachim Schmiedl

In the first half of the twentieth century a typical parish in a mid-European country such as Germany, Austria or Belgium, included a small house of religious sisters. Often there were no more than four or five sisters in such a house, and they cared for the church (i.e. sacristy and flowers, etc.), the kindergarten and the sick. Generations of parishioners passed through the hands of these sisters and received their initial education and religious socialisation from them. In 1953, there were 8,248 religious houses for sisters in Western Germany. Following the Second Vatican Council very few religious communities have been able to open new houses. On the contrary, within the course of a few decades an ageing process, which until then had not existed or been hidden, became obvious. A glance into Catholic papers today shows that reports on advanced jubilees of profession appear far more often than on vestiture ceremonies. The work of the diocesan commissions for religious is to a large extent dominated by the closure of houses.

Is it more than just a coincidence that the "turning point in the history of religious institutes"[1] is connected with the Second Vatican Council? Was the Council the cause and catalyst of the apparent decline of religious communities, or was it able to stop or slow a process that had already begun? I shall try to answer these questions in four steps.[2]

1 Haas, "Das II. Vatikanum als Wendepunkt der Ordensgeschichte".

2 A description of the preparatory phase of the Second Vatican Council and the origin of the conciliar reform of religious life is based on the author's habilitation thesis. It has an extensive reference to all relevant publications, so they are not referred to in detail in this paper. See Schmiedl, *Das Konzil und die Orden*; see also the subject survey in: Idem, "Rückkehr zum Ursprung und Anpassung ans Heute".

Religious Institutes before the Second Vatican Council Between Climax and Crisis

At first glance, religious institutes[3] experienced a boost in the years prior to the Second Vatican Council. The numbers of members grew substantially in the first decades of the twentieth century. The main growth took place in the institutes for women whose numbers worldwide grew between 1942 and 1956 from 538,708 to 730,434. In this period, all the religious communities could increase the numbers of their foundations. In some countries, such as Spain, there was a real boom in new members of religious houses.

However, this was only one side of the picture. After the Second World War, the situation in Europe changed and the growth curve declined. The signs of a crisis were clearly visible. The members of religious communities still had a leading voice in influencing public opinion, and they initiated innovative theological trends, but they were also more easily attacked by countermeasures. Theologians such as Henri de Lubac, SJ[4], Pierre Teilhard de Chardin, SJ[5], Karl Rahner, SJ[6], Yves Congar, OP[7], and Marie-Dominique Chenu, OP[8], stood for new emphases in theology, but both within their own communities as well as with the authorities in Rome, they found themselves under a cloud and were marginalised by disciplinary measures.

In the mainstream of religious life, however, they were atypical. Étienne Fouilloux has characterised the dominant mentality as that of a "fortress under siege".[9] As early as 1952, Lenten pastoral letters of the Belgian bishops described the reasons for the decline in vocations as "an increasing desire for unlimited freedom, a worldly atmosphere and a result of the opposition of

3 In what follows, 'religious institutes' includes all forms of consecrated life, that is, the traditional orders, as well as congregations, secular institutes and apostolic communities. In the words of a Vatican instruction: "Consecrated persons - monks and nuns, contemplatives, religious dedicated to the works of the apostolate, members of secular institutes and societies of apostolic life, hermits and consecrated virgins" (Kongregation für die Institute des geweihten Lebens, *Neubeginn in Christus*, no. 5).

4 Cf. de Lubac, *Meine Schriften im Rückblick*.

5 Cf. Kettern, "Teilhard de Chardin", which includes an extensive list of references.

6 On Karl Rahner and his influence on the Second Vatican Council, but also on its early life, see Wassilowsky, *Universales Heilssakrament Kirche*.

7 Cf. Congar, *Herbstgespräche*. On Congar's role during the Council, see Melloni, *Yves Congar à Vatican II*.

8 On Chenu's role during the opening phase of the Council, see his edited diary: Chenu, *Notes quotidiennes au Concile*.

9 Fouilloux, "Die vor-vorbereitende Phase", 86.

parents to the religious life", but also as "a new attitude to marriage".[10] It indicated an outside view which was largely not shared by the majority of religious institutes at that time. In the 1950s, the dominant tendency was to stick to their guns rather than a readiness to renew themselves. Although, from time to time, these communities strongly emphasised their own conservatism and anti-modernist stance as an expression of zeal for their mission, there was a growing and increasingly vocal criticism of the omnipresence of the letter of the law, of the restrictions of the cloister that were particularly felt by the communities actively engaged in the apostolate, of the anachronistic forms of religious habits, of the repression of sexuality through an overemphasis on the value of virginity, of rigid ascetical practices, and the tendencies to close communities off from the world and create a ghetto.

The 'aggiornamento' of religious institutes, their adaptation to the challenges of the times, and the modernisation of their ways of life had to be initiated from above. Pius XII was greatly interested in this, because religious communities were among his closest collaborators, and because they occupied key positions in the Roman Curia. This explains the comprehensive reform of religious communities that took place between 1947 and 1958. Secular institutes were established as a new form of consecrated life.[11] It has probably not been fully grasped even today, what an inner readjustment this required of traditional communities, and the extent to which it cast doubt on their own identity. They were suddenly confronted with a way of life within the state of perfection that was lived outside the cloister, and that was accepted and recommended by the papacy. It became possible for communities of nuns to combine the apostolic and contemplative ways of living. Smaller communities were encouraged to link together to form a federation. The superiors of communities for men and women met on national and international levels to form conferences and commissions. The examination and acceptance of rules and constitutions formed an important part of their work. Special emphasis was placed on the education and further training of religious, in particular sisters. However, the underpinning theology of a consecrated life continued to take its bearings from principles that set the religious state over that of marriage. In his encyclical, *Sacra virginitas* (1954), Pius XII stressed that sexuality is not the main motivating force in human beings, and that marriage is not

10 Quoted in: Schmiedl, *Das Konzil und die Orden*, 95.

11 An indispensable source for the study of the history and theology of secular institutes remains: Pollak, *Der Aufbruch der Säkularinstitute*.

the best way to arrive at perfection. Young people should not be prevented from responding to a religious vocation.

Pope Pius' reform of religious life was unable to offer a positive answer to the question posed by communities as to their place in a changing world. It remained "a situational reform that helped to remedy some abuses, but was only able to do limited justice to the aim of modernising the Church and renewing theology from its sources".[12]

The period of preparation for the Council also did nothing towards answering this question. The main concern of the bishops was to regulate the relationship between religious communities and the dioceses in the sense of integrating them into the pastoral structures controlled by the bishops. Since they were responsible for diocesan communities of sisters, the bishops were deeply interested in reforming their outward appearance. Hence the future Council Fathers submitted a host of suggestions aimed at simplifying the habit, reducing privileges in the field of popular liturgy, as well as stipulations regarding the enclosure and regulations limiting the confessional practice of sisters. It is remarkable that the suggestions submitted by the bishops who belonged to religious communities, as well as the superiors of communities, remained as colourless as those of the other Council Fathers. Their wishes were concentrated on detailed suggestions and the apologetic defence of privileges of exemptions already granted.

This trend continued into the preparatory phase of the Council. The draft schema on religious life, comprising 132 pages, was painstakingly worked out by the preparatory commission. To a large extent, members of religious communities were personally involved in this work. The majority lived in Rome and were either the procurators of their communities or working at the papal universities. However, it was not a great success. This was partly because of the disastrous separation of the disciplinary from the theological sections (the Theological Commission laid claim to the latter) and also because of the perspective of Canon Law, which the members and consultors of the commission were unable to set aside. In 1961, Cardinal Suenens[13] published his groundbreaking and challenging book on the crisis and renewal of communities for women[14], but the twofold perspective he offered of 'crisis' and 'renewal' was not sufficiently adopted. "The signs of crisis were described,

12 Schmiedl, *Das Konzil und die Orden*, 150.

13 Cf. his autobiography: Suenens, *Souvenirs et espérances*.

14 Cf. Idem, *Krise und Erneuerung der Frauenorden*.

but the possibilities of renewal were only approached in a defensive and cautious way. Despite some beginnings (e.g. indications of the importance of the means of communication), the tendency of religious life to turn away from the world was strengthened."[15] It is not surprising that against this background there was considerable criticism of the schema already in the first phase of examination within the central commission. However, it did not come to anything as there was too little time left before the opening of the Council.

The treatment of religious life in the preparatory phase of the Council corresponds almost exactly with the situation in the communities themselves. They moved between the feeling that they could continue as before with a few cosmetic changes, and an incipient awareness that a new era demanded other ways of life and action.

The Contribution of the Council to the Reform of Religious Communities

The Second Vatican Council also created a storm in dealing with the subject of religious communities. Until the third session, it was not clear whether it would even be debated by the Council Fathers as a whole. The way the Decree on Religious Life, *Perfectae caritatis*, came into existence serves as a model to explain the battles between the conservative and progressive forces at work among the Council Fathers. The one aimed at an exact codification of the way of life and the discipline of religious communities with a view towards their counteracting and healing of a secularised society. As part of the *ecclesia militans*, they should, in keeping with the teaching of Thomas Aquinas, represent the *status perfectionis adquirendae*, and in this way reflect the eschatological goal of the Church as a whole. The progressive camp of Council Fathers wanted to bring the mission of religious communities for the Church and world into sharper focus. As part of the Church they should, on the one hand, be a 'sign' of a future reality, while on the other hand, serving as effective helpers in the apostolic work of the diocese. These two fronts became even clearer in the course of the four sessions and their work can be seen in three main schemata:

- The Constitution on the Church, *Lumen gentium,* integrated religious communities into the new structure of ecclesiology as a specific state, but it com-

15 Schmiedl, *Das Konzil und die Orden*, 327.

bined both the clerical and lay states comprehensively (LG 43), showing that both belong to the life and the holiness of the Church (LG 43). The Constitution departed from a mentality of privilege to the extent that it based the exemption of religious communities on the requirements of the Church and its usefulness for apostolic works (LG 45). However, the Council was unable to provide a definition of religious life. In retrospect this does not seem to be a shortcoming because it opened up possibilities for a multiplicity of ways of life to develop.

- The debate on the Decree on the Pastoral Office of Bishops, *Christus dominus,* dealt mainly with the problem of exemption. Both sides, the religious communities and the dioceses, wanted to strengthen their positions. The compromise arrived at concentration on the autonomy of religious communities in 'internal matters', while obliging them to acknowledge the final responsibility of the dioceses in the exercise of the apostolate.

- Finally, the Decree on the up-to-date Renewal of Religious Life, *Perfectae caritatis*[16], bade farewell to the fiction that it was possible to command a revision from the centre. Instead the fundamental principles laid down gave sufficient room for a reform of the individual communities. Theologically, *Perfectae caritatis* continued in line with *Lumen gentium* and stressed that the ultimate goal of religious life is perfection in love. The individual types of religious communities were characterised briefly, and reference was made to the fact that the evangelical counsels are oriented to the example of Christ. Important directives were given through the emphasis laid on the education and continued training of members, the inculturation of religious life in the missionary territories, and the express demand that communities should collaborate, amalgamate and form working commissions and councils.

As a document on the way, *Perfectae caritatis* can be indicated with reference to women religious. It is one of the scandals of the Council that, except for a hasty survey of some superior generals of women's communities in the time between the third and fourth sessions, no women religious were involved in drawing up the decree, which, to a great extent, applied to them. However, at the end of the Council there was neither the necessary sensitivity nor the awareness of the problem caused by a changed insight into the role of the sexes and the theological evaluation of the role of men and women.
This would had to have found expression in a corresponding use of language

16 Cf. Schmiedl, "Theologischer Kommentar zum Dekret über die zeitgemäße Erneuerung des Ordenslebens *Perfectae caritatis*".

and in the *modus operandi* of working out the documents together in partnership.

The subject of religious communities did not take up much time in the work of the Council. Most of the work was carried out in the commissions concerned. It was characterised by a debate between two diametrically opposing trends in the religious involved. One trend is identified with the longstanding secretary of the Commission for Religious, the Canadian Oblate Father Joseph Rousseau, an outstanding procurator and representative of a centralistic and controlling position aimed at leaving the competence for renewal exclusively with the authorities in Rome. Another supporter of this position was the secretary of the Faith Commission, the Dutch Jesuit, Father Sebastian Tromp. He was the main protagonist of Pope Pius XII's ecclesiology and a close collaborator of Cardinal Alfredo Ottaviani in the Holy Office.

On the other side we find religious such as the French Dominican, Yves Congar, who was sent overseas on three occasions between 1946 and 1956, and who had to give up his professorship. However, at the Council he was one of the most influential theologians. His aim was that renewal should take place out of the spirit of the origins and the sources of the early Church. The German religious collaborated closely with Congar and other theologians from religious communities, such as Henri de Lubac, SJ, and Edward Schillebeeckx, OP, and many others. The publications of Karl Rahner, SJ, for example, had been subjected to censorship by Rome even as late as 1962. During the Council he and his Jesuit confreres, Otto Semmelroth, Alois Grillmeier and Friedrich Wulf[17], were the advisors to Cardinal Doepfner.[18] It is to his committed and uncompromising intervention that we owe the fact that the schema on religious life even came into existence.

The constellation of theologians mirrored to some extent the two fronts that existed within religious communities. So it is doubtful whether a different or better result for the communities was possible at the Council. However, the theological debate shows clearly that both positions were represented at the Council: a conservative approach oriented towards tradition, and one that was more open to the world and ready for change.

17 On the influence of Friedrich Wulf on the subject of religious communities during the Second Vatican Council and his position in the history of spiritualities in the twentieth century, see Schulte, *Aufbruch aus der Mitte*; Idem, "Friedrich Wulf SJ".

18 Cf. the first biography on Julius Doepfner: Wittstadt, *Julius Kardinal Döpfner*.

The Reception of the Reform of Religious Communities Initiated by the Council

The reform of religious communities that was inspired and required by the Council was very widespread in the years following the Council. The most important aid in putting the reforms demanded by the Council into practice was the special chapter which each community was required to hold. Paul VI published the practical norms for these chapters in his apostolic letter, *Ecclesiae sanctae*, of 6 August 1966. The General Chapter played an important role both in drawing up legislation and in providing spiritual and apostolic revitalisation. All members were called upon to cooperate, which was facilita-ted by a particularly wide-ranging consultation. A special General Chapter had to be convoked within two or three years, possibly divided into two sessions, and it was empowered to modify the constitutions and introduce experiments. The final approbation of the constitutions was reserved to the competent authority. Cloistered nuns could also hold a chapter, but they were obliged to do this under the direction of a delegate from the Holy See.

The revision of the constitutions had to take into account the following elements: the biblical and theological foundations for the religious life were to be seen in connection with the spirit of the founder; the juridical section should have defined the character, the goals and the means required to carry them out. It was important to combine the spiritual and the juridical elements. Whatever was unnecessary was to be excluded, and everything else adapted to the physical and psychological requirements of the members and the times.

These special General Chapters were conducted between 1967 and 1971 in line with the given directives. The individual members were fully involved. Individual aspects of these Chapters were:

- A new departure was the requirement to reflect on the *charism of the founder or foundress*.[19] The Council's demand that communities should "return to the sources of every Christian life and to the spirit of the origins of the individual institutes" (*Perfectae caritatis* 2) was used by many communities as an incentive to expose themselves for the first time to the inspirations provided by their history, and (without internal censorship) to study the writings of their founder or foundress. The communities rediscovered their spiritual fathers and mothers, whose lives also symbolically reflected the challenges of

19 Schmiedl, "Konkretionen des Charismas in der Evangelisierung der nachkonziliaren Kirche".

our present times. This orientation to their origins resulted in practical consequences which the Redemptorists formulated in an exemplary way with regard to their relationship to Alphonse of Liguori: to study his life, to read his works perseveringly, to be imbued with his zeal and to identify with his attitudes.

- Necessarily, it followed that the *form of the rule or constitutions* had also to change. Many communities had first to break open a tough shell before they were able to discover the unique character of their institute behind the predominantly juridical directives. In this way the Premonstratensians became aware of the character of their Augustinian Rule as "a new reflection out of the spirit of the imitation of Christ". In their new constitutions "the spiritual basis of the Order was brought into line with the norm of the Gospel".
The Ursulines reorganised their constitutions according to subjects and started with the orientation of "the spirit and nature of our Institute" to the charisma of the foundress, Angela Merici. They placed the juridical regulations in the second part. This division into the theological foundation and juridical development was typical of the work done at the special chapters. As a result, in contrast to the legal situation before the Council which described the texts of the Bible, the Church Fathers, theologians and Councils as having no place in the constitutions, a completely new situation was created. In most instances this process was accepted by the institutes.

- An important area of reform was the *way of life* of an institute. Decisions were taken to simplify the religious habit. This was the most visible change that took place. At times the meaning of the change was not grasped and some members longed nostalgically for a return to the old 'romantic' habit. Prayer times were adapted to the needs of the apostolate and, more strongly than before, became the personal responsibility of the members. The reform tried to create a new balance between the inner life and the apostolate. Many communities of sisters regulated the possibility to pay visits, and discontinued the practice that a sister might only work outside the convent when accompanied by another sister.

- These changes in the way of life also affected the *apostolate*. Communities, which in the course of time had developed too strong an orientation to the monastic tradition, became aware of the relationship between and reciprocal enrichment of contemplation and apostolate. The integration of communities into the dioceses and their pastoral concept, although a painful process for many, was seen and accepted as a task. 'Inter-church service' and 'cooperation with sections of the Church' became slogans which required a departure from ancient structures of power and organisations if they were to be applied in practice. For some communities the Council documents resulted in new tasks. During their Thirty-first General Congregation in 1966, the Jesuits consciously accepted the task Paul VI had placed before them to study and make contact with atheism. This gave rise to an ecumenical dimension in the formation, way of life and work of the members, which was formulated in clear and practical directives.

- In most communities there was a significant change in their *government*. Having entered into dialogue with one another during the preparations for the special chapters, the members developed a new appreciation for 'community' and 'sharing' as the foundation for religious life. Co-responsibility became very important. The practice of obedience entered into crisis and had to be rethought and re-evaluated. The Jesuits, for example, highlighted the value of each member's own efforts to arrive at a recognition of God's will for him, and the value of his co-responsibility. The principle of subsidiarity took on new meaning for the government of communities. A survey of 91 institutes in a variety of countries showed that with regard to the government of the institute, 75 had chosen to formulate a new text, while 16 had only added a few changes.

- With regard to *education and formation* the publication of *Renovationis causam* was an important event. Almost all the institutes which held their special chapters between 1969 and 1971 based their deliberations on this document from the Congregation for Institutes of Consecrated Life. A revision of the novitiates, the introduction of juniorates for the professional, theological and spiritual education and formation of members during the time of temporary profession, and the regulations ensuring the ongoing formation of the perpetually professed were topics dealt with by all institutes.

The special chapters gave the individual communities an opportunity to change their inner and outer features in keeping with the directives of the Council. In the process, the latent signs of crisis, which had already been present before the Council, became obvious to all. The loss of members through their leaving the communities as well as the rapid decrease in the entry of new members became the visible signs of this crisis. Far more significant was the loss of meaning which the religious life underwent, and which was part of the global process of secularisation in the second half of the 1960s. The members of religious communities faced, in a special way, the accelerating challenges of the modern times. The young people entering a community wanted to continue their already improved education also within the religious orders. They wanted to use the mass media without any restriction. They wanted to make use of their freedom, and urged their superiors to hand out a single house key for every member. The most striking change however was the loss of religious communities' exceptional position in theology. This led to an identity crisis which found expression in different ways of living according to the evangelical counsels. The Second Vatican Council's momentum of renewal could only be applied in life to a limited extent. Instead, the signs of crisis were all too evident. On the one hand, the Council had opened up the possibility to undertake a comprehensive reform, while on the other, the communities lacked secure boundaries as a result of the emphasis placed on the juridical approach to the religious life in the decades before the Council. This meant that reform had been possible to a limited extent, but its effects were more easily monitored and controlled. Seen from the point of view of the individual and the community, the time following the Council made excessive demands on them. Compared with previous crises of religious life in the course of history, this time it did not mean the dissolution of an order because of a new foundation with more practical goals and a way of life that was better adapted to circumstances in a certain part of the world. On the contrary, communities were faced with something completely new. It simultaneously affected all communities throughout the world with their very different histories and ways of life. Every community was drawn into the crisis. As a result, crisis and renewal took place together following the Council. The crisis determined the degree of renewal, and for its part the renewal intensified the crisis.

Has the Crisis of Modernisation been overcome?

In the last few years, the problems have intensified for most religious communities. 1968 usually stands for the student uprisings which gave rise to social unrest. Through the encyclical, *Humanae vitae*, and the synodal efforts in different countries, like the *Katholikentag* at Essen and the Dutch Pastoral Council, the incipient process within the Church of opening itself to the world did not pass by religious communities without leaving a trace. The increasing public presence of sexuality affected all persons who were known as not married. The crisis of celibacy and community crises to some extent became public property, although not all were as spectacular as the case of the Siegburg Benedictine Abbot, Alkuin Heising, who announced publicly that he was leaving the order. The end of a 'Catholic milieu' became very evident in the fact that after they had left their communities, theologians did not give up their public activities, but rather increased them. Examples of this are the former Benedictine Thomas Sartory, or the former Dominicans Otto Hermann Pesch and Stephan Pfuertner. Conflicts within the Church or a community no longer resulted in someone being stigmatised or losing their influence.

As a result religious communities now have their backs to the wall. From a European perspective, this is shown in a rapid decline in the numbers of their members. From the perspective of the universal Church, however, there has been a displacement of the members to the young churches of Asia and Africa, and to a lesser extent, to Latin America. Between 1965 and 1991 the Salesians declined by 21,5%, the Franciscans by 27,3%, the Jesuits by 34%, and the Benedictines even by 56,9%.[20] Nevertheless, as a result of the increase in members in Africa and Asia, a number of newer communities have been able to maintain their numbers or even increase them. The two developments are clearly out of step, not just with regard to numbers, but also in the way the religious life is being lived.

There is an ever increasing lack of clarity what religious life is really about. People have often expressed regret because the Council shied away from providing a theological definition of religious life, while today it symbolises the search of Christian spirituality which has not come to a conclusion. The ancient theology of the religious state is no longer plausible. Other concepts have come to the fore: we are concerned with a mission in the midst of the world, with a new affinity to the world rather than flight from the world, with overcoming the world and penetrating the world. The subject that played a central role in the closing stages of the Council was very apposite, also in a theological sense, to religious life. In the German-speaking world this has influenced the writings of the Jesuit theologian, Friedrich Wulf, as well as the integrative approach of the "Ordens-Christen" in the works of Anneliese Herzig[21] and the studies published by the *Arbeitsgruppe Ordenstheologie*.[22] In the French-speaking world, mention must be made of the Canadian Dominican, Jean-Marie-Roger Tillard[23], and in Italy, Enzo Bianchi.[24] For the

20 Punsmann, "Zur Komplexität religiöser Orden heute", 147.
21 Herzig, *Ordens-Christen*.
22 Schaupp and Kunz, eds, *Erneuerung oder Neugründung?*; Schambeck and Schaupp, eds, *Lebensentscheidung*; Gruber and Kiechle, eds, *Gottesfreundschaf*.
23 Tillard, *Vertrauen zur Gemeinschaft*; Idem, *Frei sein in Gott*.
24 Bianchi, "Le monachisme au seuil de l'an 2000".

English-speaking world one may look at the works of Sandra Schneiders.[25] The new ways of life that have broken through, such as the secular institutes and above all the new spiritual movements[26], pose a particular challenge to the renewal of a theology of religious communities. Men and women religious have often received new inspiration for their own religious lives as a result of their cooperation with these new spiritual movements. However, before an unprejudiced and spontaneous collaboration is possible, both sides have to overcome their resentments.

The Congregation for Institutes of Consecrated Life and Societies of Apostolic Life in Rome continues to exercise an important function in guiding religious communities. Its task lies less in the disciplinary field, although the controversies surrounding the amalgamation of Latin American religious (CLAR) or the very different directions taken in the reform of the Carmelite family might suggest the opposite. The Congregation is far more concerned with accompanying the process of renewing religious institutes through issuing circular letters on definite subjects. In this regard mention must be made of the document *Religious and Human Advancement* published in January 1981, *Fraternal Life in Community* of 1994, and the instruction *Starting afresh from Christ - a renewed commitment to consecrated life in the third millennium*, given out at Pentecost 2002. The 1994 Bishops' Synod devoted to the consecrated life, and the document *Vita consecrata* that followed it, tended more to encourage than to demarcate. The change of perspective with regard to the biblical foundations for the consecrated life, which moved from emphasising renunciation and leaving everything behind to that of sharing in the fullness of Jesus' glory as it finds expression in the events on Mount Tabor, shows that that thinking has taken a new direction.

It should not surprise us that tensions appear along the way. Religious communities felt encouraged by the Council to overcome the dichotomy between their inner, spiritual lives and the demands of the apostolate and professions. A statement made in the document *Religious and Human Advancement* takes this up. Number 13 enlarges on four great loyalties: fidelity to humanity and to our times; fidelity to Christ and to the Gospel; fidelity to the Church and to its mission in the world; fidelity to religious life and to the charisma of one's institute. Yet sixteen years later, in the post-synodal document, *Vita consecrata*, another list is presented: faithful to Christ, the Church, to your institute and to the men and women of our time (*Vita*

25 Schneiders, *New Wineskins*; Idem, *Finding the Treasure*; Idem, *Selling All*.
26 Hegge, *Rezeption und Charisma*; Cordes, *Nicht immer das alte Lied*; Wolf, ed, *Lebensaufbrüche*.

consecrata 110).[27] It would seem that at the end of the second millennium the trend has gone into reverse. Religious should first of all be aware of their religious and ecclesiastical calling, and only from there foster their involvement with the world. It is true that religious are being strongly reminded of their role in the Church. Their involvement in the pastorate at a time when there is a scarcity of priests is not only desired, it is even required. In this regard, the debate on the limitation of exemptions has clearly borne fruit. On the other hand, the experiences gained in the course of the decades since the Council have shown clearly that the centrifugal forces at work in an active, apostolic life need to be continually counteracted. As a result, on 13 May 1999, the Congregation for Institutes of Consecrated Life presented a document on the contemplative life of cloistered nuns, *Verbi sponsa,* in which cloistered nuns are described as the "soul and yeast of apostolic initiatives", whose lives become "a mysterious source of apostolic fruitfulness and a blessing for the community of Christians and the whole world".[28] This also applies to active communities. Although there was an enormous exodus from communities in the years immediately after the Council, individual communities still have to cope repeatedly with the departure of longstanding members. In this context, it is often pointed out that there has to be a balance between the different areas of life, and that every consecrated life needs to be continually re-focussed on its centre and meaning.

The years following the Council have brought about a shift of emphasis in religious communities. Immediately after the Council, the main focus was on formation, that is, the first phase of belonging to a community. Today it is on ongoing formation. The study of theology has largely been transferred outside the individual community. After the Second World War there were thirty colleges run by religious communities in Germany, today only six colleges, of which five are full faculties of theology, are still in their hands. Yet the choices for ongoing human, spiritual and professional education and formation have grown enormously. The professionalisation of many fields of activity, the human preparation to make this possible, and its development through the different phases of life have become very important to religious communities and their members.

It is significant that these developments are no longer taking place within the individual communities. A new element has entered into Church history

27 Schermann, "Ordensleben", 40. Reference is made to the commentary of Anneliese Herzig (*Ordenskorrespondenz*, 40 (1999), 152).

28 *Verbi sponsa*, No. 7.

through the solidarity of religious institutes. In Germany, for example, there is an Association of German Religious Superiors (Vereinigung Deutscher Ordensobern (VDO), founded in 1898)[29], an Association of Religious Superiors for Women's Communities in Germany (Vereinigung der Ordensoberinnen Deutschlands (VOD), founded in 1954)[30] and an Association of Religious Superiors for Orders and Congregations of Brothers (Vereinigung der Ordenobern der Bruederorden und -kongregationen (VOB), founded in 1958)[31], as well as a Commission for Secular Institutes. Different commissions serve different fields, so that members working in the same field can meet regularly to exchange experiences. For example, there are commissions for religious working in high schools or schools, for religious working with youth, for bursars and procurators. The Institute of Orders (Institut der Orden) is responsible for coordinating the education and ongoing formation of members. Even in the financial field religious communities have become mutually dependent. In the Work of Solidarity (Solidarwerk) they have taken on the obligation to create their own system of pensions and caring for their older members, thus relieving the state. The Council's recommendations concerning the formation of conferences or councils of major superiors, because they "can contribute very much to achieve the purpose of each institute; to encourage more effective cooperation for the welfare of the Church; to ensure a more just distribution of ministers of the Gospel in a given area; and finally to conduct affairs of interest to all religious" (*Perfectae caritatis* 23) has taken a qualitative leap forward in the past decades. It is possible that this solidarity of religious communities is the most important result of the post-conciliar period and the best sign of the implementation of what was described in a theological synthesis of the Council as "Communio Theology".[32]

The reception of the Second Vatican Council by religious institutes is somewhat ambivalent. The Council provided them with a means that would enable them to cope with their crisis to some extent. The fact that they reached the culmination of their expansion, while at the same time experiencing a crisis in the numbers of their members and vocations, naturally led, within the space of a few years, to a changed evaluation of themselves as well as by others. Many tasks they had taken on shortly before the Council had to be abandoned because of a lack of personnel. Others were a burden to the communi-

29 On the history of the VDO, see Leugers, *Interessenpolitik und Solidarität*; Idem, "Vereinigung Deutscher Ordensobern".

30 For the history of the VOD, see Vereinigung der Ordensoberinnen Deutschlands, ed, *Festschrift 25 Jahre VOD.*

31 For the history of the VOB, see VOB, *25 Jahre Vereinigung der Ordensobern.*

32 See a.o. Kasper, *Die Communio-Ekklesiologie*; Garijo-Guembe, "Communio-Ekklesiologie".

ties and prevented them from finding a creative solution. With regard to their way of life, the reform has to a large extent been a success. Problems have arisen mainly in communicating with others. Within the Church itself, religious communities have been subjected to a continual process of marginalisation. So it is fairly certain that not all communities will survive the transformation. The past decades have, however, shown one thing very clearly: religious communities are capable of transforming themselves and are in a position to offer an answer to the challenges of even the most difficult circumstances in an era. This will also secure for them a place in the landscape of the Church and society in the time to come.

Bibliography

Acerbi, A. "L'ecclésiologie à la base des institutions ecclésiales post-conciliaires" in: Giuseppe Alberigo, ed. *Les Églises après Vatican II. Dynamisme et prospective.* Paris, 1981, 223-258.

Acquaviva, Sabino S. *L'Eclissi del sacro nella civilta industriale.* Milan: Comunità, 1961.

Alaerts, Leen. *Door eigen werk sterk. Geschiedenis van de kajotters en kajotsters in Vlaanderen, 1924-1967.* Leuven: KADOC-K.U.Leuven in collaboration with Het Kajottershuis, 2004.

Alberigo, Angelina, ed. *Giacomo Lercaro: Vescovo della Chiesa di Dio (1891-1976).* Genoa: Marietti, 1991.

Alberigo, Giuseppe. "Le concezioni della Chiesa e i mutamenti istituzionali" in: Giuseppe Alberigo and Andrea Riccardi, eds. *Chiesa e papato nel mondo contemporaneo.* Rome: Laterza, 1990, 65-121.

Alberigo, Giuseppe, ed. *Storia del concilio Vaticano II.* Bologna: Il Mulino, 1995-2001, 5 vols.

Alberigo, Giuseppe. "Criteri ermeneutici per una Storia del Concilio Vaticano II" in: Wolfgang Weiss, ed. *Zeugnis und Dialog. Die katholische Kirche in der neuzeitlichen Welt und das II. Vatikanische Konzil. Festschrift für Karl Wittstadt.* Würzburg: Echter, 1996, 101-117.

Alberigo, Giuseppe, ed. *Giuseppe Dossetti: Prime prospettive e ipotesi di ricerca.* Bologna: Il Mulino, 1998.

Alberigo, Giuseppe. "Transizione epocale?" in: *Storia del concilio Vaticano II.* Vol. 5: *Concilio di transizione. Il quarto periodo e la conclusione del concilio (1965).* Bologna: Il Mulino, 2001, 577-664.

Allport, Gordon W. *The Nature of Prejudice.* Reading (MA) - London: Adison-Wesley, 1979 (25th anniversary edition).

Alvarez Alonso, Fermina. "Claretiani al Concilio: Arcadio M. Larraona, Arturo Tabera e Anastasio Gutierrez. Inventario dei Fondi Documentari sul Concilio Vaticano II". *Centro Vaticano II. Ricerche e Documenti*, 2 (2002), 2.

Ammerman, Nancy Tatom. *Bible Believers: Fundamentalists in the Modern World.* New Brunswick (NJ): Rutgers University Press, 1987.

Ammerman, Nancy Tatom and Farnsley, Arthur Emery, eds. *Congregation and Community.* New Brunswick (NJ): Rutgers University Press, 1997.

Anderson, Margaret L. "Piety and Politics. Recent Work on German Catholicism". *Journal of Modern History*, 63 (1991) 4, 681-716.

Anderson, Margaret L. "The Limits of Secularization. On the Problem of the Catholic Revival in Nineteenth-Century Germany". *The Historical Journal*, 38 (1995) 3, 647-670.

Anderson, Olive. "The Incidence of Civil Marriage in Victorian England and Wales". *Past & Present*, 69 (1975), 50-87.

Appleby, R. Scott. *The Ambivalence of the Sacred: Religion, Violence and Reconciliation.* Lanham (MD): Rowman & Littlefield, 2000.

Ariarajah, Wesley. "Wider Ecumenism. A Threat or a Promise?" *Ecumenical Review*, 40 (1998) 3, 321-329.

Arnal, Oscar. *Priests in Working-Class Blue: The History of the Worker-Priests (1943-1954).* New York: Paulist Press, 1986.

Astorri, Romeo. "La segreteria di stato nelle riforme di Paolo VI e di Giovanni Paolo II" in: *Les secrétaires d'État du Saint-Siège (1814-1979). Sources et méthodes.* Mélanges de l'école française de Rome. Italie et Méditerranée, 110, 2. Rome: École française de Rome, 1998, 501-518.

Astorri, Romeo. "Codex iuris canonici" in: *Enciclopedia del diritto. Aggiornamento.* Vol. 3. Milan: Giuffrè, 2000, 364-369.

Baar Statement "Theological Perspectives on Plurality". World Council of Churches, 1990. <www.wcc-coe.org/wcc/what/interreligious/baar.html> (12.06.2008).

Balandier, Georges. *Le détour.* Paris: Fayard, 1985.

Balducci, Ernesto. *Giorgio La Pira.* San Domenico di Fiesole: Edizioni Cultura della Pace, 1986.

Bank, Jan. *Opkomst en ondergang van de Nederlandse Volks Beweging (NVB).* Deventer: Kluwer, 1978.

Baptism, Eucharist and Ministry. Faith & Order Paper 111. Geneva: World Council of Churches, 1982.

Barrau, Grégory. *Le Mai 68 des catholiques.* Paris: Éditions de l'Atelier, 1998.

Barrett, David. *World Christian Encyclopedia.* Cambridge: Cambridge University Press, 2002[2], 2 vols.

Bartlett, Alan. *The Churches in Bermondsey 1880-1939.* Ph. D. thesis. Birmingham, 1987.

Becker, Henk A. "Dynamics of Life Histories and Generations Research" in: Henk A. Becker, ed. *Life Histories and Generations.* Utrecht: ISOR, 1991, 1-55.

Becker, Henk A., ed. *Dynamics of Cohort and Generations Research.* Amsterdam: Thesis Publications, 1992.

Becker, Henk A. "A Pattern of Generations and its Consequences" in: Henk A. Becker, ed. *Dynamics of Cohort and Generations Research.* Amsterdam: Thesis Publications, 1992, 219-248.

Becker, Henk A. *Generaties en hun kansen.* Amsterdam: Meulenhoff, 1992.

Bedani, Gino. *Politics and Ideology in the Italian Workers' Movement. Union Development and the Changing Role of the Catholic and Communist Subcultures in Postwar Italy.* Oxford: Berg, 1995.

Bedeschi, Lorenzo. *L'ultima battaglia di Don Mazzolari: 'Adesso' 1949-1959.* Brescia: Morcelliana, 1990.

Beerten, Wilfried. *Le rêve travailliste en Belgique. Histoire de l'UDB 1944-1947.* Brussels: Vie Ouvrière, 1990.

Behr-Sigel, Élisabeth and Ware, Kallistos. *The Ordination of Women in the Orthodox Church.* Geneva: WCC Publications, 2000.

Bellah, Robert N. *Beyond Belief. Essays on Religion in a Post-Traditional World.* New York: Harper & Row, 1970.

Bellah, Robert N. *The Good Society.* New York: Knopf, 1992.

Bendikowski, Tillmann. "'Eine Fackel der Zwiedracht'. Katholisch-protestantische Mischehen im 19. und 20. Jahrhundert" in: Olaf Blaschke, ed. *Konfessionen im Konflikt. Das zweite konfessionelle Zeitalter zwischen 1800 und 1970*. Göttingen: Vandenhoeck & Ruprecht, 2002, 215-242.

Benelli, Giovanni. "Les rapports entre le siège de Pierre et les Églises locales". *La Documentation catholique*, 55 (1973) 1644, 1070-1080.

Bennette, Rebecca Ayako. "Threatened Protestants: Confessional Conflict in the Rhine Province and Westphalia during the Nineteenth Century". *German History*, 26 (2008) 2, 168-194.

Beretta, Roberto. *Il lungo autumno: contrastoria del Sessantotto cattolico*. Milan: Rizzoli, 1998.

Berger, Peter. *The Sacred Canopy: Elements of a Sociological Theory of Religion*. Garden City (NY): Doubleday, 1967.

Berger, Peter. "Postscript" in: Linda Woodhead, Paul Heelas and David Martin, eds. *Peter Berger and the Study of Religion*. London-New York: Routledge, 2001, 189 ff.

Bernard, Jean-Pierre. *Paris rouge. Les communistes français dans la capitale*. Seyssel: Champ Vallon, 1991.

Berrar, Émile. "Caractères d'une déclaration catholique". *Conversaciones católicas internacionales. Documentos*. San Sebastian: Conversaciones católicas internacionales, (1949) 1, 42-44.

Bertini, Barbara and Casadio, Stefano. *Clero e industria a Torino. Ricerca sui rapporti tra clero e masse operaie nella capitale dell'auto dal 1943 al 1948*. Milan: Franco Angeli, 1979.

Besret, Bernard. *Incarnation ou eschatologie? Contribution à l'histoire du vocabulaire religieux contemporain, 1935-1955*. Paris: Cerf, 1964.

Best, Thomas and Robra, Martin, eds. *Ecclesiology and Ethics. Ecumenical Ethical Engagement, Moral Formation and the Nature of the Church*. Geneva: World Council of Churches, 1997.

Bianchi, Enzo. "Le monachisme au seuil de l'an 2000". *Collectanea Cisterciensia*, 61 (1999), 3-21.

Bibby, Reginald W. *Fragmented Gods: The Poverty and Potential in Canada*. Toronto: Stoddart, 1987.

Billiet, Jaak, ed. *Tussen bescherming en verovering. Sociologen en historici over zuilvorming*. KADOC-Studies 6. Leuven: Universitaire Pers Leuven, 1988.

Billiet, Jaak. "Church Involvement, Individualism, and Ethnic Prejudice among Flemish Roman Catholics". *Journal of the Scientific Study of Religion*, 34 (1995), 224-233.

Billiet, Jaak. "Social Capital, Religious-philosophical Involvement and Social Integration in Belgium. An Empirical Investigation" in: Rudi Laermans, Bryan Wilson and Jaak Billiet, eds. *Secularization and Social Integration. Papers in Honour of Karel Dobbelaere*. Leuven: Leuven University Press, 1998, 233-250.

Billiet, Jaak; Eisinga, Rob and Scheepers, Peer. "Ethnocentrism in the Low Countries: a comparative perspective". *New Community*, 22 (1996) 3, 401-416.

Billiet, Jaak and Vanhoutvinck, Jan. "Het stemgedrag van de Vlaamse bejaarden nu en morgen. Een onderzoek naar de relatie tussen stemgedrag, leeftijd, kerkelijke betrokkenheid en niveau van onderwijs" in: Frans Lammertijn and Jef Verhoeven, eds. *Tussen sociologie en beleid: vriendenboek Prof. E.J. Leemans*. Leuven-Amersfoort: Acco, 1991, 41-71.

Billiet, Jaak et al. "Church Commitment and Some Consequences in Western and Central Europe" in: Ralph L. Piedmont and David O. Moberg, eds. *Research in the Social Scientific Study of Religion*. Vol. 14. Leiden-Boston: Brill, 2003, 129-159.

Birmelé, André. *La communion ecclésiale. Progrès œcuméniques et enjeux méthodologiques.* Paris-Geneva: Cerf, 2000.

Birmelé, André. "Le Concile Vatican II vu par les observateurs des autres traditions chrétiennes" in: Joseph Doré and Alberto Melloni, eds. *Volti di fine Concilio. Studi di storia e teologia sulla conclusione del Vaticano II*. Bologna: Il Mulino, 2001, 225-264.

Blackbourn, David. "The Catholic Church in Europe. A Review Article". *Comparative Studies in Society and History*, 33 (1991) 4, 778-790.

Blaschke, Olaf. "Das 19. Jahrhundert. Ein zweites Konfessionelles Zeitalter?". *Geschichte und Gesellschaft*, 26 (2000), 38-75.

Blaschke, Olaf, ed. *Konfessionen im Konflikt. Das zweite konfessionelle Zeitalter zwischen 1800 und 1970.* Göttingen: Vandenhoeck & Ruprecht, 2002.

Bleyen, Jan. *Het taboe voorbij? Omgaan met de dood na 1950. Een microgeschiedenis van Westmalle.* Diss. Lic. K.U.Leuven, 2002.

Bleyen, Jan. *De dood in Vlaanderen. Opvattingen en praktijken na 1950*. Leuven: Davidsfonds, 2005.

Blom, Hans. "Jaren van tucht en ascese. Enige beschouwingen over de stemming in Herrijzend Nederland (1945-1950)". *Bijdragen en Mededelingen betreffende de Geschiedenis der Nederlanden*, 96 (1981), 300-333.

Blom, J.C.H. "Pillarisation in Perspective". *West European Politics*, 23 (2000) 3, 153-164.

Blom, J.C.H. and Talsma, J., eds. *De verzuiling voorbij. Godsdienst, stand en natie in de lange negentiende eeuw.* Amsterdam: Het Spinhuis, 2000.

Bole, William. "U.S. Bishops Blast Critique of Episcopal Conference". *National Catholic Reporter*, 04.11.1988, 23.

Bollen, Kenneth. *Structural Equations with Latent Variables*. New York: John Wiley, 1989.

Bologh, Roslyn Wallach. *Love or Greatness: Max Weber and Masculine Thinking: a Feminist Inquiry.* London: Unwin Hyman, 1990.

Bonnet, Piero Antonio and Gullo, Carlo, eds. *La Curia romana nella costituzione apostolica "Pastor bonus"*. Vatican City: Libreria Editrice Vaticana, 1990.

Bonnet, Serge. *A hue et à dia: les avatars du cléricalisme sous la Ve République*. Paris: Cerf, 1973.

Booth, Charles, ed. *Life and Labour of the People in London*. London: Macmillan, 1902-1903, 17 vols.

Borutta, Manuel. "Antikatholizismus, Männlichkeit und Moderne. Die diskursive Feminisierung des Katholizismus in Deutschland und Italien (1850-1900)". AIM-Gender Tagung, s.l., s.d. <www.ruendal.de/aim/pdfs/Borutta.pdf> (09.06.2008).

Bots, Jan P.M. *Kirche in Holland. Der heutige holländische Katholizismus in geschichtlicher Sicht*. Sankt Augustin: Wiersig, 1979.

Bots, Jan P.M. *Zestig jaar katholicisme in Nederland*. De Rots 11/7-8. Venlo, 1981.

Bouthillon, Fabrice. "D'une théologie à l'autre. Pie XI et le Christ-Roi" in: *Achille Ratti, pape Pie XI*. Rome: École française de Rome, 1996, 293-303.

Boy, Daniel and Michelat, Guy. "Croyances aux parasciences: dimensions sociales et culturelles". *Revue française de sociologie*, 27 (1986), 175-204.

Boy, Daniel and Michelat, Guy. *Premiers résultats de l'enquête sur les croyances aux parasciences*. Paris: Albin Michel, 1993, 209-223.

Boy, Daniel and Michelat, Guy. "Les Français et les parasciences" in: SOFRES. *L'État de l'opinion*. Paris: Seuil, 1994, 201-217.

Boylan, Anne M. *Sunday School. The Formation of an American Institution, 1790-1880.* New Haven (CT): Yale University Press, 1988.

Boym, Svetlana. *The Future of Nostalgia*. New York: Basic Books, 2001.

Brakelmann, Günter. "Evangelische Pfarrer im Konfliktfeld des Ruhrbergarbeiterstreiks von 1905" in: Jürgen Reulecke and Wolfhard Weber, eds. *Fabrik Familie Feierabend: Beiträge zur Sozialgeschichte des Alltags im Industriezeitalter.* Wuppertal: Peter Hammer, 1978, 297-314.

Braudel, Fernand. *Écrits sur l'histoire*. Paris: Flammarion, 1969.

Brehm, John and Rahn, Wendy. *Individual Level Evidence for the Causes and Consequences of Social Capital.* Unpublished paper. Durham: Duke University, 1996.

Brotherton, Anne, ed. *The Voice of the Turtledove: New Catholic Women in Europe.* New York: Paulist Press, 1992.

Broughton, David and ten Napel, Hans-Martien, eds. *Religion and Electoral Behaviour in Europe.* London-New York: Routledge-ECPR, 2000.

Brown, Callum G. *Religion and Society in Scotland since 1707*. Edinburgh: Edinburgh University Press, 1997.

Brown, Callum G. *The Death of Christian Britain: Understanding Secularisation 1800-2000.* London-New York: Routledge, 2001.

Brown, Callum G. *Religion and Society in Twentieth-Century Britain*. Harlow: Pearson Longman, 2006.

Bruce, Steve. *The Rise and Fall of the New Christian Right: Conservative Protestant Politics in America, 1978-1988*. Oxford: Clarendon Press, 1988.

Bruce, Steve. *Pray TV: Televangelism in America.* New York: Routledge, 1990.

Bruce, Steve, ed. *Religion and Modernization: Sociologists and Historians Debate the Secularization Thesis*. Oxford: Oxford University Press, 1992.

Bruce, Steve. *Religion in the Modern World: From Cathedrals to Cults*. Oxford: Oxford University Press, 1996.

Bruce, Steve. "The Curious Case of the Unnecessary Recantation: Berger and Secularization" in: Linda Woodhead, Paul Heelas and David Martin, eds. *Peter Berger and the Study of Religion*. London-New York: Routledge, 2001, 87-100.

Bruce, Steve. *Choice and Religion: A Critique of Rational Choice Theory*. Oxford: Oxford University Press, 2002.

Bruce, Steve. *God is Dead: Secularization in the West*. Oxford: Blackwell, 2002.

Bruni, Luigino. "Economy of Communion. Between Market and Solidarity" in: J. Boswell, Francis McHugh and Johan Verstraeten, eds. *Catholic Social Thought: Twilight or Renaissance?* Bibliotheca Ephemeridum Theologicarum Lovaniensium 157. Leuven: Peeters-University Press, 2000, 239-248.

Budde, Gunilla-Friederike. *Auf dem Weg ins Bürgerleben: Kindheit und Erziehung in deutschen und englischen Bürgerfamilien 1840-1914.* Göttingen: Vandenhoeck & Ruprecht, 1994.

Burleigh, Michael. *Earthly Powers: Religion and Politics in Europe from the French Revolution to the Great War.* London: Harper Collins, 2005.

Burleigh, Michael. *Sacred Causes: Religion and Politics from the European Dictators to Al Qaeda.* London: Harper Press, 2006.

Butler, Jon; Wacker, Grant and Balmer, Randall. *Religion in American Life: A Short History.* New York: Oxford University Press, 2003.

Butler, Joseph. *An Analogy of Religion, Natural and Revealed, to the Constitution and Course of Nature.* London, 1736.

Buyst, Erik et al. *CERA 1892-1998. The Power of Co-operative Solidarity.* Antwerp: Mercatorfonds, 2002.

Cahiers du G.R.M.F. Villeneuve d'Ascq: Groupement pour la Recherche sur les Mouvements Familiaux, 1983-.

Called to Common Mission: A Lutheran Proposal for Revision of the Concordat of Agreement. <www.elca.org> (12.06.2008).

Cambré, Bart. *De relatie tussen religiositeit en etnocentrisme. Een contextuele benadering met cross-culturele data.* Diss. Doct. K.U.Leuven, 2002.

Cambré, Bart; Welkenhuysen-Gybels, J. and Billiet, Jaak. "Is it Content or Style? An Evaluation of Two Competitive Measurement Models Applies to a Balanced Set of Ethnocentrism Items". *International Journal of Comparative Sociology*, 43 (2002), 1-20.

Campanini, Giorgio. *Don Primo Mazzolari fra religione e politica.* Bologna: Edizioni Dehoniane, 1989.

Campanini, Giorgio and Truffelli, Matteo, eds. *Mazzolari e 'Adesso': Cinquant'anni dopo.* Brescia: Morcelliana, 2000.

Campbell, Colin. *The Easternization of the West: A Thematic Account of Cultural Change in the Modern Era.* Boulder (CO): Paradigm, 2007.

Caprile, Giovanni. "Contributo alla storia della 'Nota explicativa praevia'" in: *Paolo VI e i problemi ecclesiologici al concilio.* Brescia: Istituto Paolo VI, 1989, 587-697.

Casanova, José. *Public Religions in the Modern World.* Chicago: University of Chicago Press, 1994.

Casula, Carlo Felice. *Cattolici-comunisti e sinistra cristiana (1938-1945).* Bologna: Il Mulino, 1976.

Catterall, Peter. "The Conservative Party and Religion" in: Anthony Seldon and Stuart Ball. *Conservative Century. The Conservative Party since 1900.* Oxford: Oxford University Press, 1994, 637-670.

Cautres, Bruno. "Religion et comportement électoral en Grande-Bretagne" in: Monica Charlot, ed. *Religion et politique en Grande-Bretagne.* Paris: Presses de la Sorbonne Nouvelle, 1994, 165-190.

Cavalli, F. "Sviluppo dell'internazionalizzazione nella Curia romana". *Civiltà cattolica*, 121 (1970) 2, 555-568.

Chadwick, Owen. *The Secularization of the European Mind in the Nineteenth Century.* Cambridge: Cambridge University Press, 1975.

Chaves, Mark. *Ordaining Women: Culture and Conflict in Religious Organizations.* Cambridge (MA): Harvard University Press, 1997.

Chaves, Mark and Cavendish, James. "Recent Changes in Women's Ordination Conflicts: The Effect of a Social Movement on Intra-organizational Controversy". *Journal for the Scientific Study of Religion*, 36 (1997) 4, 574-586.

Chaves, Mark and Gorski, Philip S. "Religious Pluralism and Religious Participation". *Annual Review of Sociology*, 27 (2001), 261-281.

Chenaux, Philippe. *Une Europe vaticane? Entre le plan Marshall et les traités de Rome.* Brussels: Éditions Ciaco, 1990.

Chenaux, Philippe. *Les rapports du "montinianisme" et du "maritanisme"*. Brescia: Istituto Paolo VI, 1994.

Chenu, Marie-Dominique. *Dimension nouvelle de la chrétienté.* Paris: Cerf, 1937.

Chenu, Marie-Dominique. "À propos des 'Mouvements de paix'". *La Vie intellectuelle*, June 1950, 745-748.

Chenu, Marie-Dominique. *Pour une théologie du travail.* Paris: Seuil, 1955.

Chenu, Marie-Dominique. "L'Église en état de mission". *Parole et Mission*, 15.10.1958, 427-430.

Chenu, Marie-Dominique. *La 'doctrine sociale' de l'Église comme idéologie.* Paris: Cerf, 1979.

Chenu, Marie-Dominique. *Une école de theologie: Le Saulchoir.* Paris: Cerf, 1985.

Chenu, Marie-Dominique. *Notes quotidiennes au Concile. Journal de Vatican II, 1962-1963.* Paris: Cerf, 1995.

Cholvy, Gérard and Hilaire, Yves-Marie. *Histoire religieuse de la France contemporaine 1930-1988.* Toulouse: Privat, 1988.

Cholvy, Gérard and Hilaire, Yves-Marie. *Histoire religieuse de la France contemporaine 1880-1930.* Toulouse: Privat, 1986.

Cholvy, Gérard and Hilaire, Yves-Marie. *Histoire religieuse de la France contemporaine 1800-1880.* Toulouse: Privat, 1990[2].

Les Chrétiens, la lutte contre la misère, le développement économique. Antsirabe: Notre Imprimerie, 1964.

Church and World. The Unity of the Church and the Renewal of Human Community. Faith & Order Paper 151. Geneva: World Council of Churches, 1990.

Clark, Christopher and Kaiser, Wolfram, eds. *Culture Wars: Secular-Catholic Conflict in Nineteenth-Century Europe.* Cambridge: Cambridge University Press, 2003.

Clarke, Peter B. "Introduction: Change and Variety in New Religious Movements in Western Europe, c. 1960 to Present" in: Elisabeth Arweck and Peter B. Clarke. *New Religious Movements in Western Europe: An Annotated Bibliography.* Westport (CT)-London: Greenwood Press, 1997, xvii-xliii.

Cobb, John B. Jr. *Reclaiming the Church.* Louisville: Westminster John Knox Press, 1997.

Cohen, Jack Simcha. "The Orthodox Synagogue: Challenges of the Inner City and Suburbia". *Jewish Life*, 2 (1977-1978), 67-72.

Coleman, James S. "Social Capital in the Creation of Human Capital". *American Journal of Sociology*, 94 (1988) (supplement), 195-210.

Coleman, James S. *Foundations of Social Theory.* Cambridge (MA): Harvard University Press, 1990.

Coleman, John A. *The Evolution of Dutch Catholicism, 1958-1974.* Berkeley: University of California Press, 1978.

Coleman, Simon. *The Globalisation of Charismatic Christianity: Spreading the Gospel of Prosperity*. Cambridge: Cambridge University Press, 2007.

Comblin, Joseph. *Échec de l'Action catholique?* Paris: Éditions universitaires, 1961.

Comité épiscopal des Migration (France). *Un peuple en devenir. L'Église et les migrants*. Paris: Éditions de l'Atelier, 1995.

Commission internationale catholique-luthérienne. *Face à l'unité.* Paris, 1986.

Compagnon, Olivier. *Jacques Maritain et l'Amérique du sud. Le modèle malgré lui.* Lille: Presses universitaires du Septentrion, 2003.

Concerns of the Churches. Amsterdam: World Council of Churches, 1948.

Confessing the One Faith. An Ecumenical Explication of the Apostolic Faith as it is Confessed in the Nicene-Constantinopolitan Creed (381). Faith & Order Paper 153. Geneva: World Council of Churches, 1991.

Congar, Yves. "La 'réception' comme réalité ecclésiologique". *Revue des sciences philosophiques et théologiques*, 56 (1972), 369-403.

Congar, Yves. "Remarques générales" in: *Paul VI et la modernité dans l'Église*. Rome: École française de Rome, 1984, 851-853.

Congar, Yves. *Herbstgespräche. Erinnerungen und Anstöße*. Theologie und Glaube. Munich: Verlag Neue Stadt, 1988.

Consensus œcuménique et différence fondamentale. Ed. Comité mixte catholique-protestant en France. Paris: Centurion, 1987.

Conway, Martin. *Collaboration in Belgium. Léon Degrelle and the Rexist Movement 1940-1944.* New Haven (CT): Yale University Press, 1993.

Conway, Martin. "Introduction" in: Martin Conway and Tom Buchanan, eds. *Political Catholicism in Europe, 1918-1965.* Oxford: Oxford University Press, 1996, 1-33.

Conway, Martin. *Catholic Politics in Western Europe 1918-1945.* London-New York: Routledge, 1997.

Conway, Martin. "Left Catholicism in Europe in the 1940s: Elements of an Interpretation" in: Gerd-Rainer Horn and Emmanuel Gerard, eds. *Left Catholicism. Catholics and Society in Western Europe at the Point of Liberation, 1943-1955.* KADOC-Studies 25. Leuven: Leuven University Press, 2001, 269-281.

Conway, Martin. "The Age of Christian Democracy: The Frontiers of Success and Failure" in: Thomas Kselman and Joseph A. Buttigieg, eds. *European Christian Democracy. Historical Legacies and Comparative Perspectives.* Notre Dame (IN): University of Notre Dame Press, 2003, 43-67.

Conway, Martin and Buchanan, Tom, eds. *Political Catholicism in Europe, 1918-1965.* Oxford: Oxford University Press, 1996.

Conzen, Kathleen N. "The Place of Religion in Urban and Community Studies". *Religion and American Culture*, 6 (1996), 108-114.

Cordes, Paul Josef. *Nicht immer das alte Lied. Die Kirchenkrise und die neuen religiösen Bewegungen*. Vienna: Molden, 1999.

Coste, René. *L'Église et la paix*. Paris: Desclée, 1979.

Cours-Saliès, Pierre. *La CFDT: un passé porteur d'avenir: pratiques syndicales et débats stratégiques depuis 1946.* Paris: La Brèche, 1988.

Cracknell, Kenneth. "Ambivalent Theology and Ambivalent Policy: The World Council of Churches and Interfaith Dialogue 1938-1999". *Studies in Interreligious Dialogue*, 9 (1999), 87-111.

Cracknell, Kenneth. *In Good and Generous Faith: Christian Responses to Religious Pluralism*. Cleveland: The Pilgrim Press, 2005.

Cuminetti, Mario. *Il dissenso cattolico in Italia, 1965-1980*. Milan: Rizzoli, 1998.

Czempiel, Ernst-Otto. "Die Christen und die Auswärtige Politik. Lehre vom Gerechter Krieg oder Praxeologie des Friedens". *Civitas. Jahrbuch für christliche Gesellschafsordnung*, 6 (1967), 20-45.

Damberg, Wilhelm. *Abschied vom Milieu? Katholizismus im Bistum Münster und in den Niederlanden 1945-1980*. Veröffentlichungen der Kommission für Zeitgeschichte, Reihe B, Forschungen 79. Paderborn: Schöningh, 1997.

Damberg, Wilhelm. "Radikal katholische Laien an die Front! Beobachtungen zur Idee und Wirkungsgeschichte der Katholischen Aktion" in: Joachim Köhler and Damian van Melis, eds. *Siegerin in Trümmern. Die Rolle der katholischen Kirche in der deutschen Nachkrieggesellschaft*. Stuttgart-Berlin-Cologne: Kohlhammer, 1998, 142-160.

Damberg, Wilhelm. "Van voorbeelden en schrikbeelden. Over de relatie tussen het Nederlandse en het Duitse katholicisme in de negentiende en twintigste eeuw". *Trajecta*, 7 (1998) 4, 319-338.

Damberg, Wilhelm. "Religiöser Wandel im Generationenwechsel". *Mitteilungsblatt des Instituts für soziale Bewegungen*, 26 (2001), 183-190.

Damberg, Wilhelm. "Pontifikate und politische Konjunkturen. Beobachtungen zur kirchlichen Zeitgeschichte" in: Catherine Bosshart-Pfluger, Joseph Jung and Franziska Metzger, eds. *Nation und Nationalismus in Europa. Kulturelle Konstruktion von Identitäten. Festschrift für Urs Altermatt*. Frauenfeld (Switz.): Huber, 2002, 749-767.

Daniélou, Jean. "Christianisme et Histoire". *Études*, 254 (1947), 166-184.

Davenson(-Marrou), Henri. *Fondements d'une culture chrétienne*. Cahier de la Nouvelle Journée 27. Paris: Bloud et Gay, 1934.

Davie, Grace. *Religion in Britain since 1945. Believing without Belonging*. Oxford: Blackwell, 1994.

Davie, Grace. *Religion in Modern Europe: A Memory Mutates*. Oxford: Oxford University Press, 2000.

Davie, Grace. *Europe: The Exceptional Case: Parameters of Faith in the Modern World*. London: Darton, Longman and Todd, 2002.

Davies, Edward T. *Religion in the Industrial Revolution in South Wales*. Cardiff: University of Wales Press, 1965.

Debès, Joseph. *Naissance de l'Action catholique ouvrière*. Paris: Éditions Ouvrières, 1982.

"Déclaration commune à propos de la doctrine de la justification". *La Documentation catholique*, 79 (1997) 18, 875-885.

de Giorgio, Michaela. "Het katholieke model" in: Georges Duby and Michelle Perrot, eds. *Geschiedenis van de vrouw*. Vol. 4: Geneviève Fraisse and Michelle Perrot, eds. *De negentiende eeuw*. Amsterdam: Agon, 1993, 125-156.

de Giuseppe, Massimo. *Giorgio La Pira: Un sindaco e le vie della pace*. Milan: Centro Ambrosiano, 2001.

de Goei, Leonie M.L.M. *De psychohygiënisten. Psychiatrie, cultuurkritiek en de beweging voor geestelijke volksgezondheid in Nederland, 1924-1970*. Nijmegen: SUN, 2001.

de Goeij, Hans J.A. "Het Verraad der Clercken". *De Tijd*, 26.07.1966.

de Groot, Kees. "Three Types of Liquid Religion". *Implicit Religion: Journal of the Centre for the Study of Implicit Religion and Contemporary Spirituality (CSIRCS)*, 11 (2008) 3, 277-286.

de Haan, Peter. *Van volgzame elitestrijder tot kritische gelovige. Geschiedenis van de Katholieke Actie in Nederland (1934-1966)*. Nijmegen: KDC, 1994.

de Jonge, Marinus. *God's Final Envoy: Early Christology and Jesus' Own View of His Mission*. Grand Rapids-Cambridge: Eerdmans, 1998.

Dekker, Gerard; de Hart, Joep and Peters, Jan. *God in Nederland. 1966-1996*. Amsterdam: Anthos, 1997.

Delbreil, Jean-Claude. "The French Catholic Left and the Political Parties" in: Gerd-Rainer Horn and Emmanuel Gerard, eds. *Left Catholicism. Catholics and Society in Western Europe at the Point of Liberation, 1943-1955*. KADOC-Studies 25. Leuven: Leuven University Press, 2001, 45-63.

Delhaye, Philippe; Guéret, Michel and Tombeur, Paul. *Concilium Vaticanum II. Concordance, index verborum, listes de fréquence, tables comparatives*. Louvain-la-Neuve: CETEDOC, 1974.

Dellepoort, Johannes Joseph, ed. *Die europäische Priesterfrage. Bericht der Internationalen Enquête in Wien 10.-12. Oktober 1958*. Vienna: Institut für Kirchliche Sozialforschung, 1959[2].

de Lubac, Henri. *Meine Schriften im Rückblick*. Theologia Romanica 21. Einsiedeln: Johannes, 1996.

De Maeyer, Jan and Hellemans, Staf. "Katholiek reveil, katholieke verzuiling en dagelijks leven" in: Jaak Billiet, ed. *Tussen bescherming en verovering. Sociologen en historici over zuilvorming*. KADOC-Studies 6. Leuven: Universitaire Pers Leuven, 1988, 171-200.

Demerath III, Nicolas Jay. *Crossing the Gods: World Religions and Worldly Politics*. New Brunswick (NJ) - London: Rutgers University Press, 2001.

de Neuville, Raphaëlle. *Jean Ousset et la Cité catholique*. Bouère: Dominique Martin Morin, 1998.

Denzinger, Henricus and Schönmetzer, Adolfus. *Enchiridion Symbolorum, definitionum et declarationum de rebus fidei et morum*. Freiburg-Basel-Vienna: Herder, 1967.

de Soignie, Philippe. *Mystique chrétienne et ascension ouvrière*. Tournai: Casterman, 1946.

Desrochers, John. *The Social Teaching of the Church*. Bangalore: John Desrochers, 1982.

d'Haens, Frans. "De Katholieke Werkgemeenschap in de Partij van de Arbeid en de politieke doorbraak". *Jaarboek van het Katholiek Documentatie Centrum*, 4 (1974), 59-98.

Diamond, Etan. *And I Will Dwell in Their Midst: Orthodox Jews in Suburbia*. Chapel Hill: University of North Carolina Press, 2000.

Diébolt, Evelyne. "Les femmes catholiques: entre Église et société" in: Kay Chadwick, ed. *Catholicism, Politics and Society, in Twentieth-Century France*. Liverpool: Liverpool University Press, 2000, 219-243.

Dierick, Gerard. "De Christofoorgroep en het tijdschrift *Te Elfder Ure* in de jaren 1945-1953". *Jaarboek van het Katholiek Documentatie Centrum*, 13 (1983), 35-90.

Dietrich, Tobias. *Konfession im Dorf. Westeuropäische Erfahrungen im 19. Jahrhundert.* Cologne: Böhlau, 2004.

di Giovanni, Stephen Michael. *Michael Augustine Corrigan and the Italian Immigrants: The Relationship between the Church and the Italians in the Archdiocese of New York, 1885-1902.* Rome: Pontificia Universitas Gregoriana, 1983.

Dillon, Michele. "Religion and Culture in Tension: The Abortion Discourses of the U.S. Catholic Bishops and the Southern Baptist Convention". *Religion and American Culture*, 5 (1995), 159-180.

Dillon, Michele. *Catholic Identity: Balancing Reason, Faith, and Power.* New York: Cambridge University Press, 1999.

Dixon, Thomas. *Failure of Protestantism in New York and its Causes.* New York: Strauss and Rehn, 1896.

Dobbelaere, Karel. "Professionalization and Secularization in the Belgian Catholic Pillar". *Japanese Journal of Religious Studies*, 6 (1979) 1-2, 39-64.

Dobbelaere, Karel. "Secularization, Pillarization, and Religious Change in the Low Countries" in: Thomas M. Gannon, ed. *World Catholicism in Transition.* New York-London: Macmillan, 1988, 80-115.

Dobbelaere, Karel. "The Surviving Dominant Church in Belgium" in: Wade Clark Roof, Jackson W. Carroll and David A. Roozen, eds. *The Post-War Generation and Establishment Religion: Cross-Cultural Perspectives.* Boulder (CO)-San Francisco-Oxford: Westview Press, 1995, 171-190.

Dobbelaere, Karel. "Towards an Integrated Perspective of the Process Related to the Descriptive Concept of Secularization". *Sociology of Religion*, 60 (1999), 229-247.

Dobbelaere, Karel. *Secularization: An Analysis at Three Levels.* Gods, humans and religions 1. Brussels: Peter Lang, 2002.

Dobbelaere, Karel. "Assessing Secularization Theory" in: Peter Antes et al., eds. *New Approaches to the Study of Religion.* Vol. 2: *Textual, Comparative, Sociological, and Cognitive Approaches.* Berlin-New York: De Gruyter, 2008, 229-253.

Dobbelaere, Karel et al. *Verloren zekerheid. De Belgen en hun waarden, overtuigingen en houdingen.* Tielt: Lannoo, 2000.

Dobbelaere, Karel and Billiet, Jaak. "Les changements internes au pilier catholique en Flandre: d'une catholicité d'Église à une chrétienté socioculturelle". *Recherches sociologiques*, 14 (1983) 2, 141-184.

Dobbelaere, Karel and Riis, Ole. "Religious and Moral Pluralism. Theories, Research Questions, and Design" in: Ralph L. Piedmont and David O. Moberg, eds. *Research in the Social Scientific Study of Religion.* Vol. 13. Leiden: Brill, 2002, 159-171.

Dobbelaere, Karel; Tomasi, Luigi and Voyé, Liliane. "Religious Syncretism" in: Ralph L. Piemond and David Moberg, eds. *Research in the Social Scientific Study of Religion.* Vol. 13. Leiden: Brill, 2002, 221-243.

Dobbelaere, Karel and Voyé, Liliane. "Western European Catholicism since Vatican II" in: Helen Rose Ebaugh, ed. *Vatican II and U.S. Catholicism.* Greenwich (CT)-London: JAI Press, 1991, 205-231.

Dobbelaere, Karel and Voyé, Liliane. "Europäische Katholiken und die katholische Kirche nach dem Zweiten Vatikanischen Konzil" in: Franz-Xaver Kaufmann and Arnold Zingerle, eds. *Vatikanum II und Modernisierung. Historische, theologische und soziologische Perspektiven.* Paderborn: Schöningh, 1996, 209-232.

Dobbelaere, Karel and Voyé, Liliane. "Religie en kerkbetrokkenheid. Ambivalentie en vervreemding" in: Karel Dobbelaere et al. *Verloren zekerheid. De Belgen en hun waarden, overtuigingen en houdingen.* Tielt: Lannoo, 2000, 117-152.

Documents pontificaux de Paul VI. Saint-Maurice: Ed. Saint-Augustin, 1963-1983, 20 vols.

Dogan, Mattei. "Class, Religion, Party: Triple Decline of Electoral Cleavages in Western Europe" in: Lauri Karvonen and Stein Kuhnle, eds. *Party Systems and Voter Alignments Revisited.* London: Routledge, 2001, 93-114.

Donohue, John J. and Esposito, John L., eds. *Islam in Transition: Muslim Perspectives.* New York-Oxford: Oxford University Press, 1982.

d'Onorio, J.-B. "Paul VI et le gouvernement central de l'Église" in: *Paul VI et la modernité dans l'Église.* Rome: École française de Rome, 1984, 615-645.

Dorr, Donal. *Option for the Poor: A Hundred Years of Vatican Social Teaching.* Rev. ed. Dublin: Gill and Macmillan, 1992.

Dowell, Susan and Williams, Jane. *Bread, Wine and Women: The Ordination Debate in the Church of England.* London: Virago, 1994.

Drehsen, Volker. *Wie religionsfähig ist die Volkskirche? Sozialisationstheoretische Erkundungen neuzeitlicher Christentumspraxis.* Gütersloh: Kaiser Verlag, 1994.

Drews, Paul. *Das kirchliche Leben der Evangelischen-Lutherischen Landeskirche im Königreich Sachsen.* Tübingen: J.C.B. Mohr, 1902.

Duff, Edward. *Social Thought of the World Council of Churches.* London: Longmans Green, 1956.

Duhamel, Éric. *L'Union démocratique et socialiste de la résistance: d'une résistance à l'autre.* Diss. Université de Paris IV, 1993.

Dunn, James D.G. *Christology in the Making: A New Testament Inquiry into the Origins of the Doctrine of the Incarnation.* London: SCM, 1980.

Dupront, Alphonse. *Qu'est-ce que les Lumières?* Paris: Gallimard, 1996.

Durand, Jean-Dominique. *L'Église catholique dans la crise de l'Italie (1943-1948).* Rome: École française de Rome, 1991.

Durand, Jean-Dominique. "La grande attaque de 1956". *Cahiers Jacques Maritain,* 30 (1995), 3-31.

Durand, Jean-Dominique. *L'Europe de la Démocratie chrétienne.* Brussels: Complexe, 1995.

Duriez, Bruno. "Left Wing Catholicism in France: From Catholic Action to the Political Left: The Mouvement Populaire des Familles" in: Gerd-Rainer Horn and Emmanuel Gerard, eds. *Left Catholicism: Catholics and Society in Western Europe at the Point of Liberation, 1943-1955.* KADOC-Studies 25. Leuven: Leuven University Press, 2001, 64-90.

Durkheim, Émile. *The Division of Labor in Society.* Transl. George Simpson. New York: The Free Press, 1964.

Durkheim, Émile. *The Elementary Forms of the Religious Life.* Transl. Joseph W. Swain. New York: The Free Press, 1965.

Duynstee, Willem J.A.J. "De verdringingstheorie, beoordeeld van thomistisch standpunt" in: *Verslag van de tweede algemeene vergadering van de Vereeniging voor Thomistische Wijsbegeerte.* Nijmegen: Dekker & Van de Vegt, 1935, 32-57.

Dwyer, Judith A. *An Analysis of Nuclear Warfare in Light of the Traditional Just War Theory: An American Rome Catholic Perspective (1945-1981)*. Ann Arbor (MI): UMI, 1986.

Eakins, Pamela. *Priestess: Woman as Sacred Celebrant*. York Beach (ME): Weiser, 1996.

Ebertz, M.N. *Kirche im Gegenwind. Zum Umbruch der religiösen Gesellschaft*. Freiburg-Basel-Vienna: Herder, 1999[3].

Eck, Diana L. "On Seeking and Finding in the World's Religions". <www.religion-online.org/cgi-bin/relsearchd.dll/showarticle?item_id=770> (26.01.2008).

"L'Église de Jésus-Christ" in: André Birmelé and Jacques Terme, eds. *Accords et dialogues œcuméniques*. Vol. 2. Paris: Les Bergers et les Mages, 1995, 81-117.

Eisinga, Rob; Felling, Albert and Peters, Jan. "Religious Belief, Church Involvement and Ethnocentrism in the Netherlands". *Journal for the Scientific Study of Religion*, 29 (1990) 1, 54-75.

Elchardus, Mark; Huyse, Luc and Hooghe, Marc, eds. *Het maatschappelijk middenveld in Vlaanderen*. Brussels: VUB Press, 2001.

Ellwood, Robert S. *The Sixties Spiritual Awakening: American Religion Moving from Modern to Postmodern*. New Brunswick (NJ): Rutgers University Press, 1994.

Emeis, Dieter. "Individualisierte Religiosität Jugendlicher und Gemeindekatechese". *Katechetische Blätter*, 121 (1996) 1, 27-31.

Erickson, Victoria Lee. *Where Silence Speaks: Feminism, Social Theory, and Religion*. Minneapolis (MN): Fortress Press, 1993.

Evans, Gillian R. *The Church and the Churches*. Cambridge: Cambridge University Press, 1997.

Les événements et la foi, 1940-1952. Jeunesse de l'Église. Paris: Seuil, 1951.

"FABC Urged to Reject Vatican Draft on Bishop's Conferences". *Asia Focus*, 07.05.1988, 1 and 5.

Fairclough, Adam. *To Redeem the Soul of America: The Southern Christian Leadership Conference and Martin Luther King, Jr*. Athens: University of Georgia Press, 1987.

Famerée, Joseph. "Vescovi e diocesi (5-15 novembre 1963)" in: Giuseppe Alberigo, ed. *Storia del concilio Vaticano II*. Vol. 3: *Il concilio adulto. Il secondo periodo e la seconda intersessione (settembre 1963-settembre 1964)*. Bologna: Il Mulino, 1998, 137-153.

Fattori, Maria Teresa and Melloni, Alberto, eds. *L'evento e le decisioni. Studi sulle dinamiche del concilio Vaticano II*. Bologna: Il Mulino, 1997.

Feifel, Erich and Kasper, Walter. *Tradierungskrise des Glaubens*. Munich: Kösel, 1987.

Felling, Albert; Peters, Jan and Schreuder, Osmund. *Geloven en leven. Een nationaal onderzoek naar de invloed van religieuze overtuigingen*. Zeist: Kerckebosch, 1986.

Ferrari, Silvio. "State Regulation of Religion in the European Democracies" in: Gabriel Motzkin and Yochi Fischer, eds. *Religion and Democracy in Contemporary Europe*. London: Alliance Publishing Trust, 2008, 103-112.

Fey, Harold E. *The Ecumenical Advance: A History of the Ecumenical Movement*. Vol. 2: *1948-1968*. London: SPCK, 1970.

Field-Bibb, Jacqueline. *Women towards Priesthood: Ministerial Politics and Feminist Praxis*. Cambridge: Cambridge University Press, 1991.

Fiévez, Marguerite and Meert, Jacques. *Cardijn*. Brussels: Vie Ouvrière, 1969.

Final Report of the Special Commission on Orthodox participation in the WCC. Geneva: Central Committee World Council of Churches, 26.8-3.9.2002. <www2.wcc-coe.org/ccdocuments.nsf/index/gen-5-en.html> (29.01.2008).

Findlay, James F. "Religion and Politics in the Sixties: The Churches and the Civil Rights Act of 1964". *Journal of American History*, 77 (1990), 66-92.

Findlay, James F. *Church People in the Struggle: The National Council of Churches and the Black Freedom Movement, 1950-1970.* New York: Oxford University Press, 1993.

Finke, Roger. "The Consequences of Religious Competition: Supply-Side Explanations for Religious Change" in: Lawrence A. Young, ed. *Rational Choice Theory and Religion: Summary and Assessment.* New York-London: Routledge, 1997, 46-65.

Finke, Roger. "The Illusion of Shifting Demand. Supply-Side Interpretations of American Religious History" in: Thomas A. Tweed, ed. *Retelling U.S. Religious History.* Berkeley-Los Angeles-London: University of California Press, 1997, 108-124.

Finke, Roger and Stark, Rodney. "Religious Economies and Sacred Canopies: Religious Mobilization in American Cities (1906)". *American Sociological Review*, 53 (1988), 41-49.

Finke, Roger and Stark, Rodney. *The Churching of America, 1776-1980: Winners and Losers in our Religious Economy.* New Brunswick (NJ): Rutgers University Press, 1992.

Focke, Franz. *Sozialismus aus christlicher Verantwortung.* Wuppertal: Peter Hammer, 1981.

Ford, Caroline. "Religion and Popular Culture in Modern Europe". *Journal of Modern History*, 65 (1993) 1, 152-175.

Ford, Caroline. *Divided Houses: Religion and Gender in Modern France.* Ithaca-London: Cornell University Press, 2005.

Fortmann, Han. "Nieuwe opvattingen omtrent de psychologie en de paedagogiek van de wil". *Dux*, 18 (1951), 446-465.

Fortmann, Han. "Gelieve de ketters niet te verbranden". *De Volkskrant*, 03.09.1966.

Fouilloux, Étienne. "Une vision eschatologique du christianisme: *Dieu vivant* (1945-1955)" in: Étienne Fouilloux. *Au cœur du XXe siècle religieux.* Paris: Éditions ouvrières, 1993, 277-305.

Fouilloux, Étienne. "La phase antépréparatoire (1959-1960)" in: Giuseppe Alberigo, ed. *Histoire du concile Vatican II (1959-1965).* Vol. 1: *Le catholicisme vers une nouvelle épreuve. L'annonce et la préparation (janvier 1959-octobre 1962).* Paris: Cerf, 1997, 69-183.

Fouilloux, Étienne. "Die vor-vorbereitende Phase (1959-1960). Der langsame Gang aus der Unbeweglichkeit" in: Giuseppe Alberigo and Klaus Wittstadt, eds. *Geschichte des Zweiten Vatikanischen Konzils (1959-1965).* Vol. 1: *Die katholische Kirche auf dem Weg in ein neues Zeitalter. Die Ankündigung und Vorbereitung des Zweiten Vatikanischen Konzils (Januar 1959 bis Oktober 1962).* Mainz-Leuven: Grünewald, 1997, 61-187.

Fouilloux, Étienne. *Une Église en quête de liberté. La pensée catholique française entre modernisme et Vatican II (1914-1962).* Paris: Desclée de Brouwer, 1998.

Frady, Marshall. *Billy Graham: A Parable of American Righteousness.* Boston: Little Brown, 1979.

Frie, Ewald. "Zwischen Katholizismus und Wohlfahrtsstaat. Skizze einer Verbandsgeschichte der Deutschen Caritas". *Jahrbuch für Christliche Sozialwissenschaften*, 38 (1997), 21-42.

Für eine Zukunft in Solidarität und Gerechtigkeit. Wort des Rates der Evangelischen Kirche in Deutschland und der Deutschen Bischofskonferenz zur wirtschaftlichen und sozialen Lage in Deutschland. Hannover: Kirchenamt der Evangelischen Kirche - Bonn: Sekretariat der Deutschen Bischofskonferenz, 1997.

Gabriel, Karl. "Tradition im Kontext enttraditionalisierter Gesellschaft" in: Dietrich Wiederkehr, ed. *Wie geschieht Tradition? Überlieferung im Lebensprozeß der Kirche*. Quaestiones disputatae 133. Freiburg-Basel-Vienna: Herder, 1991, 69-88.

Gabriel, Karl. *Christentum zwischen Tradition und Postmoderne*. Quaestiones disputatae 141. Freiburg-Basel-Vienna: Herder, 1992.

Gadbois, Geneviève. "'Vous êtes presque la seule consolation de l'Église': La foi des femmes face à la déchristianisation" in: Jean Delumeau, ed. *La religion de ma mère*. Paris: Cerf, 1992, 301-325.

Gaëlle, Cario. *Jalons pour une histoire des prêtres-ouvriers en Belgique (1944-1960)*. Diss. Lic. Université Libre de Bruxelles, 1994-1995.

Garijo-Guembe, Miguel Maria. "Communio-Ekklesiologie. Zum Schreiben der römischen Glaubenskongregation über einige Aspekte der Kirche als Communio". *Una Sancta*, 47 (1992), 323-329.

Garrow, David J. *Bearing the Cross: Martin Luther King, Jr., and the Southern Christian Leadership Conference*. New York: Vintage Books, 1986.

Gaustad, Edwin and Schmidt, Leigh. *The Religious History of America*. Rev. ed. San Francisco: Harper, 2002.

Gay, Peter. *The Enlightenment: An Interpretation*. London: Wildwood House, 1967-1973, 2 vols.

Geertz, Clifford. *The Interpretation of Cultures: Selected Essays*. New York: Basic Books, 1973.

Gehler, Michael; Kaiser, Wolfram and Wohnout, Herman, eds. *Christian Democracy in 20th Century Europe / Christdemokratie in Europa im 20. Jahrhundert / La Démocratie Chrétienne en Europe au 20e siècle*. Vienna: Böhlau, 2001.

Gehler, Michael and Kaiser, Wolfram, eds. *Christian Democracy in Europe since 1945*. London: Routledge, 2004.

Gellard, Jacques; Valadier, Paul and Donegani, Jean-Marie. *Regards sur le catholicisme français*. Paris: Cahiers Recherches-Débats, 1984.

"La genèse de la Constitution 'Regimini Ecclesiae universae'". *La Documentation catholique*, 49 (1967) 1500, 1473-1476.

Georgi, Frank. *L'invention de la CFDT, 1957-1970: syndicalisme, catholicisme et politique dans la France de l'expansion*. Paris: Éditions de l'Atelier, 1995.

Gerard, Emmanuel. *De Katholieke Partij in crisis. Partijpolitiek leven in België 1918-1940*. Leuven: Kritak, 1985.

Gerard, Emmanuel. *Église et mouvement ouvrier chrétien en Belgique. Sources inédites relatives à la direction générales des œuvres sociales 1916-1936*. Cahiers du Centre Interuniversitaire d'Histoire Contemporaine 102. Leuven-Brussels: Nauwelaerts, 1990.

Gerard, Emmanuel. "Adaptation en temps de crise (1921-1944)" in: Emmanuel Gerard and Paul Wynants, eds. *Histoire du mouvement ouvrier chrétien en Belgique*. Vol. 1. KADOC-Studies 16. Leuven: Leuven University Press, 1994, 174-245.

Gerard, Emmanuel et al. *Van arbeiderscoöperatie tot bank. De geschiedenis van BACOP*. Tielt: Lannoo, 1995.

Gibson, Ralph. *A Social History of French Catholicism 1789-1914.* London: Routledge, 1989.

Giddens, Antony. *Modernity and Self-Identity: Self and Society in the Late Modern Age.* Cambridge: Polity Press, 1991.

Gilbert, Alan D. *The Making of Post-Christian Britain.* London: Longman, 1980.

Gill, Robin. *The Myth of the Empty Church.* London: SPCK, 1993.

Gilson, Étienne. *Pour un ordre catholique.* Bruges-Paris: Desclée de Brouwer, 1934.

Ginsburg, Faye D. *Contested Lives: The Abortion Debate in an American Community.* Berkeley: University of California Press, 1989.

Giovagnoli, Agostino, ed. *1968: fra utopia e Vangelo. Contestazione e mondo cattolico.* Rome: Ave, 2000.

Giovanni Paulo II. *L'arricchimento della fede.* Vatican City: Libreria Editrice Vaticana, 1981.

Gisel, Pierre, ed. *Encyclopédie du protestantisme.* Paris-Geneva: Cerf, 1995.

Glatzel, Norbert. "Neueste kirchliche Lehrverkündigung zur Sicherheits- und Rüstungsdebatte ab 1945" in: Norbert Glatzel and Ernst-Josef Nagel, eds. *Frieden in Sicherheit. Zur Weiterentwicklung der katholischen Friedensethik.* Freiburg: Herder, 1981, 125-148.

Glendon, Mary Ann. "The Sources of 'Right Talk' - Some are Catholic". *Commonweal*, 127 (2001) 17, 11-13.

Glendon, Mary Ann. "The Forgotten Crucible: The Latin American Influence on the Universal Declaration of Human Rights Idea". Lecture at the Ateneo Pontificio Regina Apostolorum, Rome, 30.04.2001. *Harvard Human Rights Journal*, 16 (2003), 27-39.

Global Governance. Our Responsibility to Make Globalization an Opportunity for all Bishops of COMECE. Report to the Bishops of COMECE (Commission of the Bishops' Conferences of the European Community). Brussels, 2001.

Glock, Charles Y. and Stark, Rodney. *Christian Beliefs and Anti-Semitism.* New York: Harper & Row, 1966.

Goddard, Hugh P. *Muslim Perceptions of Christianity.* London: Grey Seal, 1996.

Goddijn, Walter J.J.O. *The Deferred Revolution: A Social Experiment in Church Innovation in Holland, 1960-1970.* Amsterdam: Elsevier, 1975.

Goddijn, Walter; Jacobs, Jan and van Tillo, Gerard, eds. *Tot vrijheid geroepen. Katholieken in Nederland: 1946-2000.* Baarn: Ten Have, 1999.

Godin, Henri and Daniel, Yvan. *La France, pays de mission?* Le monde en 10/18, 26. Paris: Union générale d'éditions, 1962 (1943[1]).

Götz von Olenhusen, Imtraud. "Die Feminisierung der Religion und Kirche im 19. und 20. Jahrhundert. Forschungsstand und Forschungsperspektiven" in: Imtraut Götz von Olenhusen, ed. *Frauen unter dem Patriarchat der Kirchen. Katholikinnen und Protestantinnen im 19. und 20. Jahrhundert.* Stuttgart-Berlin: Kohlhammer, 1995, 69-88.

Graf, Friedrich W. and Große Kracht, Klaus. "Einleitung: Religion und Gesellschaft im Europa des 20. Jahrhunderts" in: Friedrich W. Graf and Klaus Große Kracht, eds. *Religion und Gesellschaft: Europa im 20. Jahrhundert.* Cologne: Böhlau, 2007, 1-44.

Gramsci, Antonio. "The Intellectuals" in: Quintin Hoare and Geoffrey N. Smith, eds. *Selections from the Prison Notebooks of Antonio Gramsci.* London: Lawrence and Wishart, 1971, 5-23.

Granovetter, Mark. "Threshold Models of Collective Behavior". *American Journal of Sociology*, 83 (1977) 1, 1420-1443.

Greeley, Andrew M. *American Catholics since the Council: An Unauthorized Report*. Chicago: Thomas More Press, 1985.

Greeley, Andrew M. *The Catholic Revolution: New Wine, Old Wineskins, and the Second Vatican Council*. Berkeley-Los Angeles: University of California Press, 2004.

Greeley, Andrew M.; McCready, William C. and McCourt, Kathleen. *Catholic Schools in a Declining Church*. Kansas City (Mo): Sheet & Ward, 1976.

Groot, Jan C. "Nieuwe tendenzen in de hedendaagse theologie". *Streven*, 9 (1955-56), 793-800, 913-926.

Gros, Jeffrey; Meyer, Harding and Rusch, William, eds. *Growth in Agreement II: Reports and Agreed Statements of Ecumenical Conversations on a World Level 1982-1998*. Geneva: World Council of Churches, 2000.

Gruber, Margareta and Kiechle, Stefan, eds. *Gottesfreundschaft. Ordensleben heute denken* Würzburg: Echter, 2007.

Guasco, Maurilio and Trionfini, Paolo, eds. *Don Zeno e Nomadelfia: tra società civile e società religiosa*. Brescia: Morcelliana, 2001.

Guerrier, Claudine. *La Jeune République de 1912 à 1945*. Diss. Université de Paris II, 1979.

Guidelines for Dialogue and Relations with People of Other Religions. Document for the WCC Central Committee 26.8-3.9.2002, document GEN 11 and final version in *Current Dialogue*, 40 (2002) <www.wcc-coe.org/wcc/what/interreligious/cd40-04.html> (29.01.2008).

Gustafsson, Berndt. *Socialdemokratien och kyrkan 1881-90*. Stockholm: SKD Bokförlag, 1953.

Guyot, Claire. "Entre morale et politique: le Centre catholique des intellectuels français face à la décolonisation (1952-1966)". *Vingtième siècle. Revue d'histoire*, 63 (1999), 75-86.

Haas, Reimund. "Das II. Vatikanum als Wendepunkt der Ordensgeschichte. Vorstellung des Buches von Joachim Schmiedl 'Das Konzil und die Orden'". *Ordenskorrespondenz*, 40 (1999), 482-493.

Hahn, Ferdinand. *The Titles of Jesus in Christology: Their History in Early Christianity*. London: Lutterworth, 1969.

Hall, Mitchell K. *Because of Their Faith: CALCAV and Religious Opposition to the Vietnam War*. New York: Columbia University Press, 1991.

Halman, Loek. *The European Values Study: A Third Wave*. Tilburg: WORK, Tilburg University, 1999.

Halman, Loek, ed. *The European Values Study: A Third Wave. Source book of the 1999/2000 European Values Study Survey*. Tilburg: WORC, Tilburg University, 2001.

Hankins, Barry. *Uneasy in Babylon: Southern Baptist Conservatives and American Culture*. Tuscaloosa (AL): University of Alabama Press, 2002.

Hanley, David, ed. *Christian Democracy in Europe: A Comparative Perspective*. London-New York: Pinter, 1994.

Harris, Ruth. *Lourdes: Body and Spirit in the Secular Age*. New York: Penguin Books, 1999.

Hebblethwaite, Peter. *John XXIII, Pope of the Council*. London: Chapman, 1984.

Heelas, Paul; Woodhead, Linda et al. *The Spiritual Revolution: Why Religion is Giving Way to Spirituality*. London: Blackwell, 2005.

Hegge, Christoph. *Rezeption und Charisma. Der theologische und rechtliche Beitrag kirchlicher Bewegungen zur Rezeption des Zweiten Vatikanischen Konzils.* Forschungen zur Kirchenrechtswissenschaft 29. Würzburg: Echter, 1999.

Heinze, Andrew. *Adapting to Abundance: Jewish Immigrants, Mass Consumption, and the Search for American Identity.* New York: Columbia University Press, 1990.

Heinze, Andrew. "The First Mass Market Rabbi". *Midstream: A Monthly Jewish Review*, 42 (1996), 14-17.

Hellemans, Staf. *Strijd om de moderniteit. Sociale bewegingen en verzuiling in Europa sinds 1800.* KADOC-Studies 10. Leuven: Leuven University Press, 1990.

Hellemans, Staf. "Zuilen en verzuiling in Europa" in: Uwe Becker, ed. *Nederlandse politiek in historisch en vergelijkend perspectief.* Amsterdam: Het Spinhuis, 1993, 121-150.

Hellemans, Staf. "From 'Catholicism Against Modernity' to the Problematic 'Modernity of Catholicism'". *Ethical Perspectives*, 8 (2001) 2, 117-127.

Hellemans, Staf. "How Modern is Religion in Modernity?" in: Judith Frishman, Willemien Otten and Gerard Rouwhorst, eds. *Religious Identity and the Problem of Historical Foundation: The Foundational Character of Authoritative Sources in the History of Christianity and Judaism.* Leiden-Boston: Brill, 2004, 76-94.

Hellemans, Staf. "Die Transformation der Religion und der Grosskirchen in der zweiten Moderne aus der Sicht des religiösen Modernisierungsparadigmas". *Schweizerische Zeitschrift für Religions- und Kulturgeschichte*, 99 (2005), 11-35.

Hellemans, Staf. *Het tijdperk van de wereldreligies. Religie in agrarische civilisaties en in moderne samenlevingen.* Zoetermeer-Kapellen: Meinema-Pelckmans, 2007.

Hello, Evelyn; Scheepers, Peer and Gijsberts, Merove. "Education and Ethnic Prejudice in Europe: Explanations for Cross-national Variances in the Educational Effect on Ethnic Prejudice". *Scandinavian Journal of Educational Research*, 46 (2002) 1, 5-24.

Hendriks, Jan. *Gemeente als herberg. De kerk van 2000 - een concrete utopie.* Kampen: Kok, 2000.

Henry, Patrick. "'And I Don't Care What It Is': The Tradition-History of a Civil Religion Proof-Text". *Journal of the American Academy of Religion*, 49 (1981), 35-47.

Herberg, Will. *Protestant-Catholic-Jew: An Essay in American Religious Sociology.* Garden City (NY): Doubleday, 1955.

Herr, Edouard. *Sauver la paix. Qu'en dit l'Église?* Namur: Culture et Vérité, 1991.

Hervieu-Léger, Danièle. "Religion and Modernity in the French Context: For a New Approach to Secularization". *Sociological Analysis*, 51 (1990), 15-25.

Hervieu-Léger, Danièle. "Renouveaux émotionnels contemporains" in: Françoise Champion and Danièle Hervieu-Léger, eds. *De l'émotion en religion: renouveaux et traditions.* Paris: Le Centurion, 1990, 219-248.

Hervieu-Léger, Danièle. *La religion pour mémoire.* Paris: Cerf, 1993.

Hervieu-Léger, Danièle. *Religion as a Chain of Memory.* New Brunswick (NJ): Rutgers University Press, 2000.

Hervieu-Léger, Danièle. *Catholicisme, la fin d'un monde.* Paris: Bayard, 2002.

Herzig, Anneliese. *Ordens-Christen. Theologie des Ordenslebens in der Zeit nach dem Zweiten Vatikanischen Konzil*. Studien zur systematischen und spirituellen Theologie 3. Würzburg: Echter, 1991.

Hilaire, Yves-Marie. "Les vœux des évêques français après l'annonce du concile" in: *Le deuxième concile du Vatican (1959-1965)*. Rome: École française de Rome, 1989, 101-117.

Hobsbawm, Eric J. *The Age of Revolution 1789-1848*. New York: Mentor, 1962.

Hobsbawm, Eric J. *The Age of Capital, 1848-1875*. London: Weidenfeld, 1975.

Hobsbawm, Eric J. *The Age of Extremes 1914-1991*. London: Michael Joseph, 1994.

Hobsbawm, Eric J. and Ranger, Terence, eds. *The Invention of Tradition*. Past and Present Publications. Cambridge: Cambridge University Press, 1983.

Hoge, Dean R. *The Future of Catholic Leadership: Responses to the Priest Shortage*. Kansas City (Mo): Sheed & Ward, 1987.

Hoge, Dean R. et al., eds. *Money Matters: Personal Giving in American Churches*. Louisville: Westminster John Knox Press, 1996.

Hölscher, Lucian. "Hannover in the 19th Century". *Hispania Sacra*, 32 (1990), 405-411.

Hölscher, Lucian. "Säkularisierungsprozesse" in: Hans-Jürgen Pühle, ed. *Bürger in der Gesellschaft der Neuzeit*. Göttingen: Vandenhoeck & Ruprecht, 1991, 238-258.

Hölscher, Lucian, ed. *Datenatlas zur religiösen Geographie im protestantischen Deutschland: Von der Mitte des 19. Jahrhunderts bis zum Zweiten Weltkrieg*. Berlin: De Gruyter, 2001, 4 vols.

Hölscher, Lucian. "Konfessionspolitik in Deutschland zwischen Glaubensstreit und Koexistenz" in: Lucian Hölscher, ed. *Baupläne der sichtbaren Kirche. Sprachliche Konzepte religiöser Vergemeinschaftung in Europa*. Göttingen: Wallstein, 2007, 11-53.

Hopkins, Kathleen S. "The 'Other Priest' and the Body of Christ". *America*, 177 (1997) July 5-12, 19-22.

Horn, Gerd-Rainer. "Left Catholicism in Western Europe in the 1940s" in: Gerd-Rainer Horn and Emmanuel Gerard, eds. *Left Catholicism 1943-1955: Catholics and Society in Western Europe at the Point of Liberation*. KADOC-Studies 25. Leuven: Leuven University Press, 2001, 13-44.

Horn, Gerd-Rainer. *Western European Liberation Theology, 1924-1959: The First Wave*. Oxford: Oxford University Press, 2008.

Horn, Gerd-Rainer and Gerard, Emmanuel, eds. *Left Catholicism 1943-1955: Catholics and Society in Western Europe at the Point of Liberation*. KADOC-Studies 25. Leuven: Leuven University Press, 2001.

Hout, M. and Greeley, Andrew M. "The Center doesn't hold: Church Attendance in the United States, 1940-1984". *American Sociological Review*, 52 (1987), 325-345.

Houtepen, Anton. "Hermeneutics, Mission and Ecumenism: The Art of Understanding a Communicative God". *Exchange*, 24 (1995), 91-110.

Houtepen, Anton. "Evangelisation and Ecumenism: Contradiction and Challenge". *Religion, State & Society*, 26 (1998), 89-100.

Houtepen, Anton. "From Freedom of Religion towards Really Free Religion: Voices from Rome and Geneva". *Exchange*, 27 (1998), 290-310.

Houtepen, Anton. *God: An Open Question*. New York: Continuum, 2002.

Hudnut-Beumler, James. *Looking for God in the Suburbs: The Religion of the American Dream and its Critics.* New Brunswick (NJ): Rutgers University Press, 1994.

Huntington, Samuel. *The Clash of Civilizations and the Remaking of World Order.* New York: Simon and Schuster, 1996.

Hürten, Heinz. *Kurze Geschichte des deutschen Katholizismus 1800-1960.* Mainz: Matthias-Grünewald, 1986.

Hürten, Heinz. "Zukunftperspektiven kirchlicher Zeitgeschichtsforschung" in: Ulrich von Hehl and Konrad Repgen, eds. *Der deutsche Katholizismus in der zeitgeschichtlichen Forschung.* Mainz: Matthias-Grünewald, 1988, 97-116.

Hürten, Heinz. *Deutsche Katholiken 1918-1945.* Paderborn: Schöningh, 1992.

Hutsebaut, Dirk. *Een zekere onzekerheid. Jongeren en geloof.* Leuven: Acco, 1995.

Huyse, Luc. *De verzuiling voorbij.* Leuven: Kritak, 1987.

Iannaccone, Laurence R. "Rational Choice: Framework for the Scientific Study of Religion" in: Lawrence A. Young, ed. *Rational Choice Theory and Religion: Summary and Assessment.* New York-London: Routledge, 1997, 25-45.

Inglehart, Ronald. *Culture Shift in Advanced Industrial Society.* Princeton (NJ): Princeton University Press, 1990.

Les intellectuels dans la chrétienté. Rome: Mouvement international des intellectuels catholiques, 1948.

Les intellectuels devant la charité du Christ. Semaine des intellectuels catholiques, 1948. Paris: Éditions de Flore, 1948.

Isserman, Maurice and Kazin, Michael. *America Divided: The Civil War of the 1960s.* New York-Oxford: Oxford University Press, 2000.

Jackson, Kenneth T. *Crabgrass Frontier: The Suburbanization of the United States.* New York: Oxford University Press, 1985.

Jacobs, Jan. *'Naar één oecumenische beweging'. De Katholieke Conferentie voor Oecumenische Vragen: een leerschool en gids, 1951-1965.* Tilburg: Tilburg University Press, 1991.

Jacobs, Jan. "Het verval van de katholieke zuil. Over de dynamiek van de katholieke beweging" in: Jan Jacobs et al. *Daarom toch katholiek. Opstellen rond een kentering.* Nijmegen: Valkhof Pers, 2004.

Jadoulle, Jean-Louis. "Les visages de l'Église de Belgique à la veille du Concile Vatican II" in: Claude Soetens, ed. *Vatican II et la Belgique.* Ottignies: Quorum, 1996, 11-70.

Jadoulle, Jean-Louis. *Chrétiens modernes? L'engagement des intellectuels catholiques "progressistes" belges de 1945 à 1948.* Louvain-la-Neuve: Bruylant-Academia, 2003.

Jagodzinski, Wolfgang and Dobbelaere, Karel. "Secularization and Church Religiosity" in: Jan W. van Deth and Elinor Scarbrough, eds. *The Impact of Values. Beliefs in Government.* Vol. 4: *The Impact of Values.* Oxford-New York: Oxford University Press, 1995, 117-152.

Jankowiak, François. *La Curie romaine de Pie IX à Pie X. Le gouvernement central de l'Église et la fin des États pontificaux (1846-1914).* Rome: École française de Rome, 2007.

Janssen, Jacques and Prins, Maarten. "'Let's reinvent the Gods'. De religie van Nederlandse jongeren in een Europese context". *J* Tijdschrift over jongeren*, 1 (2000) 4, 4-14.

Janssen, Marie-José. *Naar een kerk op twee benen. Studie over de pastoraalwerkster in de R.K. kerk.* Aalsmeer: Luyten, 1988.

Jean-Paul II. *Qu'ils soient un.* Paris: Cerf, 1995.

Jenkins, Philip. *God's Continent. Christianity, Islam, and Europe's Religious Crisis.* Oxford: Oxford University Press, 2007.

John Paul II. *Sources of Renewal: The Implementation of the Second Vatican Council.* London: Collins, 1980.

"Joint Declaration on the Doctrine of Justification". *Origins*, 28 (1998) 8, 120-126.

Jöreskog, Karl and Sörbom, Dag. *LISREL 8 User's Reference Guide.* Chicago: Scientific Software International, 1993.

Journet, Charles. "Le régime de la chrétienté profane" in: Charles Journet. *L'Église du Verbe incarné. Essai de théologie spéculative.* Vol. 1: *La hiérarchie apostolique.* Bruges-Paris: Desclée de Brouwer, 1941, 243-252.

Journet, Charles. "Le philosophe de la cité" in: *Recherches et débats du Centre catholique des intellectuels français.* Cahier 19. Paris: Fayard, 1957, 136-147.

Het jubeljaar 2000. Verklaring van de bisschoppen van België 25. Brussel: Licap, 1999.

Kaelin, Jean de la Croix. "L'inspiration évangélique dans la pensée de Jacques Maritain" in: *Recherches et débats du Centre catholique des intellectuels français.* Cahier 19. Paris: Fayard, 1957, 188-205.

Kaiser, Wolfram. "Review Article: Christian Democracy in Twentieth Century Europe". *Journal of Contemporary History*, 39 (2004) 1, 127-135.

Kaiser, Wolfram and Wohnout, Helmut, eds. *Political Catholicism in Europe 1918-45.* London: Routledge, 2004.

Kalyvas, Stathis N. *The Rise of Christian Democracy in Europe.* Ithaca (NY)-London: Cornell University Press, 1996.

Kasper, Walter. *Die Communio-Ekklesiologie als Grundlage für eine erneuerte Pastoral. Überlegungen zur pastoralen Bedeutung der ekklesiologischen Leitidee des II. Vatikanischen Konzils.* Rottenburg a.N.: Bischöfliches Ordinariat, 1990.

Kaufmann, Franz-Xaver. *Kirche begreifen: Analysen und Thesen zur gesellschaftlichen Verfassung des Christentums.* Freiburg: Herder, 1979.

Kaufmann, Franz-Xavier and Stachel, Günter. "Religiöse Sozialisation" in: *Christlicher Glaube in moderner Gesellschaft.* Vol. 25. Freiburg-Basel-Vienna: Herder, 1980, 117-164.

Kaufmann, Ludwig. "Ansätze einer Theologie der Befreiung in Europa? M.-D. Chenu (1895-1990), eine notwendige Erinnerung an französische Impulse" in: Heiner Ludwig and Wolfgang Schroeder, eds. *Sozial- und Linkskatholizismus. Erinnerung, Orientierung, Befreiung.* Frankfurt am Main: Josef Knecht, 1990, 261-284.

Kay, William and Francis, Leslie. *Drift from the Churches. Attitudes towards Christianity during Childhood and Adolescence.* Cardiff: University of Wales Press, 1996.

Keck, Thierry. *Jeunesse de l'Église, 1936-1955. Aux sources de la crise progressiste en France.* Paris: Karthala, 2004.

Keenan, Marjorie - Pontifical Council for Justice and Peace. *Care for Creation: Human Activity and the Environment.* Vatican City: Libreria Editrice Vaticana, 2000.

Keenan, Marjorie. *From Stockholm to Johannesburg: An Historical Overview of the Concern of the Holy See for the Environment, 1972-2002*. Vatican City: Pontifical Council for Justice and Peace, 2002.

Kelly, Dean M. *Why Conservative Churches are Growing: A Study in the Sociology of Religion*. New York: Harper & Row, 1972.

Kettern, Bernd. "Teilhard de Chardin, Marie-Joseph-Pierre" in: Traugott Bautz, ed. *Biographisch-Bibliographisches Kirchenlexikon*. Vol. 11. Herzberg: Bautz, 1996, 606-621.

Khadduri, Majid. *War and Peace in the Law of Islam*. New York: AMS, 1979 (London: Luzac, 1940).

King, Martin Luther et al. *Dr. Martin Luther King, Jr., Dr. John C. Bennett, Dr. Henry Steele Commager, Rabbi Abraham Heschel Speak on the War in Vietnam*. New York: Clergy and Laymen Concerned About Vietnam, 1967.

Kinnamon, Michael, ed. *Signs of the Spirit: Official Report Seventh Assembly, Canberra, Australia, 7-20 February 1991*. Geneva-Grand Rapids: World Council of Churches - Eerdmans, 1999.

Kits, Ans. *De pastor is een vrouw*. Gorinchem: Narratio, 2000.

Knippenberg, Hans G. "Europäische Religionsgeschichte: Schauplatz vom Pluralisierung und Modernisierung der Religionen" in: Friedrich W. Graf and Klaus Große Kracht, eds. *Religion und Gesellschaft: Europa im 20. Jahrhundert*. Cologne: Böhlau, 2007, 45-72.

Knitter, Paul F. *No Other Name? A Critical Survey of Christian Attitudes Toward the World Religions*. London: SCM, 1985.

Köcher, R. "Religiös in einer säkularisierten Welt" in: Elisabeth Noelle-Neuman and Renate Köcher. *Die verletzte Nation. Über den Versuch der Deutschen ihren Charakter zu ändern*. Stuttgart: Deutsche Verlags-Anstalt, 1987, 164-281.

Komonchak, Joseph. "Le débat théologique". *Concilium*, (1986) 208, 69-80.

Komonchak, Joseph. "The Silencing of John Courtney Murray" in: Alberto Melloni, ed. *Cristianesimo nella storia. Saggi in onore di Giuseppe Alberigo*. Bologna: Il Mulino, 1996, 657-702.

Kongregation für die Institute des geweihten Lebens und die Gesellschaften des apostolischen Lebens. *Neubeginn in Christus. Ein neuer Aufbruch des geweihten Lebens im dritten Jahrtausend. Instruktion (19. Mai 2002)*. <www.vatican.va/roman_curia/congregations/ccscrlife/documents/rc_con_ccscrlife_doc_20020614_ripartire-da-cristo_ge.html> (16.06.2008).

Korte, Anne-Marie. "Erkenning van religieus leiderschap van vrouwen: een 'moderne' kwestie?" *Tijdschrift voor Theologie*, 43 (2003) 2, 113-123.

Korte, Anne-Marie and Sanders, José. "Vrouwen en kerkelijk leiderschap. De nota 'Meewerken in het pastoraat' in het licht van het leidinggevend optreden van vrouwen in de kerkelijke organisatie" in: A.H.C. van Eijk and A.P.H. Meijers, eds. *Gedoopt, gevormd, gezonden. Status en statuut van de pastoraal werk(st)er*. Zoetermeer: Meinema, 2001, 62-89.

Korte, Anne-Marie and Sanders, José. "Mannenbolwerk of vrouwenorganisatie? Bestandsopname van de katholieke kerk" in: Yvonne Benschop and Freda Dröes, eds. *Op de voet gevolgd. Gender en emancipatiebeleid*. Amsterdam: SWP, 2002, 106-122.

Kretschmann, Carsten and Pahl, Henning. "Ein 'Zweites konfessionelles Zeitalter'? Vom Nutzen und Nachteil einer neuen Epochensignatur". *Historische Zeitschrift*, 276 (2003), 369-392.

Kselman, Thomas. "The Varieties of Religious Experience in Urban France" in: Hugh McLeod, ed. *European Religion in the Age of Great Cities*. London: Routledge, 1995, 165-190.

Küng, Hans. *Projekt Weltethos*. Munich-Zurich: Piper, 1990.

Küppers, Kurt. "Martin von Cochem" in: *Lexikon für Theologie und Kirche*. Vol. 6. Freiburg i.Br. 1997³, 1432 ff.

Kuschel, Karl-Josef. *Streit um Abraham*. Munich: Piper, 1994.

Laermans, Rudi. *In de greep van de Moderne Tijd: modernisering en verzuiling. Evoluties binnen de ACW-vormingsorganisaties*. Leuven-Apeldoorn: Garant, 1992.

Laeyendecker, Leo. "The Case of the Netherlands" in: Wade Clark Roof, Jackson W. Carroll and David A. Roozen, eds. *The Post-War Generation and Establishment Religion: Cross-Cultural Perspectives*. Boulder-San Francisco-Oxford: Westview Press, 1995, 131-150.

Laidlaw, Walter. "Christ and the City". *Christian City*, 10 (1898), 497-502.

Laidlaw, Walter. "Third Sociological Canvass: The Twenty-First Assembly District". *Federation [Appendix D to 1899 Annual Report of The Federation of Churches and Christian Workers of New York City]*, 1 (1899), 1-92.

Laíz, Consuelo. *La lucha final: Los partidos de la izquierda radical durante la transición española*. Madrid: Los Libros de la Catarata, 1995.

Lambert, Yves. *Dieu change en Bretagne. La religion à Limerzel de 1900 à nos jours*. Paris: Cerf, 1985.

Lambert, Yves. "Religion: l'Europe à un tournant?" *Futuribles*, 277 (2002), 129-159.

Lamberts, Emiel, ed. *Christian Democracy in the European Union (1945-1995)*. KADOC-Studies 21. Leuven: Leuven University Press, 1997.

Langan, John. "The Just War Theory After the Gulf War". *Theological Studies*, 53 (1992), 95-112.

Langlois, Claude. *Le catholicisme au féminin*. Paris: Cerf, 1983.

Langlois, Claude. "Féminisation du catholicisme" in: Jacques Le Goff and René Rémond, eds. *Histoire de la France religieuse*. Vol. 3. Paris: Seuil, 1991, 292-310.

Lankard, Frank G. *A History of the American Sunday School Curriculum*. New York-Cincinnati: Abingdon Press, 1927.

Lannon, Frances. *Privilege, Persecution and Prophecy: The Catholic Church in Spain 1875-1975*. Oxford: Clarendon Press, 1987.

Lausanne 77: Fifty Years of Faith and Order. Faith and Order Paper 82. Geneva: World Council of Churches, 1977.

Lefèvre, Luc J. "Les droits de l'homme et la chrétienté". *Conversaciones católicas internacionales. Documentos*. San Sebastian: Conversaciones católicas internacionales, (1950) 4, 107-121.

Legrand, Hervé; Manzanares, Julio and Garcia y Garcia, Antonio, eds. *Les Conférences épiscopales: théologie, statut canonique, avenir*. Paris: Cerf, 1988.

Legrand, Hervé. "Églises locales, Églises régionales et Église entière" in: Michel Deneken et al. *L'Église à venir: Mélanges offerts à Joseph Hoffmann*. Paris: Cerf, 1999, 277-308.

Lehmann, Hartmut, ed. *Säkularisierung, Dechristianisierung, Rechristianisierung im neuzeitlichen Europa: Bilanz und Perspektiven der Forschung*. Göttingen: Vandenhoeck & Ruprecht, 1997.

Leirvik, Oddbjørn. *Images of Jesus Christ in Islam*. Uppsala: Swedish Institute of Missionary Research, 1999.

Letamendia, Pierre. *Le Mouvement Républicain Populaire. Histoire d'un grand parti français*. Paris: Beauchesne, 1995.

Leugers, Antonia. "Vereinigung Deutscher Ordensobern 1898 bis 1998". *Ordenskorrespondenz*, (39) 1998, 412-444.

Leugers, Antonia. *Interessenpolitik und Solidarität. 100 Jahre Superioren-Konferenz Vereinigung Deutscher Ordensobern*. Frankfurt: Knecht, 1999.

Lidtke, Vernon L. *The Alternative Culture: Socialist Labor in Imperial Germany*. New York: Oxford University Press, 1985.

Lienesch, Michael. *Redeeming America: Piety and Politics in the New Christian Right*. Chapel Hill: University of North Carolina Press, 1993.

Lienkamp, Andreas. "Socialism Out of Christian Responsibility: The German Experiment of Left Catholicism (1945-1949)" in: Gerd-Rainer Horn and Emmanuel Gerard, eds. *Left Catholicism: Catholics and Society in Western Europe at the Point of Liberation, 1943-1955*. KADOC-Studies 25. Leuven: Leuven University Press, 2001, 192-227.

Lipset, Seymour M. and Rokkan, Stein, eds. *Party Systems and Voter Alignments: Cross-National Perspectives*. New York: The Free Press, 1967.

Loeff, Jan J. *Verhouding staat en rechtsgemeenschap, mede in verband met de traditionele katholieke staatsleer*. Leiden: Stenfert Kroese, 1955.

López García, Basilisa. *Aproximación a la historia de la HOAC: 1946-1981*. Madrid: Ediciones HOAC, 1995.

Lovsky, Fadiey. *La Déchirure de l'absence. Essai sur les rapports de l'Église du Christ et du peuple d'Israël*. Paris: Calmann-Lévy, 1971.

Luckmann, Thomas. *The Invisible Religion: The Problem of Religion in Modern Society*. New York: Macmillan, 1967.

Luhmann, Niklas. *Funktion der Religion*. Frankfurt am Main: Suhrkamp, 1977.

Luhmann, Niklas. *Essays on Self-Reference*. New York: Columbia University Press, 1990.

Luykx, Paul. "Erger dan de Reformatie? Katholieken in de jaren vijftig" in: Paul Luykx and Pim Slot, eds. *Een stille revolutie? Cultuur en mentaliteit in de lange jaren vijftig*. Hilversum: Verloren, 1997, 67-88.

Luyckx, Paul. *Andere katholieken. Opstellen over Nederlandse katholieken in de twintigste eeuw*. Nijmegen: SUN, 2000.

Luykx, Paul and Slot, Pim, eds. *Een stille revolutie? Cultuur en mentaliteit in de lange jaren vijftig*. Hilversum: Verloren, 1997.

Lynch, Christopher. *Selling Catholicism: Bishop Sheen and the Power of Television*. Lexington: University Press of Kentucky, 1999.

Lyotard, Jean-François. *The Postmodern Condition*. Minneapolis: University of Minnesota Press, 1984.

Madeley, John. "Politics and Religion in Western Europe" in: George Moyser, ed. *Politics and Religion in the Modern World*. London: Routledge, 1991, 28-66.

Madeley, John T.S. and Enyedi, Zsolt, eds. *Church and State in Contemporary Europe: The Chimera of Neutrality*. Special issue of *West European Politics*, 26 (2003) 1.

Malgeri, Francesco. *La Sinistra cristiana (1937-1945)*. Brescia: Morcelliana, 1982.

Manzanares, J. "La reforma de la curia romana por Pablo VI" in: *Paul VI et les réformes institutionnelles dans l'Église*. Brescia: Instituo Paolo VI, 1987, 49-69.

Maraviglia, Mariangela. *Chiesa e storia in 'Adesso' (1949-1959)*. Bologna: Edizioni Dehoniane, 1991.

Margotti, Marta. *Preti e operai. La Mission de Paris dal 1943 al 1954*. Turin: Paravia, 2000.

Maritain, Jacques. *Humanisme intégral. Problèmes temporels et spirituels d'une nouvelle chrétienté*. Paris: Aubier, 1936[1], 1946[2] and 2000[4] (foreword René Rémond).

Maritain, Jacques. "Les civilisations humaines et le rôle des chrétiens" in: *Les intellectuels dans la chrétienté*. Rome: Mouvement international des intellectuels catholiques, 1948, 85-105.

Maritain, Jacques. *Le Paysan de la Garonne. Un vieux laïc s'interroge à propos du temps présent*. Paris: Desclée de Brouwer, 1966.

Martin, David. *The Religious and the Secular: Studies in Secularization*. London: Routledge & Kegan Paul, 1969.

Martin, David. *Pentecostalism: The World Their Parish*. London: Blackwell, 2001.

Martínez Hoyos, Francisco. *Ja JOC a Catalunya (1947-1975). Els senyals d'una Església del demà*. Barcelona: Editorial Mediterrània, 2000.

Marwick, Arthur. *The Sixties*. Oxford: Oxford University Press, 1988.

Mary, André. *Le défi du syncrétisme. Le travail symbolique de la religion d'Eboga (Gabon)*. Paris: Éditions EHESS, 1999.

Mason, Orioldo and Villa, Roberto, eds. *Giuseppe Dossetti. Il circuito delle due parole*. Portogruaro: Ediciclo, 2000.

Massa, Mark Stephen. *Catholics and American Culture: Fulton Sheen, Dorothy Day, and the Notre Dame Football Team*. New York: Crossroad, 1999.

Mattioli, Aram. *Gonzague de Reynold, idéologue d'une Suisse autoritaire*. Fribourg: Éditions universitaires, 1997.

Mayer, Arno. *Why Did the Heavens Not Darken?* New York: Pantheon, 1990.

Mayeur, Jean-Marie. *Catholicisme social et Démocratie chrétienne: principes romains, expériences françaises*. Paris: Cerf, 1986.

Mazzolari, Primo. *Rivoluzione Cristiana*. Bologna: Edizioni Dehoniane, 1995.

McCormick, Richard A. "Laborem Exercens and Social Morality" in: Charles E. Curran and Richard A. McCormick, eds. *Official Catholic Social Teaching*. Readings in Moral Theology 5. New York: Paulist Press, 1986, 219-232.

McGirr, Lisa. *Suburban Warriors: The Origins of the New American Right*. Princeton (NJ): Princeton University Press, 2001.

McLeod, Hugh, ed. *European Religion in the Age of Great Cities*. London: Routledge, 1995.

McLeod, Hugh. *Piety and Poverty: Working Class Religion in Berlin, London and New York 1870-1914*. New York: Holmes & Meier, 1996.

McLeod, Hugh. *Religion and Society in England 1850-1914*. Basingstoke: Macmillan, 1996.

McLeod, Hugh. *Religion and the People of Western Europe 1789-1989*. Oxford: Oxford University Press, 1997.

McLeod, Hugh. "Comparing Secularisations: Germany and Britain" in: Anselm Doering-Manteuffel and Kurt Nowak, eds. *Religions-politik in Deutschland*. Stuttgart: Kohlhammer, 1999, 177-194.

McLeod, Hugh. "New Perspectives on the Religious History of Western and Northern Europe 1815-1960". *Kyrkohistorisk årsskrift*, 2000, 135-145.

McLeod, Hugh. *Secularisation in Western Europe 1848-1914*. Basingstoke: Macmillan, 2000.

McLeod, Hugh. *The Religious Crisis of the 1960s*. Oxford: Oxford University Press, 2007.

McLeod, Hugh and Ustorf, Werner, eds. *The Decline of Christendom in Western Europe, 1750-2000*. Cambridge: Cambridge University Press, 2003.

McPhillips, Kathleen. "Modernity, Rationality and the Problem of Women's Religious Agency". *Australian Feminist Studies*, 14 (1999) 30, 293-303.

McSweeney, Bill. *Roman Catholicism: The Search for Relevance*. Oxford: Blackwell, 1980.

The Meissen Common Statement. On the Way to Visible Unity. CCU Occasional Papers 2. London: Council for Christian Unity, 1992.

Melloni, Alberto. "Yves Congar à Vatican II. Hypothèses et pistes de recherche" in: André Vauchez, ed. *Cardinal Yves Congar, 1904-1995. Actes du colloque réuni à Rome les 3-4 juin 1996*. Paris: Cerf, 1999, 117-164.

Menozzi, Daniele. *Sacro Cuore. Un culto tra devozione interiore e restaurazione cristiana della società*. Rome: Viella, 2001.

Merton, Robert K. *Social Theory and Social Structure*. New York: The Free Press, 1957.

Messer, Donald E. *Send Me? The Itineracy in Crisis*. Nashville: Abingdon Press, 1991.

Methuen, Charlotte. "Women Priests Have Real Presence: Reflections on Liturgy and Presidency" in: Susan K. Roll et al., eds. *Women, Ritual and Liturgy*. Yearbook of the European Society of Women in Theological Research 9. Leuven: Peeters, 2001, 241-250.

Meyer, Harding and Vischer, Lukas, eds. *Growth in Agreement: Reports and Agreed Statements of Ecumenical Conversations on a World Level*. New York-Geneva: Paulist Press - World Council of Churches, 1984.

Mich, Marvin L. Krier. *Catholic Social Teaching and Movements*. Mystic (CT): Twenty-Third Publications, 1998.

Miller, Robert Moats. *Bishop G. Bromley Oxnam: Paladin of Liberal Protestantism*. Nashville: Abingdon Press, 1990.

Miller, Zane L. *Suburb: Neighborhood and Community in Forest Park, Ohio, 1935-1976*. Knoxville: University of Tennessee Press, 1981.

Milza, Pierre and Bernstein, Serge. *Le fascisme italien 1919-1945*. Paris: Seuil, 1980.

Moderamen des reformierten Bundes. *Das Bekenntnis zu Jesus Christus und die Friedens-verantwortung der Kirche*. Gütersloh, 1982.

Moreira Neves, L. "Paul VI et la réforme de la Curie". *Istituto Paolo VI. Notiziario*, 8 (1984), 51-66.

Mortimer, Edward. *Faith and Power*. London: Faber & Faber, 1982.

Motzkin, Gabriel and Fischer, Yochi, eds. *Religion and Democracy in Contemporary Europe*. London: Alliance Publishing Trust, 2008.

Moule, Charles F.D. *The Origin of Christology.* Cambridge: Cambridge University Press. 1977.

Mounier, Emmanuel. "L'agonie du christianisme". *Esprit*, May 1946, 717-730.

Mounier, Emmanuel. *Carnets de route*. 1: *Feu la chrétienté*. Paris: Seuil, 1950.

Müller, Hubert and Pottmeyer, Hermann-Josef. *Die Bischofskonferenz: theologischer und juridischer Status*. Düsseldorf: Patmos, 1989.

Nagel, Ernst-Josef and Oberhem, Harald. *Dem Frieden verpflichtet. Konzeptionen und Entwicklungen der katholischen Friedensethik seit dem Zweiten Weltkrieg*. Munich-Mainz: Kaiser, 1982.

Nash, David. "Reconnecting Religion with Social and Cultural History: Secularization's Failure as a Master Narrative". *Cultural and Social History*, 1 (2004), 302-325.

Neckebrouck, Valeer. *De stomme duivelen. Het antimissionaire syndroom in de westerse kerk.* Leuven: Acco, 2002[2].

Nesbitt, Paula D. "Clergy Feminization: Controlled Labor or Transformative Change?" *Journal for the Scientific Study of Religion*, 36 (1997) 4, 585-599.

Nesbitt, Paula D. *Feminization of the Clergy in America: Occupational and Organizational Perspectives.* New York: Oxford University Press, 1997.

Nipperdey, Thomas. *Deutsche Geschichte 1800-1866.* Munich: C.H. Beck, 1983.

Nipperdey, Thomas. *Religion im Umbruch: Deutschland 1870-1918.* Munich: C.H. Beck, 1988.

Njoku, Jude. *Examining the Foundations of Solidarity in the Social Encyclicals of John Paul II.* Diss. Doct. K.U.Leuven, 2004.

Noirjean de Ceuninck, Martine and Borie, Jean, eds. *De l'amitié. Hommage à Albert Béguin (1901-1957).* Geneva: Droz, 2001.

Norris, Pippa and Inglehart, Ronald. *Sacred and Secular: Religion and Politics Worldwide.* Cambridge: Cambridge University Press, 2004.

La nouvelle organisation de la Curie Romaine (juin 1988). Paris, 1988.

Novak, Michael. *The Catholic Ethic and the Spirit of Capitalism.* New York: The Free Press, 1993.

Obelkevich, James. "The Religion of Music" in: James Obelkevich, Lyndal Roper and Raphael Samuel, eds. *Disciplines of Faith.* London: Routledge, 1987, 550-565.

O'Brien, William V. *Morality, Nuclear War and the Schema on the Church in the Modern World.* CAIP New, 1964.

O'Malley, John W. *Trent and All That: Renaming Catholicism in the Early Modern Age.* Cambridge (MA): Harvard University Press, 2002.

Oomen-van der Vegt, R.A.J. *Vrouwen in het pastoraal werk. Een onderzoek naar de positie van vrouwelijke pastores in de katholieke kerk.* Tilburg: Theologische Faculteit Tilburg, 1995.

"Openheid en geslotenheid van de katholieken in Nederland". *Binnenlands apostolaat*, 8 (1957), 117-163.

Ormières, Jean-Louis. "Les rouges et les blancs" in: Pierre Nora, ed. *Les lieux de mémoire.* Vol. 3. Paris: Gallimard, 1997[2], 2395-2432.

Orsi, Robert A. *The Madonna of 115th Street: Faith and Community in Italian Harlem, 1880-1950.* New Haven: Yale University Press, 1985.

Paiano, Maria. "Les travaux de la Commission liturgique conciliaire" in: M. Lamberigts, C. Soetens and J. Grootaers, eds. *Les commissions conciliaires à Vatican II*. Instrumenta theologica 18. Leuven: Bibliotheek van de Faculteit Godgeleerdheid, 1996, 1-26.

Palathinkal, Abraham. *Goods of the Earth Destined for All: The Evolution in the Socio-Economic Vision of the Catholic Social Teachings: From Private Property to Universal Destination.* Diss. Doct. K.U.Leuven, 1998.

Panikkar, Raimundo. *The Unknown Christ of Hinduism*. New York: Orbis, 1981.

Panikkar, Raimundo. *The Cosmotheandric Experience*. New York: Orbis, 1993.

Pannenberg, Wolfhart. *Systematische Theologie.* Vol. 1. Göttingen: Vandenhoeck & Ruprecht, 1988.

Pannenberg, Wolfhart. "Die Wirklichkeit Gottes und der Götter in der Erfahrung der Religionen" in: Wolfhart Pannenberg. *Systematische Theologie.* Vol. 1. Göttingen: Vandenhoeck & Ruprecht, 1988, 133-206.

Pannet, Robert. *Le catholicisme populaire: 30 ans après "La France pays de mission?"* Paris: Le Centurion, 1974.

Parisella, Antonio, ed. *Gerardo Bruni e i cristiano-sociali.* Rome: Edizioni Lavoro, 1984.

Parisella, Antonio. "Christian Movements and Parties of the Left in Italy (1938-1958)" in: Gerd-Rainer Horn and Emmanuel Gerard, eds. *Left Catholicism: Catholics and Society in Western Europe at the Point of Liberation, 1943-1955.* KADOC-Studies 25. Leuven: Leuven University Press, 2001, 142-173.

Pasture, Patrick. *Kerk, politiek en sociale actie. De unieke positie van de christelijke arbeidersbeweging in België (1944-1973).* HIVA-reeks 14. Leuven-Apeldoorn: Garant, 1992.

Pasture, Patrick. "Diverging Paths: The Development of Catholic Labour Organisations in France, the Netherlands and Belgium since 1945". *Revue d'histoire ecclésiastique*, 88 (1994) 1, 54-90.

Pasture, Patrick. "Entre Église et citoyen. Le PSC/CVP et sa base organisée" in: Wilfried Dewachter et al. *Entre État et société. Les sociaux-chrétiens en Belgique.* Louvain-la-Neuve: Duculot, 1995, 265-295.

Pasture, Patrick. Review of Peter de Haan, *Van volgzame elitestrijder tot kritische gelovige. Geschiedenis van de Katholieke Actie in Nederland (1934-1966)* (Nijmegen, 1994). *Trajecta*, 4, (1995) 3, 274-275.

Pasture, Patrick. "Divergent Developments, Regional Alliances and the Need for National Solidarity in Belgium" in: Johan Wets, ed. *Cultural Diversity in Trade Unions: A Challenge to Class Identity?* Aldershot: Ashgate, 2000, 35-70.

Pasture, Patrick. "Modèles internationaux d'action ouvrière catholique" in: Bruno Duriez et al., eds. *Chrétiens et ouvriers en France 1937-1970.* Paris: Éditions de l'Atelier, 2001, 245-257.

Pasture, Patrick. "Christendom and the Legacy of the Sixties: Between the Secular City and the Age of Aquarius". *Revue d'histoire ecclésiastique*, 99 (2004) 1, 82-117.

Pasture, Patrick. "Window of Opportunities or *trompe l'œil*? The Myth of Labour Unity in Western Europe After 1944" in: Gerd-Rainer Horn and Padraic Kenney, eds. *Transnational Moments of Change: Europe 1945, 1968, 1989.* Lanham (MD): Rowman & Littlefield, 2004, 27-49.

Pasture, Patrick. "Building the Social Security State: A Comparative History of Belgium, the Netherlands and Germany, from the Nineteenth Century to the 1960s" in: Lex Heerma van Voss, Patrick Pasture and Jan De Maeyer, eds. *Between Cross and Class: Comparative Histories of Christian Labor in Europe 1840-2000.* Bern: Peter Lang, 2005, 252-284.

Pasture, Patrick. "Religion in Contemporary Europe: Contrasting Perceptions and Dynamics". *Archiv für Sozialgeschichte*, 2009, (forthcoming).

Pasture, Patrick. "Beyond the Feminisation Thesis. Gendering the History of Christianity in the 19th and 20th Century" in: Jan Art et al., eds. *'Dieu changea de sexe'? Christian Feminisation and Masculinisation in Western Europe 18th-20th c.* Leuven (forthcoming).

Pasture, Patrick. "Christianity in a De-traditionalising World: A GG-CT Interpretation of the Transformations of the 1960s" in: Erik Sidenval, ed. *Transforming European Religion - Secularisation in the long 1960s.* Stockholm (forthcoming).

Patterson, James T. *Grand Expectations: The United States, 1945-1975.* New York-Oxford: Oxford University Press, 1996.

Peale, Norman Vincent. *The Power of Positive Thinking.* New York: Prentice-Hall, 1952.

Pelletier, Denis. *La crise catholique. Religion, société, politique.* Paris: Payot, 2002.

Pennings, Paul. "Jongeren en ontzuiling, 1950-1970" in: Tjitske Akkerman and Siep Stuurman, eds. *De zondige riviera van het katholicisme. Een lokale studie over feminisme en ontzuiling 1950-1975.* Amsterdam: SUA, 1985, 74-116.

Pérouas, Louis. *Refus d'une religion, religion d'un refus en Limousin rural 1880-1940.* Paris: Éditions de l'École des Hautes Études en Sciences Sociales, 1985.

Philips, Gérard. *L'Église et son mystère au IIe Concile du Vatican: histoire, texte et commentaire de la Constitution Lumen Gentium.* Paris: Desclée, 1967-1968, 2 vols.

Piemont, Ralph L. and Moberg, David O., eds. *Research in the Social Scientific Study of Religion.* Vol. 13-14. Leiden-Boston: Brill, 2002-2003.

Pieper, Jos et al. *Charisma, ambt, professionaliteit. Theologische reflecties bij een onderzoek onder pastoraal werk(st)ers in het bisdom Roermond.* Nijmegen: Theologische Faculteit KU-Nijmegen, 1999.

Piras, Pierine. "Nouveaux mysticismes". *Le Monde diplomatique. Manière de voir*, 48 (1999), 90-93.

Platti, Emilio. *Wat gelooft een goede moslim?* Amsterdam: Muntinga - Averbode: Altiora, 1996.

Pollack, Detlef. "Wiederkehr des Religiösen? Neue religiöse Bewegungen im Kontext des religiösen und gesellschaftlichen Wandels". *Sociologia Internationalis*, 38 (2000), 13-45.

Pollack, Detlef. *Säkularisierung - ein moderner Mythos?* Tübingen: Mohr Siebeck, 2003.

Pollack, Detlef. "Religion und Moderne. Zur Gegenwart der Säkularisierung in Europa" in: Friedrich W. Graf and Klaus Große Kracht, eds. *Religion und Gesellschaft: Europa im 20. Jahrhundert.* Cologne: Böhlau, 2007, 73-104.

Pollak, Gertrud. *Der Aufbruch der Säkularinstitute und ihr theologischer Ort. Historisch-systematische Studien.* Vallendar-Schönstatt: Patris, 1986.

Polner, Murray and O'Grady, Jim. *Disarmed and Dangerous: The Radical Lives and Times of Daniel and Philip Berrigan.* New York: Basic Books, 1997.

Pombeni, Paolo. *Le 'Cronache Sociali' di Dossetti 1947-1951: Geografia di un movimento di opinione.* Florence: Vallecchi, 1976.

Pombeni, Paolo. *Il gruppo dossettiano e la fondazione della democrazia italiana (1938-1948).* Bologna: Il Mulino, 1979.

Pontifical Commission Iustitia et Pax. *Ways of Peace: Papal Messages for the World Days of Peace (1968-1986).* Vatican City, s.d.

Pontifical Council for Justice and Peace. *From Stockholm to Johannesburg: A Historical Overview of the Concern of the Holy See for the Environment, 1972-2002.* Vatican City, 2002.

Poortinga, Y.H. "Equivalence of Cross-Cultural Data: An Overview of Basic Issues". *International Journal of Psychology*, 24 (1989) 6, 737-756.

Pope, Stephen J. "You Can't Keep a Good Theory Down: The Just War, the Gulf War and Beyond". *Commonweal*, 12 February 1993, 9-12.

Porter, Roy and Teich, Mikulas, eds. *The Enlightenment in National Context.* Cambridge: Cambridge University Press, 1981.

Porterfield, Amanda. *The Transformation of American Religion: The Story of a Late-Twentieth-Century Awakening.* New York-Oxford: Oxford University Press, 2001.

The Porvoo Common Statement. Together in Mission and Ministry. London: Church House Publishing, 1993.

Poulat, Émile. *"Humanisme intégral* dans la culture des années trente. Un projet pour le monde". *Le Supplément*, December 1993, 139-174.

Poulat, Émile. *Les prêtres-ouvriers. Naissance et fin.* Paris: Cerf, 1999.

Pranger, Jan H. *Redeeming Tradition: Inculturation, Contextualization, and Tradition in a Postcolonial Perspective.* Diss. Groningen, 2003.

Prévotat, Jacques. "Fondements d'une culture chrétienne" in: Yves-Marie Hilaire, ed. *De Renan à Marrou. L'histoire du christianisme et les progrès de la méthode historique (1863-1968).* Lille: Presses universitaires du Septentrion, 1999, 117-131.

Pruvot, Samuel. *Monseigneur Charles, aumônier de la Sorbonne.* Paris: Cerf, 2002.

Punsmann, Hermann. "Zur Komplexität religiöser Orden heute". *Wissenschaft und Weisheit*, 61 (1998), 137-169.

Putnam, Robert D. *Making Democracy Work: Civic Traditions in Italy.* Princeton: Princeton University Press, 1993.

Putnam, Robert D. "Bowling alone: America's Declining Social Capital". *Journal of Democracy*, 6 (1995) 1, 65-78.

"Quas primas" in: *Actes de Pie XI pour les années 1925 et 1926.* Paris: Bonne Presse, 1927.

Raab, Kelly A. *When Women Become Priests: The Catholic Women's Ordination Debate.* New York: Columbia University Press, 2000.

Rahner, Karl. "Christianity and the Non-Christian Religions" in: Karl Rahner. *Theological Investigations.* Vol. 5. Baltimore: Helicon, 1966, 115-134.

Rahner, Karl. "Anonymous Christianity and the Missionary Task of the Church" in: Karl Rahner. *Theological Investigations.* Vol. 12. New York: Seabury, 1974, 161-178.

Rahner, Karl. "Observations on the Problem of the 'Anonymous Christian'" in: Karl Rahner. *Theological Investigations.* Vol. 14. New York: Seabury, 1976, 280-294.

Rahner, Karl and Fries, Heinrich. *Einheit der Kirche - reale Möglichkeit.* Quaestiones disputatae 100. Freiburg: Herder, 1983.

Raiser, Konrad. *For a Culture of Life. Transforming Globalization and Violence.* Geneva: World Council of Churches, 2002.

Ratzinger, Joseph. *Einführung in das Christentum. Vorlesungen über das Apostolische Glaubensbekenntnis.* Munich: Kösel, 1969.

Ratzinger, Joseph and Messori, Vittorio. *Entretien sur la foi.* Paris: Fayard, 1985.

Ratzinger, Joseph and Messori, Vittorio. *Rapporto sulla fede. Vittorio Messori a colloquio con il cardinale Joseph Ratzinger.* Cinisello Balsamo: Edizioni Paoline, 1985.

Reed, Ralph. *Active Faith: How Christians Are Changing the Soul of American Politics.* New York: The Free Press, 1996.

Reeves, Thomas C. *America's Bishop: The Life and Times of Fulton J. Sheen.* San Francisco: Encounter Books, 2001.

Rémond, René. "Bonne volonté et réalités politiques". *La Vie intellectuelle,* October 1948, 64-78. Reproduced with a testimony of the author in: René Rémond. *Le catholicisme français dans la société politique.* Paris: Éditions de l'Atelier, 1995, 61-72.

Rémond, René. *Le catholicisme français dans la société politique.* Paris: Éditions de l'Atelier, 1995.

Remy, Jean and Voyé, Liliane. "L'Église catholique de Belgique et la transaction avec la modernité. Quelques initiatives à portée internationale" in: Liliane Voyé et al., eds. *La Belgique et ses dieux. Églises, mouvements religieux et laïques.* Louvain-la-Neuve: Cabay, 1985, 11-29.

Rensvold, R.B. and Chung, G.W. "Testing Measurement Models for Factorial Invariance: A Systematic Approach". *Educational and Psychological Measurement,* 58 (1998) 6, 1017-1034.

Reskin, Barbara F. and Roos, Patricia A. et al. *Job Queues, Gender Queues: Explaining Women's Inroads into Male Occupations.* Philadelphia: Temple University Press, 1990.

"Response to Vatican Working Paper on Bishop's Conferences". *Origins,* 13 (1988) 25, 397-402.

Reychler, Luc. "Religion and Conflict". *International Journal of Peace Studies,* 2 (1997) 1, 19-38.

Ribbe, Wolfgang. "Zur Entwicklung und Funktion der Pfarrgemeinden in der Evangelischen Kirche Berlins bis zum Ende der Monarchie" in: Kaspar Elm and Hans-Dietrich Loock, eds. *Seelsorge und Diakonie in Berlin.* Berlin: De Gruyter, 1990, 233-263.

Riccardi, Andrea. *Il "partito romano" nel secondo dopoguerra (1945-1954).* Brescia: Morcelliana, 1983.

Riccardi, Andrea. "Preparare il Concilio: Papa e Curia alla vigilia del Vaticano II" in: *Le Deuxième Concile du Vatican (1959-1962).* Rome: École française de Rome, 1989, 181-205.

Riccardi, Andrea. "I 'vota' romani" in: M. Lamberigts and Cl. Soetens, eds. *À la veille du concile Vatican II. Vota et réactions en Europe et dans le catholicisme oriental.* Instrumenta theologica 9. Leuven: Bibliotheek van de Faculteit Godgeleerdheid, 1992, 146-168.

Riccardi, Andrea. *Le politiche della Chiesa.* Cinisello Balsamo: San Paolo, 1997.

Righart, Hans. *De katholieke zuil in Europa. Het ontstaan van verzuiling onder katholieken in Oostenrijk, Zwitserland, België en Nederland.* Meppel-Amsterdam: Boom, 1986.

Robbrecht, Paul. *Mariaverering te Scherpenheuvel. Proeve van een hedendaagse pastoraal in een Mariaal bedevaartsoord.* Diss. Lic. K.U.Leuven, 1986.

Robinson, John A.T. *Honest to God.* London: SCM, 1963.

Roof, Wade Clark. *Spiritual Marketplace. Baby Boomers and the Remaking of American Religion.* Princeton: Princeton University Press, 1999.

Rossi, O. "Le tappe della preparazione della costituzione apostolica *Pastor bonus*" in: *La Curia romana: aspetti ecclesiologici, pastorali e istituzionali.* Vatican City: Libreria Editrice Vaticana, 1989, 103-110.

Rossinow, Douglas C. *The Politics of Authenticity: Liberalism, Christianity, and the New Left in America.* New York: Columbia University Press, 1998.

Rousseau, Olivier. "Vatican II". *Irénikon*, 38 (1965) 4, 447.

Roustang, François. "Le troisième homme". *Christus*, 52 (1966), 561-567.

Routhier, Gilles. *La réception d'un concile.* Paris: Cerf, 1993.

Routhier, Gilles. "Il Vaticano II: avvio di riforma della curia romana" in: *Il Concilio Vaticano II. Recezione ed ermeneutica.* Milan: Vita e pensiero, 2007, 133-164.

Saltini, Zeno. *La Rivoluzione Sociale di Gesù Cristo.* San Giacomo Roncole: Opera Piccoli Apostoli, 1946.

"The San Antonio Conference". *International Review of Mission*, 78 (1989) 311/312.

Sanders, Ed Parish. *The Historical Figure of Jesus.* London: Allen Lane/The Penguin Press, 1993.

Sanders, José. *Vrouw en beleid. Belemmeringen en stimulansen voor de doorstroom van vrouwen naar beleidsbepalende functies in de kerkelijke organisatie.* Rapport No 482. Nijmegen: KASKI, 2001.

Sani, Roberto. *Da de Gasperi a Fanfani. "La Civiltà Cattolica" e il mondo cattolico italiano nel secondo dopoguerra (1945-1962).* Brescia: Morcelliana, 1986.

Sauvage, Pierre. *"La Cité chrétienne" (1926-1940). Une revue autour de Jacques Leclercq.* Gembloux: Duculot, 1987.

Sauvage, Pierre. *Jacques Leclercq, 1891-1971. Un arbre en plein vent.* Gembloux: Duculot, 1992.

Schambeck, Mirjam and Schaupp, Walter, eds. *Lebensentscheidung - Projekt auf Zeit oder Bindung auf Dauer? Zu einer Frage des Ordenslebens heute.* Würzburg: Echter, 2004.

Schauffler, Adolphus F. "The Present Condition of New York City below Fourteenth Street, 1888" in: *The Religious Condition of New York City.* New York: Baker and Taylor, 1888, 15-25.

Schaupp, Klemens and Kunz, Claudia Edith, eds. *Erneuerung oder Neugründung? Wie Orden und kirchliche Gemeinschaften lebendig bleiben können.* Mainz: Mattthias-Grünewald-Verlag, 2002.

Scheepers, Peer; Gijsberts, Merove and Hello, Evelyn. "Religiosity and Prejudice against Ethnic Minorities in Europe: Cross-national Tests on a Controversial Relationship". *Review of Religious Research*, 43 (2002) 3, 242-265.

Schermann, Hans. "Ordensleben unter den Bedingungen heutiger Kultur". *Ordensnachrichten*, 39 (2000) 3, 36-43.

Schillebeeckx, Edward. *Jesus: An Experiment in Christology.* New York: Seabury, 1979.

Schillebeeckx, Edward. *Mensen als verhaal van God*. Baarn: Nelissen, 1989.

Schmidt, Stjepan. *Augustin Bea. Der Kardinal der Einheit*. Graz: Styria, 1989.

Schmidt-Lux, Thomas. *Wissenschaft als Religion: Szientismus im ostdeutschen Säkularisierungsprozess*. Würzburg: Ergon, 2008.

Schmiedl, Joachim. *Das Konzil und die Orden. Krise und Erneuerung des gottgeweihten Lebens*. Vallendar-Schönstatt: Patris, 1999.

Schmiedl, Joachim. "Rückkehr zum Ursprung und Anpassung ans Heute. Der Erneuerungsimpuls des II. Vatikanums für die Orden". *Regnum*, 35 (2001), 29-44.

Schmiedl, Joachim. "Konkretionen des Charismas in der Evangelisierung der nachkonziliaren Kirche" in: Peter Hünermann and Bernd Jochen Hilberath, eds. *Herders Theologischer Kommentar zum Zweiten Vatikanischen Konzil*. Vol. 5. Freiburg: Herder, 2005, 296-302.

Schmiedl, Joachim. "Theologischer Kommentar zum Dekret über die zeitgemäße Erneuerung des Ordenslebens *Perfectae caritatis*" in: Peter Hünermann and Bernd Jochen Hilberath, eds. *Herders Theologischer Kommentar zum Zweiten Vatikanischen Konzil*. Vol. 3. Freiburg: Herder, 2005, 491-550.

Schnackenburg, Rudolf. *Jesus in the Gospels: A Biblical Christology*. Louisville: Westminster John Knox Press, 1995.

Schneider, Bernhard. "Feminisierung der Religion im 19. Jahrhundert. Perspektiven einer These im Kontext des deutschen Katholizismus". *Trierer theologische Zeitschrift*, 111 (2002), 123-147.

Schneiders, Sandra M. *New Wineskins: Re-Imagining Religious Life Today*. New York: Paulist Press, 1986.

Schneiders, Sandra M. *Finding the Treasure: Locating Catholic Religious Life in a New Ecclesial and Cultural Context*. Religious Life in a New Millennium 1. New York: Paulist Press, 2000.

Schneiders, Sandra M. *Selling All: Commitment, Consecrated Celibacy, and Community in Catholic Religious Life*. Religious Life in a New Millennium 2. New York: Paulist Press, 2001.

Schoenherr, Richard A. and Yamane, David. *Goodbye Father: The Celibate Male Priesthood and the Future of the Catholic Church*. New York: Oxford University Press, 2002.

Schoenherr, Richard A.; Young, Lawrence A. and Cheng, Tsan-Yuang. *Full Pews and Empty Altars: Demographics of the Priest Shortage in United States Catholic Dioceses*. Madison: University of Wisconsin Press, 1993.

Schreiter, Robert. *The New Catholicity*. New York: Orbis, 1997.

Schreuder, Osmund. "Die deprivierte Mitte" in: Walter Weymann-Weyhe, ed. *Die offene Kirche. Analysen zur Situation - Modelle der Praxis*. Düsseldorf: Patmos Verlag, 1974, 234-264.

Schulte, Ludger. *Aufbruch aus der Mitte. Zur Erneuerung der Theologie christlicher Spiritualität im 20. Jahrhundert - im Spiegel von Wirken und Werk Friedrich Wulfs SJ (1908-1990)*. Würzburg: Echter, 1998.

Schulte, Ludger. "Friedrich Wulf SJ und sein Einfluß auf Entwicklung und Rezeption des Ordensdekretes 'Perfectae caritatis'". *Geist und Leben*, 72 (1999), 212-224.

Sered, Susan Starr. *Priestess, Mother, Sacred Sister: Religions Dominated by Women*. New York: Oxford University Press, 1994.

Sesboüé, Bernard. *Le magistère à l'épreuve: autorité, vérité et liberté dans l'Église*. Paris: Desclée de Brouwer, 2001.

Sethi, S. Prakash and Williams, Oliver. *Economic Imperatives and Ethical Values in Global Business*. Notre Dame (IN): University of Notre Dame Press, 2001.

Sheen, Fulton J. *Peace of Soul*. New York: McGraw-Hill, 1949.

Sheenan, Thomas. "Revolution in the Church". *The New York Review of Books*, 14.06.1984.

Sheenan, Thomas. "On Satan & Catholic Liberals". *Commonweal*, 14.09.1984.

Sher, Richard. *Church and University in the Scottish Enlightenment.* Edinburgh: Edinburgh University Press, 1985.

Sibalis, Michael D. "Paris" in: David Higgs, ed. *Queer Sites: Gay Urban Histories since 1600.* London: Routledge, 1999, 10-37.

Silk, Mark. *Spiritual Politics: Religion and America since World War II*. New York: Simon and Schuster, 1988.

Simons, Ed and Winkeler, Lodewijk. *Het Verraad der Clercken. Intellectuelen en hun rol in de ontwikkelingen van het Nederlandse katholicisme na 1945*. Baarn: Arbor, 1987.

Sirico, Robert A. "Latin America Imprisoned in Liberation Theology". *Religion and Liberty*, 13 (2003) 4.

Smith, Wilfred Cantwell. "The Christian in a Religiously Plural World" in: Jon Hick and Brian Hebblethwaite, eds. *Christianity and Other Religions*. Glasgow: Collins, 1980, 87-107.

Sociaal en Cultureel Planbureau. *Sociaal en Cultureel Rapport 2000.* Rijswijk: SCP, 2000.

Soen, Violet. "Ieder huisje heeft zijn kruisje. Een studie over het sociaal(-religieus) veld rond het Waregemse jeugdcentrum". *Jaarboek van de Geschied- en Heemkundige Kring De Gaverstreke*, 29 (2001), 215-256.

Solms, Friedhelm. "The World Council of Churches on Disarmament and Peace" in: *Peace and Disarmament: Documents of the World Council of Churches and the Roman Catholic Church*. Geneva: WCC - Vatican City: PCJP, 1982, 1-13.

Sommerville, C.J. "Secular Society Religious Population: Our Tacit Rules for Using the Term Secularization". *Journal for the Scientific Study of Religion*, 37 (1998) 2, 249-253.

Spalding, John Lancaster. *The Religious Mission of the Irish People and Catholic Colonization*. New York: Catholic Colonization Society, 1880.

Sperber, Jonathan. *The Kaiser's Voters: Electors and Elections in Imperial Germany.* Cambridge: Cambridge University Press, 1997.

Sperber, Jutta. *Christians and Muslims: The Dialogue Activities of the World Council of Churches and their Theological Foundation.* Berlin-New York: De Gruyter, 2000.

Stark, Rodney. "Bringing Theory Back In" in: Lawrence A. Young, ed. *Rational Choice Theory and Religion: Summary and Assessment*. New York-London: Routledge, 1997, 3-24.

Stark, Rodney and Finke, Roger. *Acts of Faith: Explaining the Human Side of Religion.* Berkeley-Los Angeles-London: University of California Press, 2000.

Starkey, Pat. "Women Religious and Religious Women. Faith and Practice in Women's Lives" in: Deborah Simonton, ed. *The Routledge History of Women since 1700*. London-New York: Routledge, 2007, 98-207.

"Statut théologique et juridique des Conférences épiscopales. Rapport du cardinal B. Gantin". *La Documentation catholique*, 69 (1987) 19, 1009.

Steenbrink, Karel. *Adam redivivus: Muslim Elaborations of the Adam Saga with Special Reference to the Indonesian Literary Traditions.* Zoetermeer: Meinema, 1998.

Steinhoff, Antony. "Ein zweites konfessionelles Zeitalter? Nachdenken über die Religion im langen 19. Jahrhundert". *Geschichte und Gesellschaft,* 30 (2004), 549-570.

Steur, Klaas. *Liefdesleven. Conferenties voor jonggehuwden.* Bussum: Paul Brand, 1947.

Steur, Klaas. *Liefdesstreven. Conferenties voor verloofden.* Bussum: Paul Brand, 1947.

Steur, Klaas. *Algemeen priesterschap der gelovigen. Beschouwing in het licht der nieuwe theologie.* The Hague: Katholieke Actie Bisdom Haarlem, 1953.

Suenens, Léon-Joseph. *Krise und Erneuerung der Frauenorden.* Salzburg: Müller, 1962.

Suenens, Léon-Joseph. *Souvenirs et espérances.* Paris: Fayard, 1991.

Suhard, Emmanuel. *Essor ou déclin de l'Église. Lettre pastorale, Carême de l'an de grâce 1947.* Livre de vie 32. Paris: Lahure, 1962.

Sullivan, Francis A. *Salvation Outside the Church? Tracing the History of the Catholic Response.* New York-Mahwah: Paulist Press, 1992.

Sundermeier, Theo. *Den Fremden wahrnehmen. Studien zum Verstehen fremder Religionen.* Gütersloh: G. Mohn, 1992.

Sundermeier Theo. *Den Fremden verstehen. Eine praktische Hermeneutik.* Göttingen: Vandenhoeck & Ruprecht, 1996.

Sussman, Lance J. "The Suburbanization of American Judaism as Reflected in Synagogue Building and Architecture, 1945-1975". *American Jewish History,* 75 (1985), 31-47.

Swanson Guy E. *The Birth of the Gods: The Origin of Primitive Beliefs.* Ann Arbor: University of Michigan Press, 1960.

Tellegen, Frans Ph.A. "Verdraagzaamheid en verzuiling. Een verkenning" in: *Verdraagzaamheid.* Utrecht-Antwerp: Het Spectrum, 1957, 86-96.

Terruwe, Anna A.A. *De neurose in het licht van de rationele psychologie.* Roermond: Romen, 1949 (*The Neurosis in the Light of Rational Psychology.* New York: Kenedy, 1960).

Theobald, Christoph. "Le devenir de la théologie catholique depuis le concile Vatican II" in: Jean-Marie Mayeur, ed. *Histoire du christianisme.* Vol. 13: *Crises et renouveau (de 1958 à nos jours).* Paris: Desclée, 2000, 169-217.

Thils, Gustave. *Théologie des réalités terrestres.* Vol. 1: *Préludes.* Vol. 2: *Théologie de l'histoire.* Bruges-Paris: Desclée De Brouwer, 1946 and 1949, 2 vols.

Thomas, Cal and Dobson, Ed. *Blinded by Might: Can the 'Religious Right' Save America?* Grand Rapids (MI): Zondervan, 1999.

Thomas, George M. *Revivalism and Cultural Change: Christianity, Nation Building, and the Market in the Nineteenth-Century United States.* Chicago: University of Chicago Press, 1989.

Thomas, M.M. *The Acknowledged Christ of the Indian Renaissance.* London: SCM, 1969.

Thomas, M.M. "Jesus Christ Frees and Unites" in: M.M. Thomas. *Towards a Theology of Contemporary Ecumenism.* Madras: Christian Literature Society - Geneva: World Council of Churches, 1978, 288-317.

Thomas, M.M. "Christ-Centered Syncretism". *Religion and Society,* 29 (1979), 25-40.

Thomas, M.M. "Modern Man and the New Humanity in Christ" in: Emerito P. Nacpil and Douglas J. Elwood, eds. *The Human and the Holy: Asian Perspectives in Christian Theology.* New York: Orbis, 1980, 313-317.

Thurlings, Jan G.M. *De wankele zuil. Nederlandse katholieken tussen assimilatie en pluralisme.* Deventer: Van Loghum Slaterus, 1978².

Thurlings, Jan G.M. "Pluralism and Assimilation in the Netherlands, with Special Reference to Dutch Catholicism". *International Journal of Comparative Sociology*, 19 (1979), 82-100.

Tillard, Jean-Marie R. *Vertrauen zur Gemeinschaft. Geistliche Grundlegung des Ordenslebens heute.* Freiburg: Herder, 1973.

Tillard, Jean-Marie R. *Frei sein in Gott. Zur Praxis des Ordenslebens heute*. Freiburg-Basel-Vienna: Herder, 1979.

Trimbos, Cees. *Gehuwd en ongehuwd.* Hilversum: Paul Brand, 1961.

Toupin-Guyot, Claire. *Les intellectuels catholiques dans la société française. Le Centre catholique des intellectuels français (1941-1976).* Rennes: Presses universitaires de Rennes, 2002.

Touraine, Alain. *Le retour de l'acteur: essai de sociologie*. Paris: Fayard, 1984.

Toward the Future. Lay Commission on Catholic Social Thinking and the U.S. Economy. New York: Lay Commission, 1984.

Towards a Common Understanding and Vision of the World Council of Churches: A Policy Statement adopted by the Central Committee of the World Council of Churches and commended to member churches and ecumenical partners for study and action in September 1997. <www.oikoumene.org/?id=1561> (29.01.2008).

Tranvouez, Yvon. *Catholiques d'abord. Approches du mouvement catholique en France, XIXe-XXe siècle.* Paris: Éditions Ouvrières, 1988.

A Treasure in Earthen Vessels. An Instrument for an Ecumenical Reflection on Hermeneutics. Faith & Order Paper 182. Geneva: World Council of Churches, 1998.

Trumbach, Randolph. "London" in: David Higgs, ed. *Queer Sites: Gay Urban Histories.* London: Routledge, 1999, 89-111.

Tschannen, Olivier. *Les théories de la sécularisation*. Geneva: Droz, 1992.

Ucko, Hans. "Reflections on International and Global Multifaith Initiatives". *Current Dialogue*, 39 (2001). <www.wcc-coe.org/wcc/what/interreligious/cd39-14.html> (26.01.2008).

Uertz, Rudolf. *Christentum und Sozialismus in der frühen CDU.* Stuttgart: Deutsche Verlags-Anstalt, 1981.

Uginet, Fr.-Ch. "La constitution 'Regimini ecclesiae universae'" in: *Paul VI et la modernité dans l'Église*. Rome: École française de Rome, 1984, 569-601.

Ukken, Shaju. *The Contributions of Jacques Maritain to the Universal Declaration of Human Rights*. Diss. Lic. K.U.Leuven, 2002.

"U.S. Bischöfe. Kritik an römischen Vorstellungen über Bischofskonferenzen". *Herder Korrespondenz*, 43 (1989) 1, 12-13.

van der Grinten, Tom. *De vorming van de ambulante geestelijke gezondheidszorg. Een historisch beleidsonderzoek*. Baarn: Ambo, 1987.

Van Dijck, Maarten. *Entreprendre avec du capital coopératif. Le Groupe ARCO 1935-2005*. Tielt: Lannoo, 2005.

van Harskamp, Anton. "Simply astounding. Ongoing secularization in the Netherlands?" in: Erik Sengers, ed. *The Dutch and Their Gods. Secularization and Transformation of Religion in the Netherlands since 1950*. Hilversum: Verloren, 2005, 43-57.

van Hemert, Martinus M. J. *En zij verontschuldigden zich: de ontwikkeling van het misbezoekcijfer 1966-1979*. The Hague: Instituut voor sociaal-wetenschappelijk onderzoek, studie en advies, 1980.

Van Isacker, Karel. *Ontwijding*. Leuven: Davidsfonds, 1989.

van Luijk, Henk. "De ontreddering van katholiek Nederland". *Elseviers Magazine*, 18.01.1985.

Van Meerbeeck, Anne. "Dopen: waarom niet? Een sociologische verkenning van de betekenis van dopen in Vlaanderen" in: Lambert Leijssen, Michel Cloet and Karel Dobbelaere, eds. *Levensrituelen. Geboorte en doopsel*. KADOC-Studies 13. Leuven: Universitaire Pers Leuven, 1996, 199-216.

Van Meerbeeck, Anne. *Het doopsel: een familieritueel. Een sociologische analyse van de betekenissen van dopen in Vlaanderen*. Diss. Doct. K.U.Leuven, 2001.

van Melsen, Andries G.M. *Geloof, wetenschap en maatschappelijke omwentelingen. Wijsgerige beschouwingen over de crisis in de cultuur*. Baarn: Ambo, 1977.

Van Osselaer, Tine. "Christening Masculinity? Adult Catholic Action Movements in Interwar Belgium". *Gender & History*, 21 (2009) 2, 380-401.

Van Osselaer, Tine. *The Pious Sex. Catholic Constructions of Masculinity and Femininity in Belgium c. 1800-1940*. Diss. Doct. K.U.Leuven, 2009.

Van Osselaer, Tine and Buerman, Thomas. "Feminization Thesis. A Survey of International Historiography and a Probing on Belgian Grounds". *Revue d'histoire ecclésiastique*, 103 (2008) 2, 497-544.

van Ouwerkerk, C. "De moraaltheologische discussie over de moderne oorlog". *Concilium*, 2 (1966) 5, 115-123.

Vecchio, Giorgio. "'Left Catholicism' and the Experiences 'On the Frontier' of the Church and Italian Society (1939-1958)" in: Gerd-Rainer Horn and Emmanuel Gerard, eds. *Left Catholicism: Catholics and Society in Western Europe at the Point of Liberation, 1943-1955*. KADOC-Studies 25. Leuven: Leuven University Press, 2001, 174-195.

Vecoli, Rudolph J. "Prelates and Peasants: Italian Immigrants and the Catholic Church". *Journal of Social History*, 2 (1969), 217-268.

Verba, Sidney; Scholzman, Kay Lehman and Brady, Henry E. *Voice and Equality: Civic Voluntarism in American Politics*. Cambridge (MA): Harvard University Press, 2002.

Vereinigung der Ordensoberinnen Deutschlands, ed. *Festschrift 25 Jahre VOD Vereinigung der Ordensoberinnen Deutschlands: 1954-1979*. Trier, 1979.

Verlinden, Anne. *Het ongewone alledaagse. Over zwarte katten, horoscopen en miraculeuze genezingen*. Leuven: Acco, 1999.

Vermès, Géza. *Jesus and the World of Judaism*. London: SCM, 1983.

Verstraeten, Johan, ed. *Economie en rechtvaardigheid. Een uitdaging van de Amerikaanse bisschoppen*. Leuven: Acco, 1989.

Verstraeten, Johan. "Solidarity and Subsidiarity" in: David A. Boileau, ed. *Principles of Catholic Social Teaching.* Marquette Studies in Theology 14. Milwaukee (WI): Marquette University Press, 1998, 133-147.

Verstraeten, Johan. "Debt Forgiveness, Social Justice and Solidarity: A Theological and Ethical Reflection". *Ethical Perspectives*, 8 (2001) 1, 18-26.

Verstraeten, Johan and Van Liedekerke, Luc. *Naar een samenleving met een menselijk gelaat. Kritische beschouwingen over de encycliek Centesimus annus.* Leuven: Acco, 1992.

Verweij, Johan and Ester, Peter. "Secularization as an Economic and Cultural Phenomenon: A Cross-national Analysis". *Journal for the Scientific Study of Religion*, 36 (1997) 2, 309-325.

Visser 't Hooft, Willem A. "The Word Ecumenical - Its History and Use" in: Ruth Rouse and Stephen Neill. *A History of the Ecumenical Movement, 1517-1948.* London: SPCK, 1954, 735-740.

Voas, David; Olson, Daniel V.A. and Alasdair Cockett. "Religious Pluralism and Participation: Was Everybody Wrong". *American Sociological Review*, 67 (2002) 2, 212-230.

VOB, ed. *25 Jahre Vereinigung der Ordensobern der Brüderorden und -kongregationen Deutschlands 1958-1983.* Furth, 1983.

von Greyerz, Kaspar. *Religion and Culture in Early Modern Europe, 1500-1800.* Oxford: Oxford University Press, 2008.

Vos, Louis. "Het dubbelspoor van de Katholieke Actie tijdens het interbellum" in: Maurits De Vroede and An Hermans, eds. *Vijftig jaar Chiroleven 1934-1984. Aspecten uit het verleden en heden van een jeugdbeweging.* Leuven: Universitaire Pers, 1985, 29-52.

Voyé, Liliane. "Au-dela de la sécularisation". *Lettres Pastorales. Informations officielles du diocèse de Tournai*, 25 (1985), 253-274.

Voyé, Liliane. "Approche méthodologique du sacré" in: Michel Cloet and Frank Daelemans, eds. *Religion, mentalités et vie quotidienne - Godsdienst, mentaliteit en dagelijks leven: religieuze geschiedenis in België sinds 1970.* Brussels: Archief- en Bibliotheekwezen in België, 1988, 255-277.

Voyé, Liliane. "Prolongements et perspectives. Le point de vue d'un sociologue" in: Jean-Louis Schlegel et al. *Le religieux en Occident. Pensées des déplacements.* Brussels: FUSL, 1988, 127-133.

Voyé, Liliane. "Religion populaire et pèlerinages en Europe" in: *Marche vers la Splendeur. Ton Dieu marche avec toi. Actes du premier Congrès mondial de la Pastorale des sanctuaires et pèlerinages.* Rome: Conseil Pontifical pour la Pastorale des Migrants et Itinérants, 1992, 78-103.

Voyé, Liliane. "From Institutional Catholicism to 'Christian Inspiration': Another Look at Belgium" in: Wade Clark Roof, Jackson W. Caroll and David A. Roozen, eds. *The Post-War Generation and Established Religion: Cross-Cultural Perspectives.* Boulder (CO): Westview, 1995, 191-206.

Voyé, Liliane. "Le rite en question" in: René Devisch et al. *Le rite, source et ressources.* Publications des Facultés universitaires Saint-Louis 69. Brussels: FUSL, 1995, 105-135.

Voyé, Liliane. "Belgique: Crise de la civilisation paroissiale et recompositions du croire" in: Grace Davie and Danièle Hervieu-Léger, eds. *Identités religieuses en Europe.* Paris: La Découverte, 1996, 195-213.

Voyé, Liliane. "Religion in Modern Europe: Pertinence of the Globalization Theories" in: Nobutaka Inoue, ed. *Globalization and Indigenous Culture*. Tokyo: Institute for Japanese Culture and Classics, 1997, 155-186.

Voyé, Liliane. "Death and Christmas Revisited" in: Rudi Laermans, Bryan Wilson and Jaak Billiet, eds. *Secularization and Social Integration: Papers in Honor of Karel Dobbelaere*. Leuven: Leuven University Press, 1998, 287-305.

Voyé, Liliane. "Popular Religion and Pilgrimages in Western Europe" in: William H. Swatos and Luigi Tomasi, eds. *From Medieval Pilgrimage to Religious Tourism*. Westport: Praeger, 2002, 115-135.

Wald, Kenneth D. *Crosses on the Ballot*. Princeton (NJ): Princeton University Press, 1983.

Wallace, Ruth. *They Call Her Pastor: A New Role for Catholic Women*. Albany (NY): State University of New York Press, 1992.

Walser Smith, Helmut and Clark, Chris. "The Fate of Nathan" in: Helmut Walser Smith, ed. *Protestants, Catholics and Jews in Germany, 1800-1914*. Oxford: Berg, 2001, 3-29.

Wassilowsky, Günther. *Universales Heilssakrament Kirche. Karl Rahners Beitrag zur Ekklesiologie des II. Vatikanums*. Innsbrucker theologische Studien 59. Innsbruck: Tyrolia, 2001.

Watt, William Montgomery. *Islamic Political Thought*. Islamic Surveys 6. Edinburgh: Edinburgh University Press, 1968.

Weaver, Mary Jo. *New Catholic Women: A Contemporary Challenge to Traditional Religious Authority*. San Francisco: Harper & Row, 1985.

Weber, Max. *Gesammelte Aufsätze zur Religionssoziologie*. Tübingen: Mohr Siebeck, 1920-1921, 3 vols.

Wessinger, Catherine, ed. *Religious Institutions and Women's Leadership: New Roles inside the Mainstream*. Columbia: University of South Carolina Press, 1996.

Westhoff, Hanneke. *Geestelijke bevrijders. Nederlandse katholieken en hun beweging voor geestelijke volksgezondheid in de twintigste eeuw*. Nijmegen: Valkhof Pers, 1996.

Westhoff, Hanneke and Roes, Jan. "Seelische versus geistliche Fürsorge. Die Rolle der psychohygiënischen Bewegung bei der Transformation des niederländischen Katholizismus im 20. Jahrhundert". *Kirchliche Zeitgeschichte*, 7 (1994), 137-160.

White, Gaylor I. "A City Block in 1896: Study of Gold Street, between Concord and Tillary Streets, Brooklyn". *Charities*, 5 (1900), 2-6.

Wilson, A.N. *God's Funeral*. London: Abacus, 1999.

Wilson, Bryan R. *Religion in a Secular Society: A Sociological Moment*. London: Watts, 1966.

Wilson, Bryan. "Aspects of Secularization in the West". *Japanese Journal of Religious Studies*, 3 (1976), 259-276.

Wilson, Bryan R. *Contemporary Transformations of Religion*. London: Oxford University Press, 1976.

Wilson, Bryan. "Secularization: The Inherited Model" in: Phillip Hammond, ed. *The Sacred in a Secular Age*. Berkeley: University of California Press, 1985, 9-20.

Wilson, Bryan and Cresswell, Jamie, eds. *New Religious Movements: Challenge and Response*. London: Routledge, 1999.

Winkeler, Lodewijk. "Verdringing van de moraal. De discussie rond het proefschrift van mevr. dr. A.A.A. Terruwe". *Jaarboek van het Katholiek Documentatie Centrum*, 10 (1980), 118-134.

Winkeler, Lodewijk. "Neothomisme en emancipatie. Verkenningen rond een hypothese" in: *De praktische Thomas. Thomas van Aquino: de consequenties van zijn theologie voor hedendaags gedrag.* Theologie en Samenleving 10. Hilversum: Gooi & Sticht, 1987, 102-112.

Winkeler, Lodewijk. "Ten dienste der seminaristen. Handboeken op de Nederlandse priesteropleidingen, 1800-1967" in: *Jaarboek van het Katholiek Documentatie Centrum*, 17 (1987), 12-56.

Winkeler, Lodewijk. *Stromingen in katholiek Nederland*. Kampen: Kok, 2004.

Winter, Gibson. *Suburban Captivity of the Churches: An Analysis of Protestant Responsibility in the Expanding Metropolis.* New York: Doubleday, 1961.

Winthrop, John. "Model of Christian Charity" in: *The Winthrop Papers*. Vol. 2. Boston: Massachusetts Historical Society, 1931, 294-295.

Wintle, Michael. "Pillarisation, Consociation, and Vertical Pluralism in the Netherlands Revisited: A European View". *West European Politics*, 23 (2000) 3, 139-152.

Witte, John Jr., ed. *Christianity and Democracy in Global Context.* Boulder (CO): Westview Press, 1993.

Wittstadt, Klaus. *Julius Kardinal Döpfner (1913-1976). Anwalt Gottes und der Menschen.* Munich: Don Bosco, 2001.

Wolf, Peter, ed. *Lebensaufbrüche. Geistliche Bewegungen in Deutschland. Mit einem Beitrag von Joseph Kardinal Ratzinger*. Vallendar-Schönstatt: Patris, 2000.

Wolff, Richard J. and Hoensch, Jörg K., eds. *Catholics, the State and the European Radical Right, 1919-1945.* New York-Boulder-Highland Lakes (NJ): Atlantic Research and Publications, 1987.

Wolffe, John. *Great Deaths.* Oxford: Oxford University Press, 2000.

Wuthnow, Robert. *The Restructuring of American Religion. Society and Faith since World War II.* Princeton (NJ): Princeton University Press, 1988.

Yonnet, Paul. *Jeux, modes et masses. La société française et le moderne*. Paris: Gallimard, 1985.

Young, Lawrence A., ed. *Rational Choice Theory and Religion. Summary and Assessment.* New York-London: Routledge, 1997.

Ziemann, Benjamin. "Das Ende der Milieukoalition. Differenzierung und Fragmentierung der katholischen Sozialmilieus nach 1945". *Komparativ*, 2 (1999), 89-101.

Ziemann, Benjamin. "Säkularisierung, Konfessionalisierung, Organisationsbildung. Dimensionen der Sozialgeschichte der Religion im langen 19. Jahrhundert". *Archiv für Sozialgeschichte*, 47 (2007), 485-508.

Ziemann, Benjamin. "The Theory of Functional Differentiation and the History of Modern Society. Reflections on the Reception of Systems Theory in Recent Historiography". *Soziale Systeme*, 13 (2007), 220-229.

Ziemann, Benjamin. *Sozialgeschichte der Religion. Von der Reformation bis zur Gegenwart.* Frankfurt am Main: Campus, 2009.

Zizola, Giancarlo. *La restaurazione di papa Wojtyla.* Rome-Bari: Laterza, 1985.

Zulehner, Paul. *Wie Europa lebt und glaubt. Europäische Wertestudie*. Düsseldorf: Patmos, 1993.

Colophon

Editors
Jaak Billiet is PhD in Social Sciences (K.U.Leuven) and emeritus professor at the K.U.Leuven. His research focuses on pillarisation and statistical methods. He is member of the central coordination team of the European Social Survey.

Leo Kenis is PhD in Theology (K.U.Leuven) and professor in History of Church and Theology at the K.U.Leuven. His research focuses on the history of Church and Theology in the 19th and 20th centuries.

Patrick Pasture is PhD in History (K.U.Leuven) and associate professor in History at the K.U.Leuven, where he co-ordinates the research unit Modernity & Society 1800-2000 (MoSa). His research focuses on European labour history and the social history of Christendom in Europe and North America.

Final Editing
Lieve Claes
Luc Vints

Lay-out
Alexis Vermeylen

KADOC
Documentation and Research Centre for Religion, Culture and Society
Vlamingenstraat 39 B - 3000 Leuven
tel. +32 16 32 35 00 fax +32 16 32 35 01
e-mail: postmaster@kadoc.kuleuven.be
website: http://kadoc.kuleuven.be